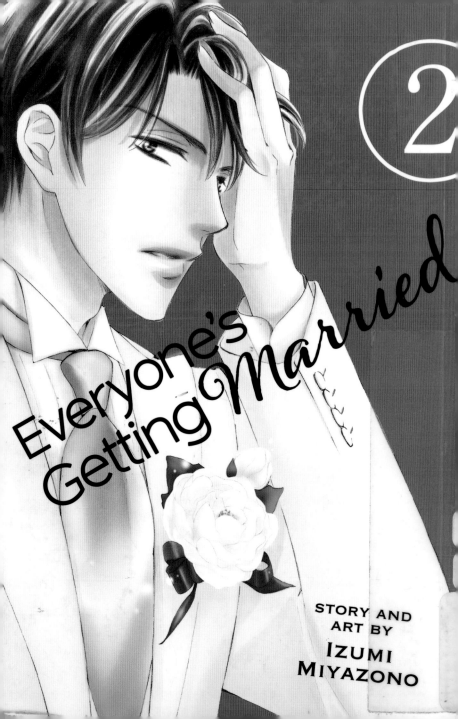

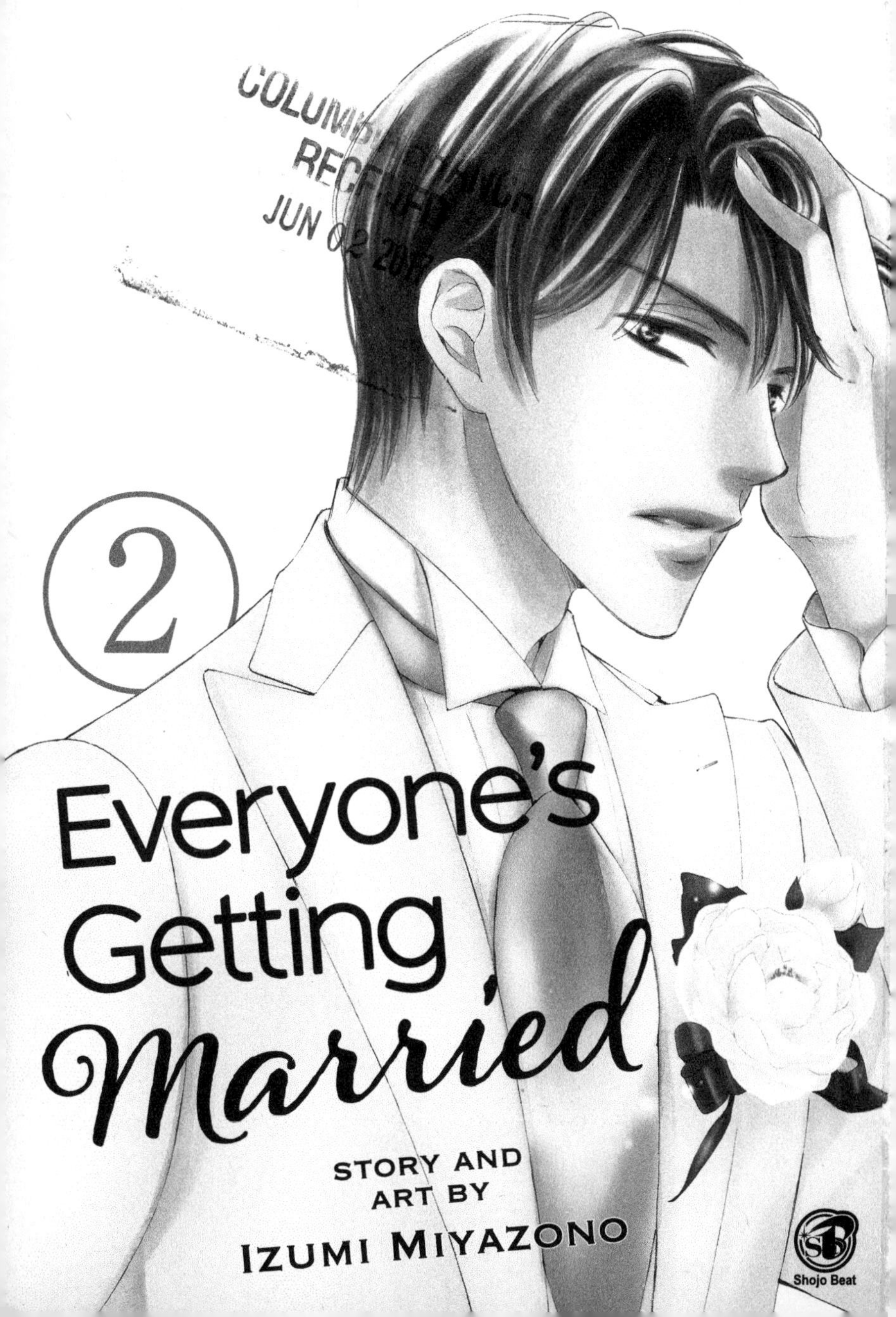
2
Everyone's Getting Married
STORY AND ART BY
IZUMI MIYAZONO
Shojo Beat

CHARACTERS

THE MAN WHO DOESN'T WANT TO GET MARRIED

Ryu Nanami

The handsome, up-and-coming newscaster at PTV. He's returned from the New York office.

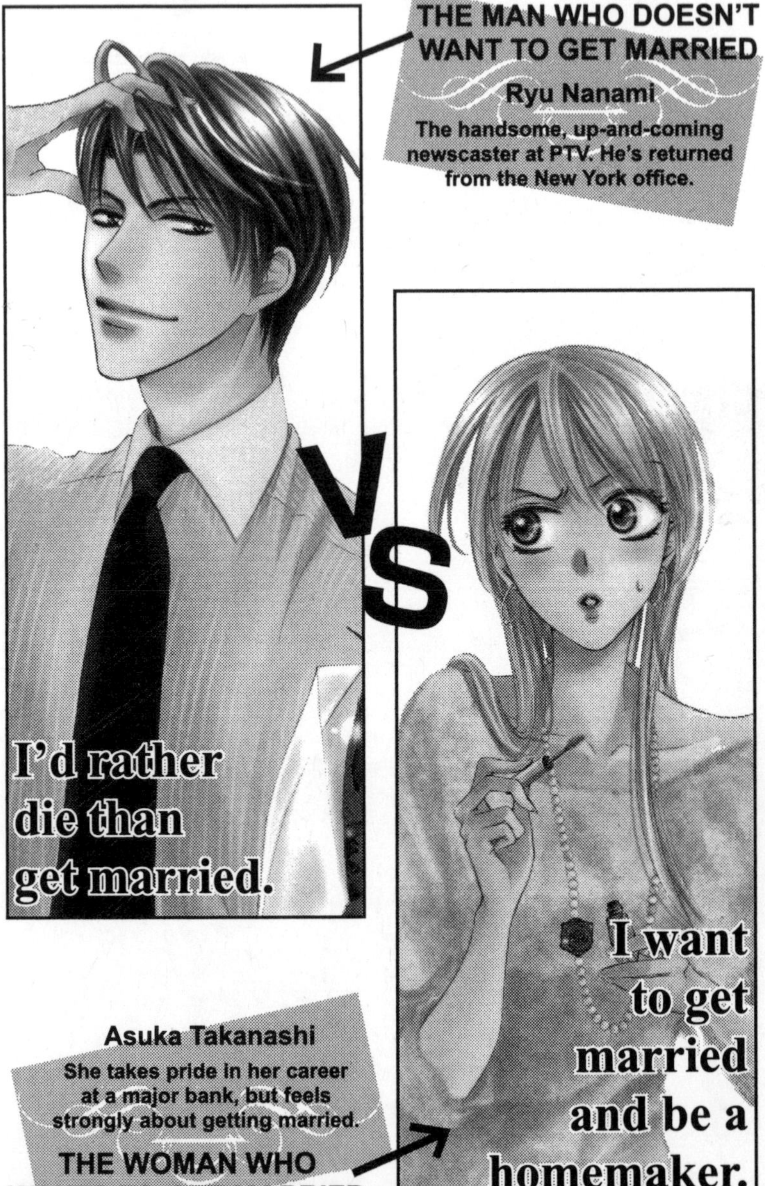
VS
I'd rather die than get married.
I want to get married and be a homemaker.

Asuka Takanashi

She takes pride in her career at a major bank, but feels strongly about getting married.

THE WOMAN WHO WANTS TO GET MARRIED

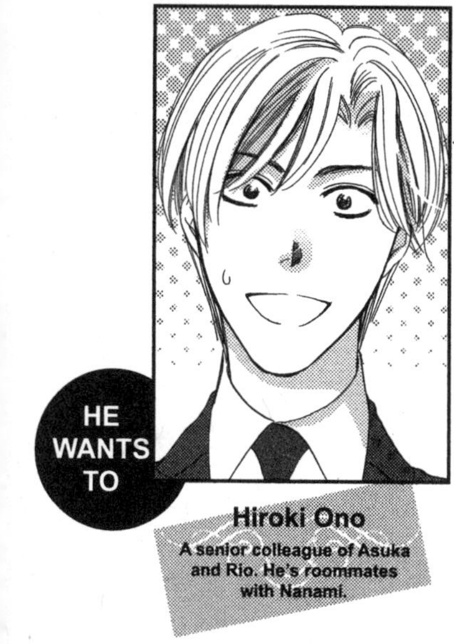

HE WANTS TO

Hiroki Ono

A senior colleague of Asuka and Rio. He's roommates with Nanami.

IN A RELATIONSHIP♥
(with no plans to marry in the future)

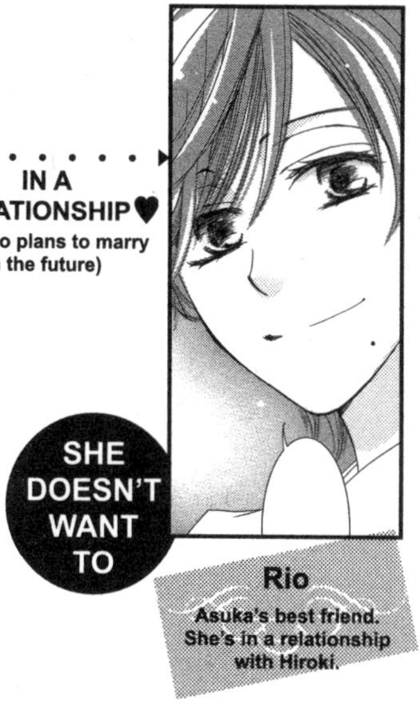

SHE DOESN'T WANT TO

Rio

Asuka's best friend. She's in a relationship with Hiroki.

STORY THUS FAR

Asuka Takanashi works at a major bank and dreams of becoming a full-time homemaker. She thinks marriage is right around the corner, but suddenly her long-term boyfriend breaks up with her.

The one who cheers up the brokenhearted Asuka is Ryu Nanami, a handsome newscaster she met previously at a wedding ceremony. Ryu is the best friend from college and roommate of Asuka's colleague from work, Hiroki Ono. Ryu and Asuka meet again when she drops by their apartment.

Asuka is attracted to Ryu's kindness, but he boldly proclaims he'd rather die than ever get married! Ryu had an affair with a married actress in the past, and he doesn't see any value in marriage.

Though Asuka and Ryu don't see eye to eye regarding marriage, for some reason they can't help falling in love with each other, and they decide to start a relationship!

Contents

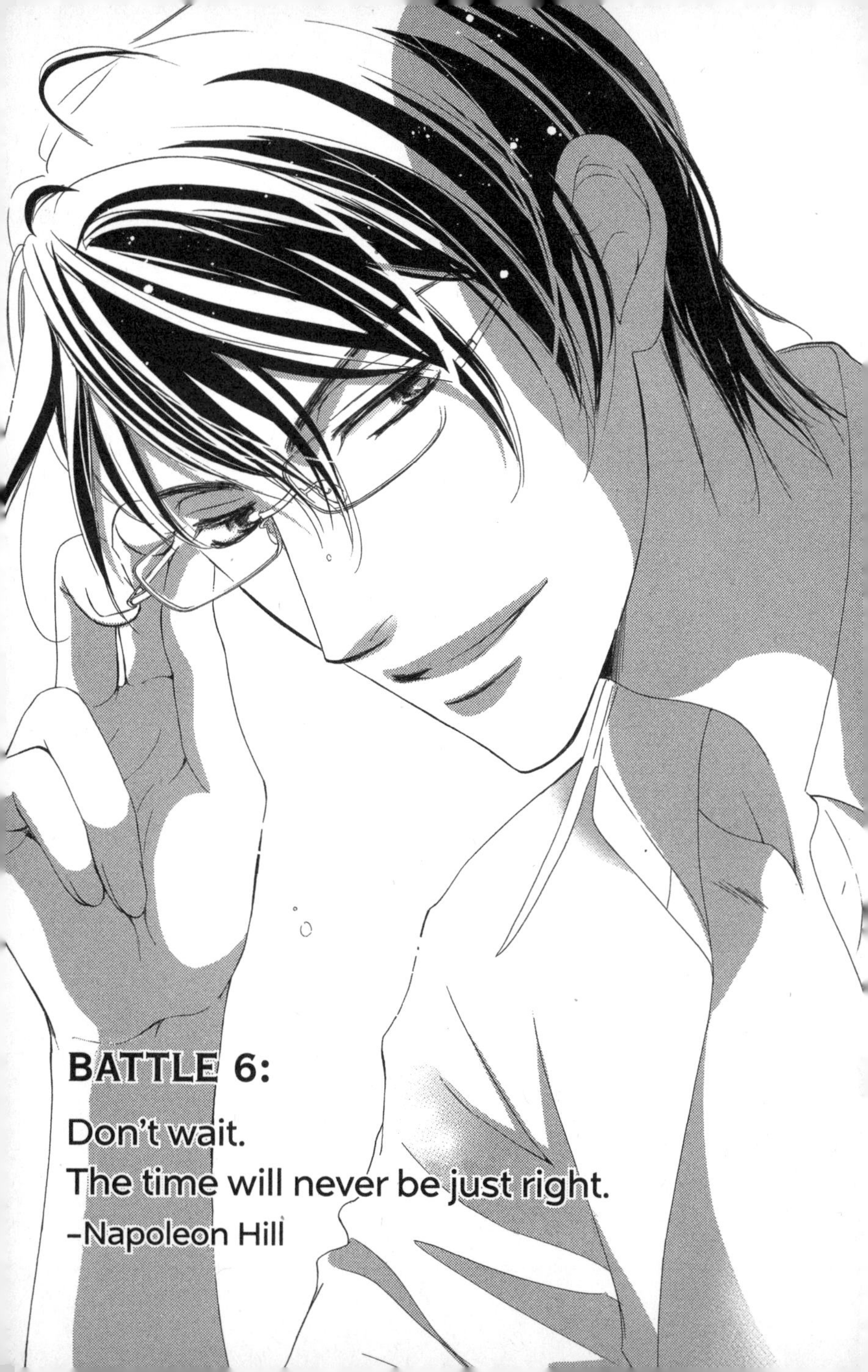

BATTLE 6:

Don't wait.
The time will never be just right.
–Napoleon Hill

I WANT TO GET MARRIED, BUT...

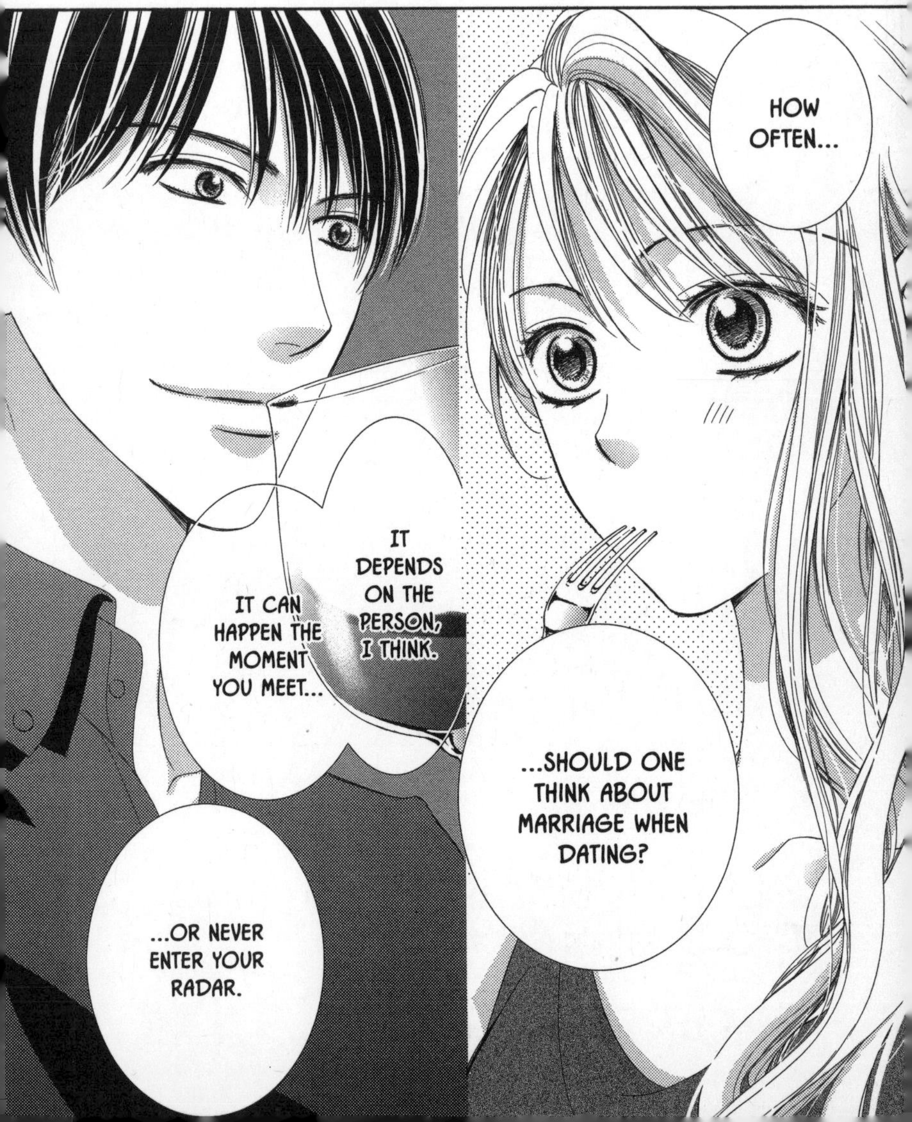
HOW OFTEN...
...SHOULD ONE THINK ABOUT MARRIAGE WHEN DATING?
IT DEPENDS ON THE PERSON, I THINK.
IT CAN HAPPEN THE MOMENT YOU MEET...
...OR NEVER ENTER YOUR RADAR.

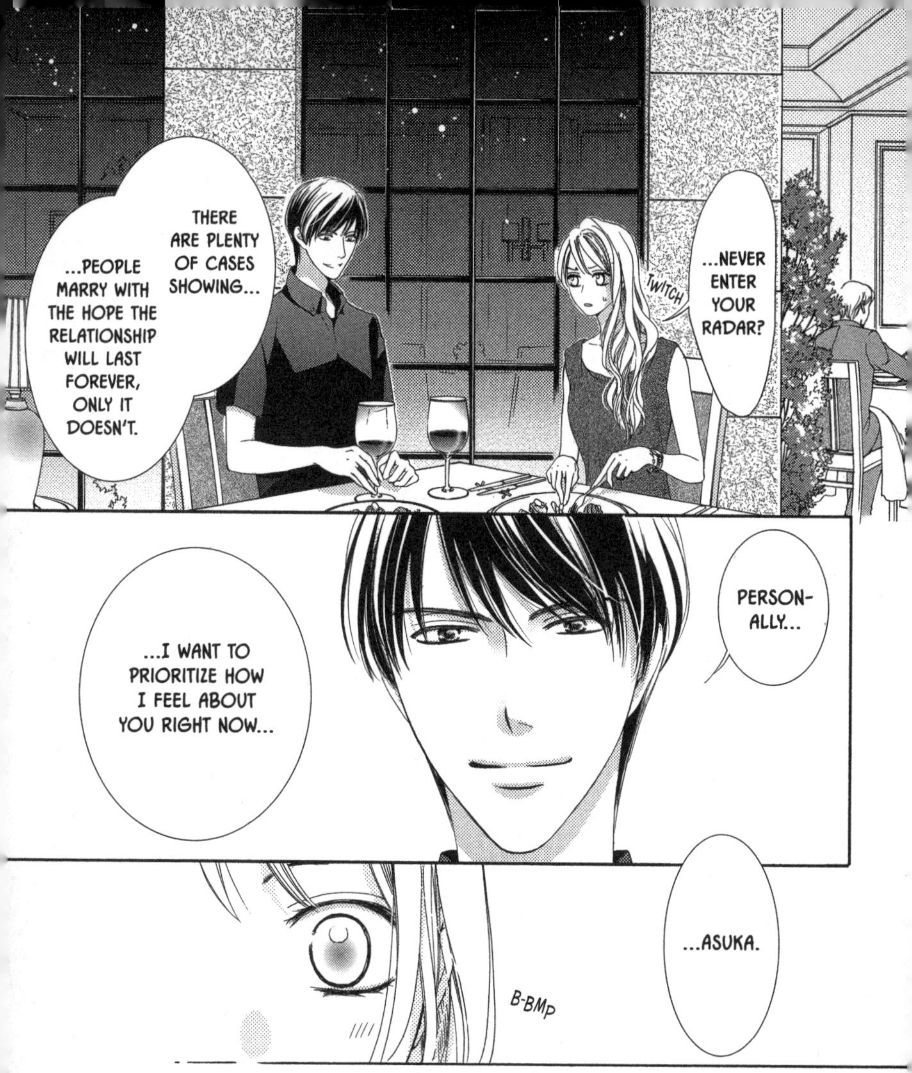
...NEVER ENTER YOUR RADAR?
TWITCH
THERE ARE PLENTY OF CASES SHOWING...
...PEOPLE MARRY WITH THE HOPE THE RELATIONSHIP WILL LAST FOREVER, ONLY IT DOESN'T.
PERSON-ALLY...
...I WANT TO PRIORITIZE HOW I FEEL ABOUT YOU RIGHT NOW...
...ASUKA.
B-BMP

...THE MAN I LOVE DOESN'T WANT TO.

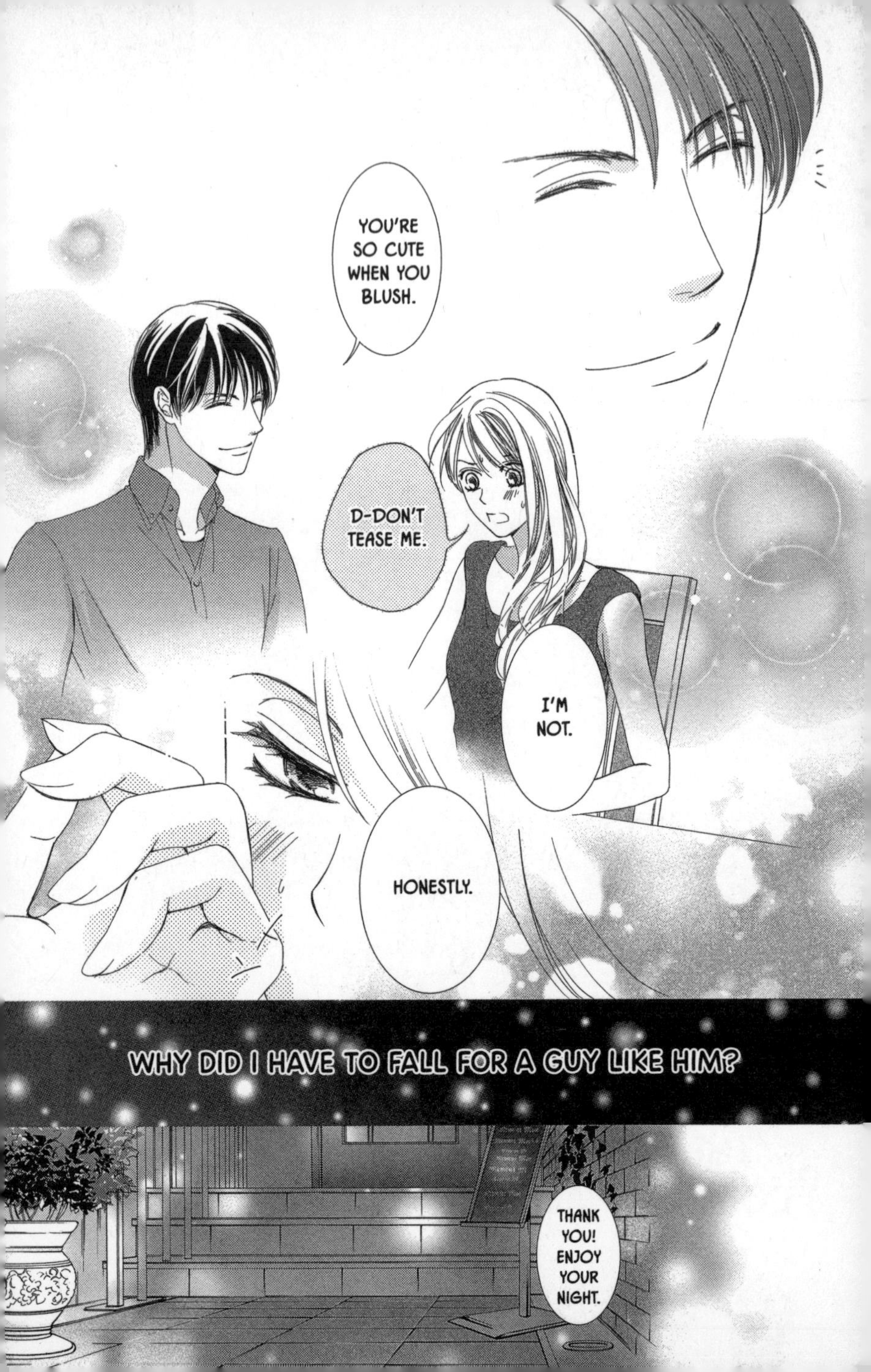
YOU'RE SO CUTE WHEN YOU BLUSH.
D-DON'T TEASE ME.
I'M NOT.
HONESTLY.
WHY DID I HAVE TO FALL FOR A GUY LIKE HIM?
THANK YOU! ENJOY YOUR NIGHT.

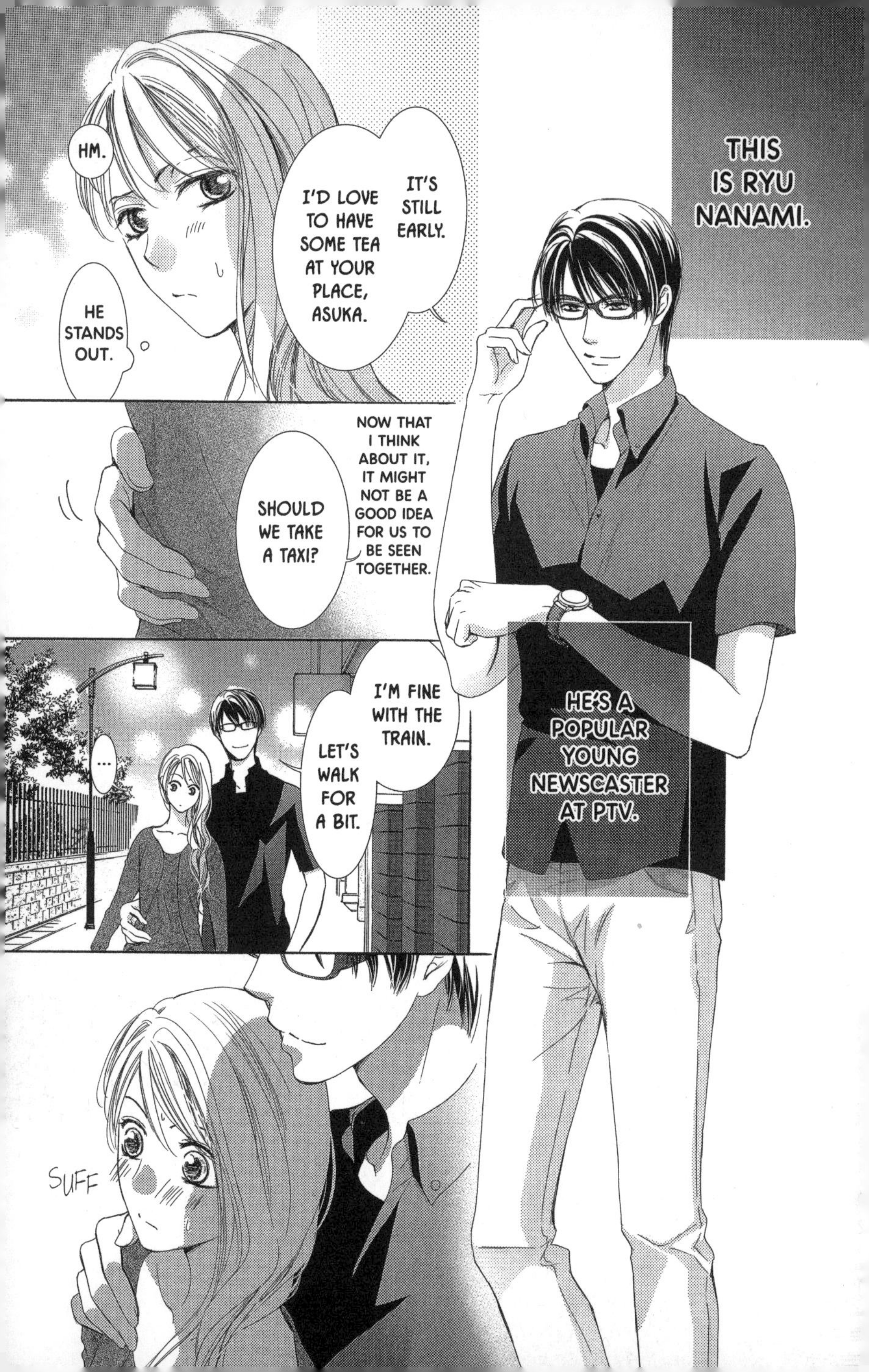
THIS IS RYU NANAMI.
HE'S A POPULAR YOUNG NEWSCASTER AT PTV.
IT'S STILL EARLY.
I'D LOVE TO HAVE SOME TEA AT YOUR PLACE, ASUKA.
HM.
HE STANDS OUT.
NOW THAT I THINK ABOUT IT, IT MIGHT NOT BE A GOOD IDEA FOR US TO BE SEEN TOGETHER.
SHOULD WE TAKE A TAXI?
I'M FINE WITH THE TRAIN.
LET'S WALK FOR A BIT.
...
SUFF

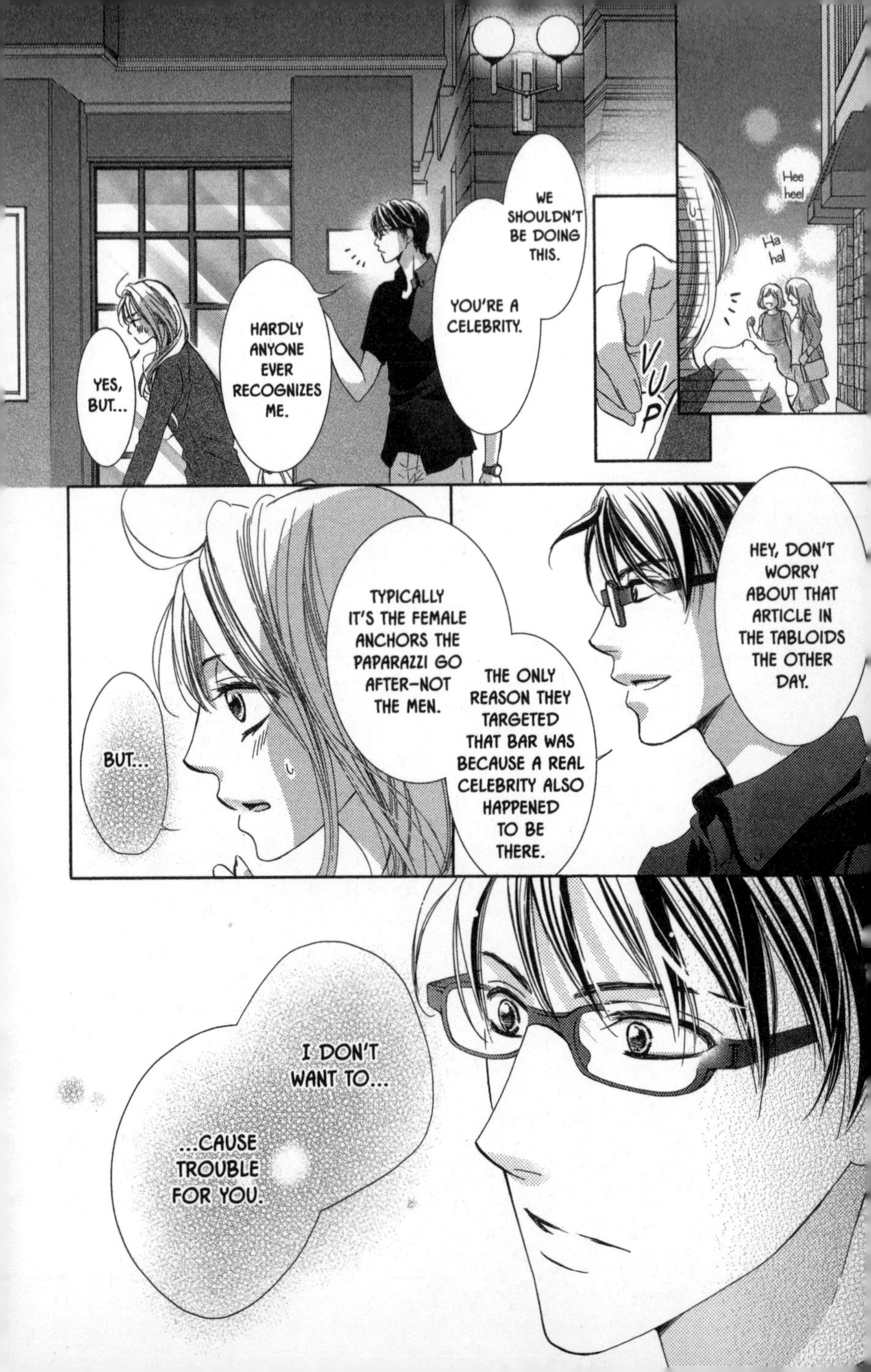
Hee hee!
Ha ha!
VUP
WE SHOULDN'T BE DOING THIS.
YOU'RE A CELEBRITY.
HARDLY ANYONE EVER RECOGNIZES ME.
YES, BUT...
HEY, DON'T WORRY ABOUT THAT ARTICLE IN THE TABLOIDS THE OTHER DAY.
TYPICALLY IT'S THE FEMALE ANCHORS THE PAPARAZZI GO AFTER–NOT THE MEN.
THE ONLY REASON THEY TARGETED THAT BAR WAS BECAUSE A REAL CELEBRITY ALSO HAPPENED TO BE THERE.
BUT...
I DON'T WANT TO...
...CAUSE TROUBLE FOR YOU.

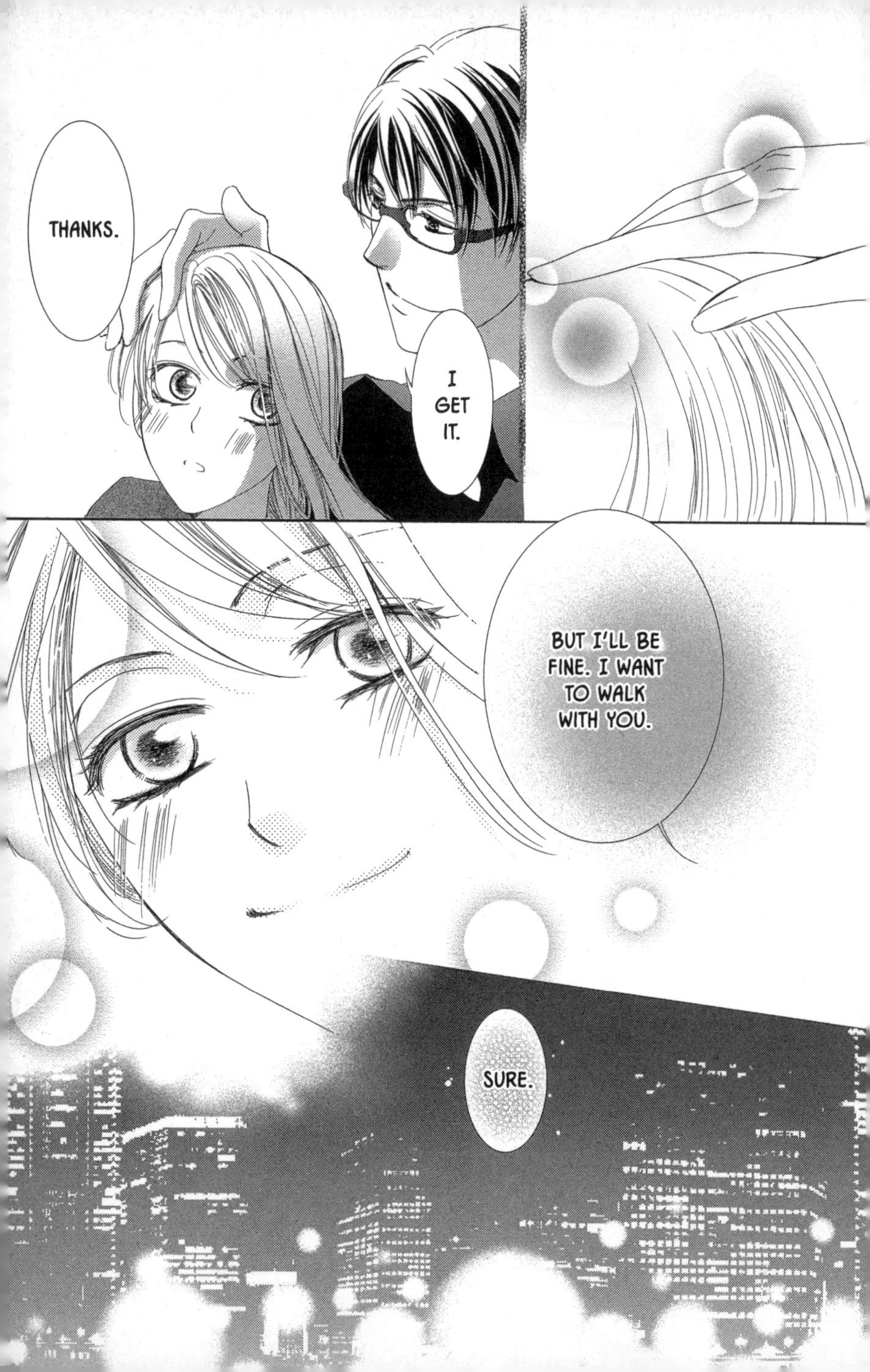
I GET IT.
THANKS.
BUT I'LL BE FINE. I WANT TO WALK WITH YOU.
SURE.

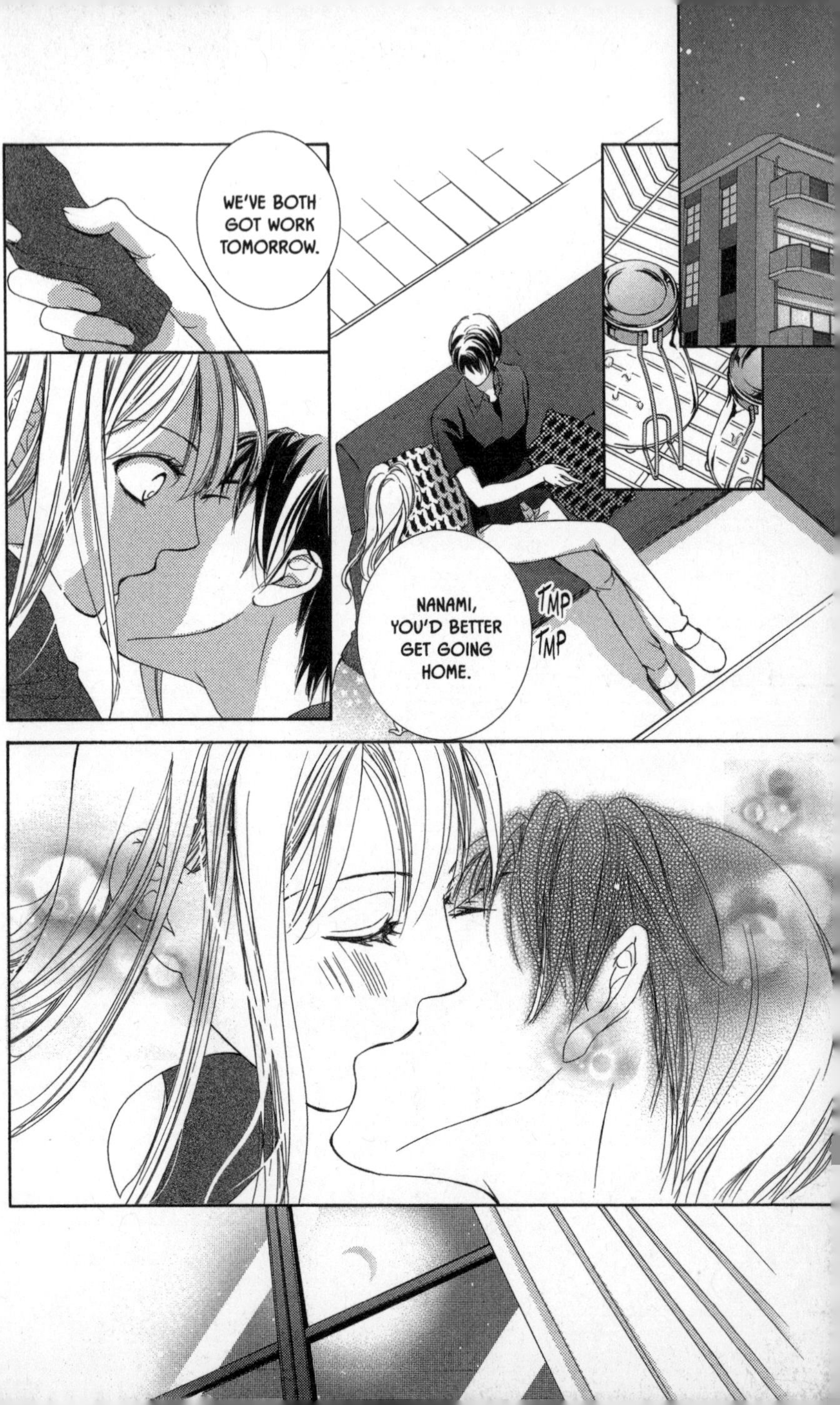
TMP
TMP
NANAMI, YOU'D BETTER GET GOING HOME.
WE'VE BOTH GOT WORK TOMORROW.

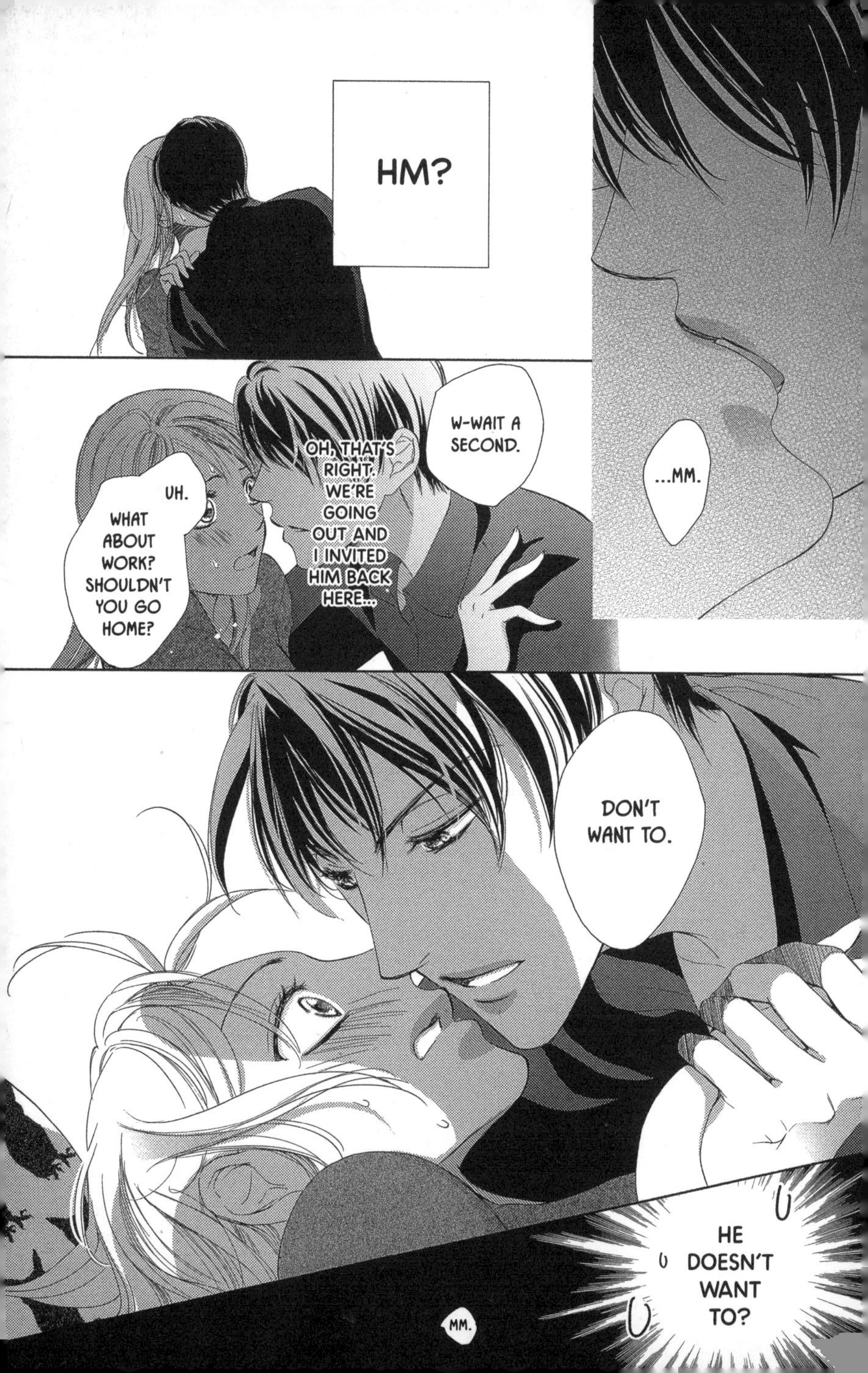
...MM.
HM?
W-WAIT A SECOND.
OH, THAT'S RIGHT. WE'RE GOING OUT AND I INVITED HIM BACK HERE...
UH.
WHAT ABOUT WORK? SHOULDN'T YOU GO HOME?
DON'T WANT TO.
HE DOESN'T WANT TO?
MM.

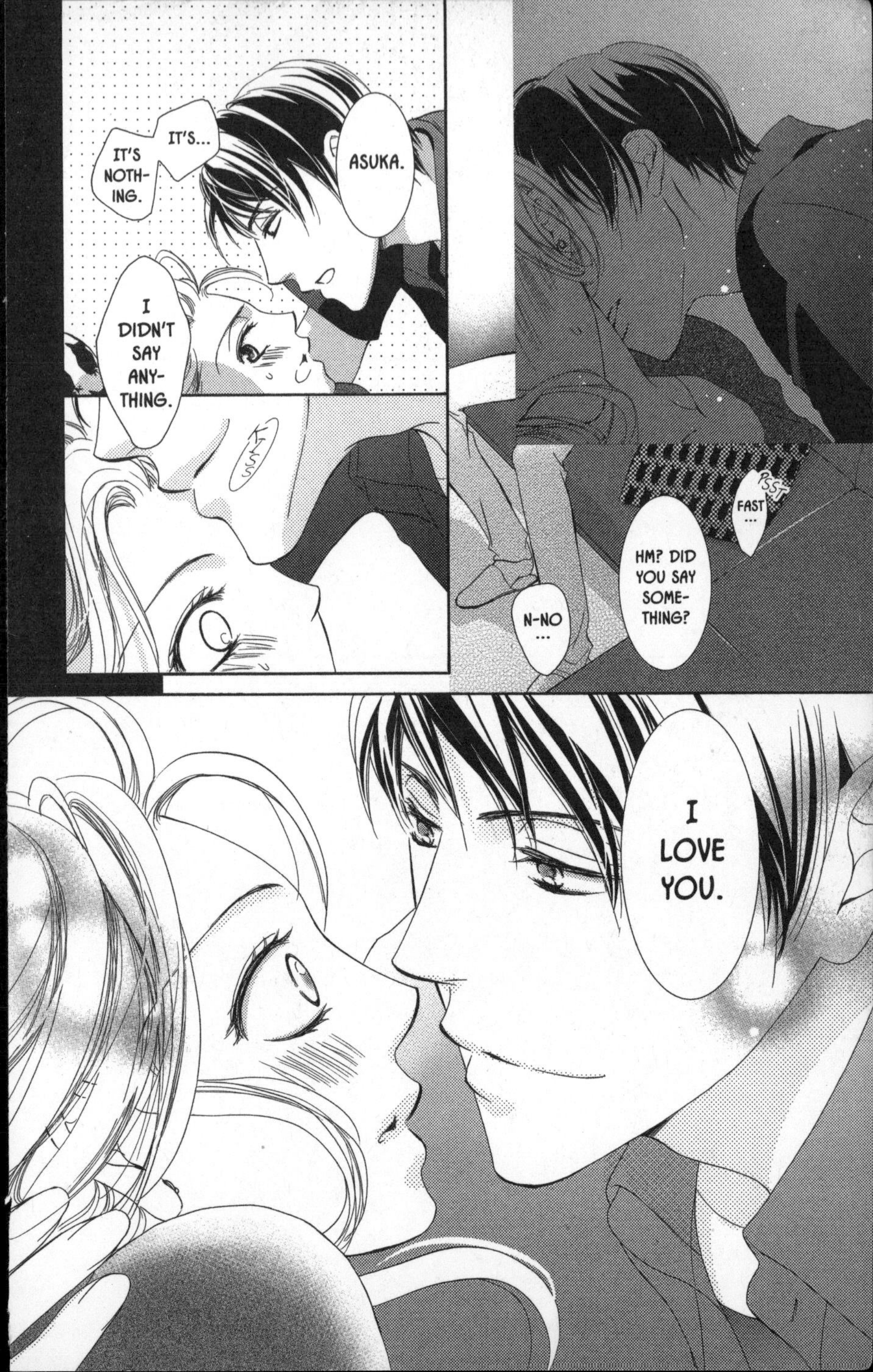
ASUKA.
IT'S...
IT'S NOTHING.
I DIDN'T SAY ANYTHING.
PSST
FAST...
HM? DID YOU SAY SOMETHING?
N-NO...
KISS
I LOVE YOU.

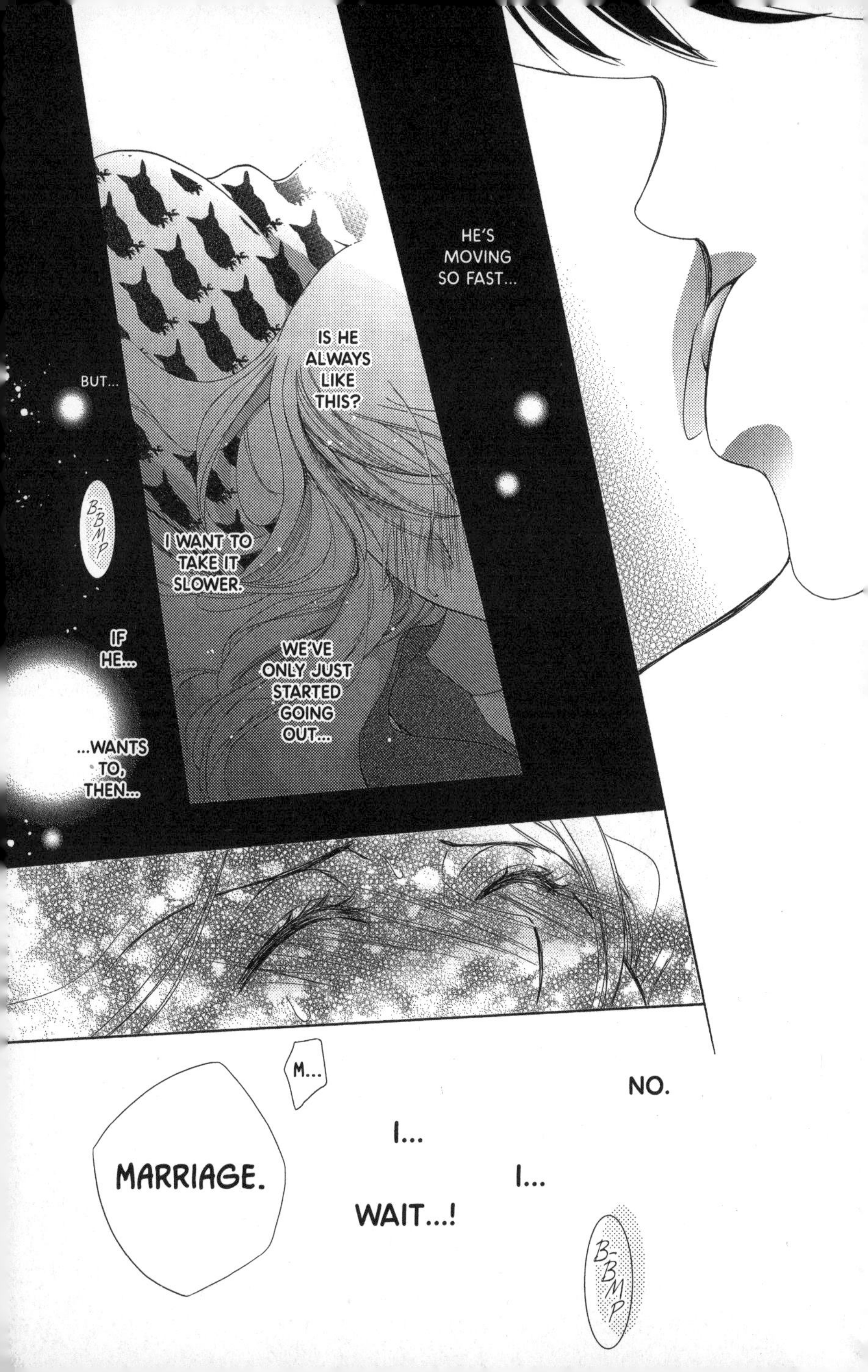
HE'S MOVING SO FAST...
IS HE ALWAYS LIKE THIS?
WE'VE ONLY JUST STARTED GOING OUT...
I WANT TO TAKE IT SLOWER.
BUT...
B-BMP
IF HE...
...WANTS TO, THEN...
NO.
M...
I...
I...
WAIT...!
MARRIAGE.
B-BMP

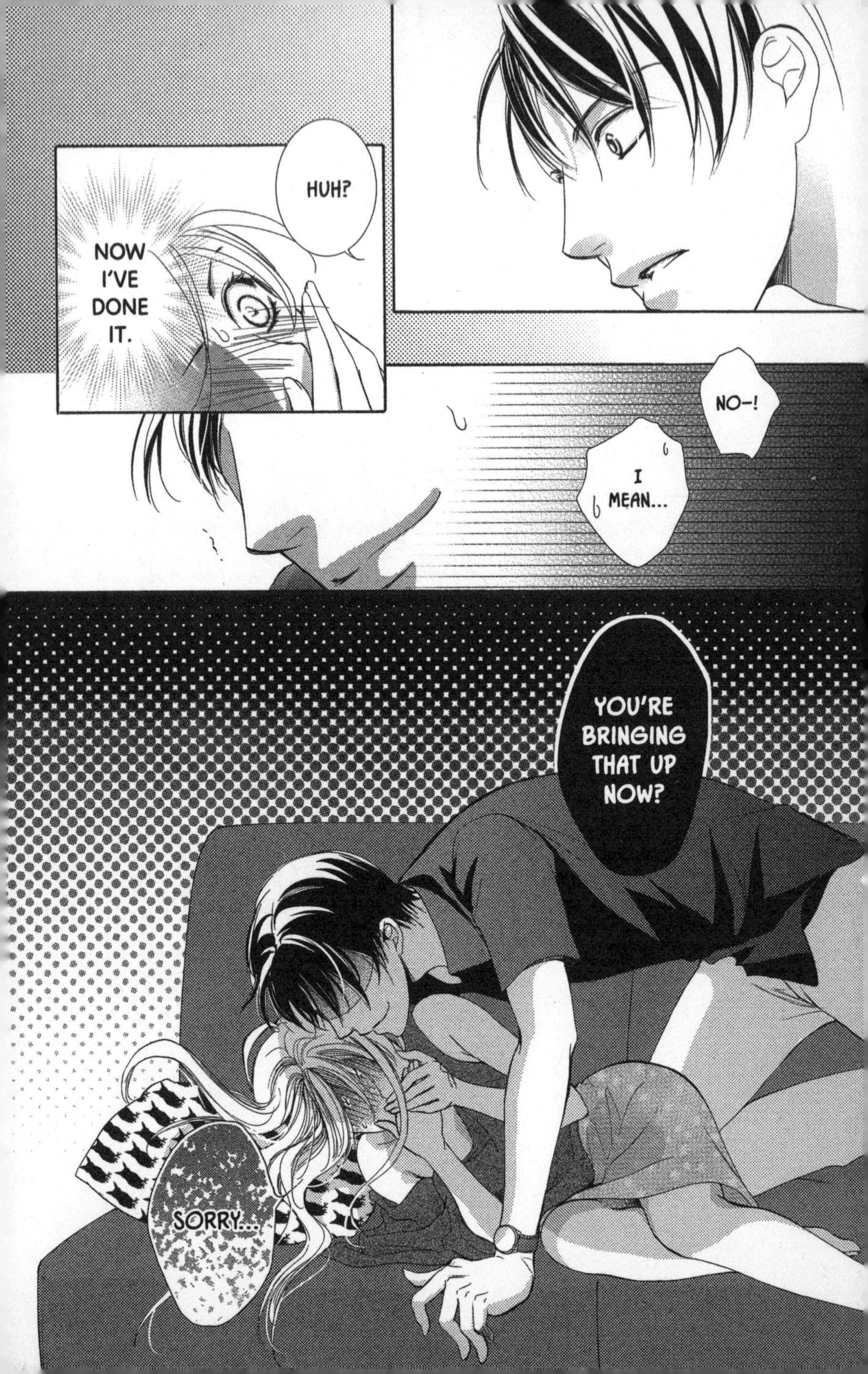
HUH?
NOW I'VE DONE IT.
NO-!
I MEAN...
YOU'RE BRINGING THAT UP NOW?
SORRY...

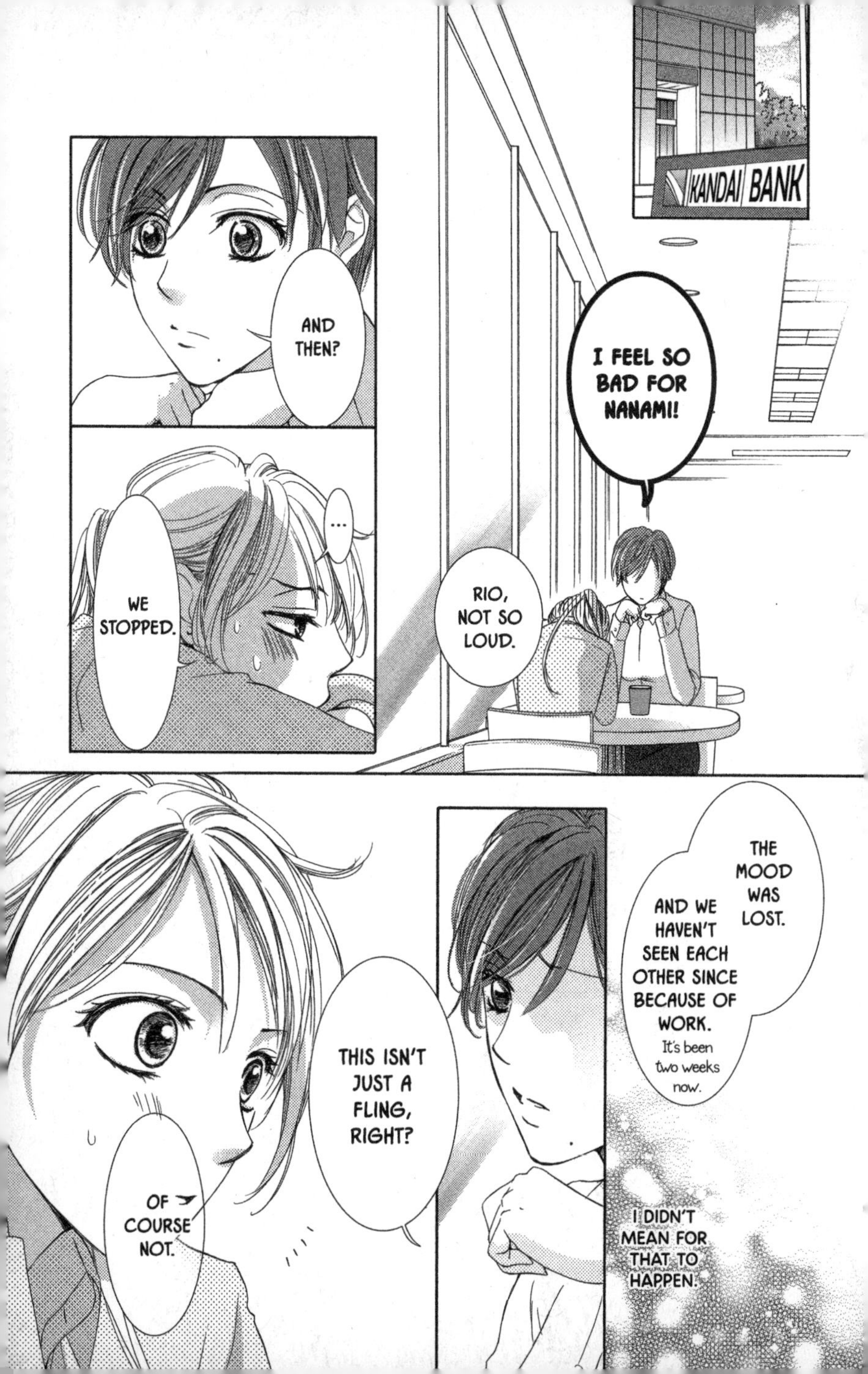
KANDAI BANK
I FEEL SO BAD FOR NANAMI!
RIO, NOT SO LOUD.
AND THEN?
...
WE STOPPED.
THE MOOD WAS LOST.
AND WE HAVEN'T SEEN EACH OTHER SINCE BECAUSE OF WORK.
It's been two weeks now.
I DIDN'T MEAN FOR THAT TO HAPPEN.
THIS ISN'T JUST A FLING, RIGHT?
OF COURSE NOT.

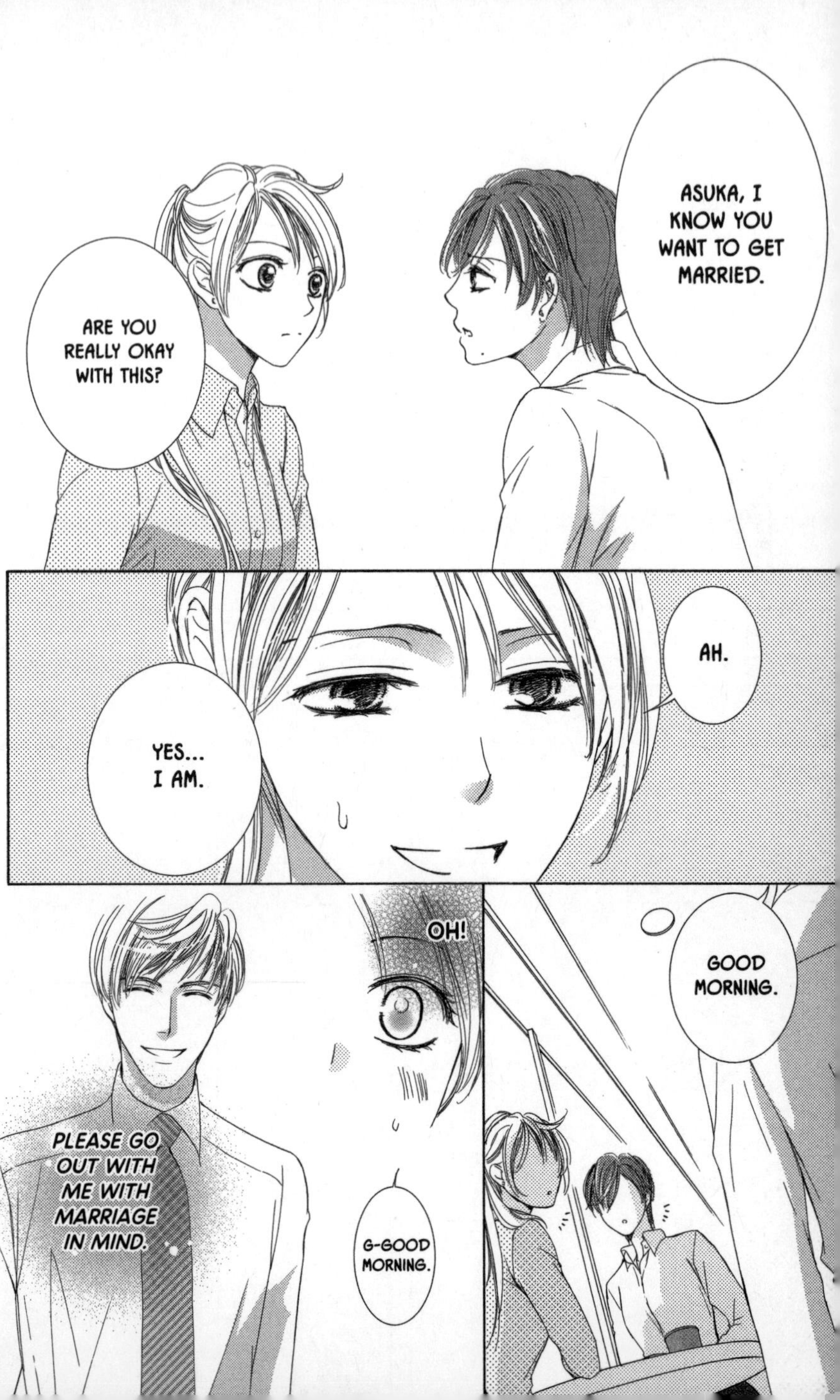
ASUKA, I KNOW YOU WANT TO GET MARRIED.
ARE YOU REALLY OKAY WITH THIS?
AH.
YES... I AM.
GOOD MORNING.
OH!
G-GOOD MORNING.
PLEASE GO OUT WITH ME WITH MARRIAGE IN MIND.

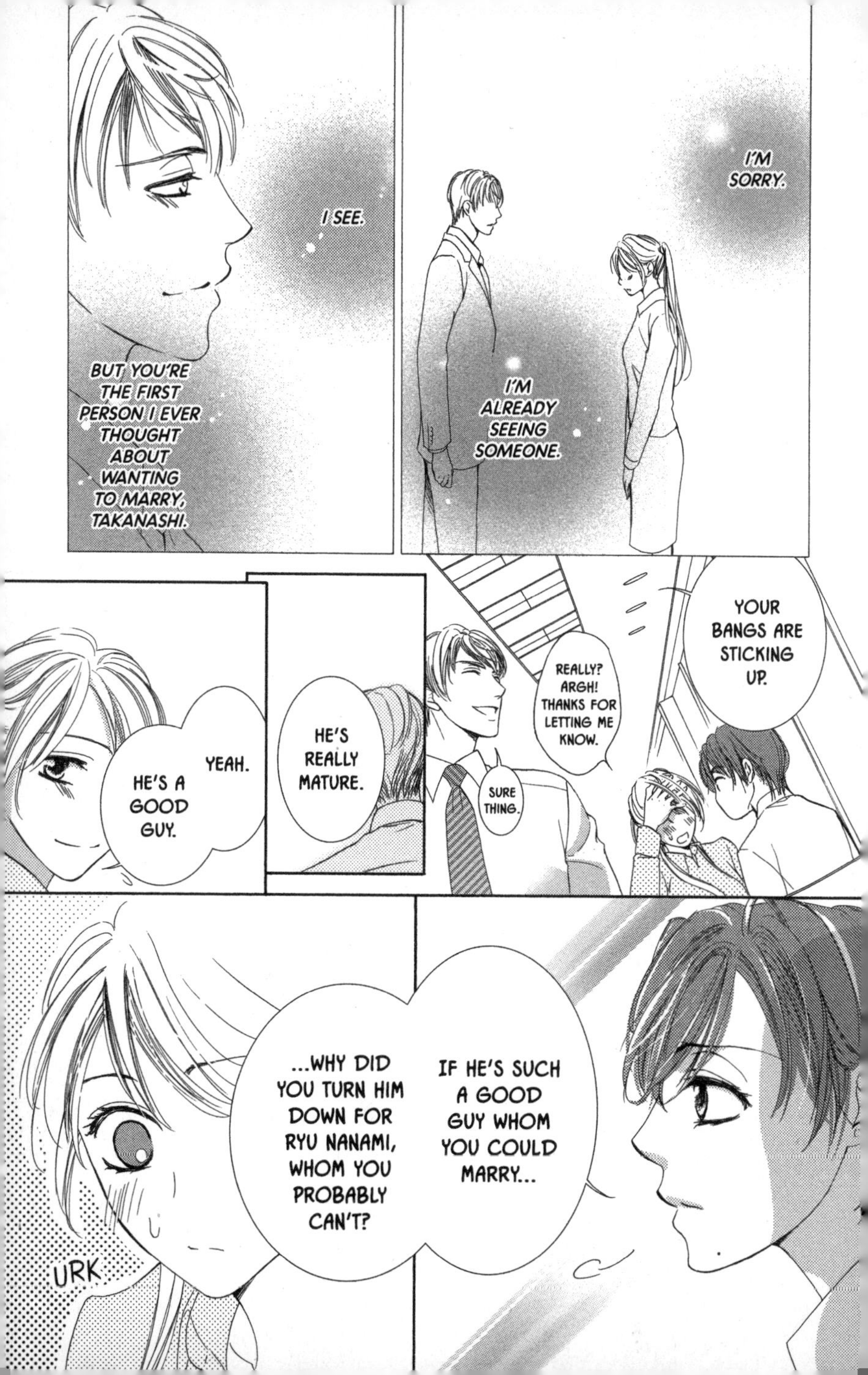
I'M SORRY.
I'M ALREADY SEEING SOMEONE.
I SEE.
BUT YOU'RE THE FIRST PERSON I EVER THOUGHT ABOUT WANTING TO MARRY, TAKANASHI.
YOUR BANGS ARE STICKING UP.
REALLY? ARGH! THANKS FOR LETTING ME KNOW.
SURE THING.
HE'S REALLY MATURE.
YEAH.
HE'S A GOOD GUY.
IF HE'S SUCH A GOOD GUY WHOM YOU COULD MARRY...
...WHY DID YOU TURN HIM DOWN FOR RYU NANAMI, WHOM YOU PROBABLY CAN'T?
URK

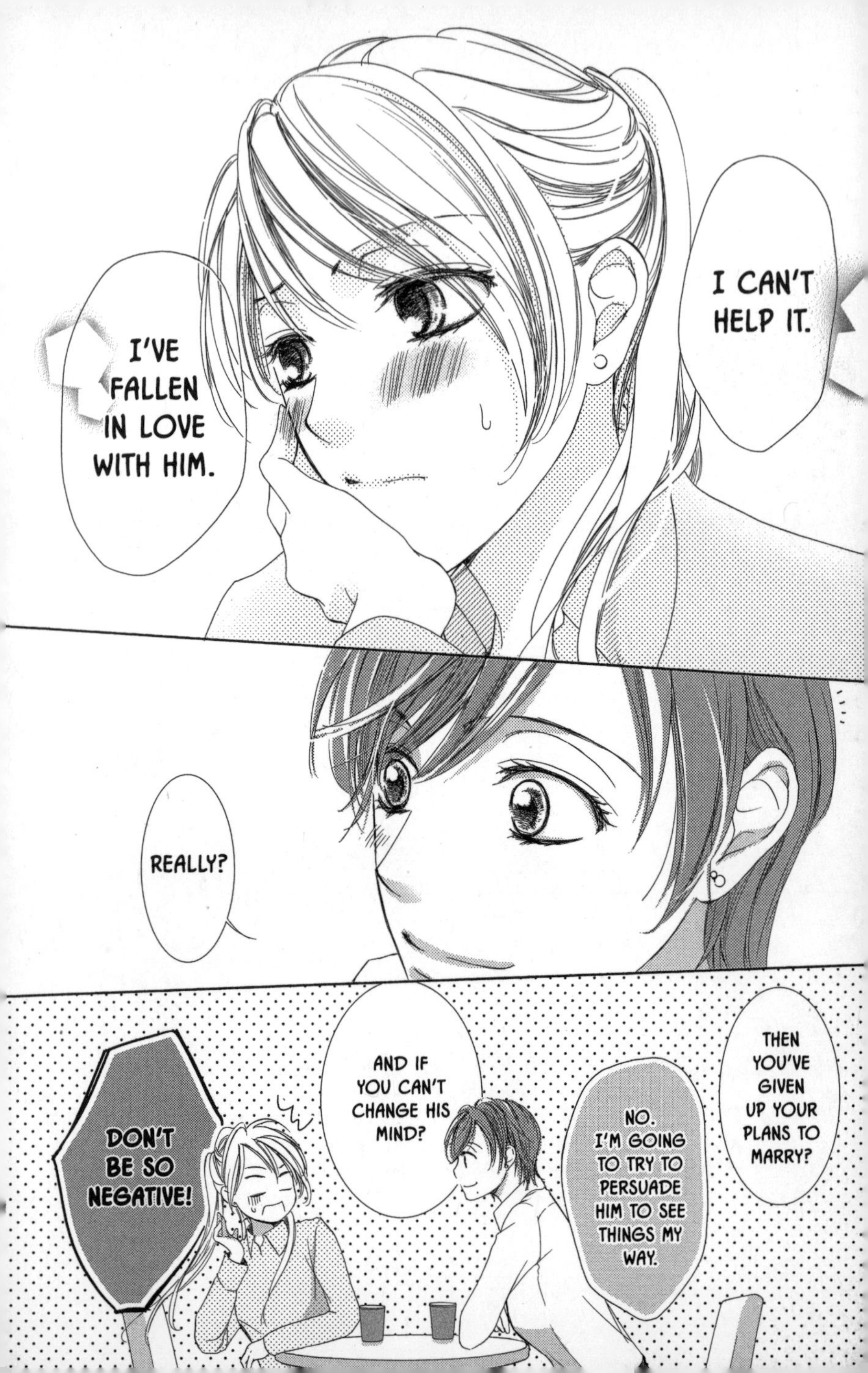
I CAN'T HELP IT.
I'VE FALLEN IN LOVE WITH HIM.
REALLY?
THEN YOU'VE GIVEN UP YOUR PLANS TO MARRY?
NO. I'M GOING TO TRY TO PERSUADE HIM TO SEE THINGS MY WAY.
AND IF YOU CAN'T CHANGE HIS MIND?
DON'T BE SO NEGATIVE!

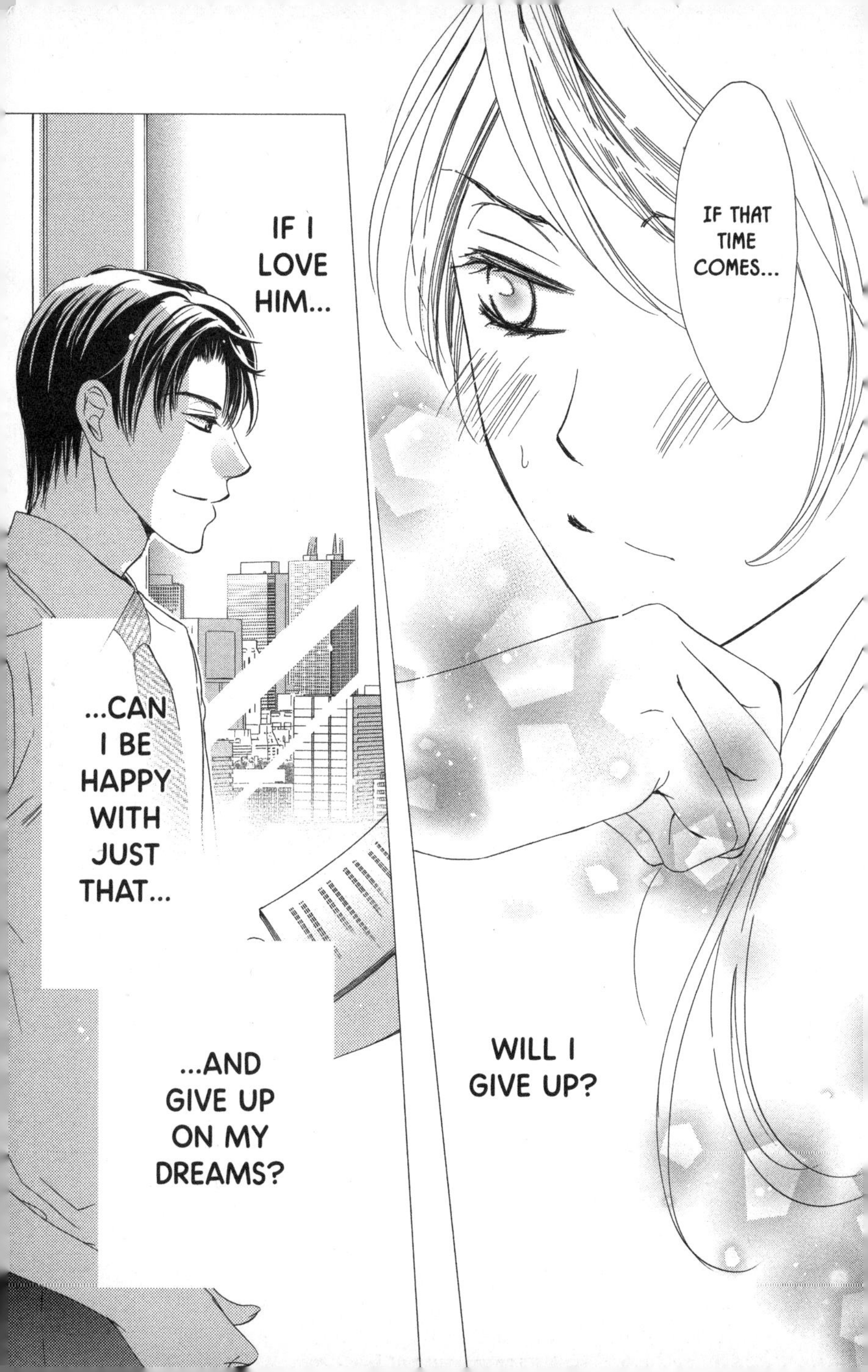
IF THAT TIME COMES...
WILL I GIVE UP?
IF I LOVE HIM...
...CAN I BE HAPPY WITH JUST THAT...
...AND GIVE UP ON MY DREAMS?

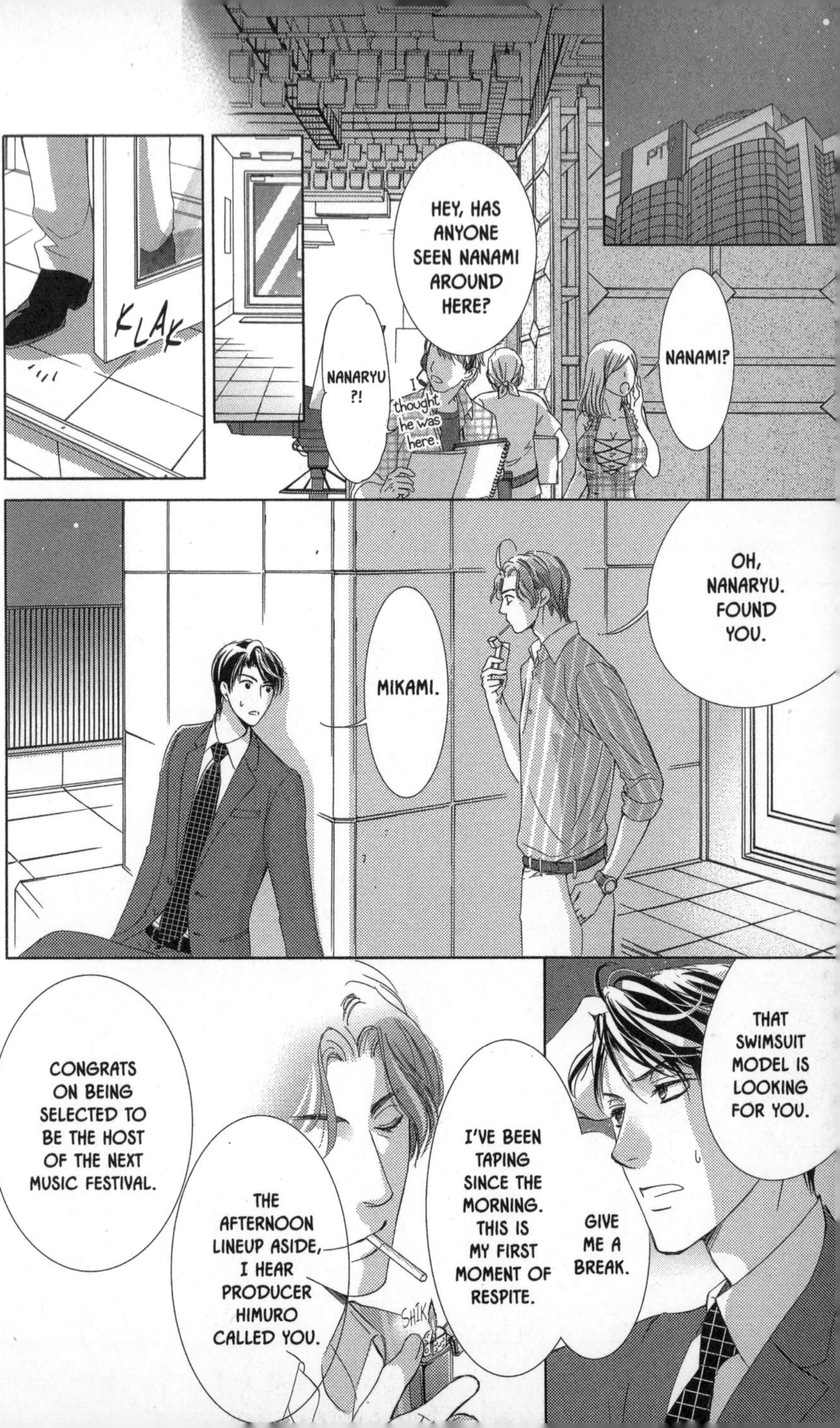
HEY, HAS ANYONE SEEN NANAMI AROUND HERE?
NANAMI?
NANARYU?!
I thought he was here.
KLAK
OH, NANARYU. FOUND YOU.
MIKAMI.
THAT SWIMSUIT MODEL IS LOOKING FOR YOU.
I'VE BEEN TAPING SINCE THE MORNING. THIS IS MY FIRST MOMENT OF RESPITE.
GIVE ME A BREAK.
CONGRATS ON BEING SELECTED TO BE THE HOST OF THE NEXT MUSIC FESTIVAL.
THE AFTERNOON LINEUP ASIDE, I HEAR PRODUCER HIMURO CALLED YOU.
SHIK

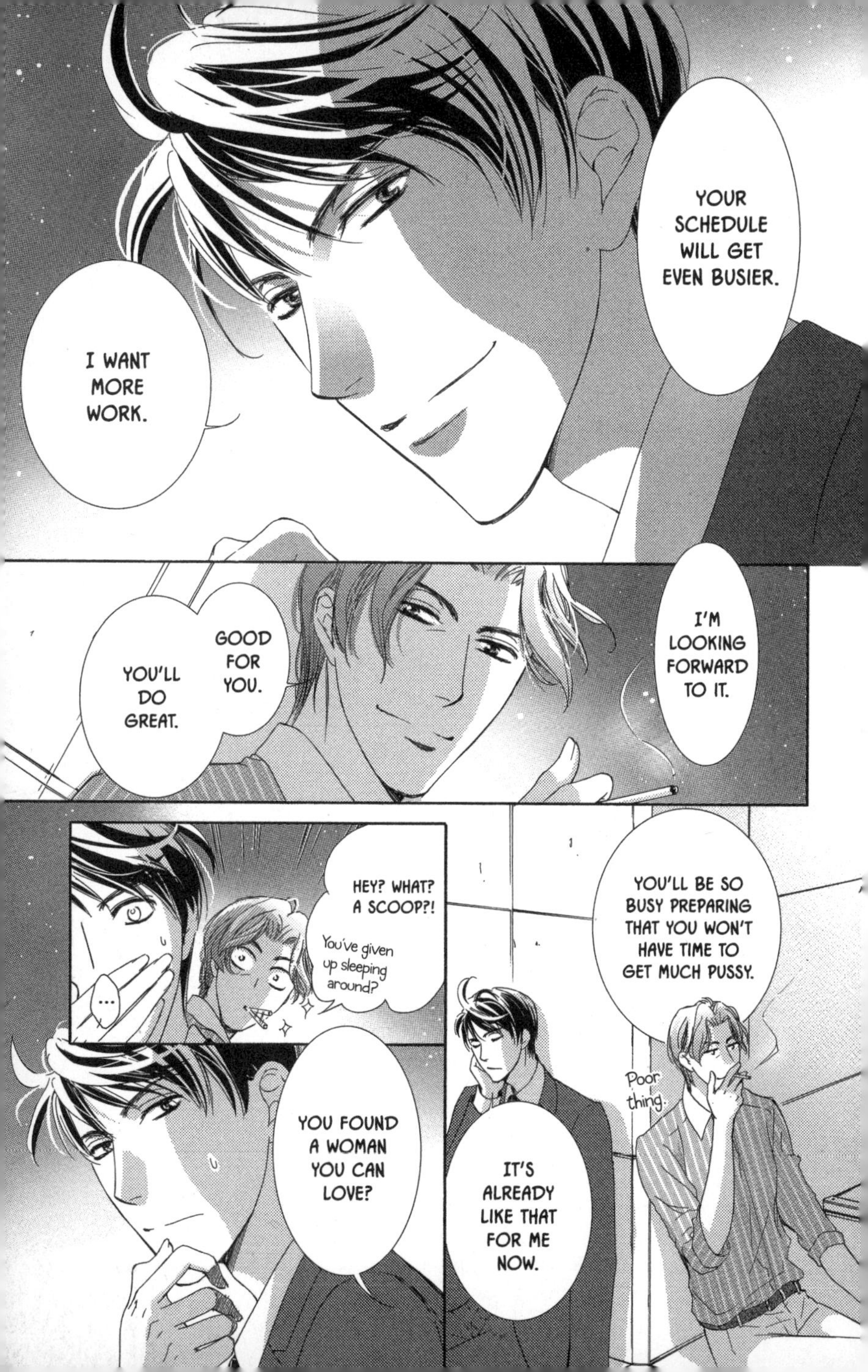
YOUR SCHEDULE WILL GET EVEN BUSIER.
I WANT MORE WORK.
I'M LOOKING FORWARD TO IT.
GOOD FOR YOU.
YOU'LL DO GREAT.
YOU'LL BE SO BUSY PREPARING THAT YOU WON'T HAVE TIME TO GET MUCH PUSSY.
Poor thing.
IT'S ALREADY LIKE THAT FOR ME NOW.
HEY? WHAT? A SCOOP?!
You've given up sleeping around?
...
YOU FOUND A WOMAN YOU CAN LOVE?

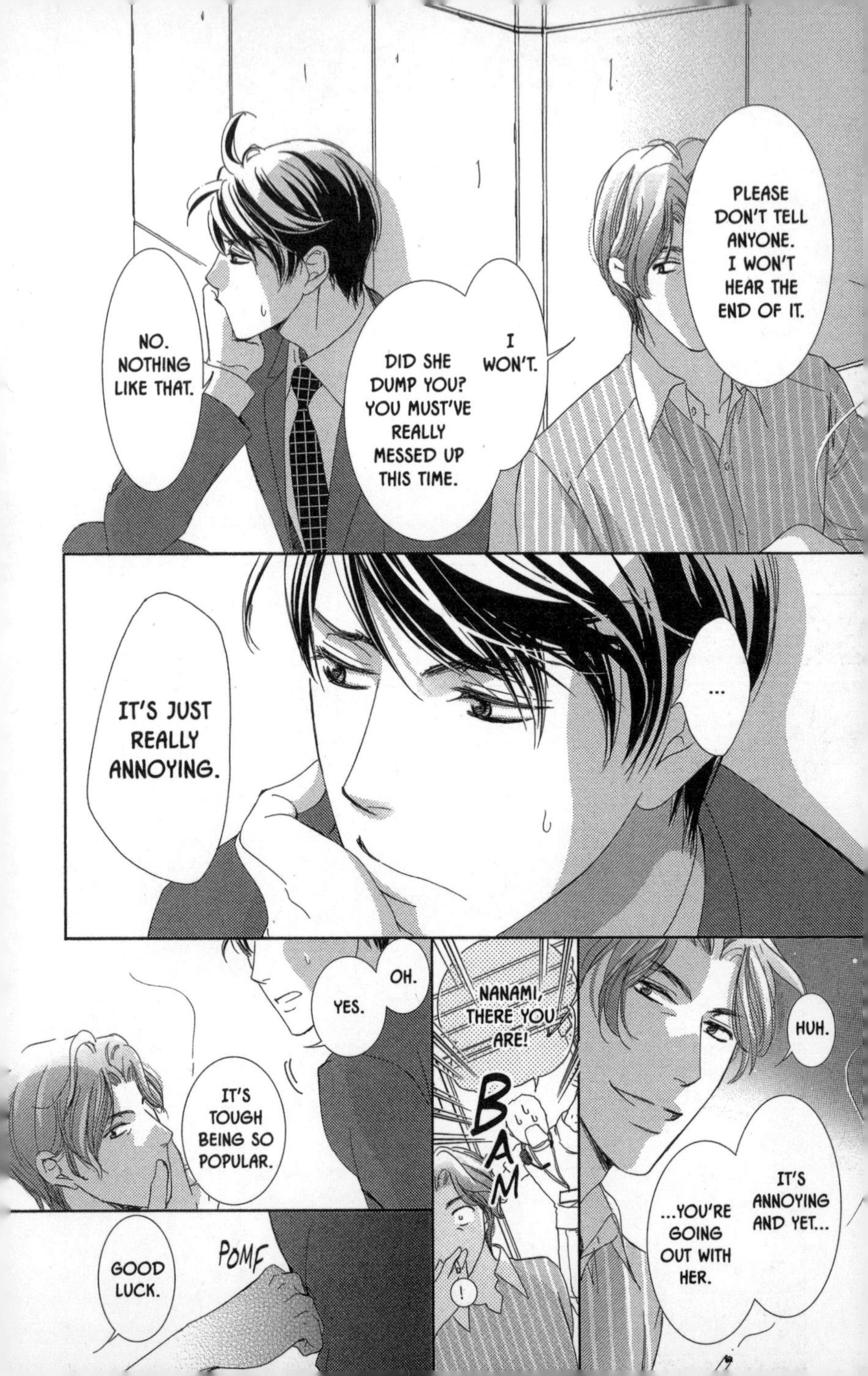
PLEASE DON'T TELL ANYONE. I WON'T HEAR THE END OF IT.
I WON'T.
DID SHE DUMP YOU? YOU MUST'VE REALLY MESSED UP THIS TIME.
NO. NOTHING LIKE THAT.
...
IT'S JUST REALLY ANNOYING.
HUH.
IT'S ANNOYING AND YET...
...YOU'RE GOING OUT WITH HER.
NANAMI, THERE YOU ARE!
BAM
!
OH.
YES.
IT'S TOUGH BEING SO POPULAR.
POMF
GOOD LUCK.

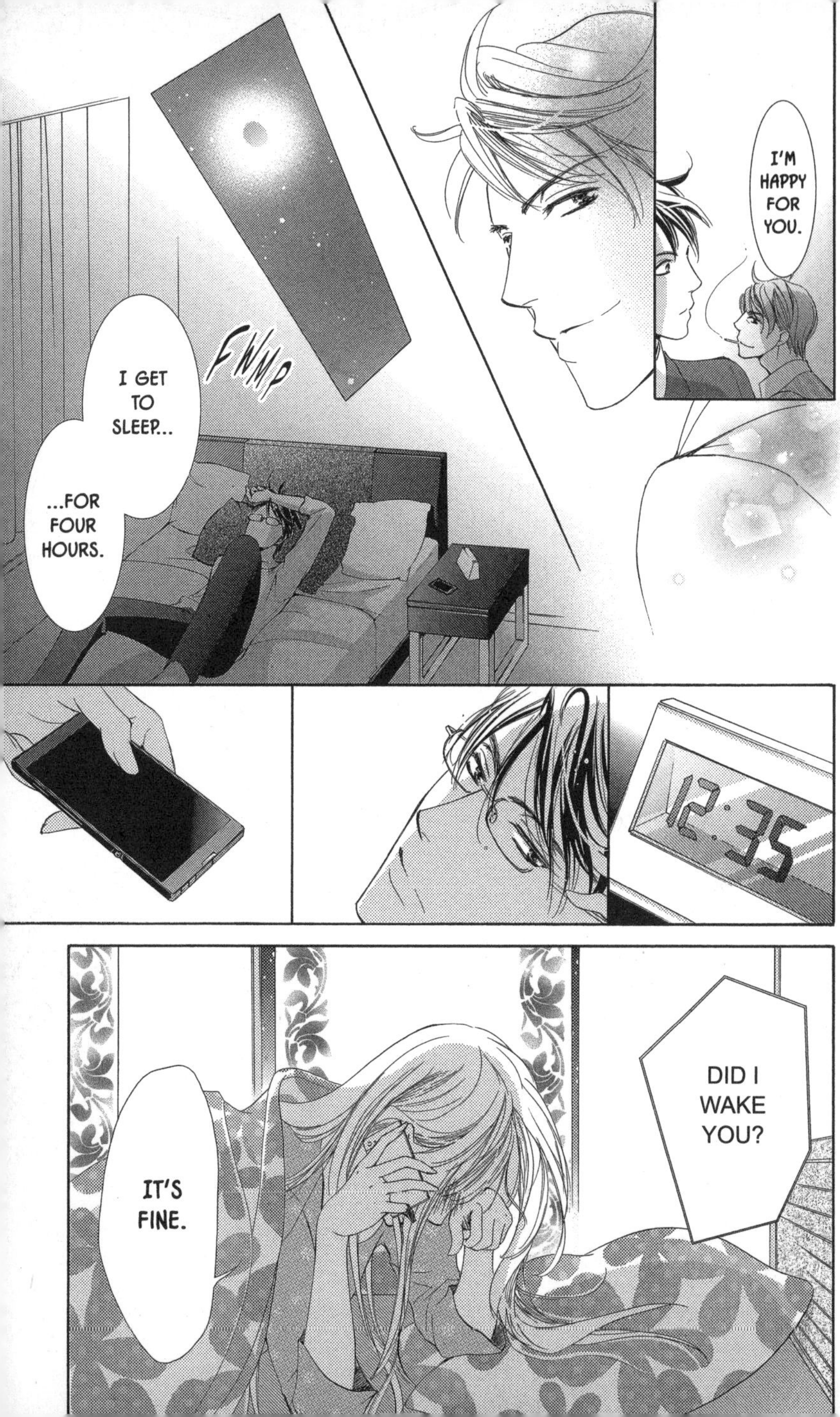
I'M HAPPY FOR YOU.
FWMP
I GET TO SLEEP...
...FOR FOUR HOURS.
12:35
DID I WAKE YOU?
IT'S FINE.

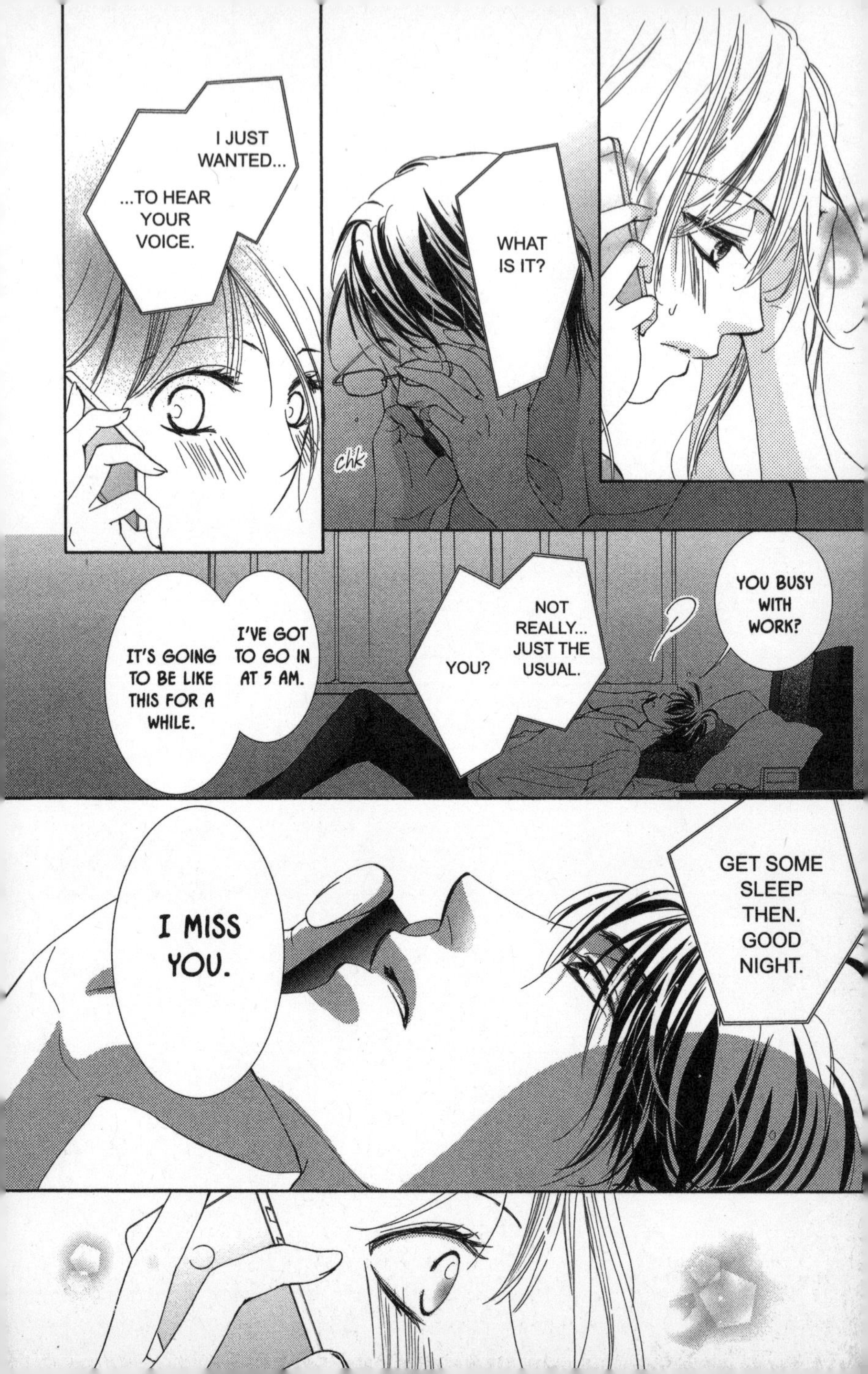
WHAT IS IT?
chk
I JUST WANTED...
...TO HEAR YOUR VOICE.
YOU BUSY WITH WORK?
NOT REALLY... JUST THE USUAL.
YOU?
I'VE GOT TO GO IN AT 5 AM.
IT'S GOING TO BE LIKE THIS FOR A WHILE.
GET SOME SLEEP THEN. GOOD NIGHT.
I MISS YOU.

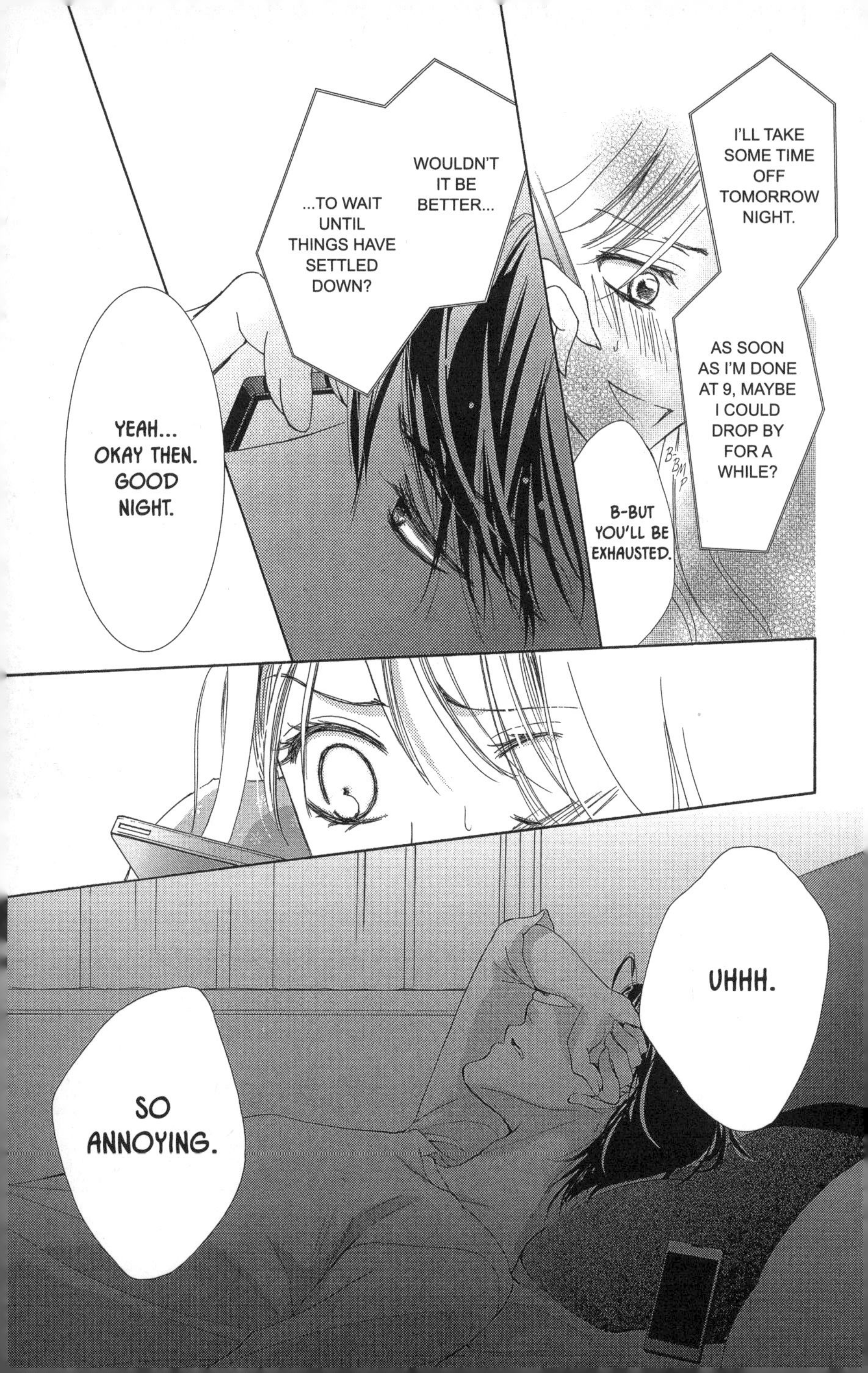
I'LL TAKE SOME TIME OFF TOMORROW NIGHT.
AS SOON AS I'M DONE AT 9, MAYBE I COULD DROP BY FOR A WHILE?
B-BMP
B-BUT YOU'LL BE EXHAUSTED.
WOULDN'T IT BE BETTER...
...TO WAIT UNTIL THINGS HAVE SETTLED DOWN?
YEAH... OKAY THEN. GOOD NIGHT.
UHHH.
SO ANNOYING.

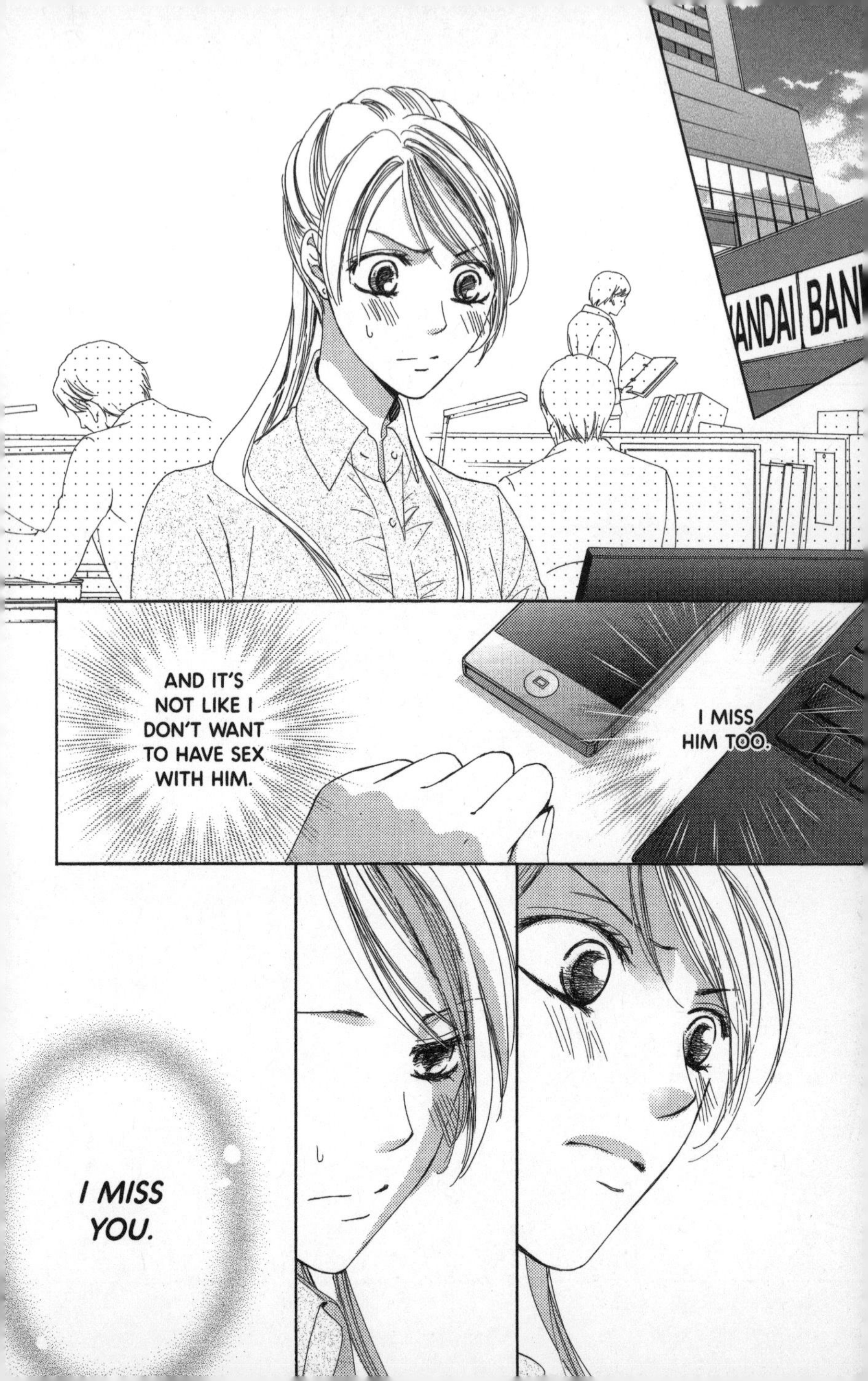
I MISS HIM TOO.
AND IT'S NOT LIKE I DON'T WANT TO HAVE SEX WITH HIM.
I MISS YOU.

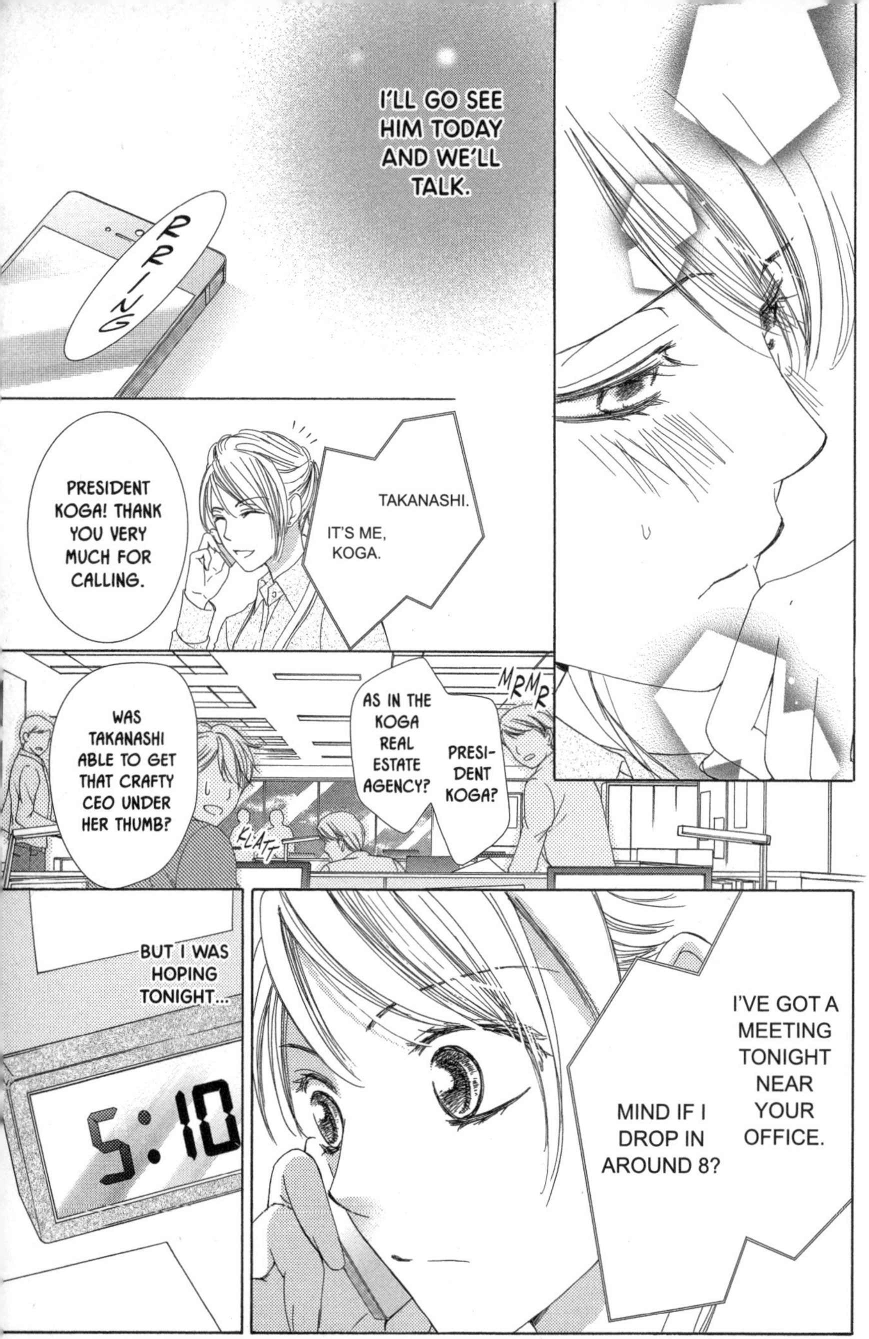
I'LL GO SEE HIM TODAY AND WE'LL TALK.
RRING
TAKANASHI.
IT'S ME, KOGA.
PRESIDENT KOGA! THANK YOU VERY MUCH FOR CALLING.
MRMR
PRESI-DENT KOGA?
AS IN THE KOGA REAL ESTATE AGENCY?
WAS TAKANASHI ABLE TO GET THAT CRAFTY CEO UNDER HER THUMB?
KLATT
I'VE GOT A MEETING TONIGHT NEAR YOUR OFFICE.
MIND IF I DROP IN AROUND 8?
BUT I WAS HOPING TONIGHT...
5:10

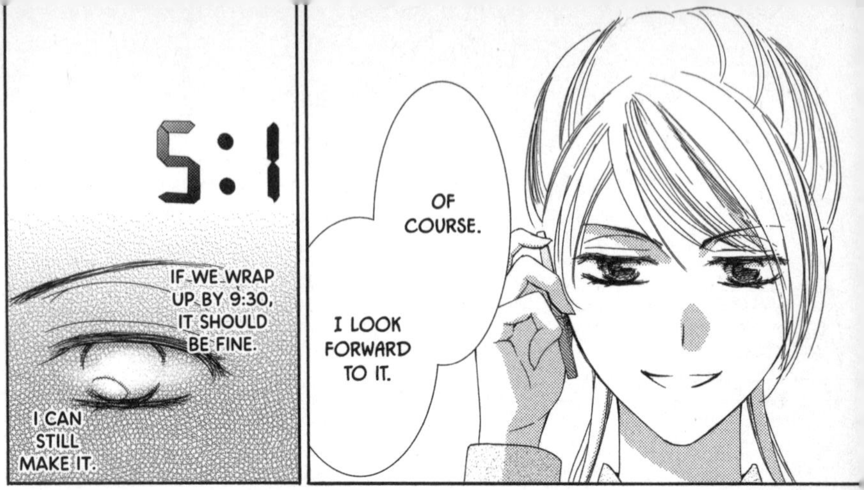
OF COURSE.
I LOOK FORWARD TO IT.
5:1
IF WE WRAP UP BY 9:30, IT SHOULD BE FINE.
I CAN STILL MAKE IT.

8:31 PM

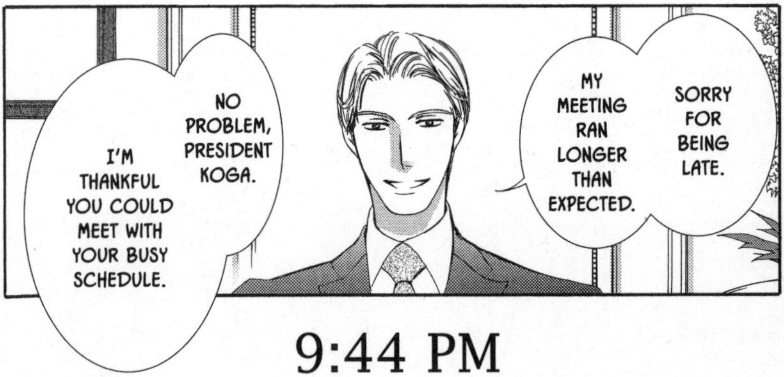
SORRY FOR BEING LATE.
MY MEETING RAN LONGER THAN EXPECTED.
NO PROBLEM, PRESIDENT KOGA.
I'M THANKFUL YOU COULD MEET WITH YOUR BUSY SCHEDULE.

9:44 PM

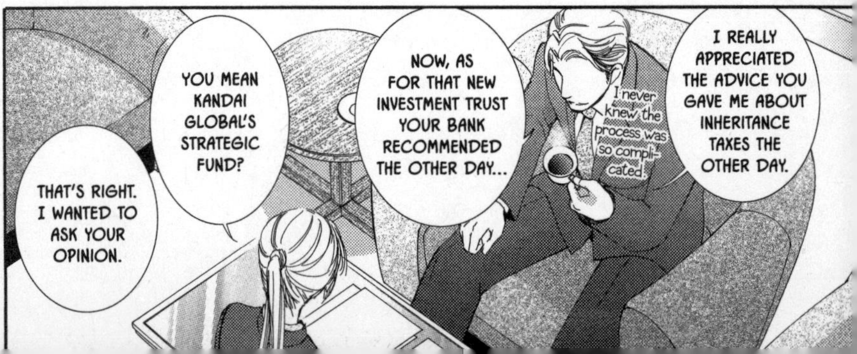
I REALLY APPRECIATED THE ADVICE YOU GAVE ME ABOUT INHERITANCE TAXES THE OTHER DAY.
I never knew the process was so compli-cated.
NOW, AS FOR THAT NEW INVESTMENT TRUST YOUR BANK RECOMMENDED THE OTHER DAY...
YOU MEAN KANDAI GLOBAL'S STRATEGIC FUND?
THAT'S RIGHT. I WANTED TO ASK YOUR OPINION.

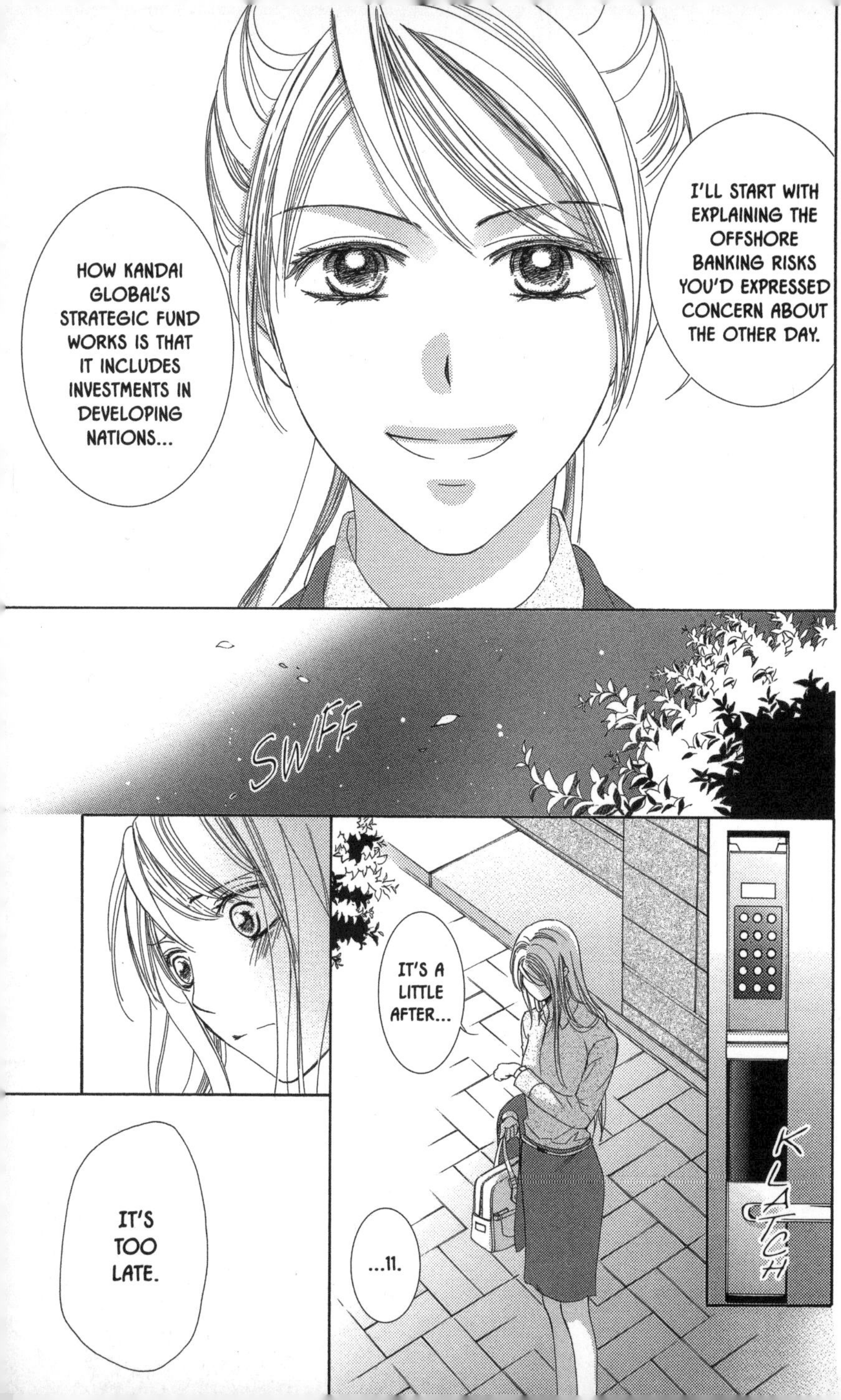
I'LL START WITH EXPLAINING THE OFFSHORE BANKING RISKS YOU'D EXPRESSED CONCERN ABOUT THE OTHER DAY.
HOW KANDAI GLOBAL'S STRATEGIC FUND WORKS IS THAT IT INCLUDES INVESTMENTS IN DEVELOPING NATIONS...
SWFF
KLATCH
IT'S A LITTLE AFTER...
...11.
IT'S TOO LATE.

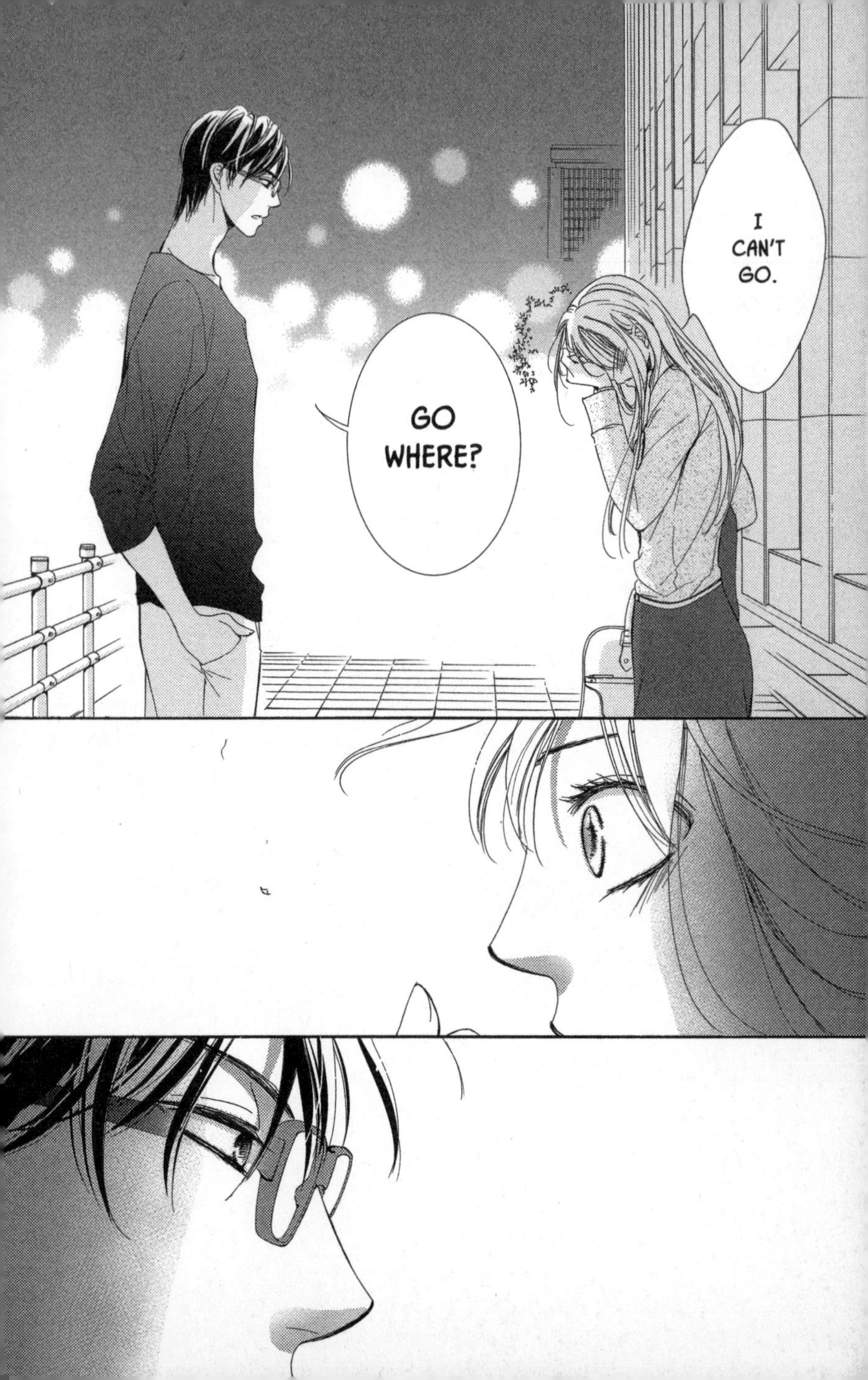
I CAN'T GO.
GO WHERE?

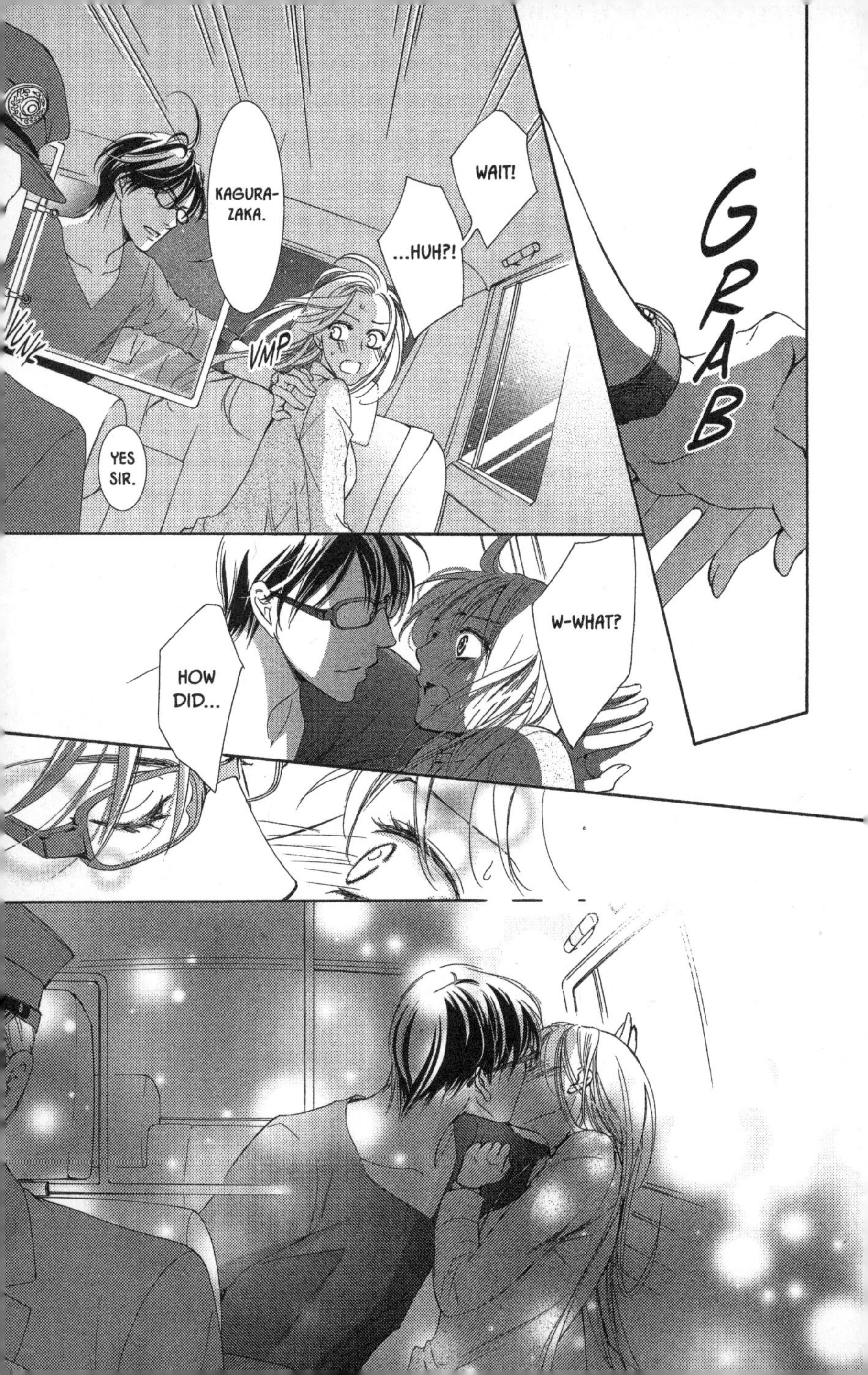
GRAB
WAIT!
...HUH?!
KAGURA-
ZAKA.
VMP
YES
SIR.
W-WHAT?
HOW
DID...

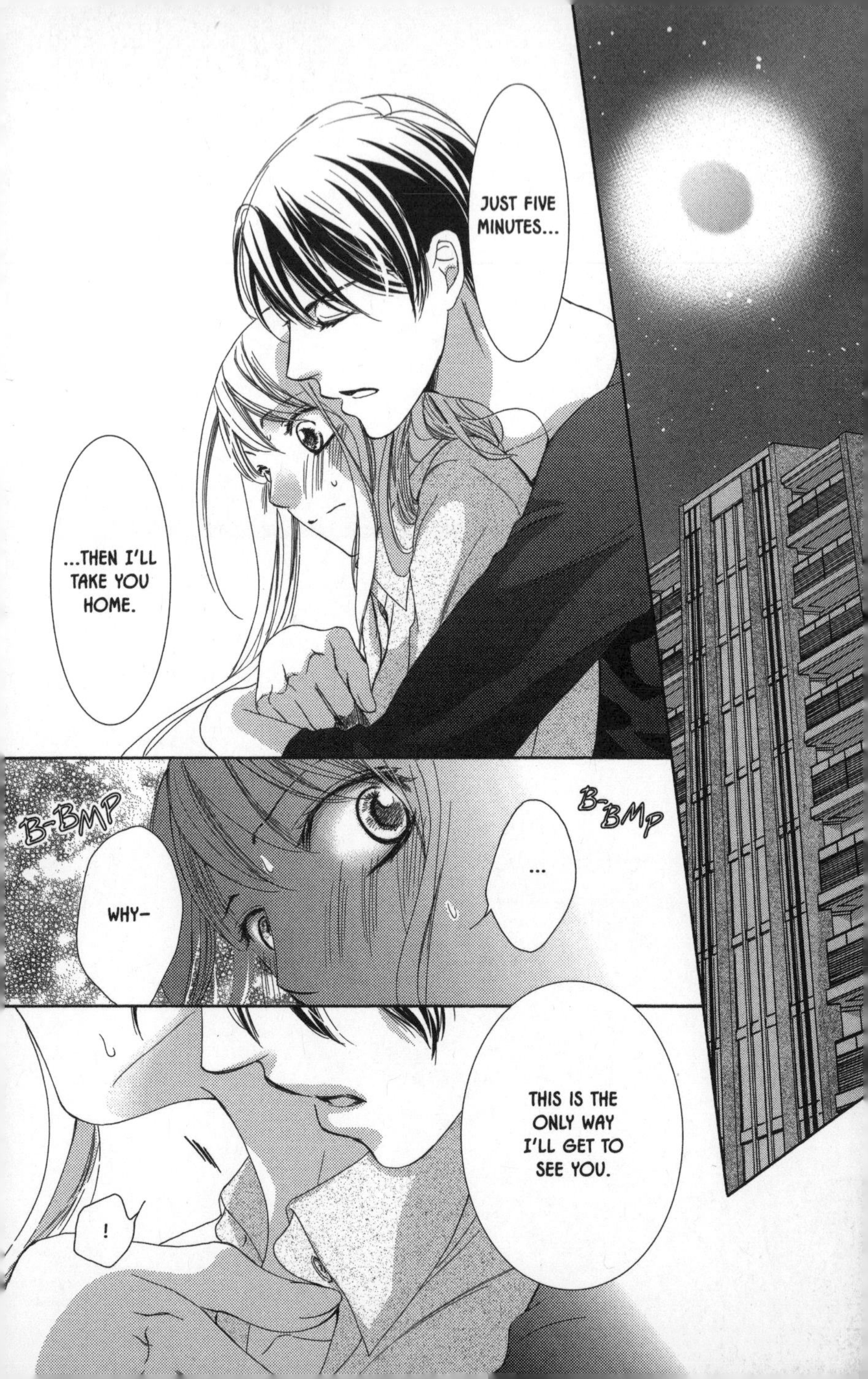
JUST FIVE MINUTES...
...THEN I'LL TAKE YOU HOME.
B-BMP
...
WHY-
B-BMP
THIS IS THE ONLY WAY I'LL GET TO SEE YOU.
!

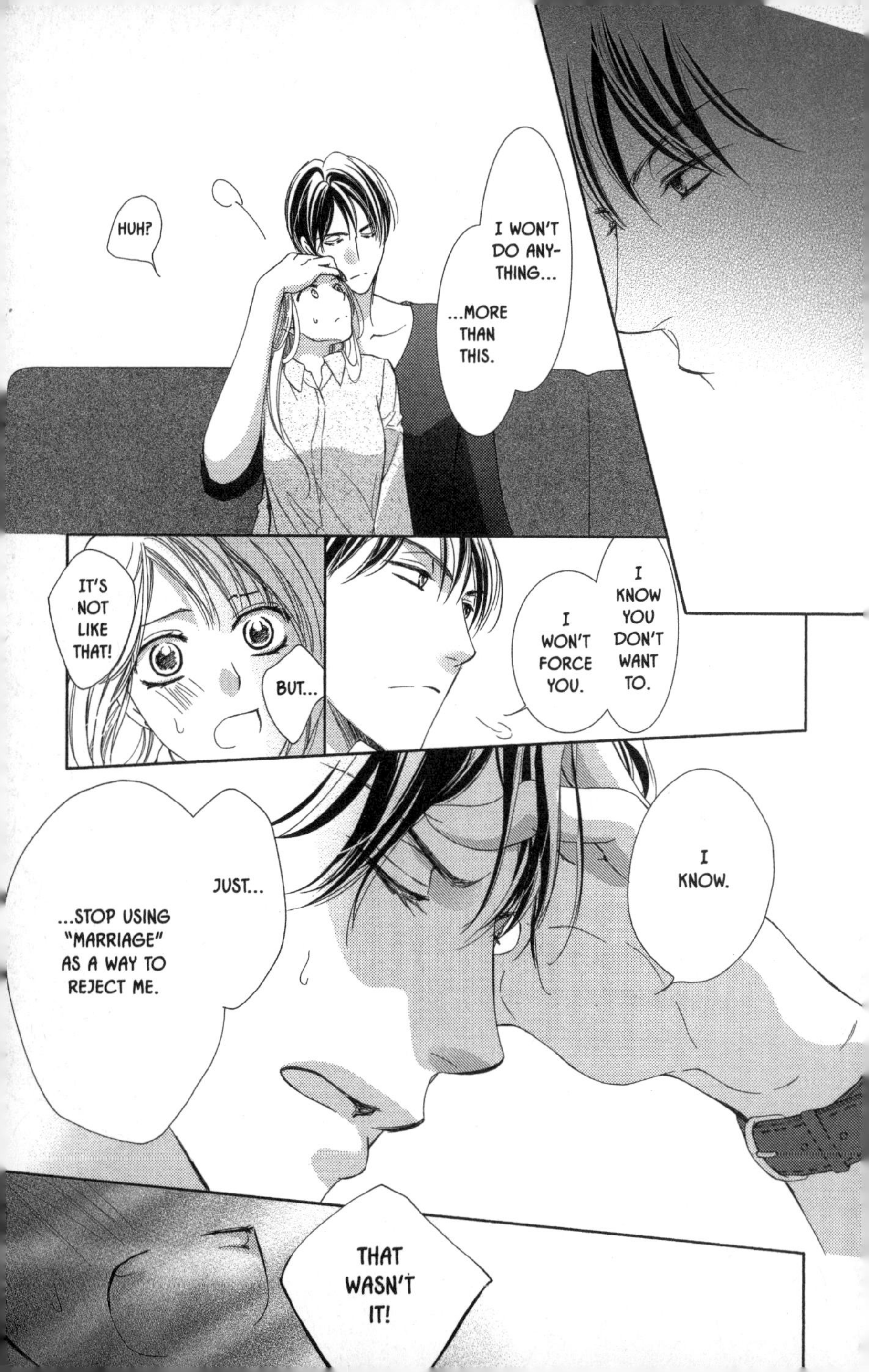
I WON'T DO ANYTHING...
...MORE THAN THIS.
HUH?
I KNOW YOU DON'T WANT TO.
I WON'T FORCE YOU.
IT'S NOT LIKE THAT!
BUT...
I KNOW.
JUST...
...STOP USING "MARRIAGE" AS A WAY TO REJECT ME.
THAT WASN'T IT!

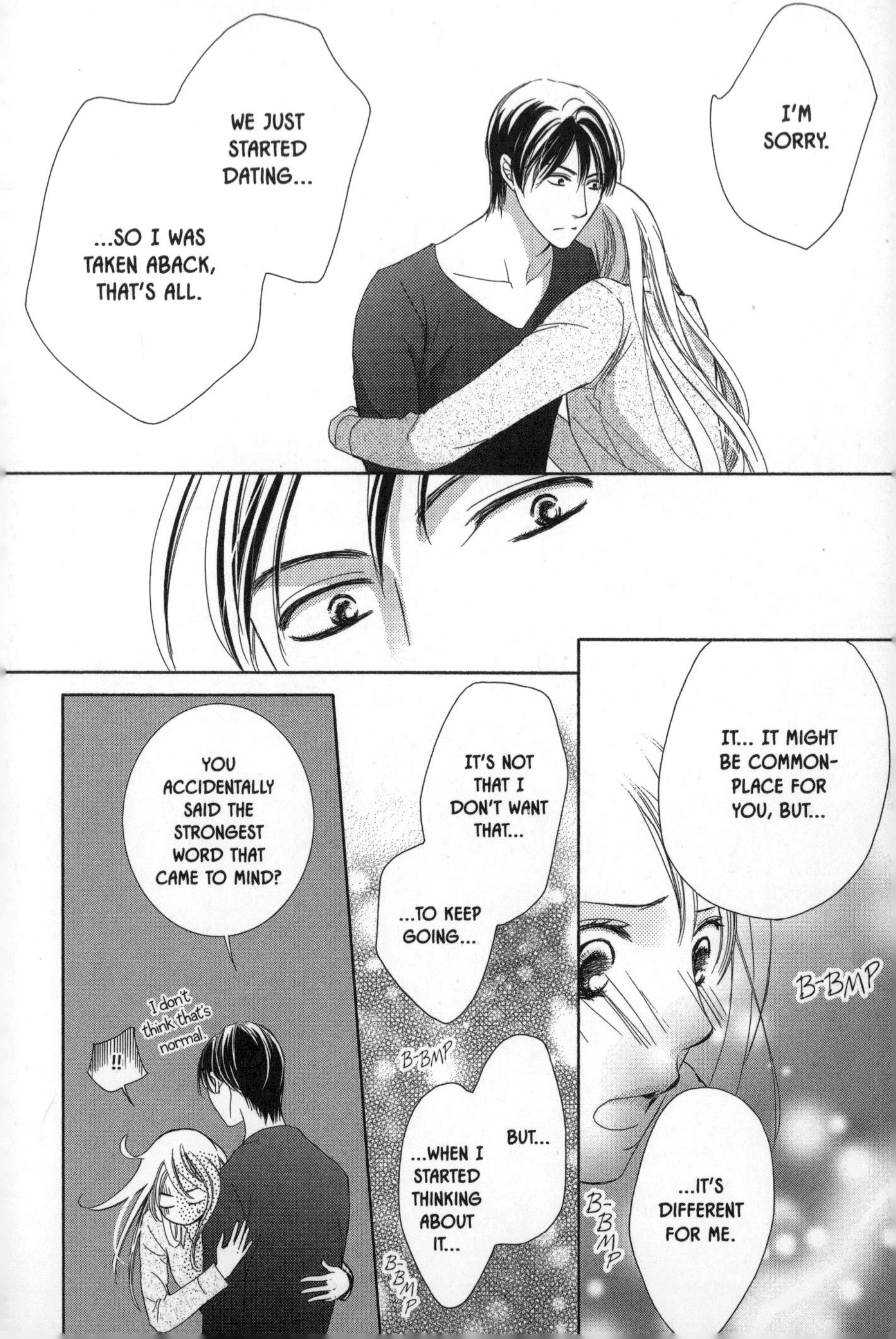
I'M SORRY.
WE JUST STARTED DATING...
...SO I WAS TAKEN ABACK, THAT'S ALL.
IT... IT MIGHT BE COMMON-PLACE FOR YOU, BUT...
B-BMP
...IT'S DIFFERENT FOR ME.
B-BMP
IT'S NOT THAT I DON'T WANT THAT...
...TO KEEP GOING...
B-BMP
BUT...
...WHEN I STARTED THINKING ABOUT IT...
B-BMP
YOU ACCIDENTALLY SAID THE STRONGEST WORD THAT CAME TO MIND?
I don't think that's normal.
!!

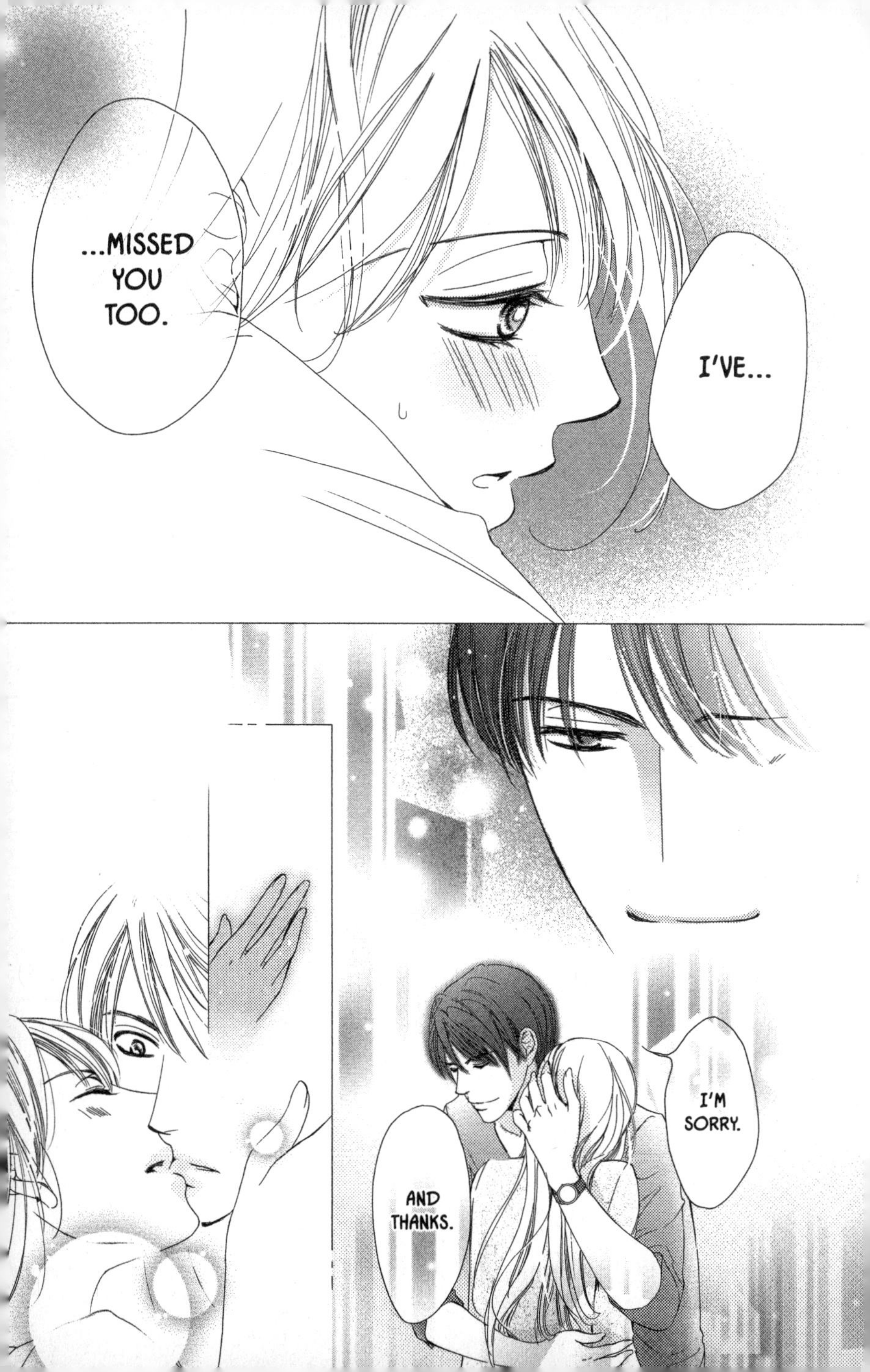
I'VE...
...MISSED YOU TOO.
I'M SORRY.
AND THANKS.

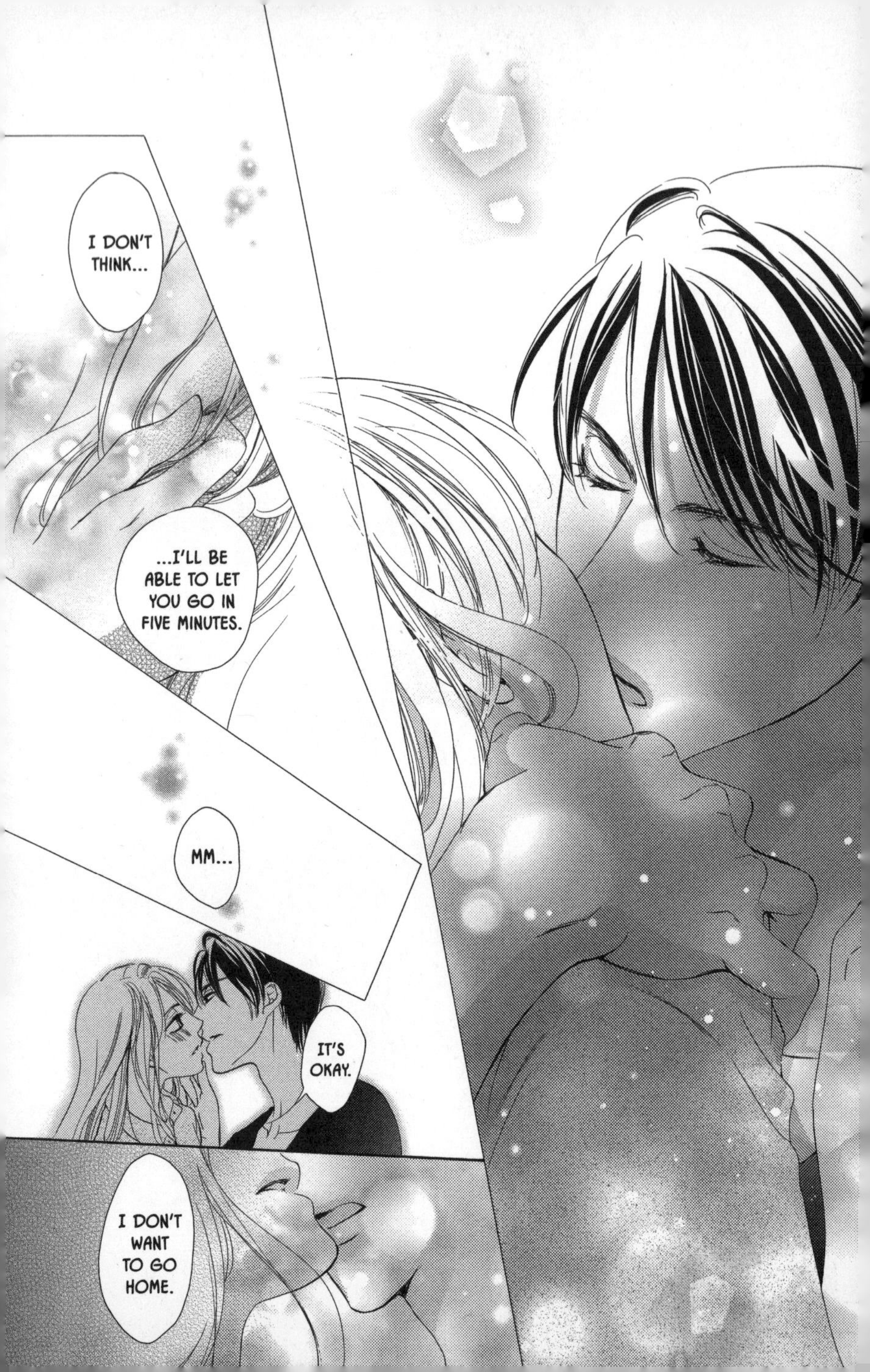
I DON'T THINK...
...I'LL BE ABLE TO LET YOU GO IN FIVE MINUTES.
MM...
IT'S OKAY.
I DON'T WANT TO GO HOME.

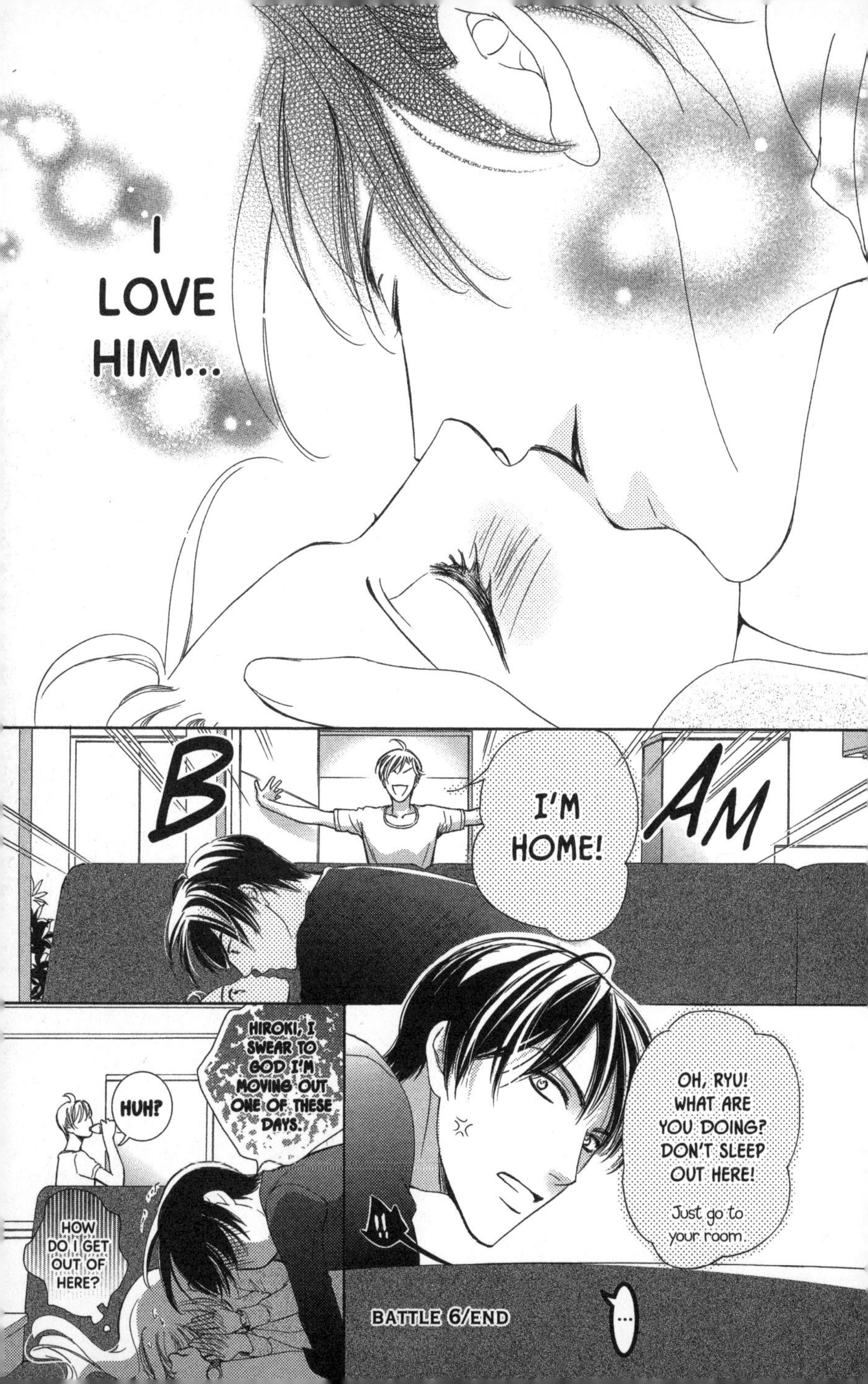
I LOVE HIM...
BAM
I'M HOME!
OH, RYU! WHAT ARE YOU DOING? DON'T SLEEP OUT HERE!
Just go to your room.
!!
...
BATTLE 6/END
HIROKI, I SWEAR TO GOD I'M MOVING OUT ONE OF THESE DAYS.
HUH?
HOW DO I GET OUT OF HERE?

I love you,
so...

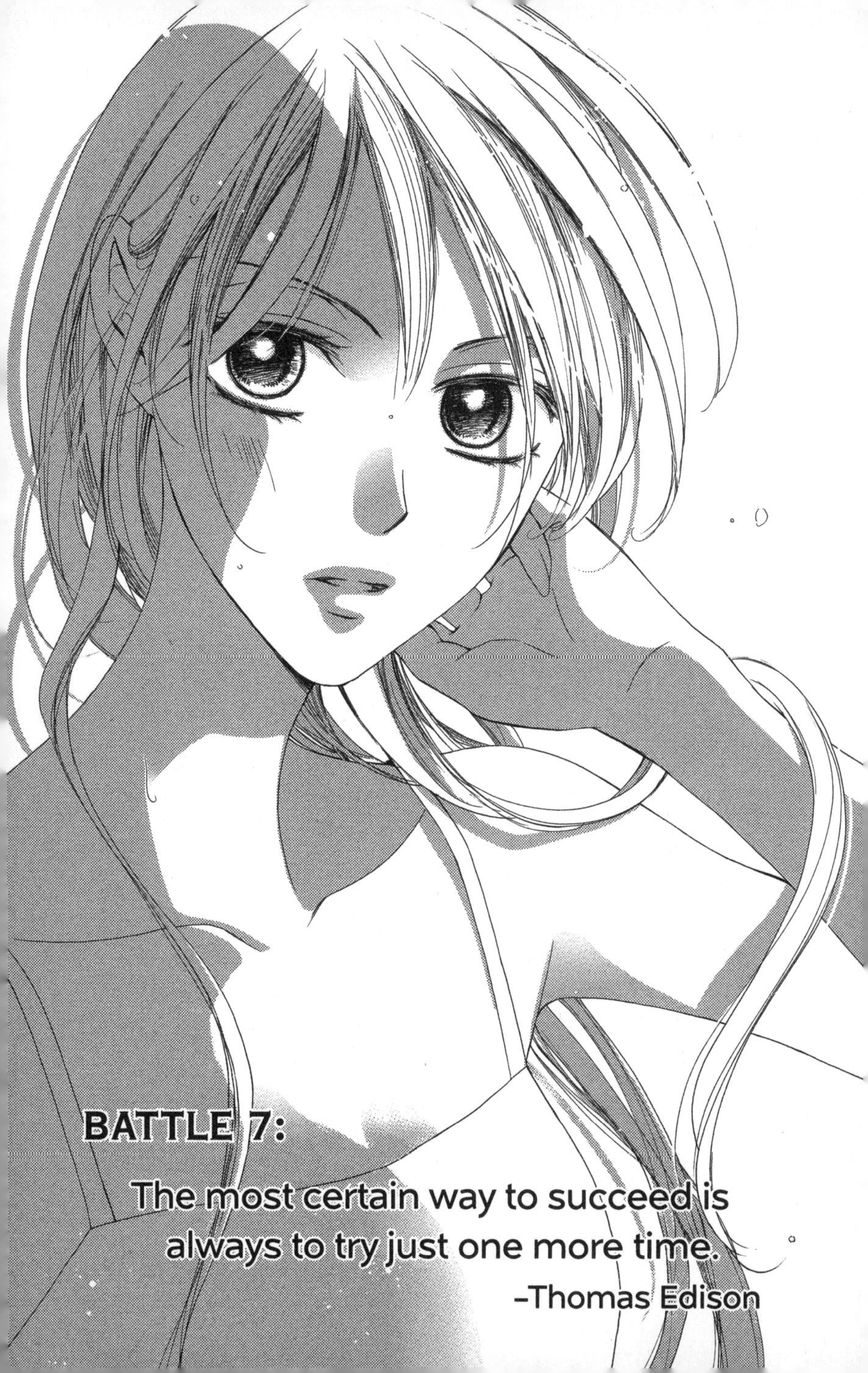
BATTLE 7:
The most certain way to succeed is always to try just one more time.
–Thomas Edison

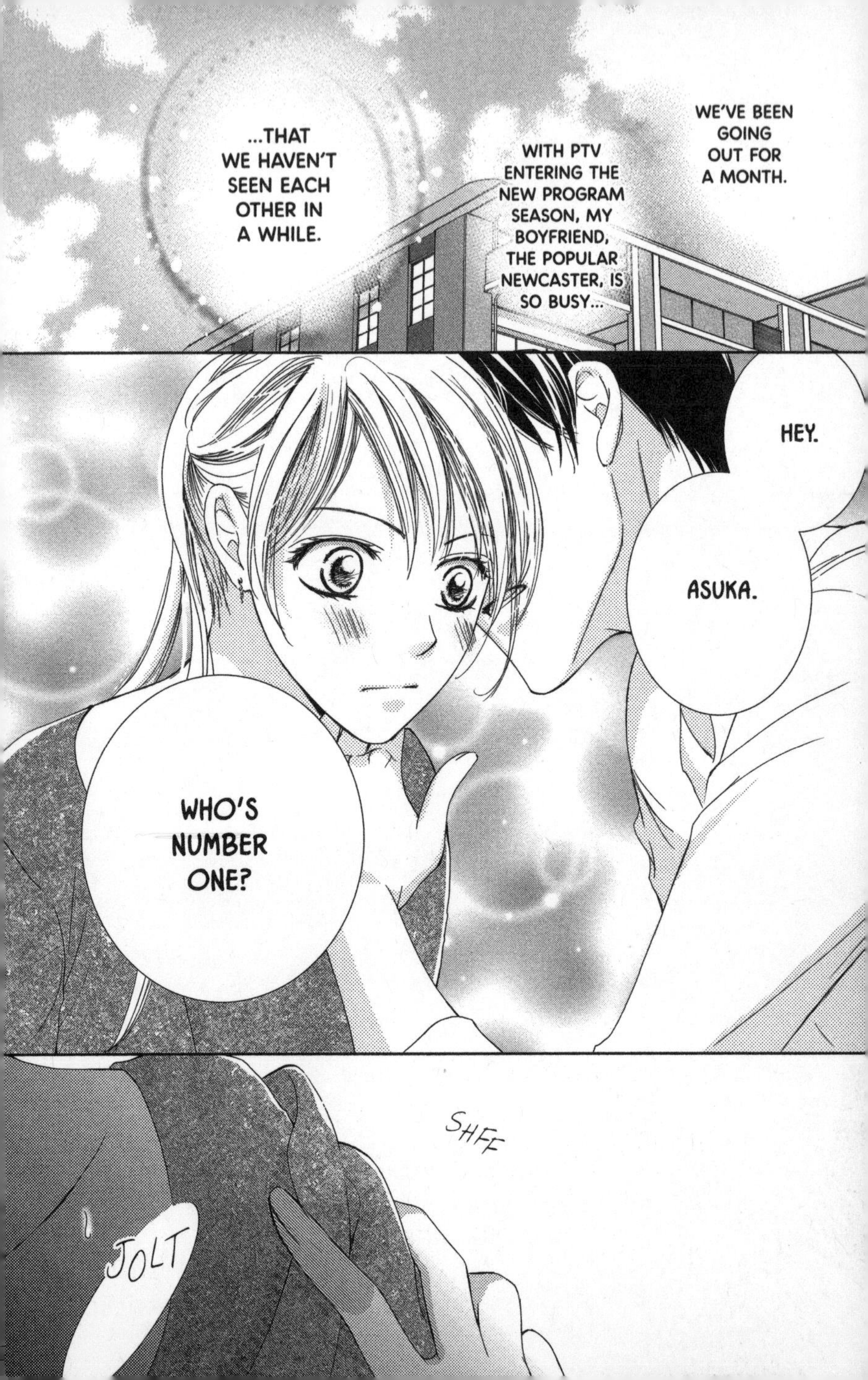
WE'VE BEEN GOING OUT FOR A MONTH.
WITH PTV ENTERING THE NEW PROGRAM SEASON, MY BOYFRIEND, THE POPULAR NEWCASTER, IS SO BUSY...
...THAT WE HAVEN'T SEEN EACH OTHER IN A WHILE.
HEY.
ASUKA.
WHO'S NUMBER ONE?
SHFF
JOLT

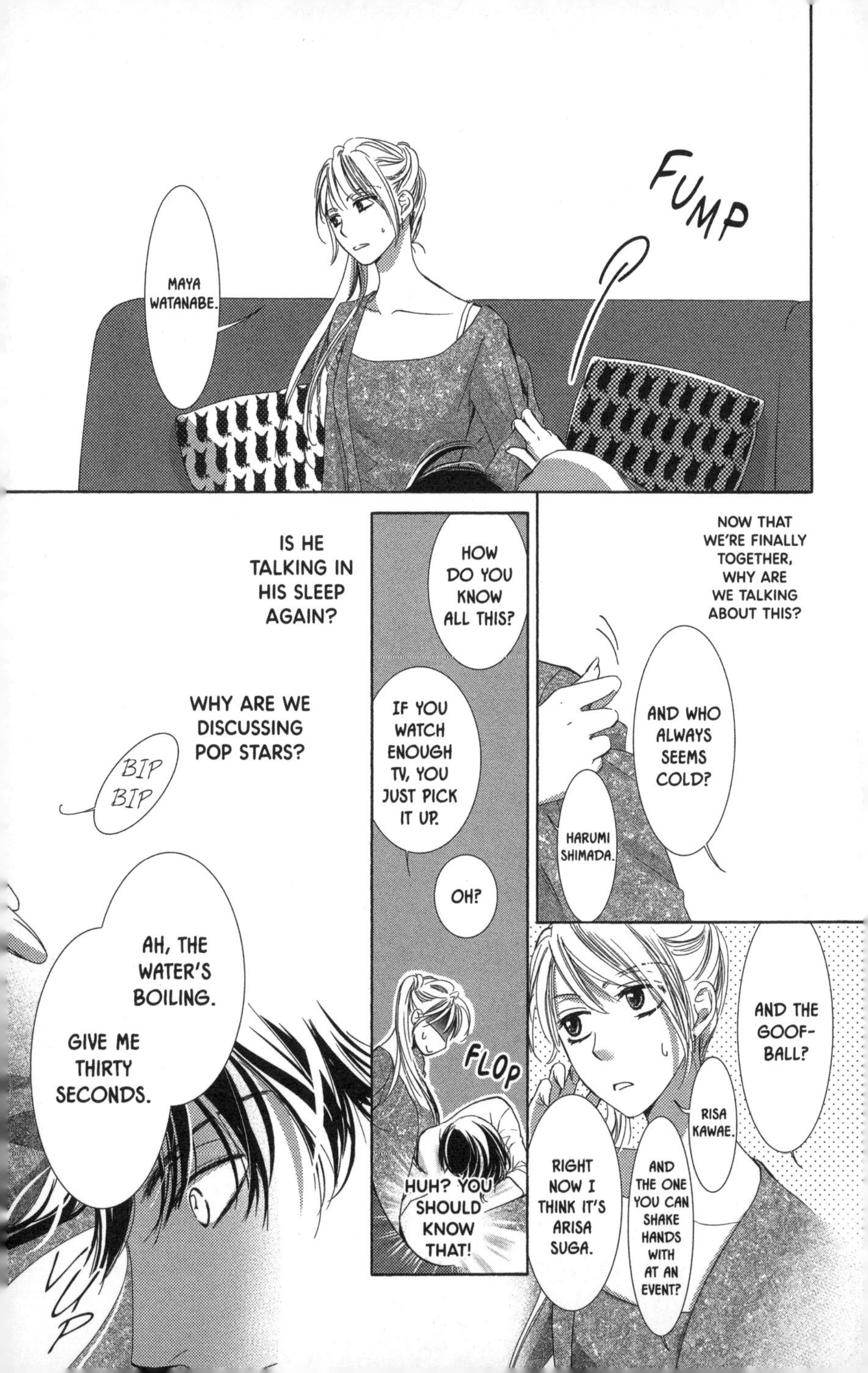
FUMP
MAYA WATANABE.
NOW THAT WE'RE FINALLY TOGETHER, WHY ARE WE TALKING ABOUT THIS?
AND WHO ALWAYS SEEMS COLD?
HARUMI SHIMADA.
AND THE GOOF-BALL?
RISA KAWAE.
AND THE ONE YOU CAN SHAKE HANDS WITH AT AN EVENT?
RIGHT NOW I THINK IT'S ARISA SUGA.
HOW DO YOU KNOW ALL THIS?
IF YOU WATCH ENOUGH TV, YOU JUST PICK IT UP.
OH?
FLOP
HUH? YOU SHOULD KNOW THAT!
IS HE TALKING IN HIS SLEEP AGAIN?
WHY ARE WE DISCUSSING POP STARS?
BIP BIP
AH, THE WATER'S BOILING.
GIVE ME THIRTY SECONDS.
VUP

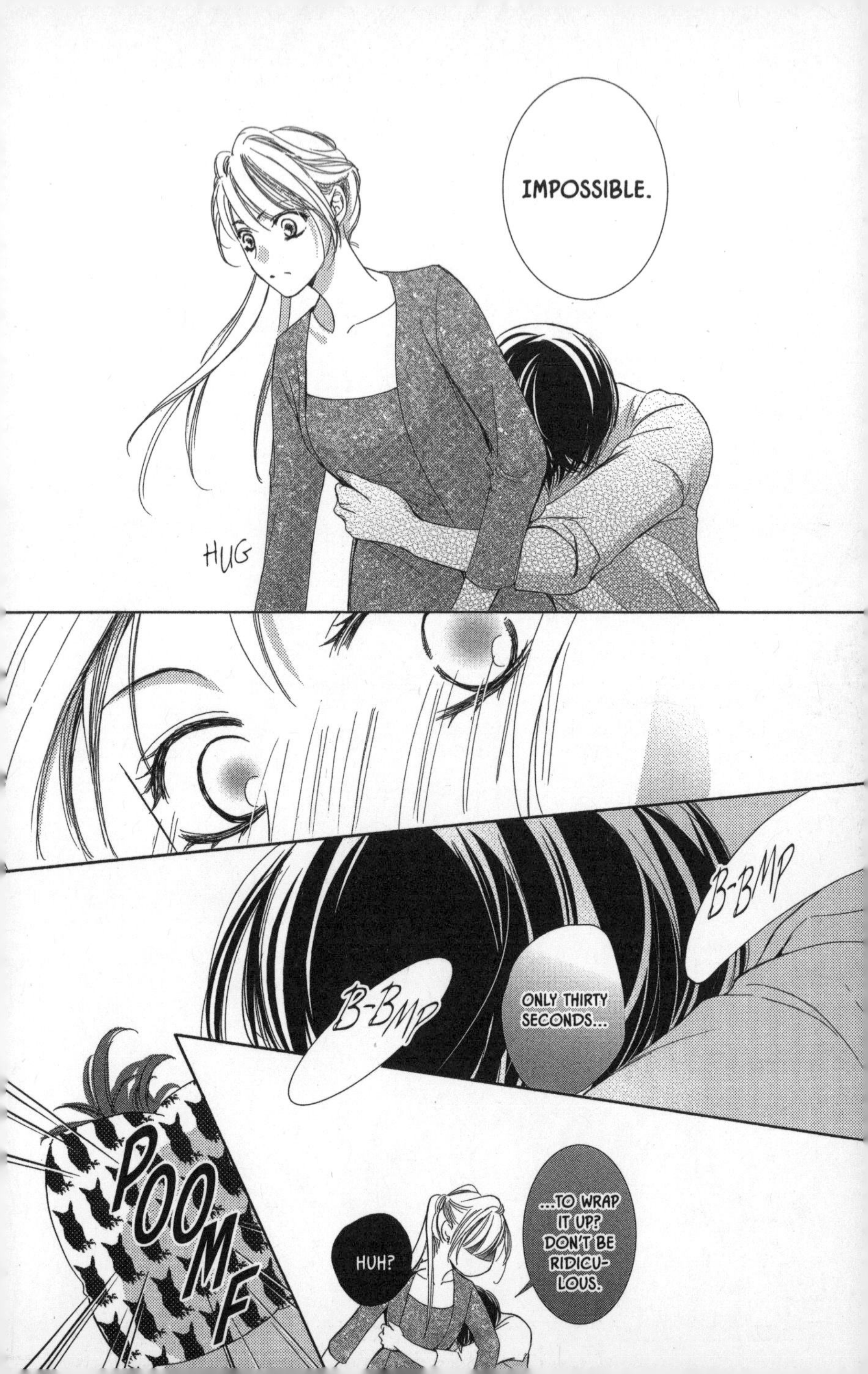
IMPOSSIBLE.
HUG
B-BMP
ONLY THIRTY SECONDS...
B-BMP
...TO WRAP IT UP? DON'T BE RIDICU- LOUS.
HUH?
POOMF

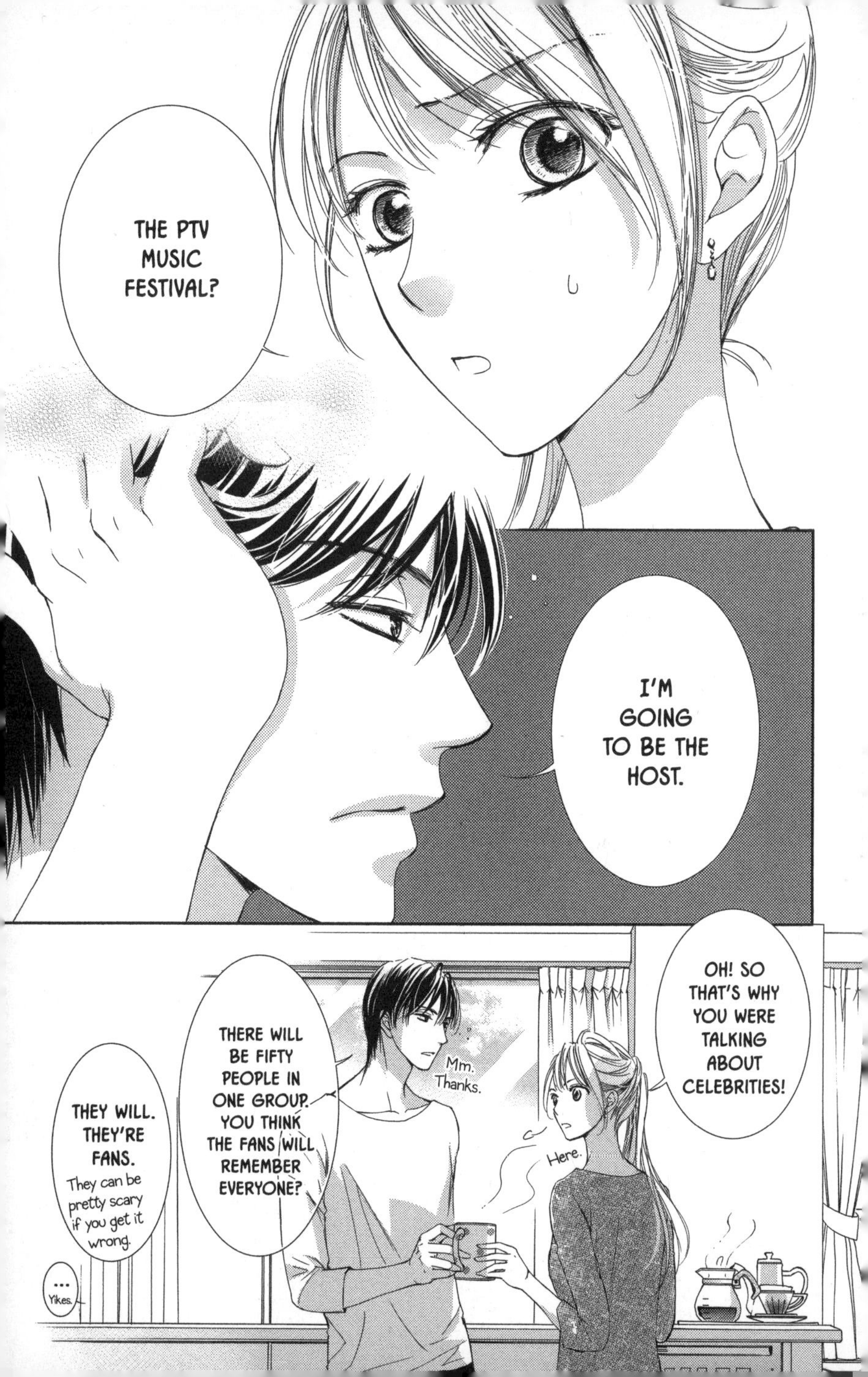
THE PTV MUSIC FESTIVAL?
I'M GOING TO BE THE HOST.
OH! SO THAT'S WHY YOU WERE TALKING ABOUT CELEBRITIES!
Here.
Mm. Thanks.
THERE WILL BE FIFTY PEOPLE IN ONE GROUP. YOU THINK THE FANS WILL REMEMBER EVERYONE?
THEY WILL. THEY'RE FANS.
They can be pretty scary if you get it wrong.
... Yikes.

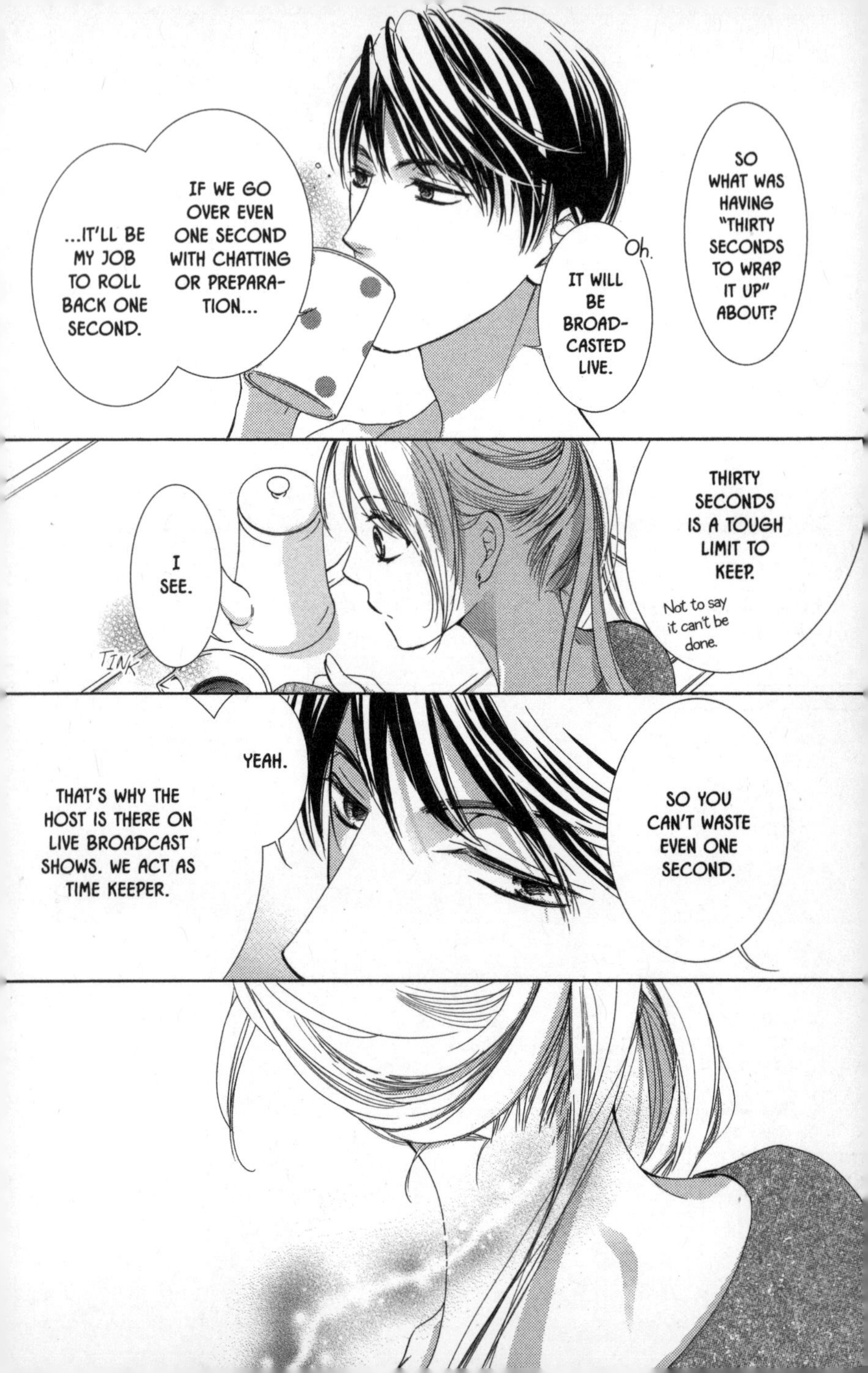

SO WHAT WAS HAVING "THIRTY SECONDS TO WRAP IT UP" ABOUT?
Oh.
IT WILL BE BROADCASTED LIVE.
IF WE GO OVER EVEN ONE SECOND WITH CHATTING OR PREPARATION...
...IT'LL BE MY JOB TO ROLL BACK ONE SECOND.
THIRTY SECONDS IS A TOUGH LIMIT TO KEEP.
Not to say it can't be done.
I SEE.
TINK
SO YOU CAN'T WASTE EVEN ONE SECOND.
YEAH.
THAT'S WHY THE HOST IS THERE ON LIVE BROADCAST SHOWS. WE ACT AS TIME KEEPER.

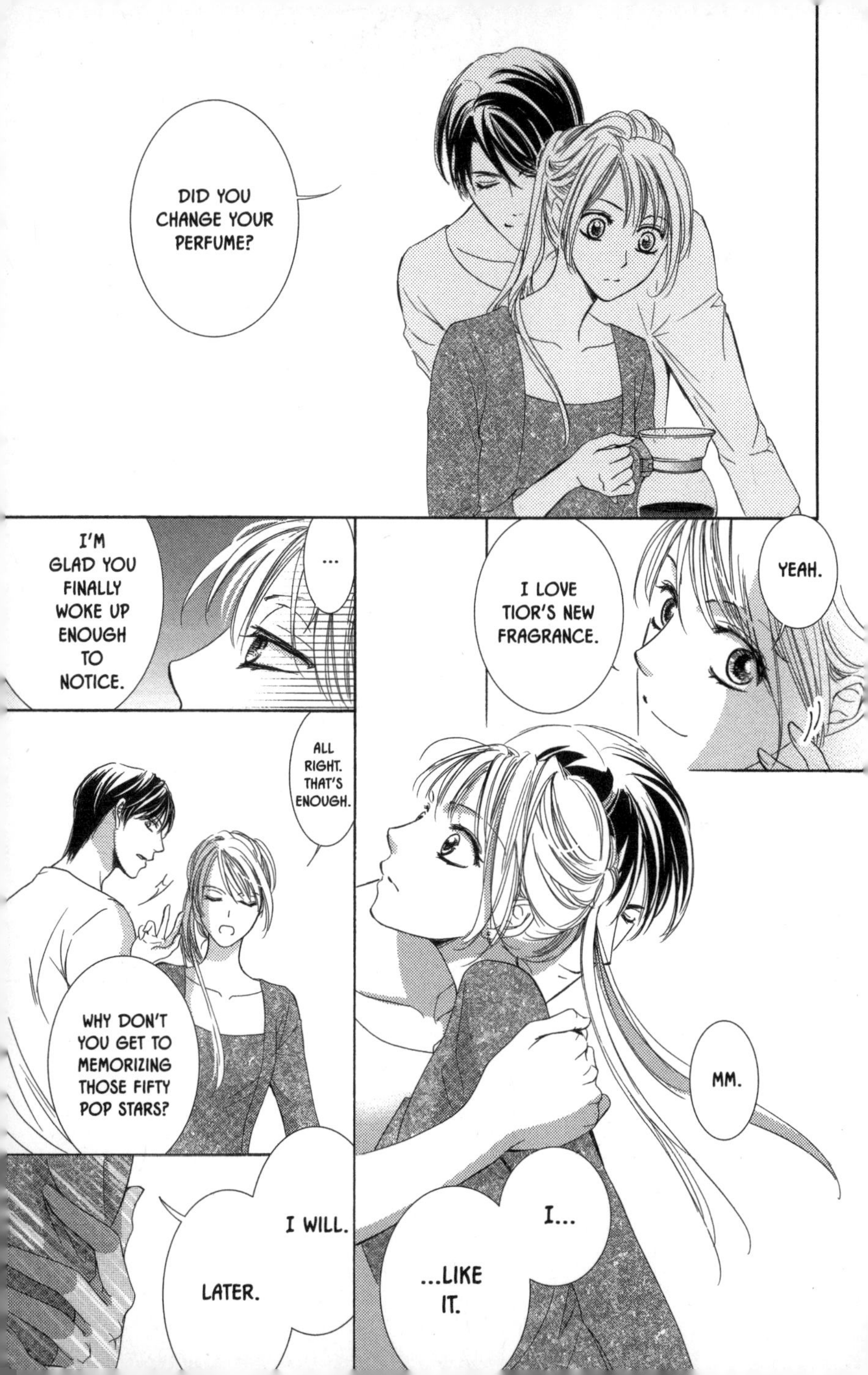
DID YOU CHANGE YOUR PERFUME?
YEAH.
I LOVE TIOR'S NEW FRAGRANCE.
...
I'M GLAD YOU FINALLY WOKE UP ENOUGH TO NOTICE.
MM.
I...
...LIKE IT.
ALL RIGHT. THAT'S ENOUGH.
WHY DON'T YOU GET TO MEMORIZING THOSE FIFTY POP STARS?
I WILL.
LATER.

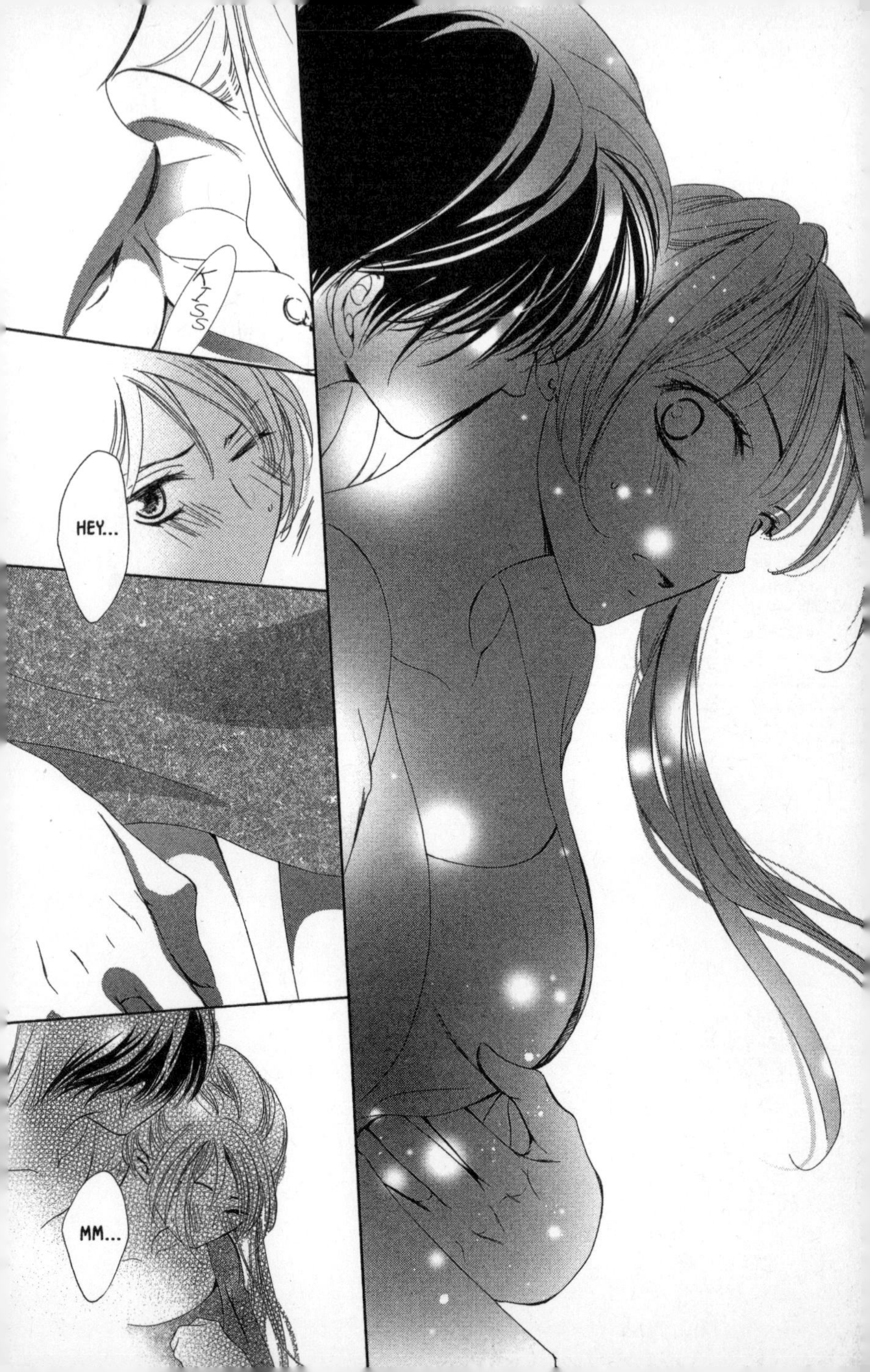
KISS
HEY...
MM...

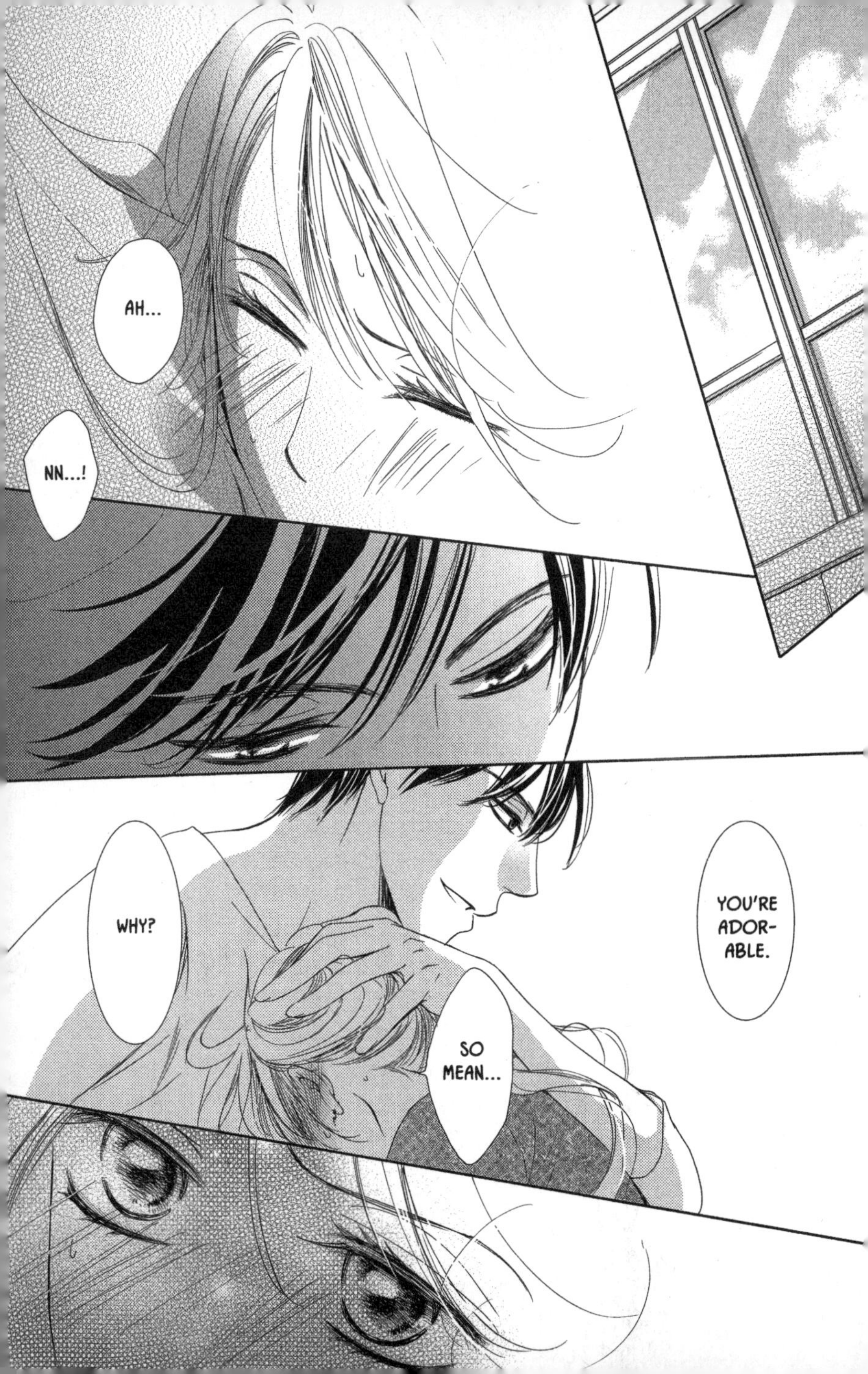
AH...
NN...!
YOU'RE ADOR-ABLE.
SO MEAN...
WHY?

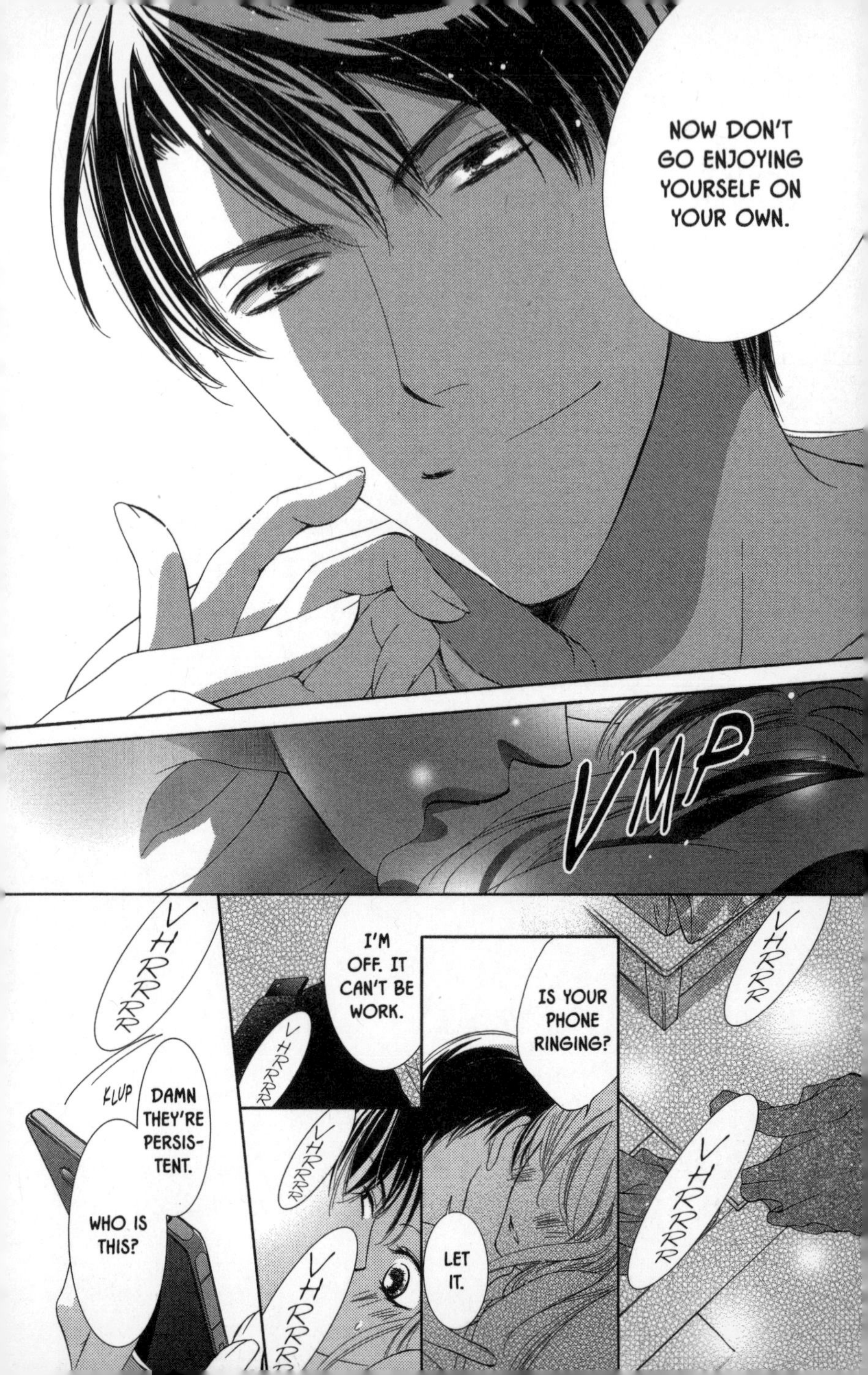

NOW DON'T GO ENJOYING YOURSELF ON YOUR OWN.
VMP
VHRRRR
IS YOUR PHONE RINGING?
VHRRRRR
I'M OFF. IT CAN'T BE WORK.
VHRRRRR
LET IT.
VHRRRR
VHRRRR
VHRRRRR
KLUP
DAMN THEY'RE PERSIS-TENT.
WHO IS THIS?

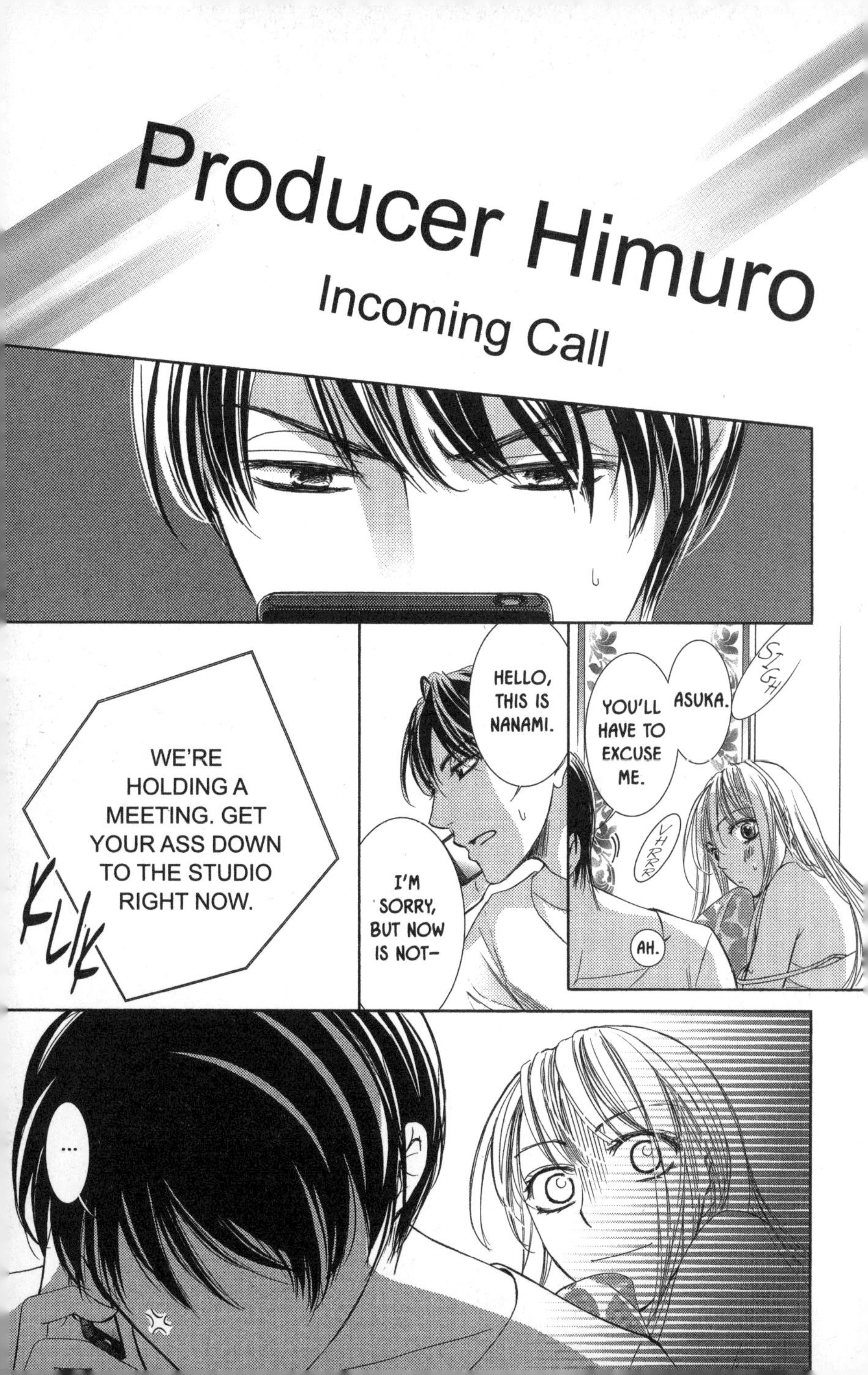
Producer Himuro
Incoming Call
SIGH
ASUKA.
YOU'LL HAVE TO EXCUSE ME.
VHRRR
AH.
HELLO, THIS IS NANAMI.
I'M SORRY, BUT NOW IS NOT–
WE'RE HOLDING A MEETING. GET YOUR ASS DOWN TO THE STUDIO RIGHT NOW.
KLIK
...

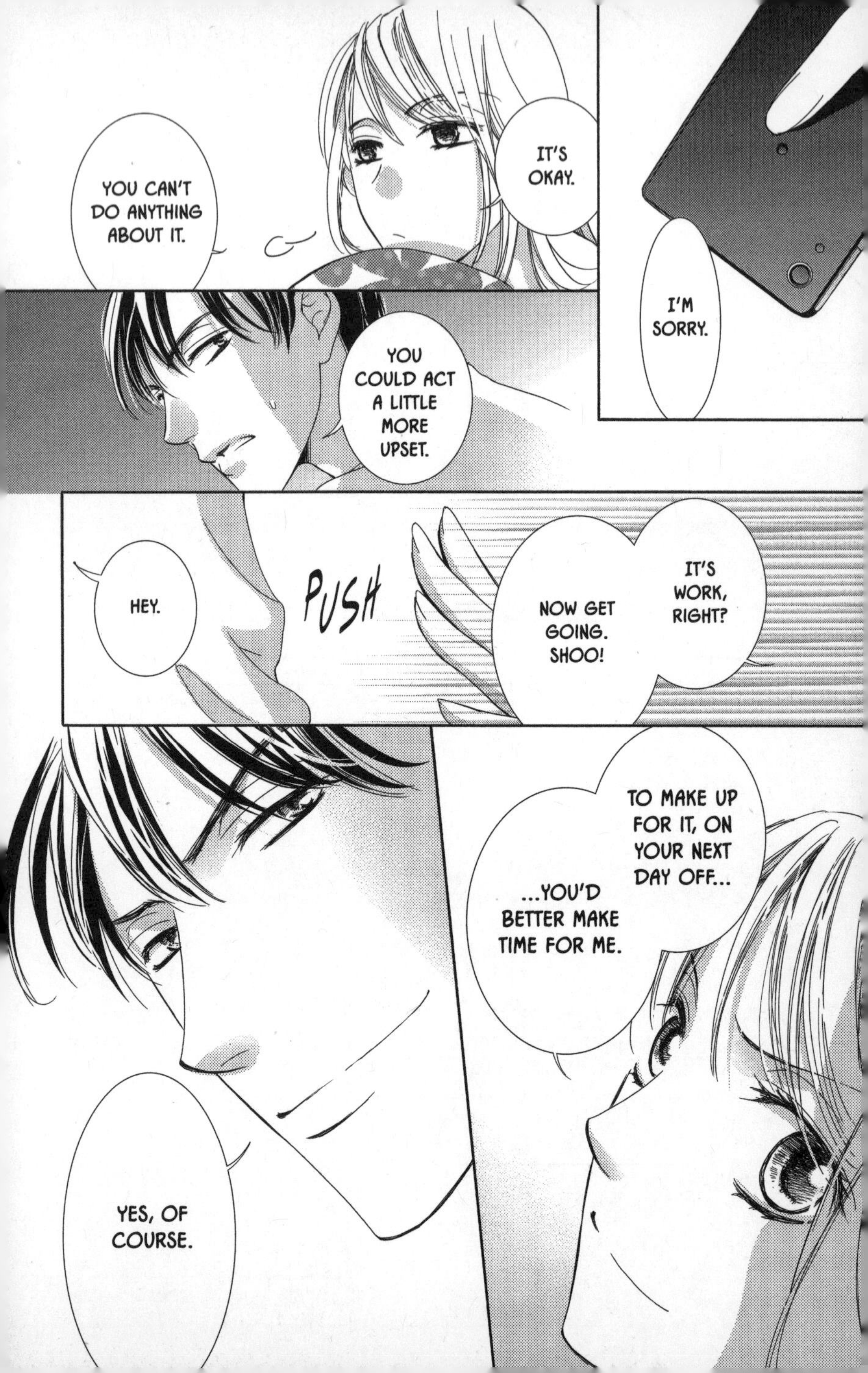
I'M SORRY.
IT'S OKAY.
YOU CAN'T DO ANYTHING ABOUT IT.
YOU COULD ACT A LITTLE MORE UPSET.
IT'S WORK, RIGHT?
NOW GET GOING. SHOO!
PUSH
HEY.
TO MAKE UP FOR IT, ON YOUR NEXT DAY OFF...
...YOU'D BETTER MAKE TIME FOR ME.
YES, OF COURSE.

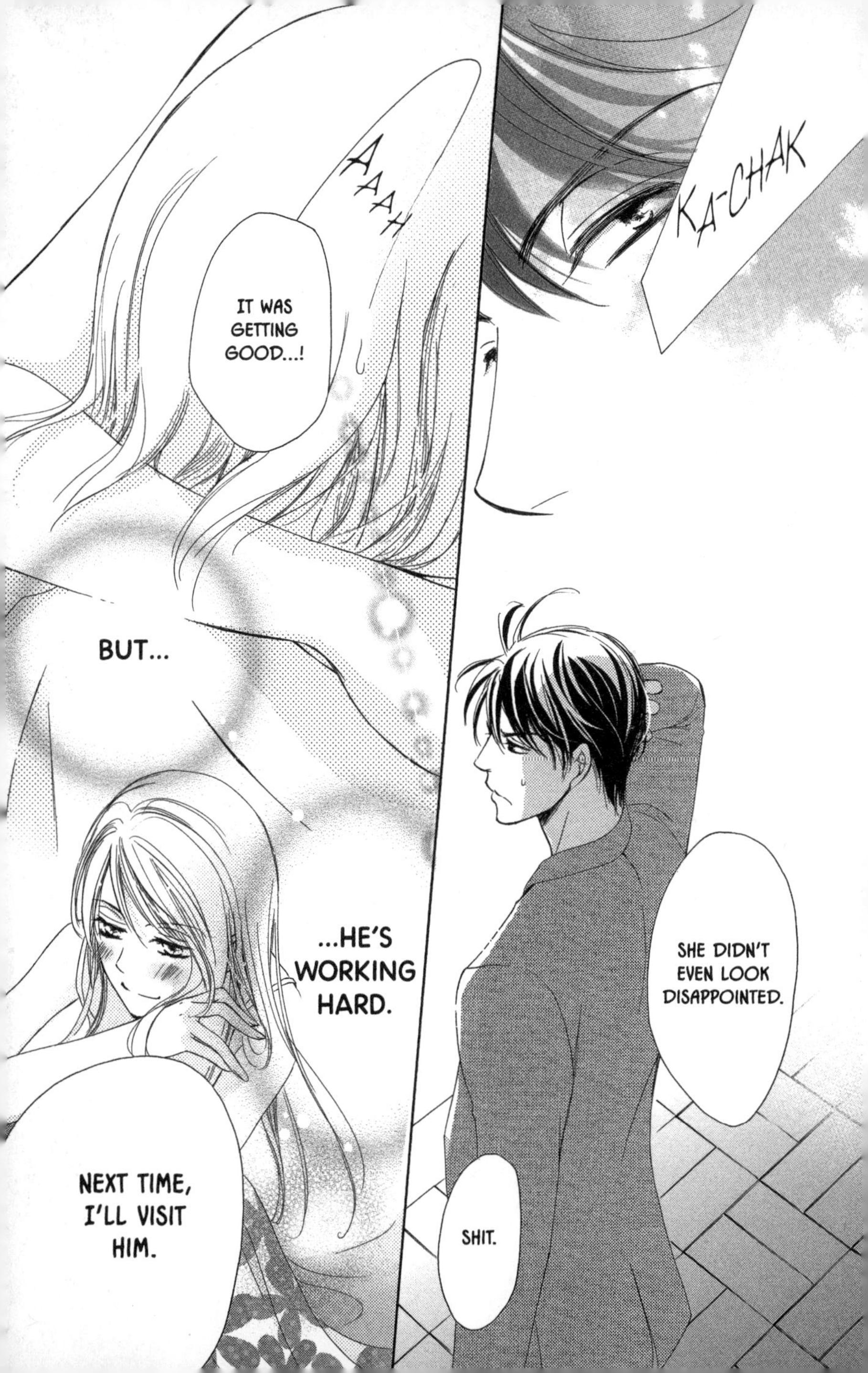
KA-CHAK
SHE DIDN'T EVEN LOOK DISAPPOINTED.
SHIT.
AAAH
IT WAS GETTING GOOD...!
BUT...
...HE'S WORKING HARD.
NEXT TIME, I'LL VISIT HIM.

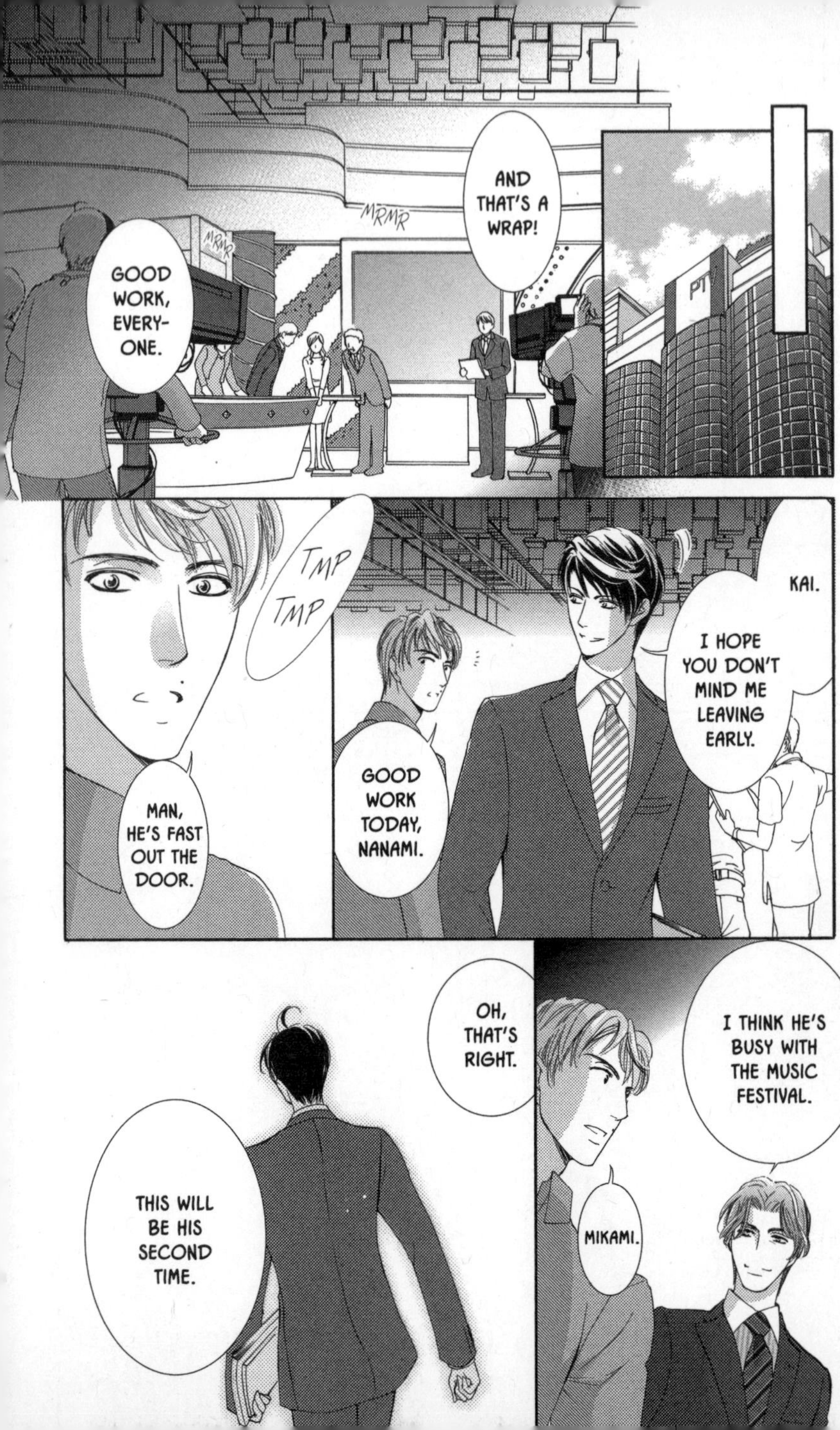
AND THAT'S A WRAP!
MRMR
GOOD WORK, EVERY-ONE.
MRMR
KAI.
I HOPE YOU DON'T MIND ME LEAVING EARLY.
GOOD WORK TODAY, NANAMI.
TMP TMP
MAN, HE'S FAST OUT THE DOOR.
I THINK HE'S BUSY WITH THE MUSIC FESTIVAL.
MIKAMI.
OH, THAT'S RIGHT.
THIS WILL BE HIS SECOND TIME.

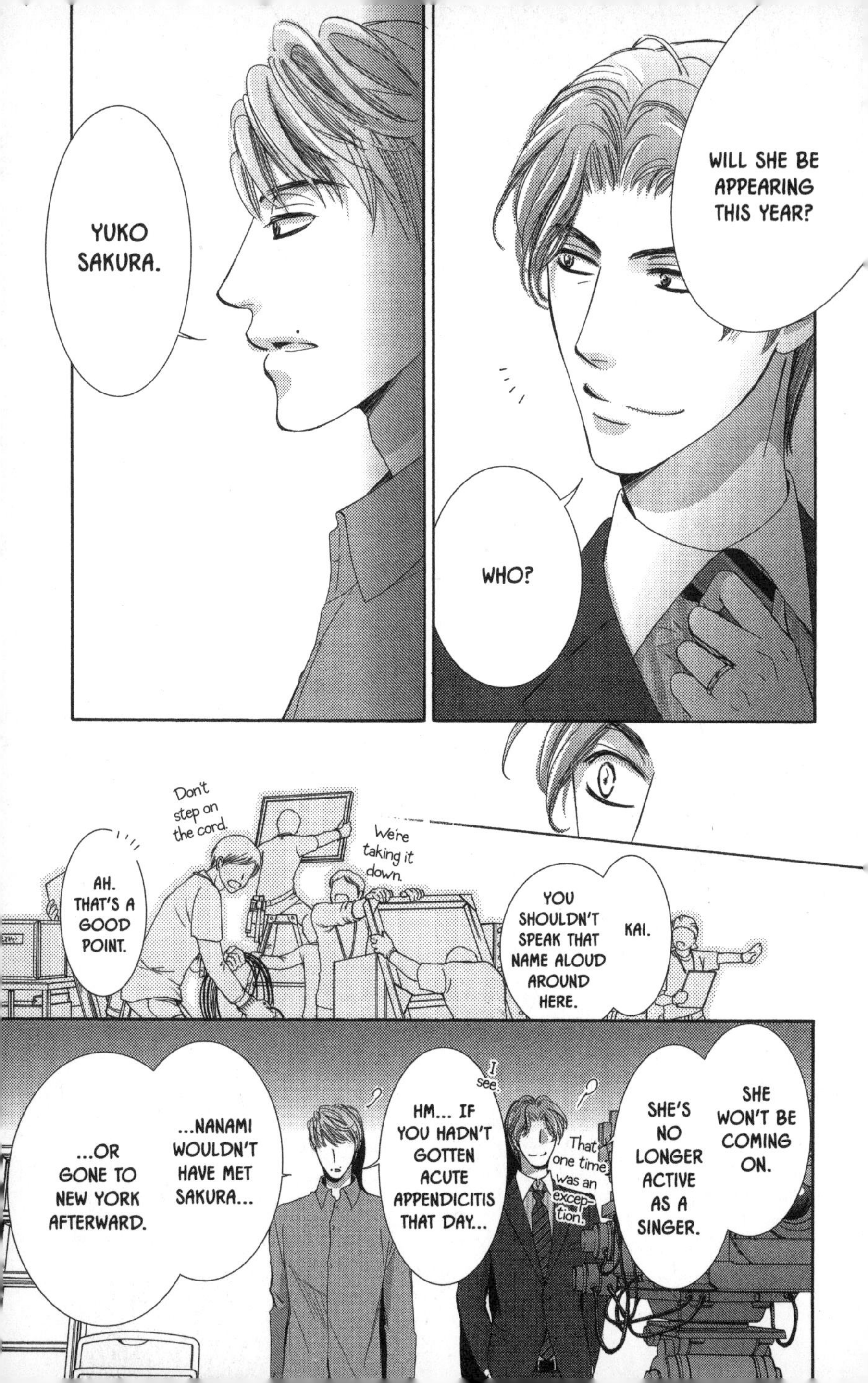
WILL SHE BE APPEARING THIS YEAR?
WHO?
YUKO SAKURA.
KAI.
YOU SHOULDN'T SPEAK THAT NAME ALOUD AROUND HERE.
We're taking it down.
Don't step on the cord.
AH. THAT'S A GOOD POINT.
SHE WON'T BE COMING ON.
SHE'S NO LONGER ACTIVE AS A SINGER.
That one time was an exception.
I see.
HM... IF YOU HADN'T GOTTEN ACUTE APPENDICITIS THAT DAY...
...NANAMI WOULDN'T HAVE MET SAKURA...
...OR GONE TO NEW YORK AFTERWARD.

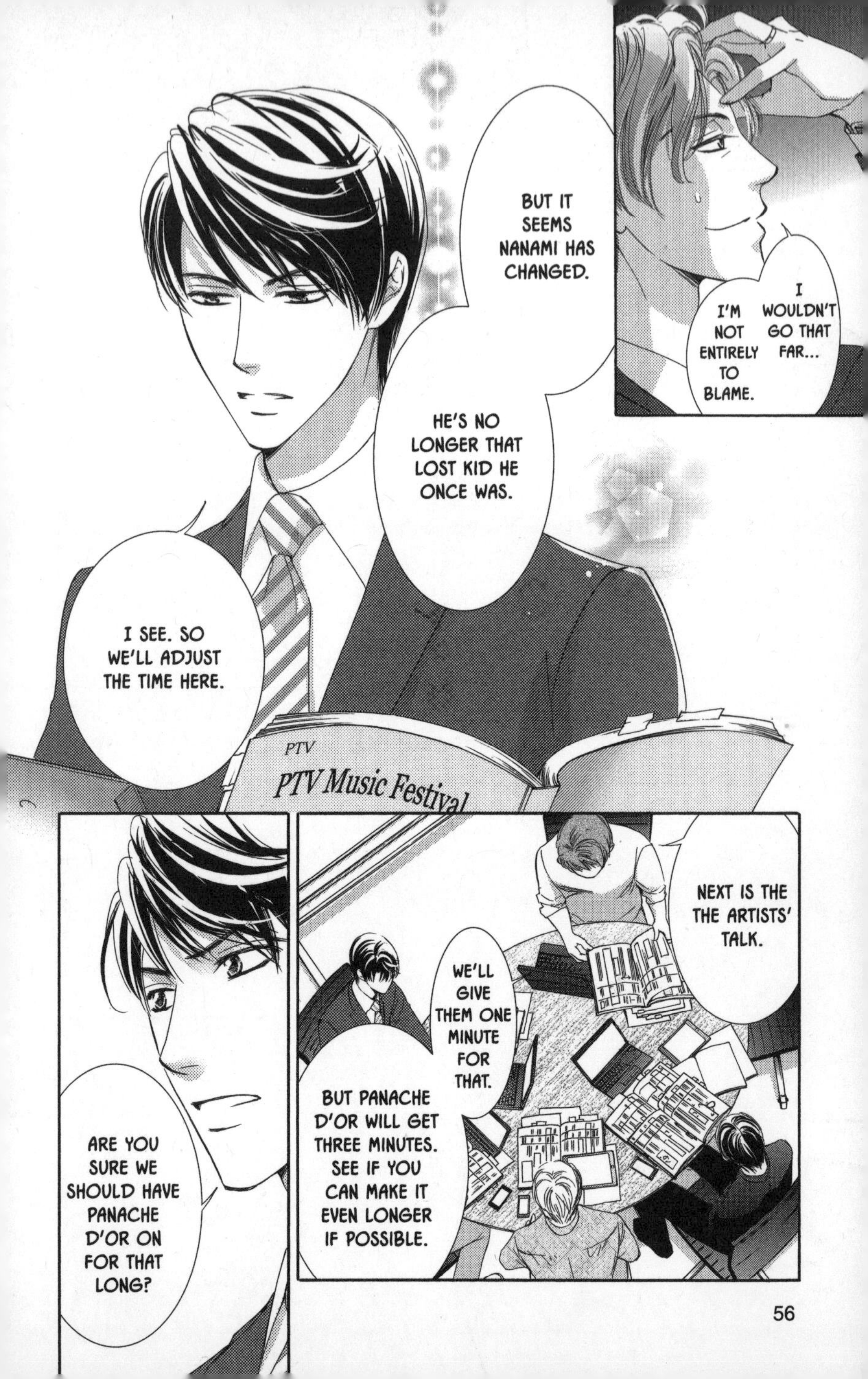
I WOULDN'T GO THAT FAR...
I'M NOT ENTIRELY TO BLAME.
BUT IT SEEMS NANAMI HAS CHANGED.
HE'S NO LONGER THAT LOST KID HE ONCE WAS.
I SEE. SO WE'LL ADJUST THE TIME HERE.
PTV
PTV Music Festival
NEXT IS THE THE ARTISTS' TALK.
WE'LL GIVE THEM ONE MINUTE FOR THAT.
BUT PANACHE D'OR WILL GET THREE MINUTES. SEE IF YOU CAN MAKE IT EVEN LONGER IF POSSIBLE.
ARE YOU SURE WE SHOULD HAVE PANACHE D'OR ON FOR THAT LONG?

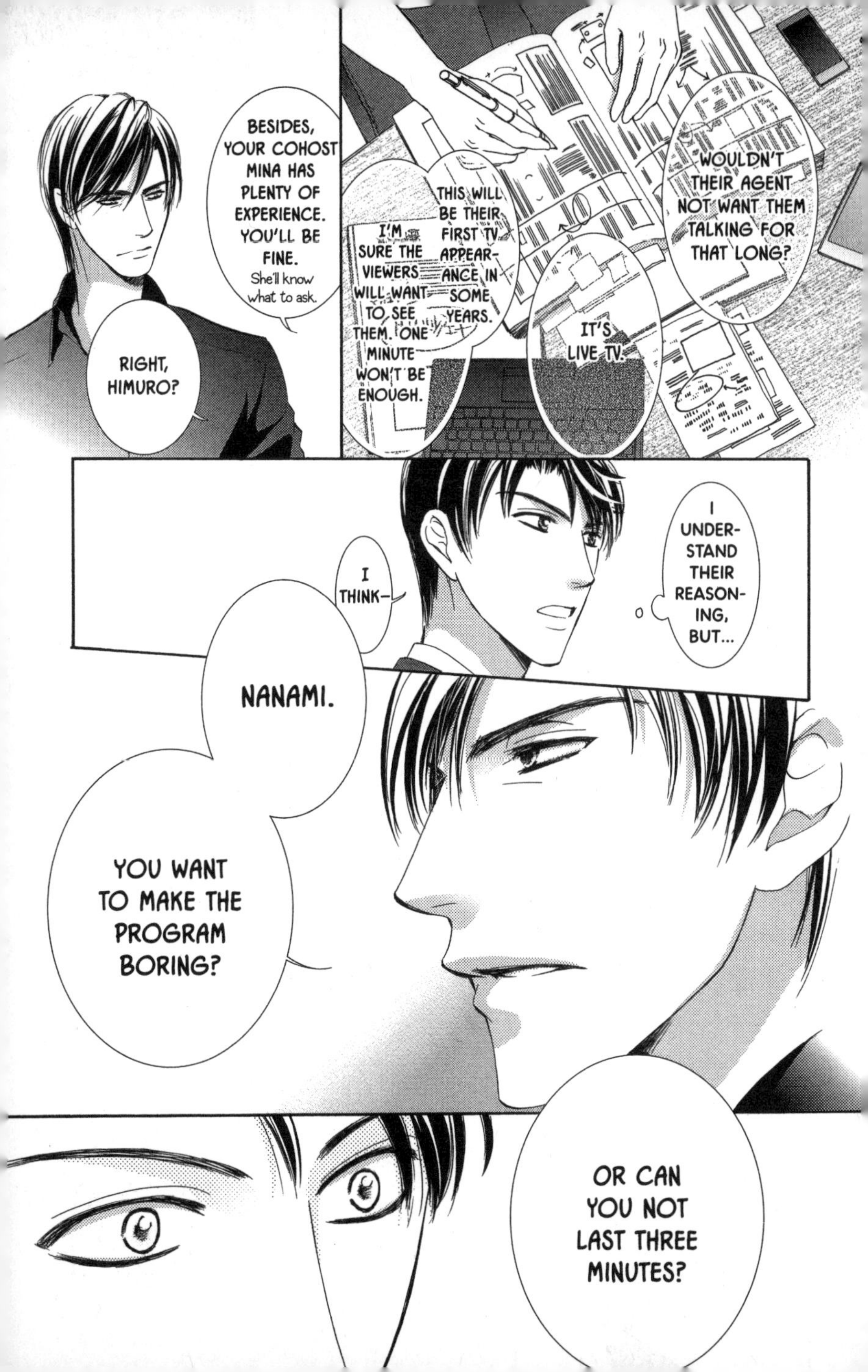
WOULDN'T THEIR AGENT NOT WANT THEM TALKING FOR THAT LONG?
IT'S LIVE TV.
THIS WILL BE THEIR FIRST TV APPEARANCE IN SOME YEARS.
I'M SURE THE VIEWERS WILL WANT TO SEE THEM. ONE MINUTE WON'T BE ENOUGH.
BESIDES, YOUR COHOST MINA HAS PLENTY OF EXPERIENCE. YOU'LL BE FINE.
She'll know what to ask.
RIGHT, HIMURO?
I UNDERSTAND THEIR REASONING, BUT...
I THINK—
NANAMI.
YOU WANT TO MAKE THE PROGRAM BORING?
OR CAN YOU NOT LAST THREE MINUTES?

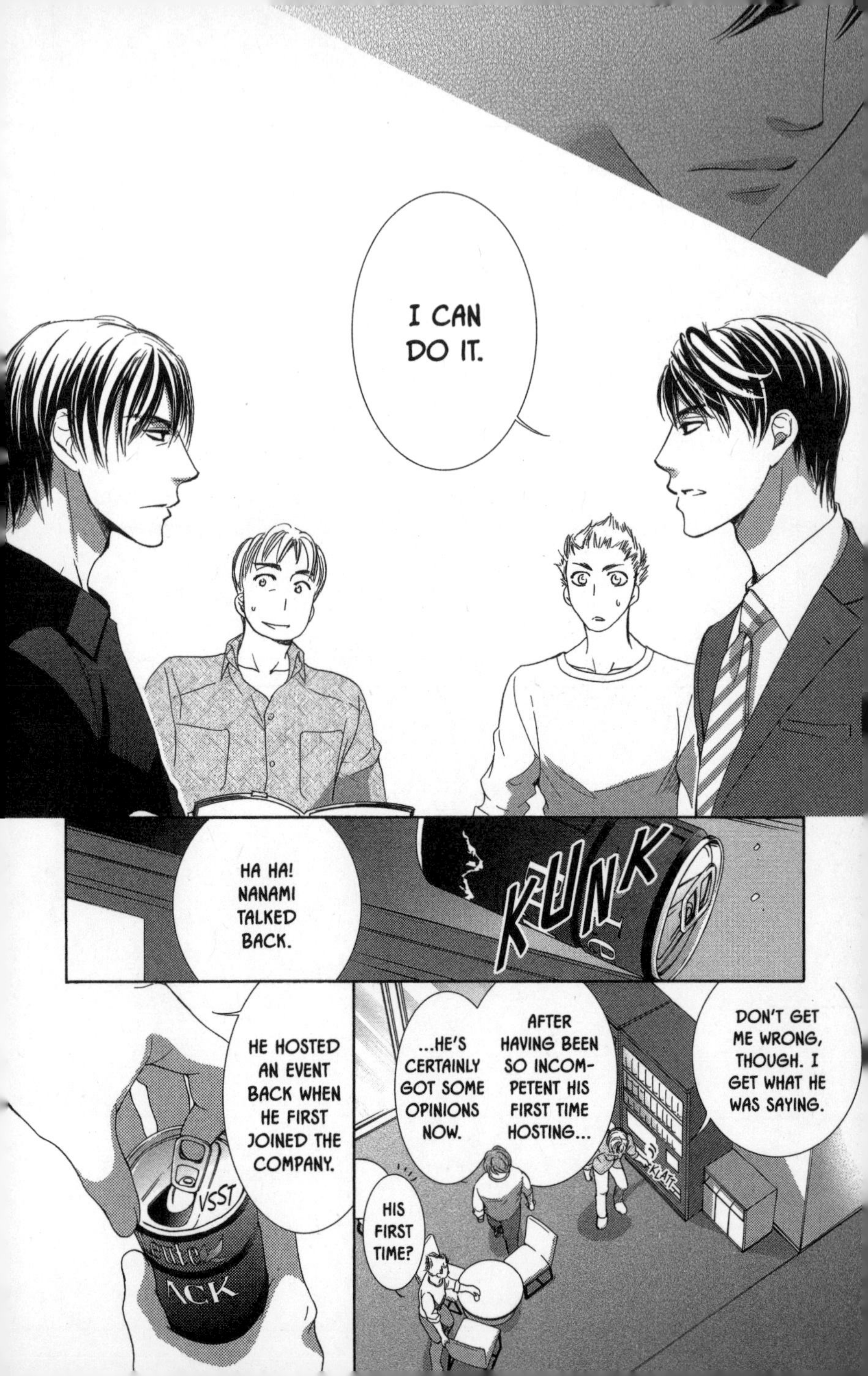
I CAN DO IT.
HA HA! NANAMI TALKED BACK.
KUNK
DON'T GET ME WRONG, THOUGH. I GET WHAT HE WAS SAYING.
AFTER HAVING BEEN SO INCOM-PETENT HIS FIRST TIME HOSTING...
...HE'S CERTAINLY GOT SOME OPINIONS NOW.
KLAT
HIS FIRST TIME?
HE HOSTED AN EVENT BACK WHEN HE FIRST JOINED THE COMPANY.
VSST

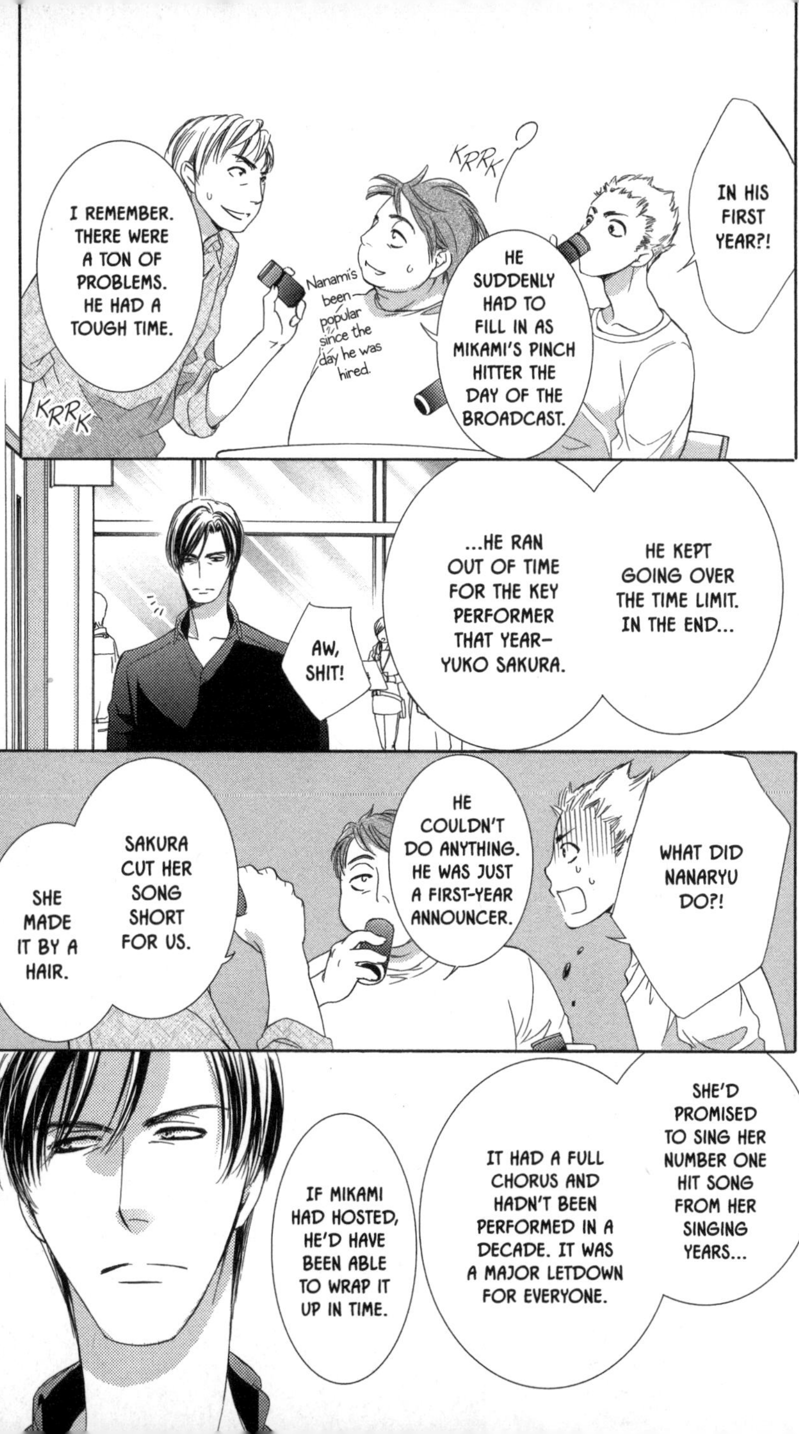
IN HIS FIRST YEAR?!
KRRK
HE SUDDENLY HAD TO FILL IN AS MIKAMI'S PINCH HITTER THE DAY OF THE BROADCAST.
Nanami's been popular since the day he was hired.
I REMEMBER. THERE WERE A TON OF PROBLEMS. HE HAD A TOUGH TIME.
KRRK
HE KEPT GOING OVER THE TIME LIMIT. IN THE END...
...HE RAN OUT OF TIME FOR THE KEY PERFORMER THAT YEAR—YUKO SAKURA.
AW, SHIT!
WHAT DID NANARYU DO?!
HE COULDN'T DO ANYTHING. HE WAS JUST A FIRST-YEAR ANNOUNCER.
SAKURA CUT HER SONG SHORT FOR US.
SHE MADE IT BY A HAIR.
SHE'D PROMISED TO SING HER NUMBER ONE HIT SONG FROM HER SINGING YEARS...
IT HAD A FULL CHORUS AND HADN'T BEEN PERFORMED IN A DECADE. IT WAS A MAJOR LETDOWN FOR EVERYONE.
IF MIKAMI HAD HOSTED, HE'D HAVE BEEN ABLE TO WRAP IT UP IN TIME.

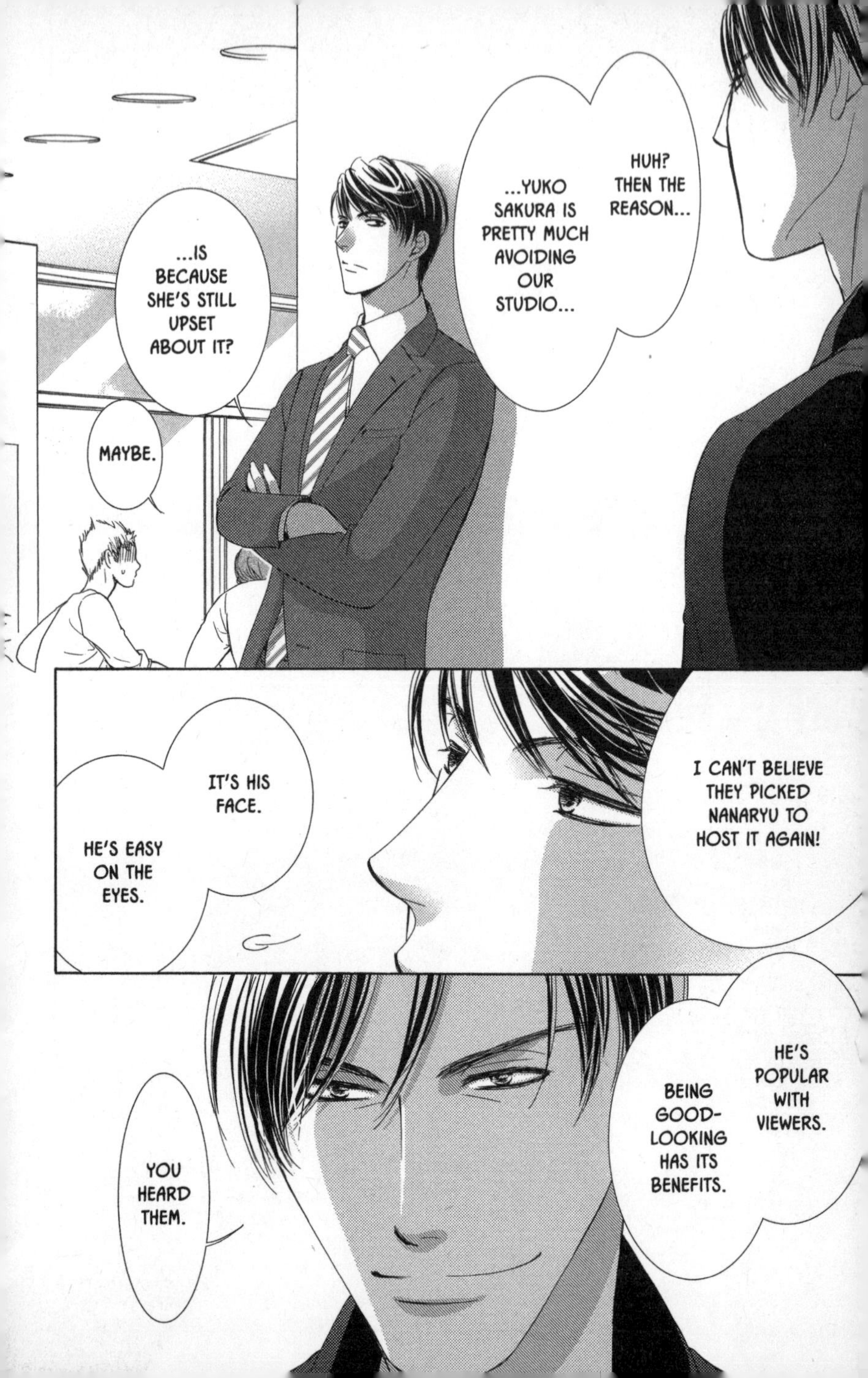
HUH? THEN THE REASON...
...YUKO SAKURA IS PRETTY MUCH AVOIDING OUR STUDIO...
...IS BECAUSE SHE'S STILL UPSET ABOUT IT?
MAYBE.
I CAN'T BELIEVE THEY PICKED NANARYU TO HOST IT AGAIN!
IT'S HIS FACE.
HE'S EASY ON THE EYES.
HE'S POPULAR WITH VIEWERS.
BEING GOOD-LOOKING HAS ITS BENEFITS.
YOU HEARD THEM.

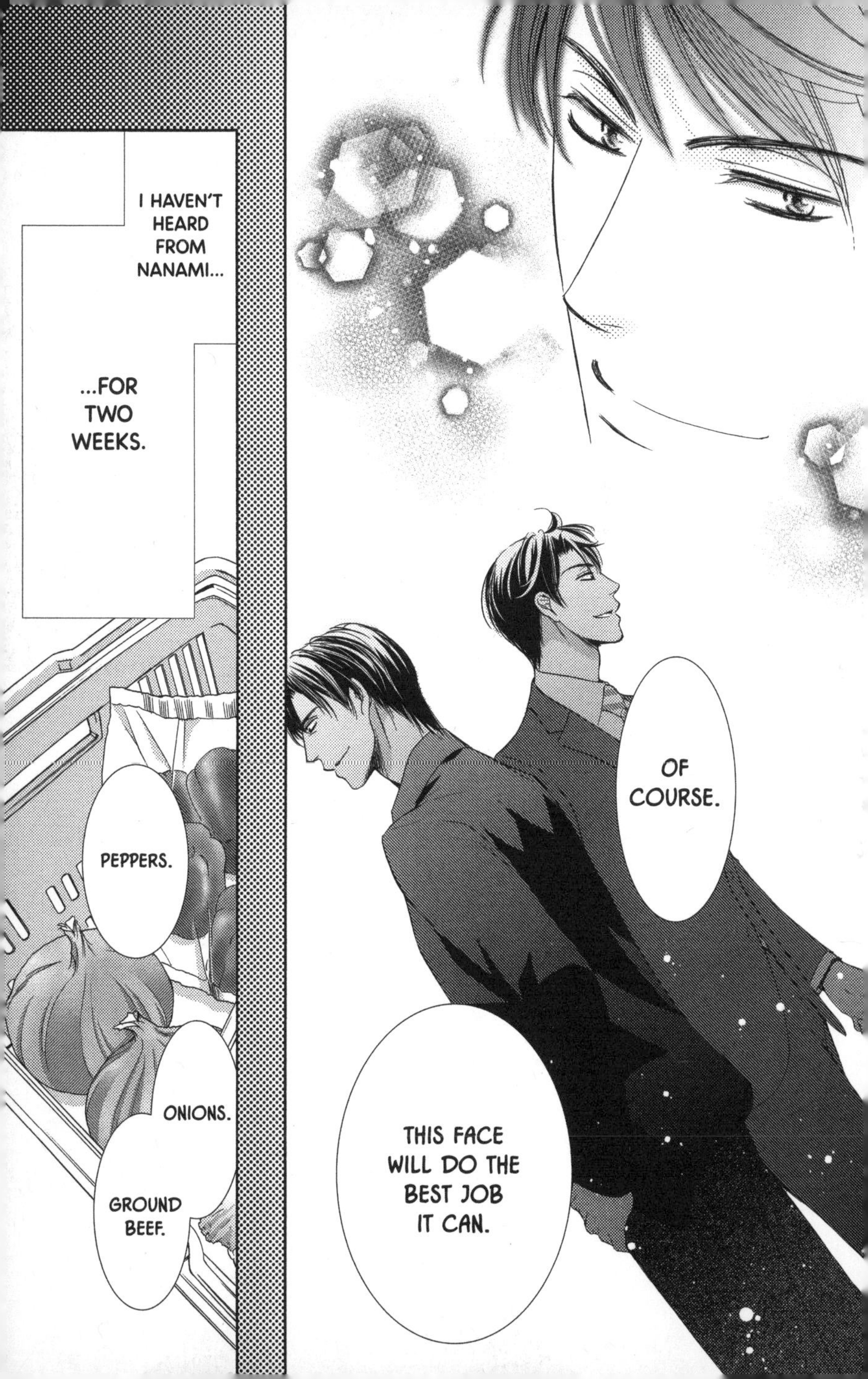
OF COURSE.
THIS FACE WILL DO THE BEST JOB IT CAN.
I HAVEN'T HEARD FROM NANAMI...
...FOR TWO WEEKS.
PEPPERS.
ONIONS.
GROUND BEEF.

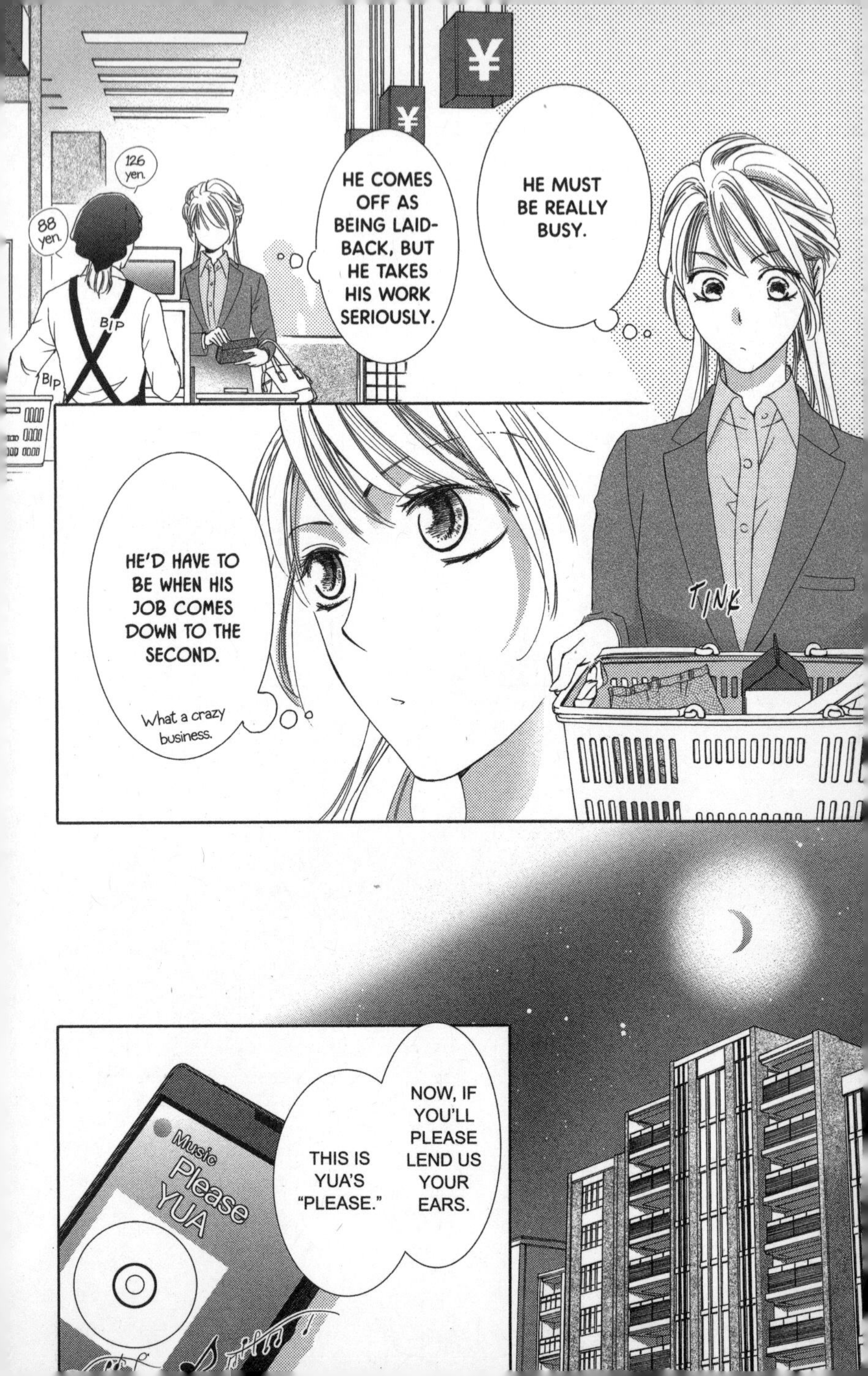
HE MUST BE REALLY BUSY.
TINK
HE COMES OFF AS BEING LAID-BACK, BUT HE TAKES HIS WORK SERIOUSLY.
126 yen.
88 yen.
BIP
BIP
HE'D HAVE TO BE WHEN HIS JOB COMES DOWN TO THE SECOND.
What a crazy business.
THIS IS YUA'S "PLEASE."
NOW, IF YOU'LL PLEASE LEND US YOUR EARS.
Music
Please
YUA

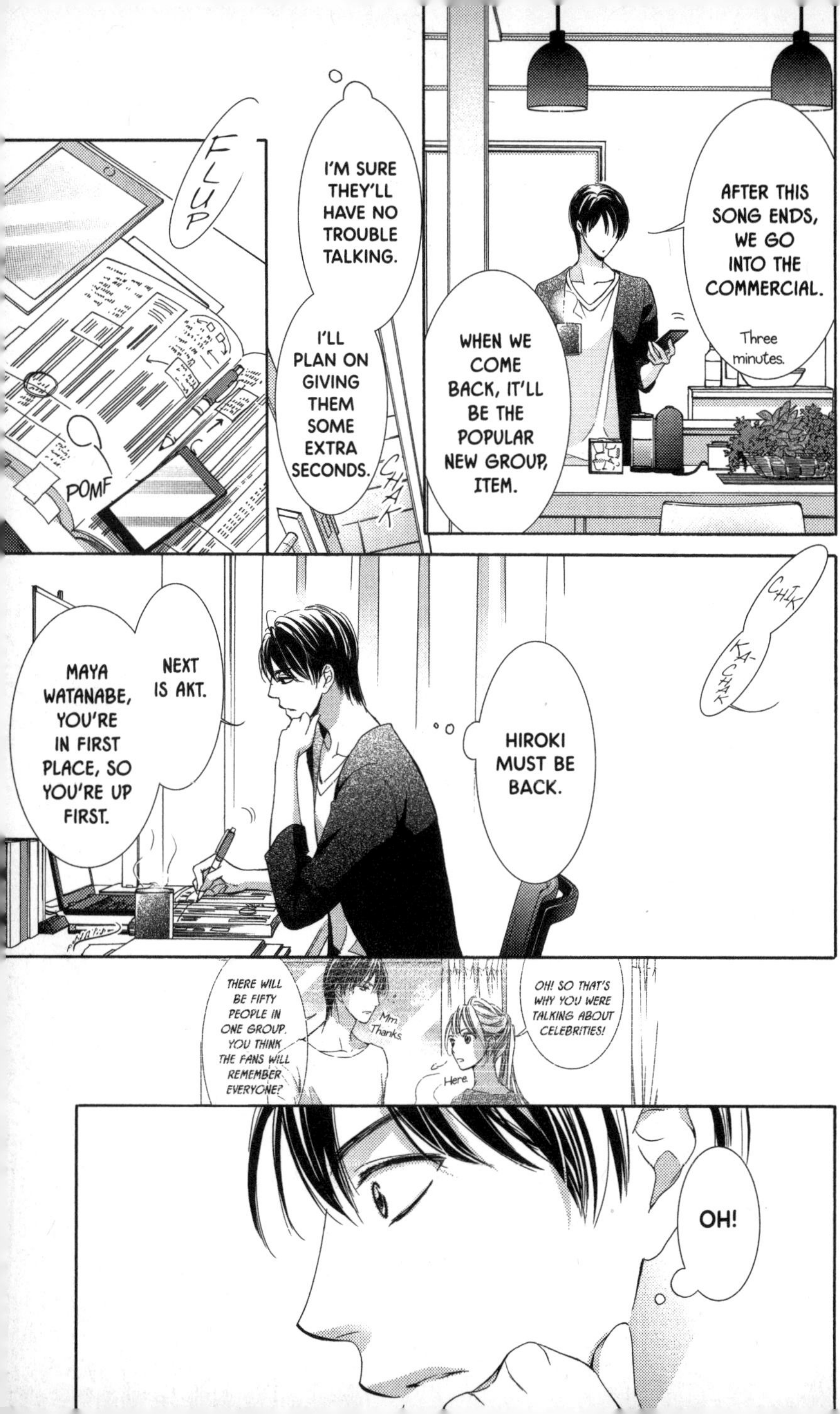
AFTER THIS SONG ENDS, WE GO INTO THE COMMERCIAL.
Three minutes.
WHEN WE COME BACK, IT'LL BE THE POPULAR NEW GROUP, ITEM.
I'M SURE THEY'LL HAVE NO TROUBLE TALKING.
I'LL PLAN ON GIVING THEM SOME EXTRA SECONDS.
FLUP
POMF
CHAK
CHIK
KA-CHAK
HIROKI MUST BE BACK.
NEXT IS AKT.
MAYA WATANABE, YOU'RE IN FIRST PLACE, SO YOU'RE UP FIRST.
OH! SO THAT'S WHY YOU WERE TALKING ABOUT CELEBRITIES!
Here.
Mm. Thanks.
THERE WILL BE FIFTY PEOPLE IN ONE GROUP. YOU THINK THE FANS WILL REMEMBER EVERYONE?
OH!

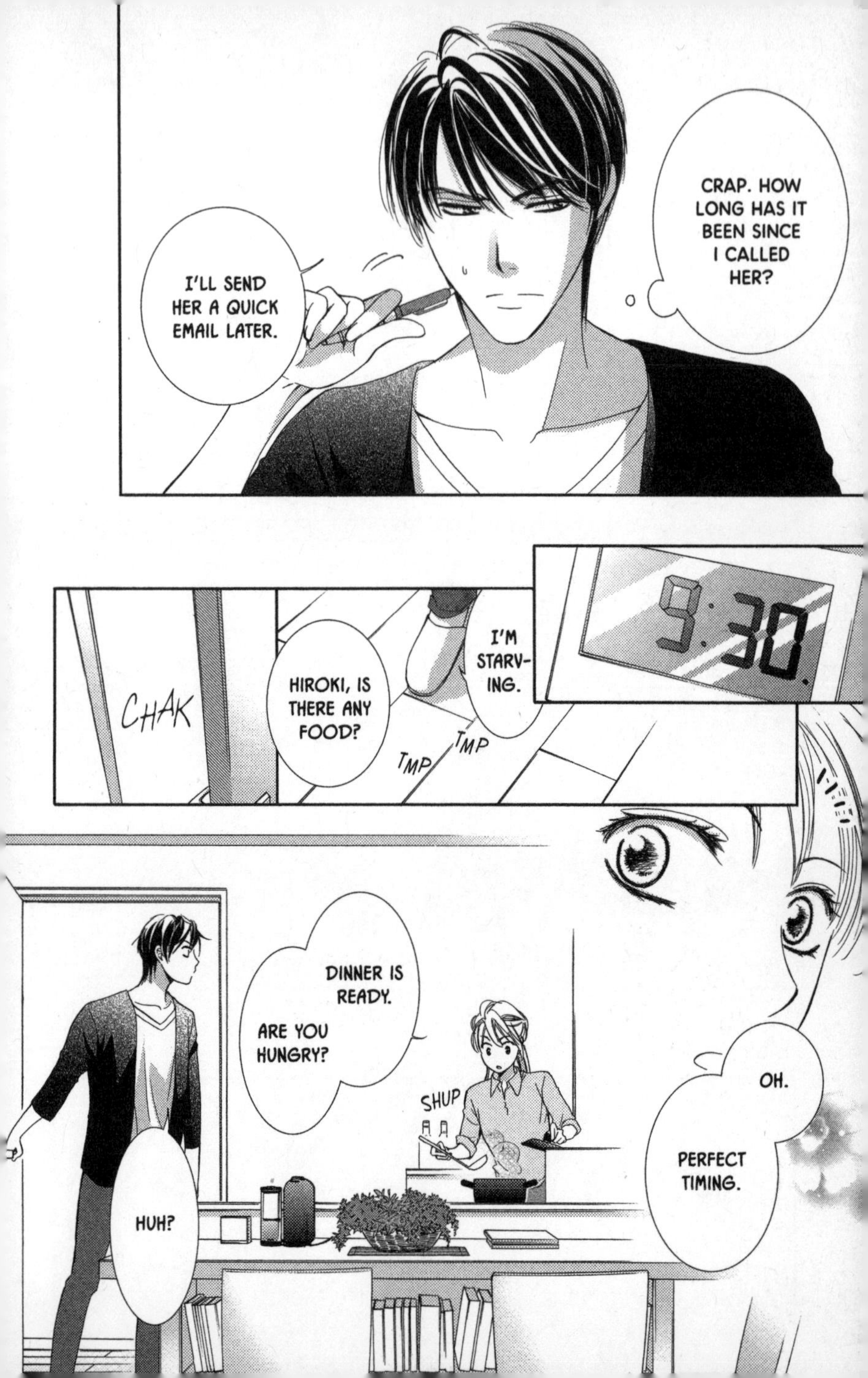
CRAP. HOW LONG HAS IT BEEN SINCE I CALLED HER?
I'LL SEND HER A QUICK EMAIL LATER.
9:30
I'M STARV-ING.
HIROKI, IS THERE ANY FOOD?
TMP
TMP
CHAK
OH.
PERFECT TIMING.
DINNER IS READY.
ARE YOU HUNGRY?
SHUP
HUH?

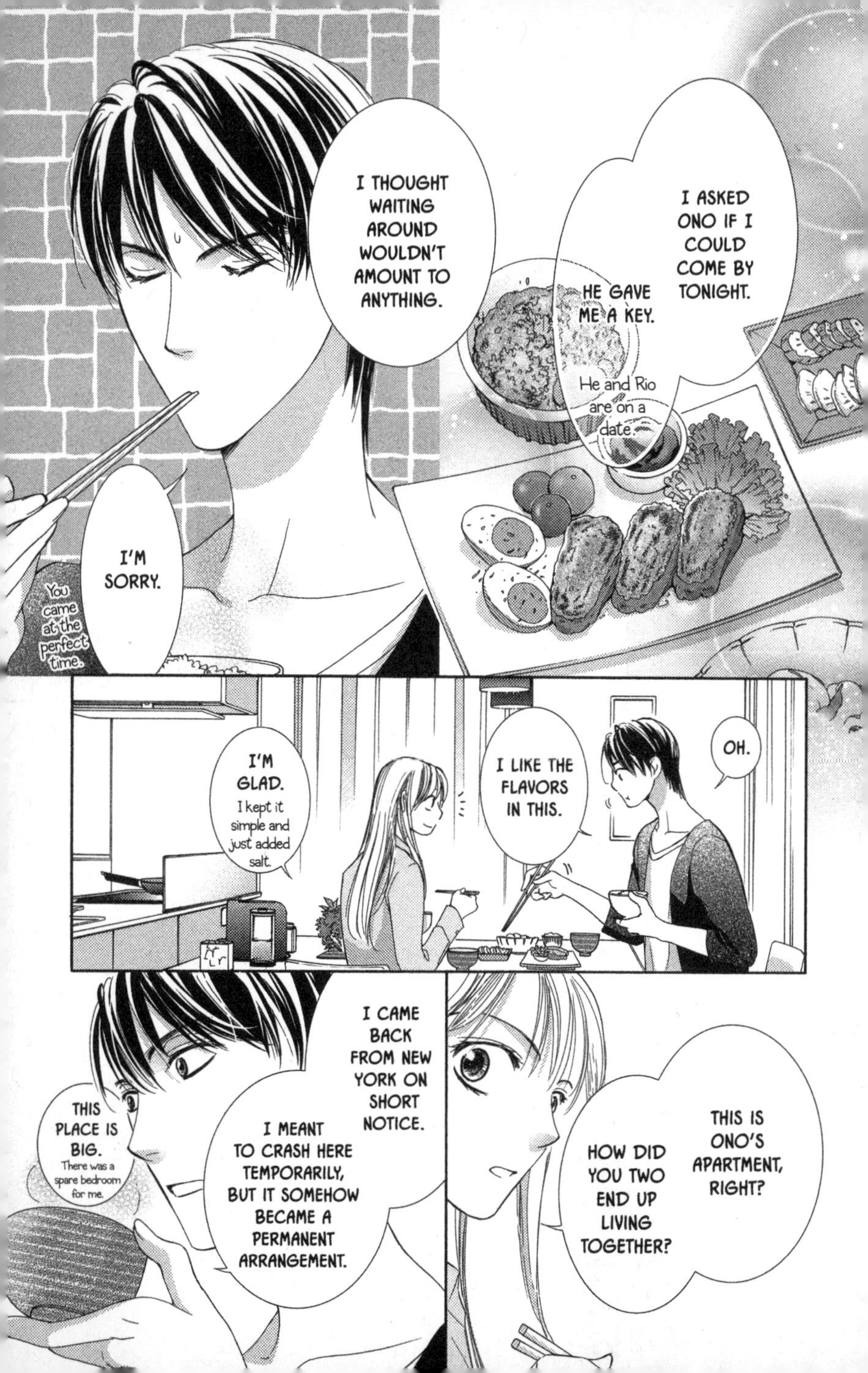
I ASKED ONO IF I COULD COME BY TONIGHT.
HE GAVE ME A KEY.
He and Rio are on a date.
I THOUGHT WAITING AROUND WOULDN'T AMOUNT TO ANYTHING.
I'M SORRY.
You came at the perfect time.
OH.
I LIKE THE FLAVORS IN THIS.
I'M GLAD.
I kept it simple and just added salt.
THIS IS ONO'S APARTMENT, RIGHT?
HOW DID YOU TWO END UP LIVING TOGETHER?
I CAME BACK FROM NEW YORK ON SHORT NOTICE.
I MEANT TO CRASH HERE TEMPORARILY, BUT IT SOMEHOW BECAME A PERMANENT ARRANGEMENT.
THIS PLACE IS BIG.
There was a spare bedroom for me.

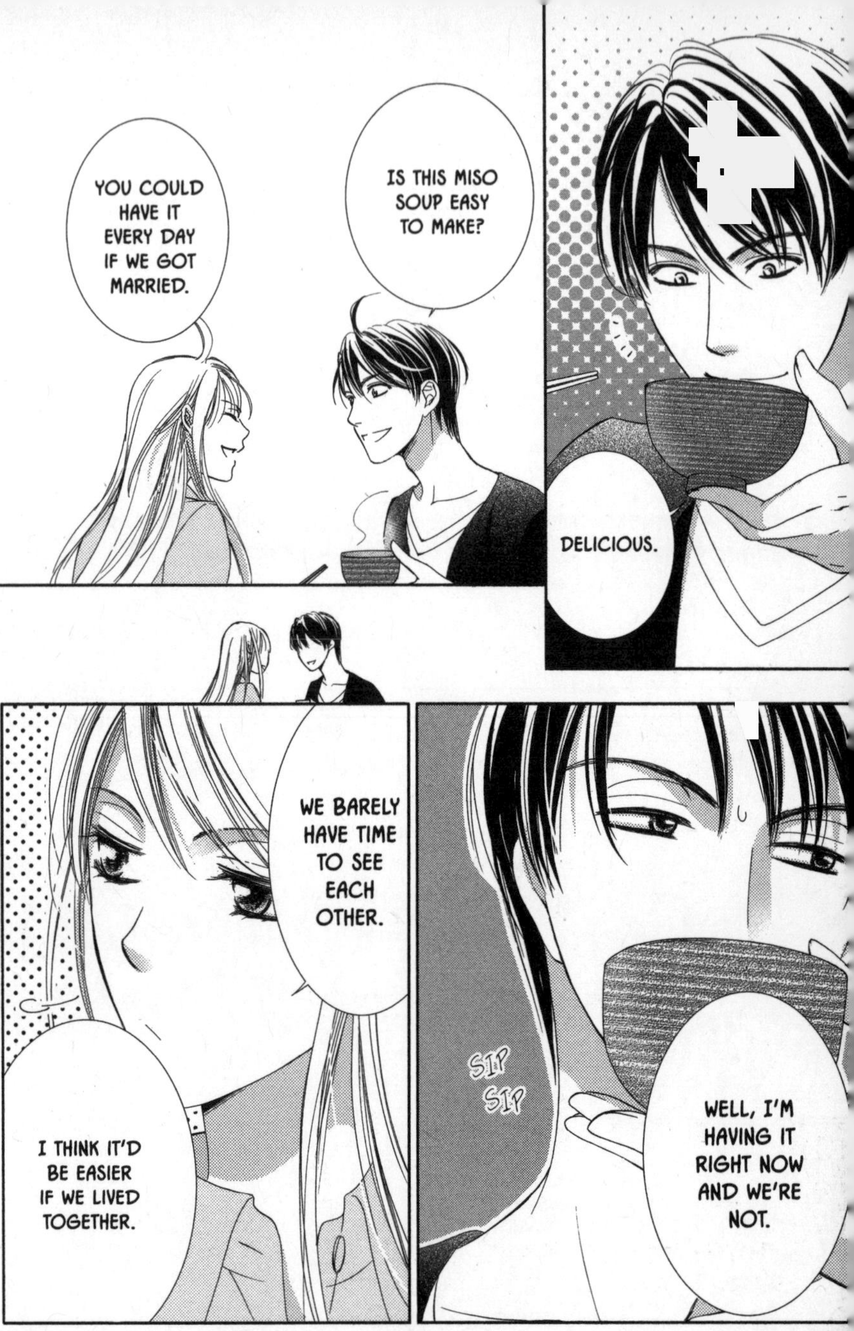
DELICIOUS.
IS THIS MISO SOUP EASY TO MAKE?
YOU COULD HAVE IT EVERY DAY IF WE GOT MARRIED.
SIP SIP
WELL, I'M HAVING IT RIGHT NOW AND WE'RE NOT.
WE BARELY HAVE TIME TO SEE EACH OTHER.
I THINK IT'D BE EASIER IF WE LIVED TOGETHER.

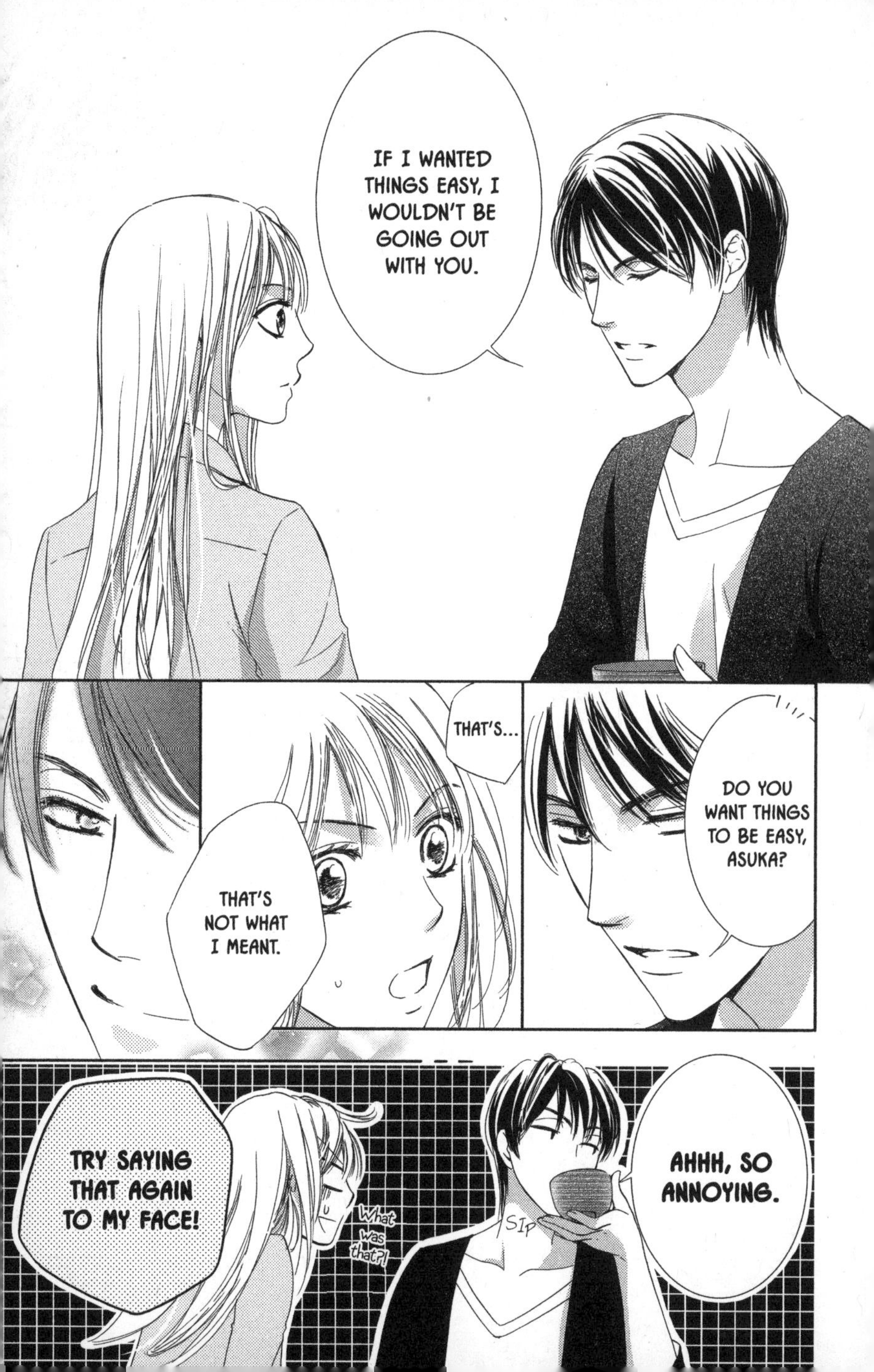
IF I WANTED THINGS EASY, I WOULDN'T BE GOING OUT WITH YOU.
DO YOU WANT THINGS TO BE EASY, ASUKA?
THAT'S...
THAT'S NOT WHAT I MEANT.
AHHH, SO ANNOYING.
SIP
What was that?!
TRY SAYING THAT AGAIN TO MY FACE!

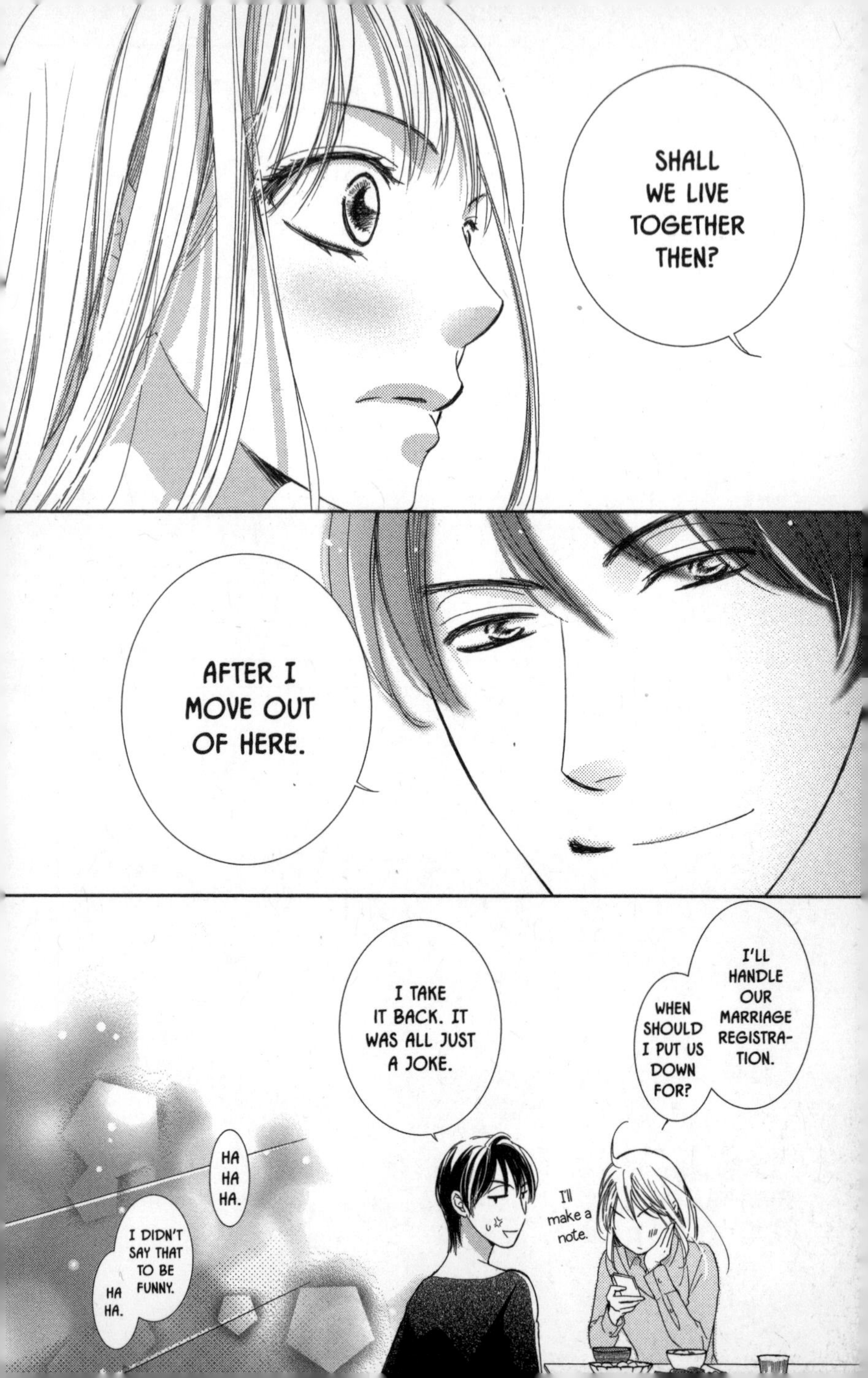
SHALL WE LIVE TOGETHER THEN?
AFTER I MOVE OUT OF HERE.
I'LL HANDLE OUR MARRIAGE REGISTRATION.
WHEN SHOULD I PUT US DOWN FOR?
I TAKE IT BACK. IT WAS ALL JUST A JOKE.
I'll make a note.
HA HA HA.
I DIDN'T SAY THAT TO BE FUNNY.
HA HA.

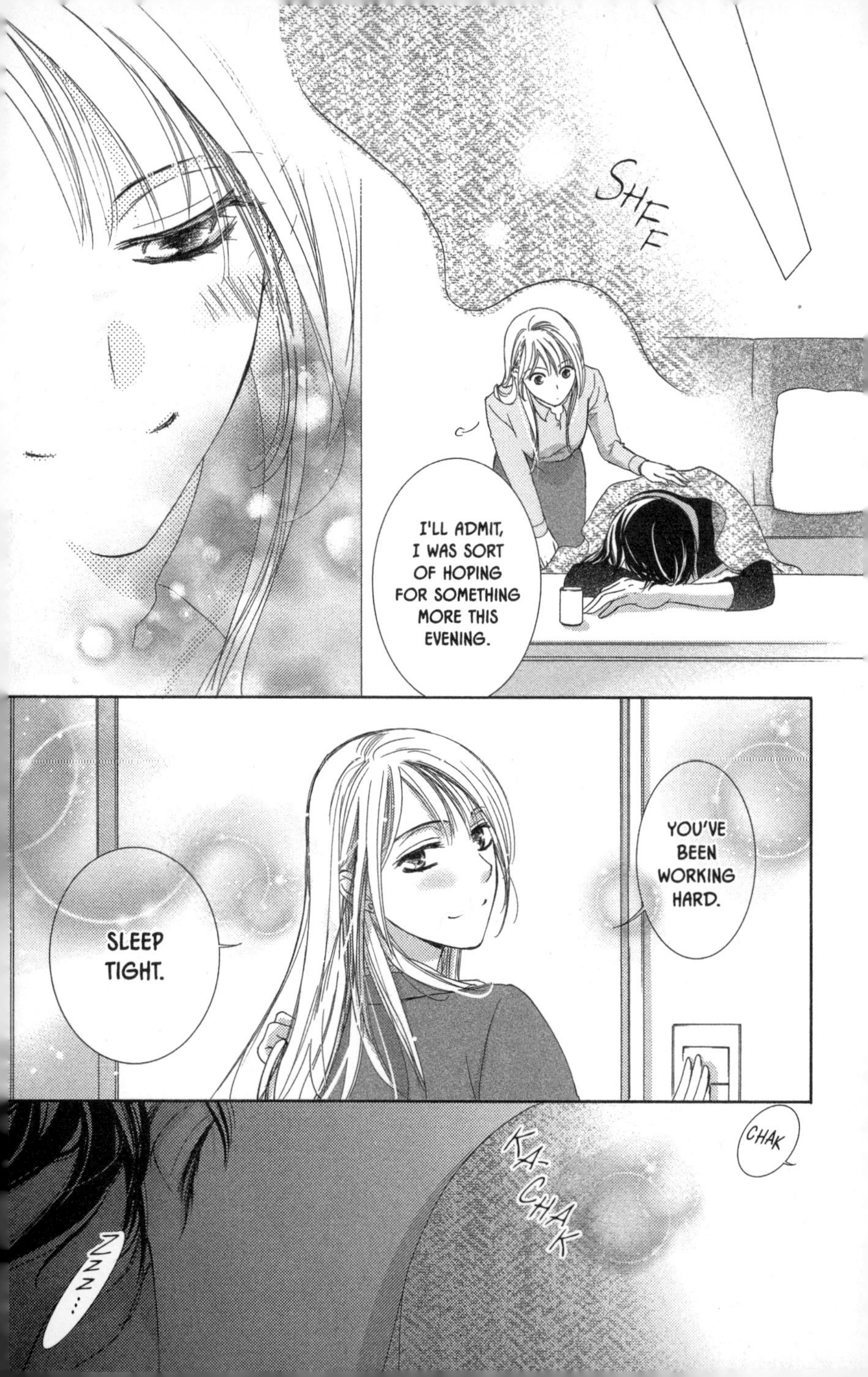
SHFF
I'LL ADMIT, I WAS SORT OF HOPING FOR SOMETHING MORE THIS EVENING.
YOU'VE BEEN WORKING HARD.
SLEEP TIGHT.
CHAK
KA-CHAK
ZZZ...

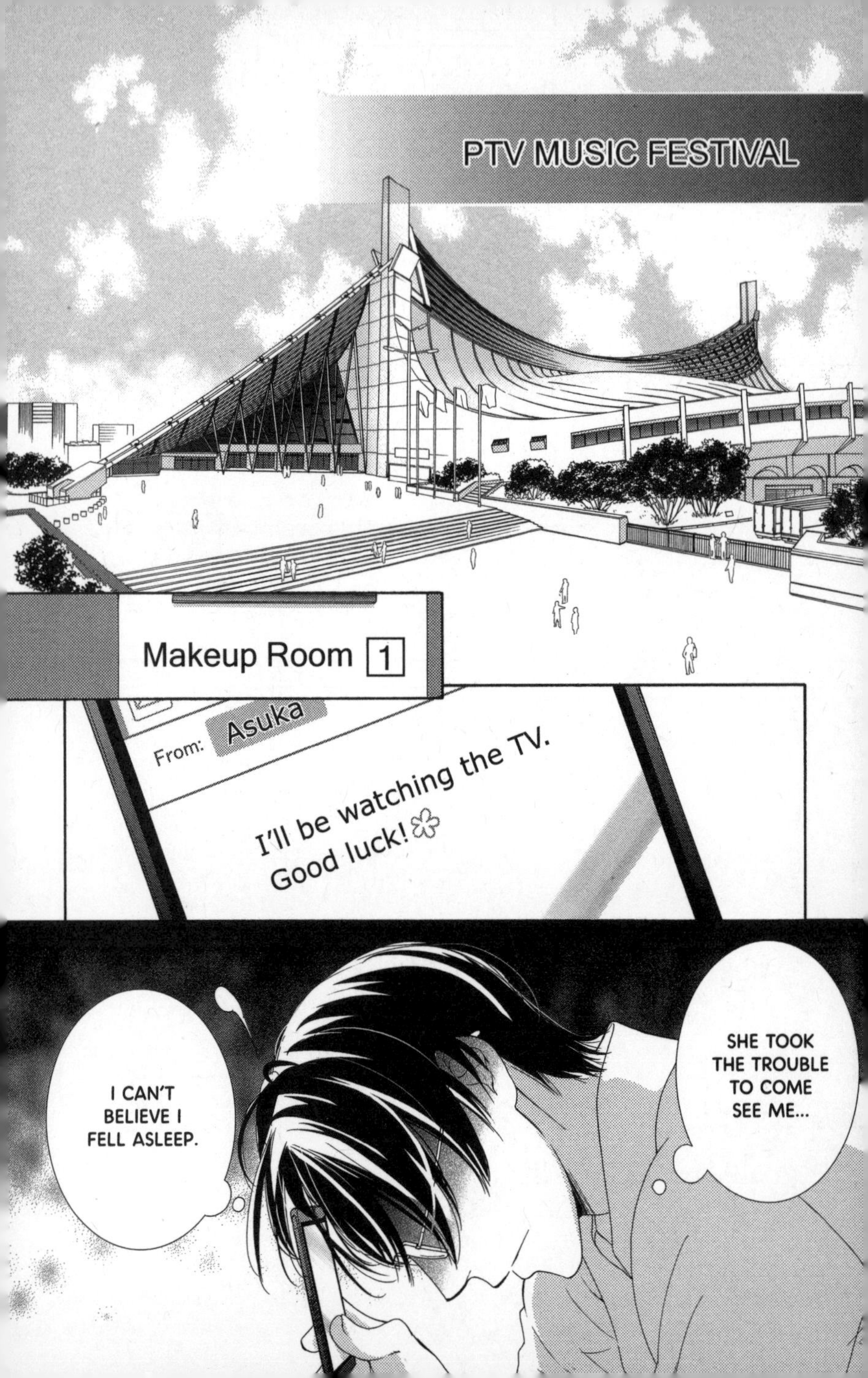
PTV MUSIC FESTIVAL
Makeup Room 1
From: Asuka
I'll be watching the TV. Good luck!
SHE TOOK THE TROUBLE TO COME SEE ME...
I CAN'T BELIEVE I FELL ASLEEP.

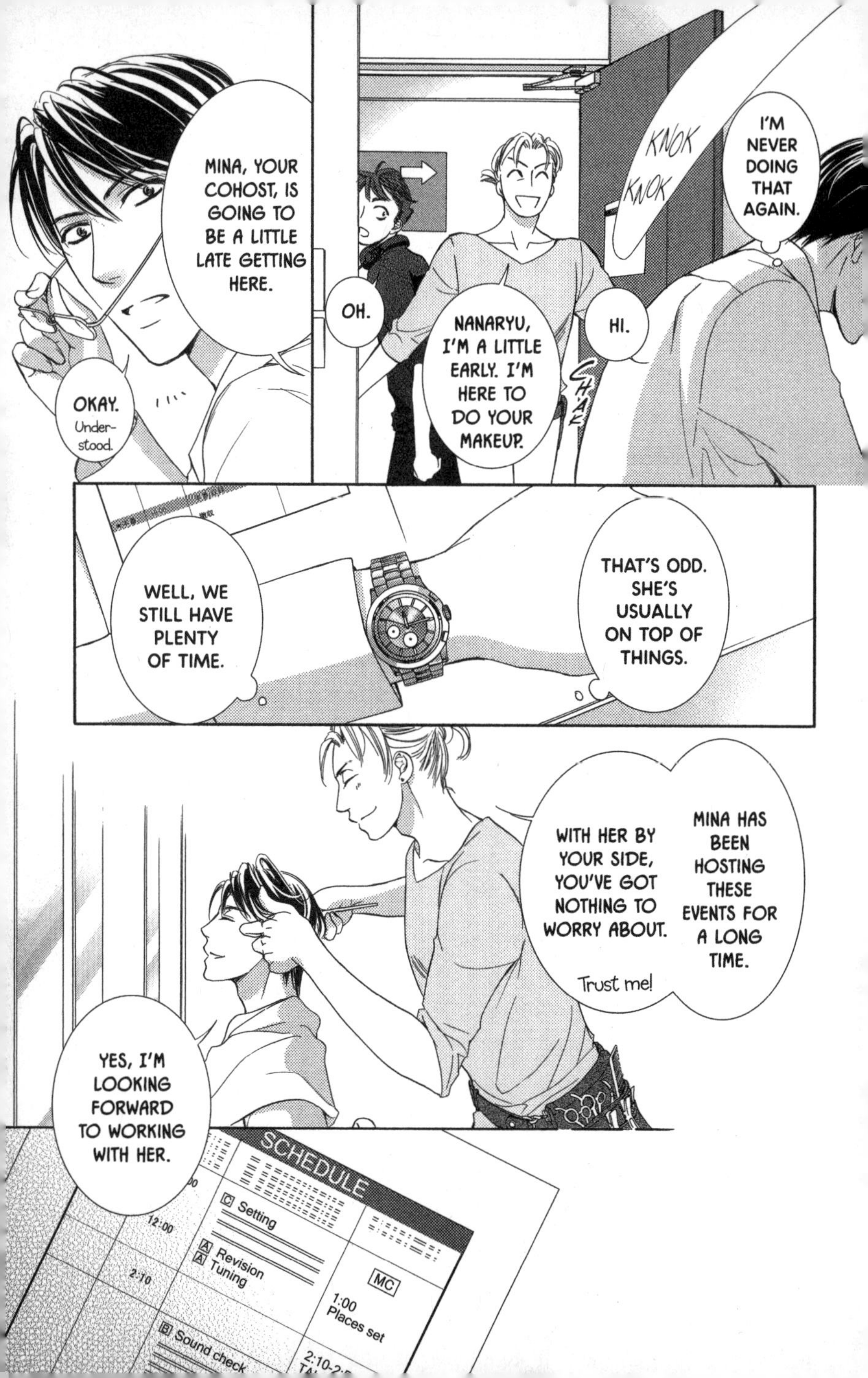
I'M NEVER DOING THAT AGAIN.
KNOK KNOK
HI.
CHAK
NANARYU, I'M A LITTLE EARLY. I'M HERE TO DO YOUR MAKEUP.
OH.
MINA, YOUR COHOST, IS GOING TO BE A LITTLE LATE GETTING HERE.
OKAY. Understood.
THAT'S ODD. SHE'S USUALLY ON TOP OF THINGS.
WELL, WE STILL HAVE PLENTY OF TIME.
MINA HAS BEEN HOSTING THESE EVENTS FOR A LONG TIME.
WITH HER BY YOUR SIDE, YOU'VE GOT NOTHING TO WORRY ABOUT.
Trust me!
YES, I'M LOOKING FORWARD TO WORKING WITH HER.
SCHEDULE
C Setting
12:00
A Revision
A Tuning
2:10
MC
1:00
Places set
B Sound check

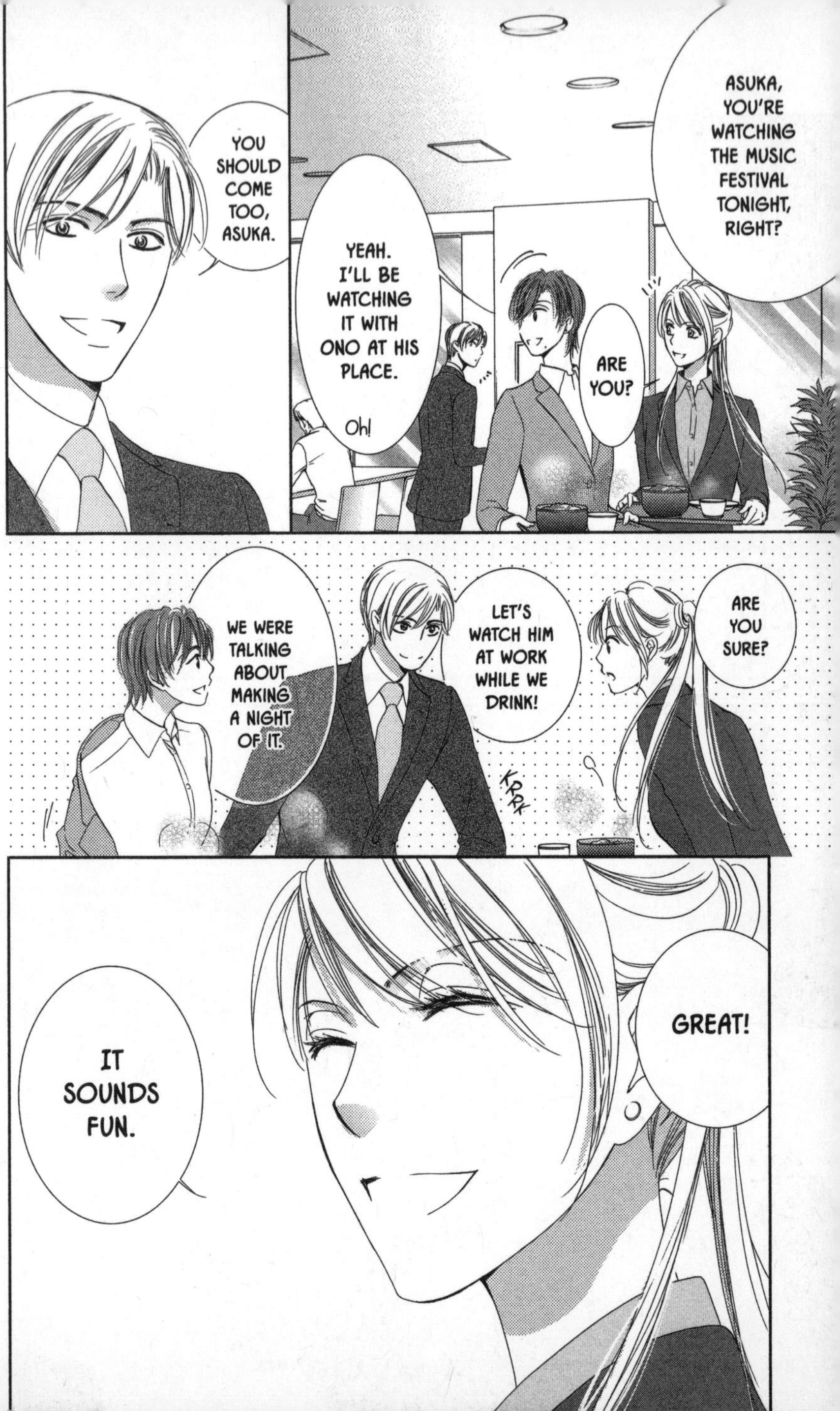
ASUKA, YOU'RE WATCHING THE MUSIC FESTIVAL TONIGHT, RIGHT?
ARE YOU?
YEAH. I'LL BE WATCHING IT WITH ONO AT HIS PLACE.
Oh!
YOU SHOULD COME TOO, ASUKA.
ARE YOU SURE?
LET'S WATCH HIM AT WORK WHILE WE DRINK!
KRRK
WE WERE TALKING ABOUT MAKING A NIGHT OF IT.
GREAT!
IT SOUNDS FUN.

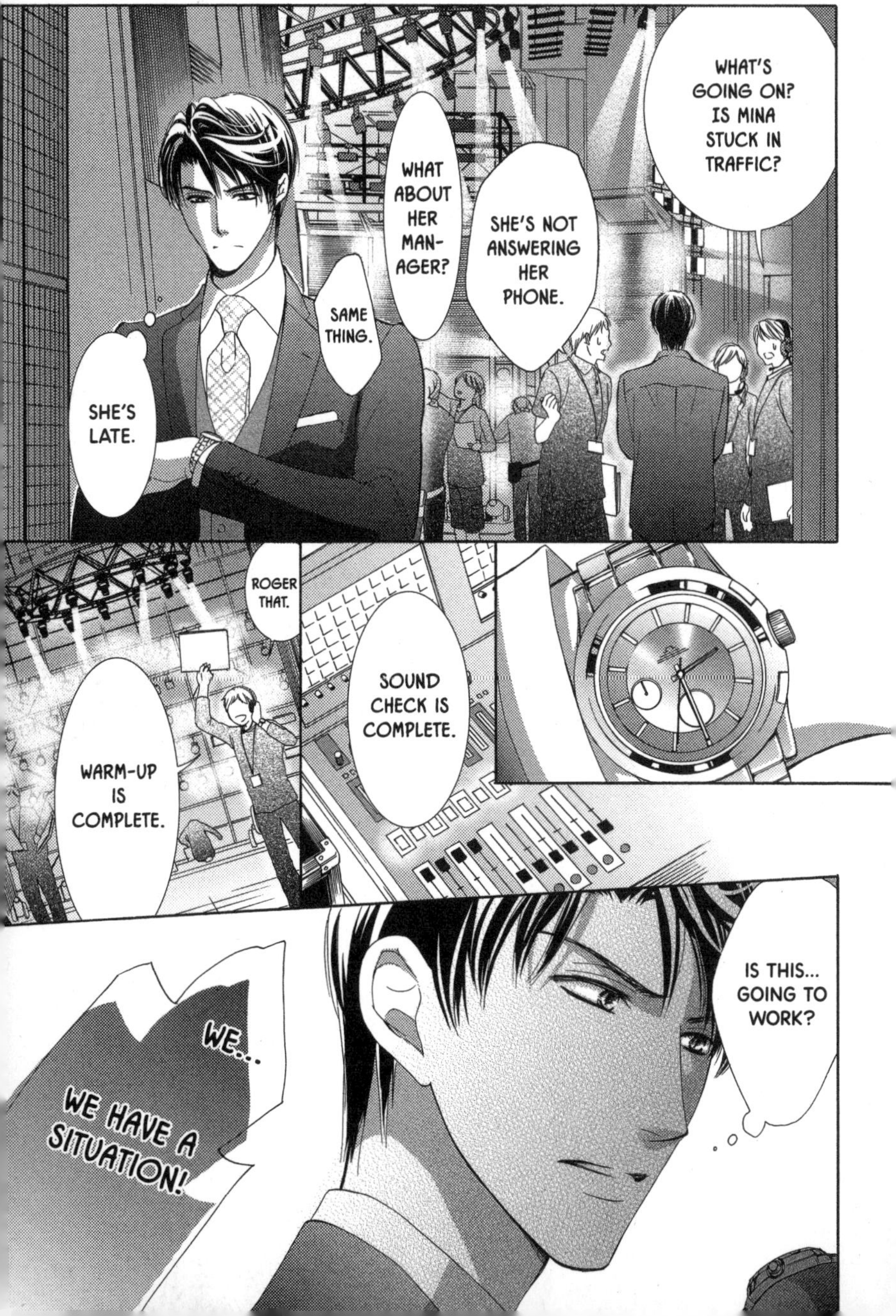
WHAT'S GOING ON? IS MINA STUCK IN TRAFFIC?
SHE'S NOT ANSWERING HER PHONE.
WHAT ABOUT HER MAN-AGER?
SAME THING.
SHE'S LATE.
SOUND CHECK IS COMPLETE.
ROGER THAT.
WARM-UP IS COMPLETE.
IS THIS... GOING TO WORK?
WE...
WE HAVE A SITUATION!

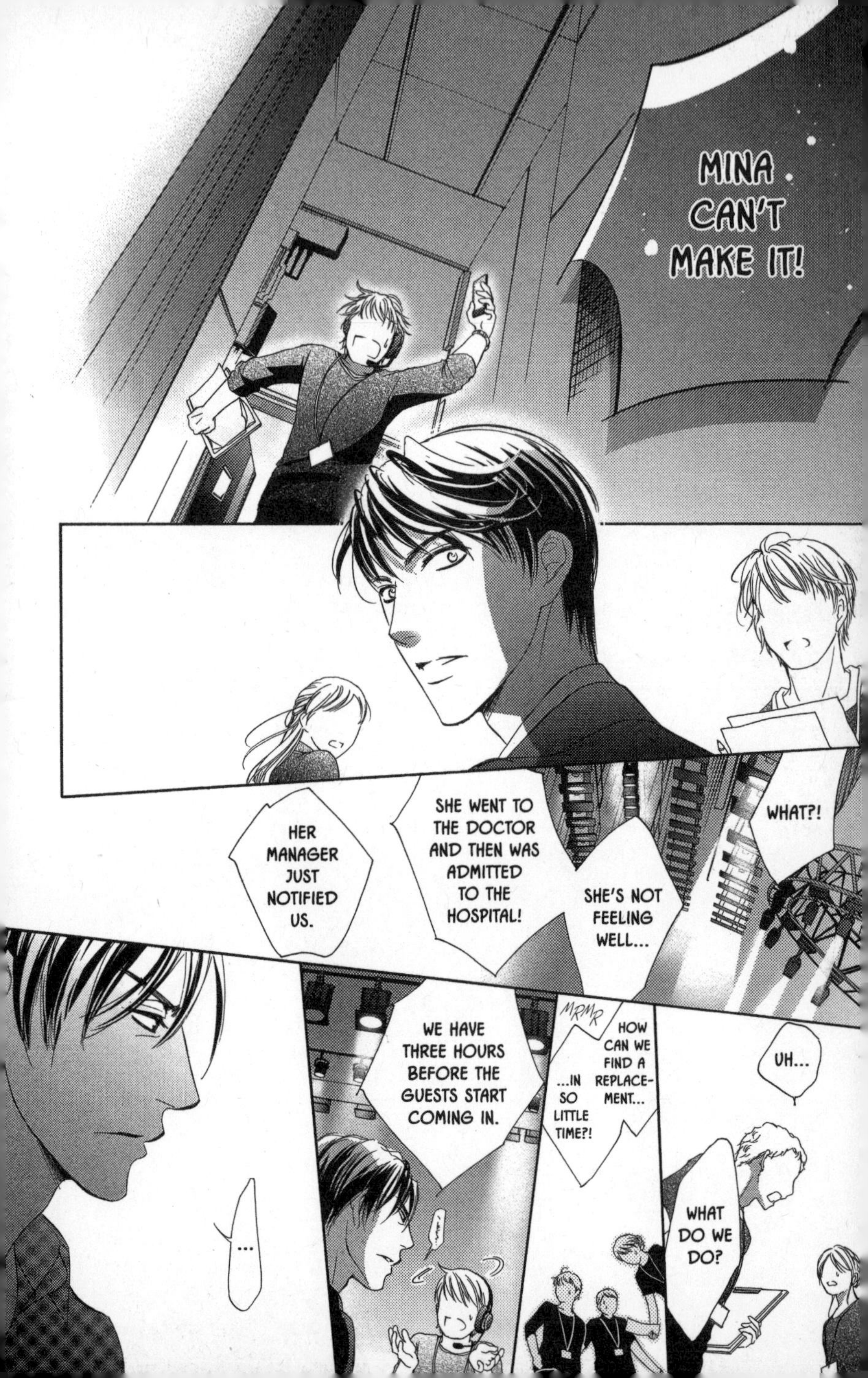
MINA CAN'T MAKE IT!
WHAT?!
SHE'S NOT FEELING WELL...
SHE WENT TO THE DOCTOR AND THEN WAS ADMITTED TO THE HOSPITAL!
HER MANAGER JUST NOTIFIED US.
UH...
WHAT DO WE DO?
MRMR
HOW CAN WE FIND A REPLACEMENT...
...IN SO LITTLE TIME?!
WE HAVE THREE HOURS BEFORE THE GUESTS START COMING IN.
...

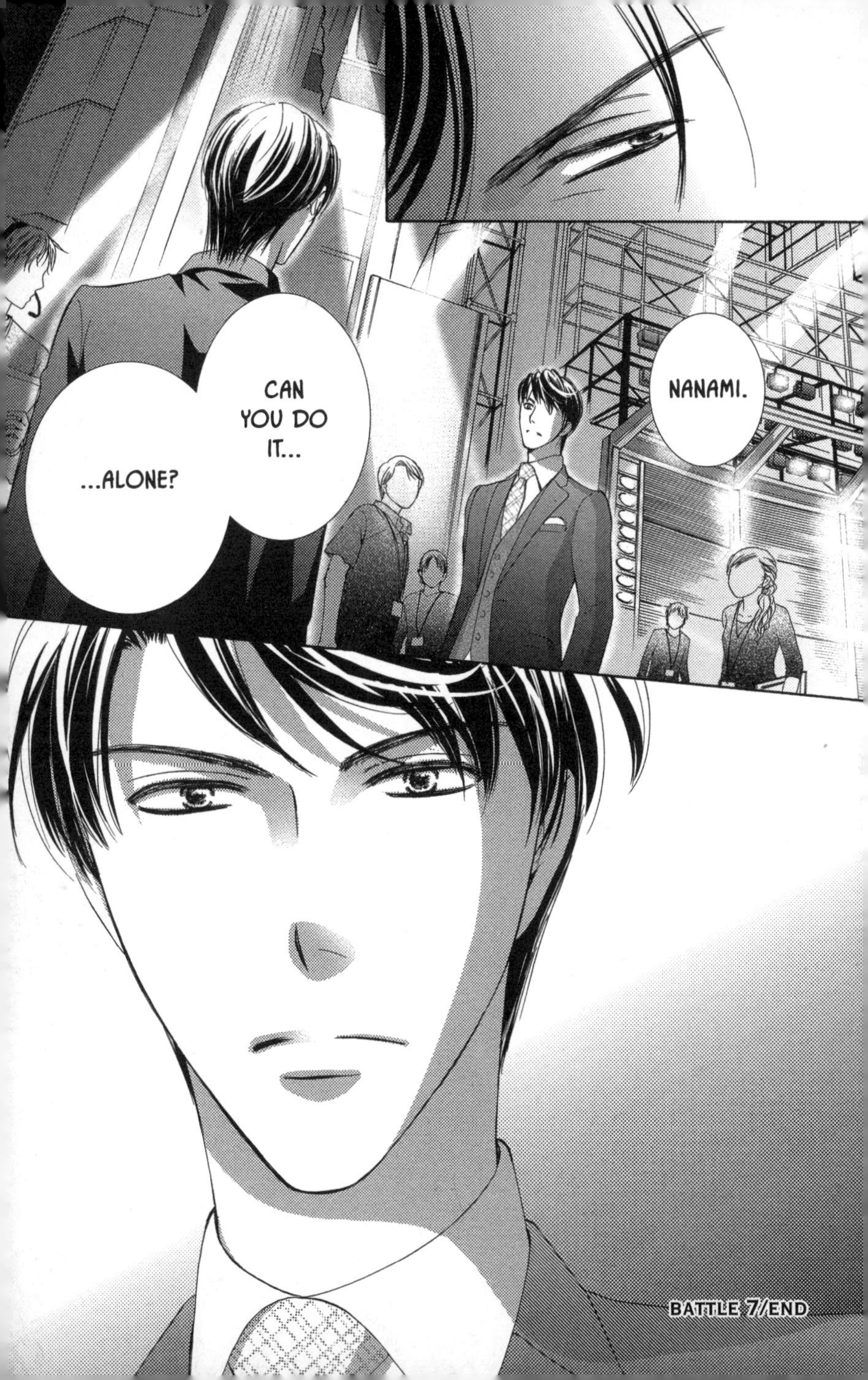
NANAMI.
CAN YOU DO IT...
...ALONE?
BATTLE 7/END

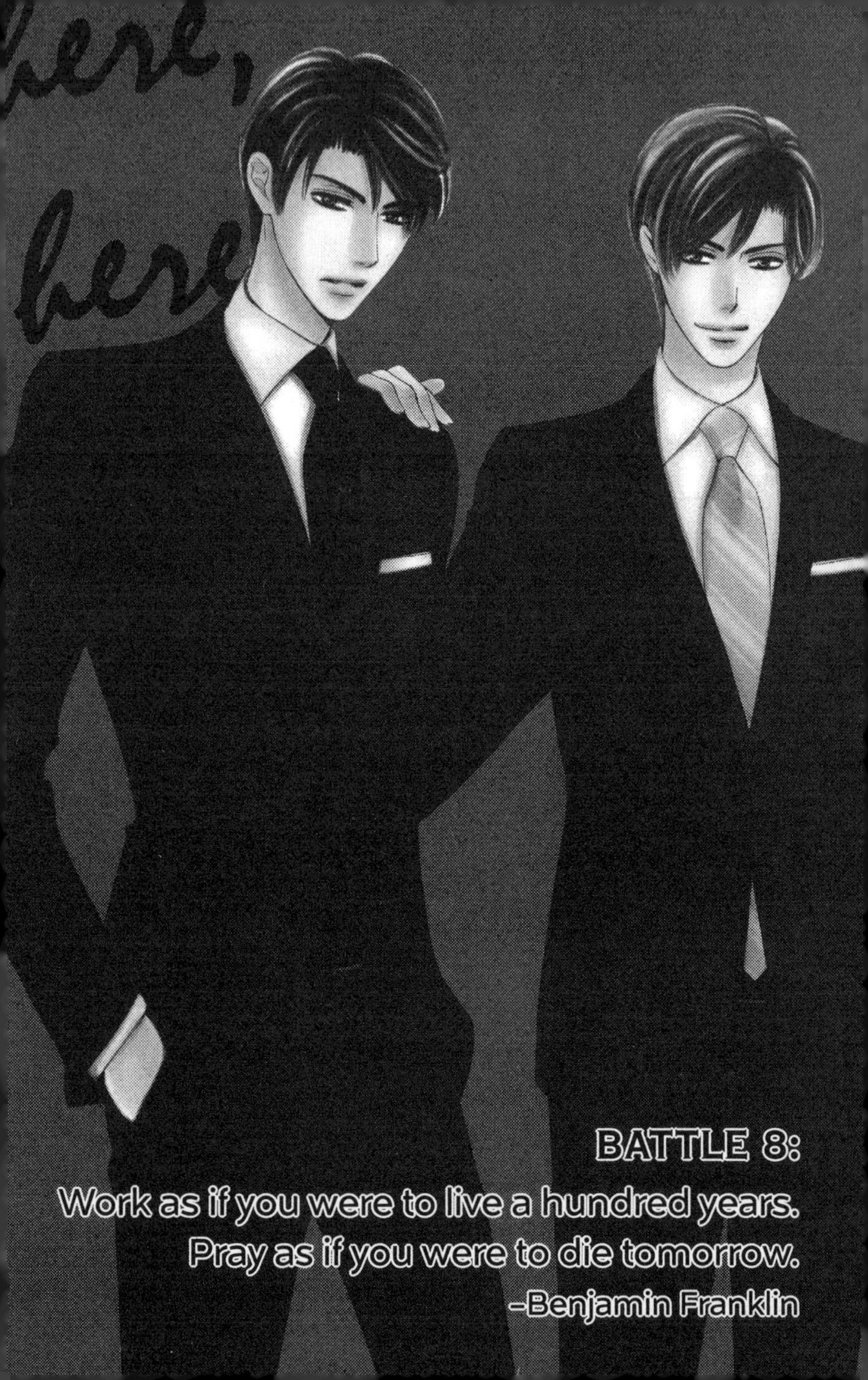

BATTLE 8:

Work as if you were to live a hundred years.
Pray as if you were to die tomorrow.
–Benjamin Franklin

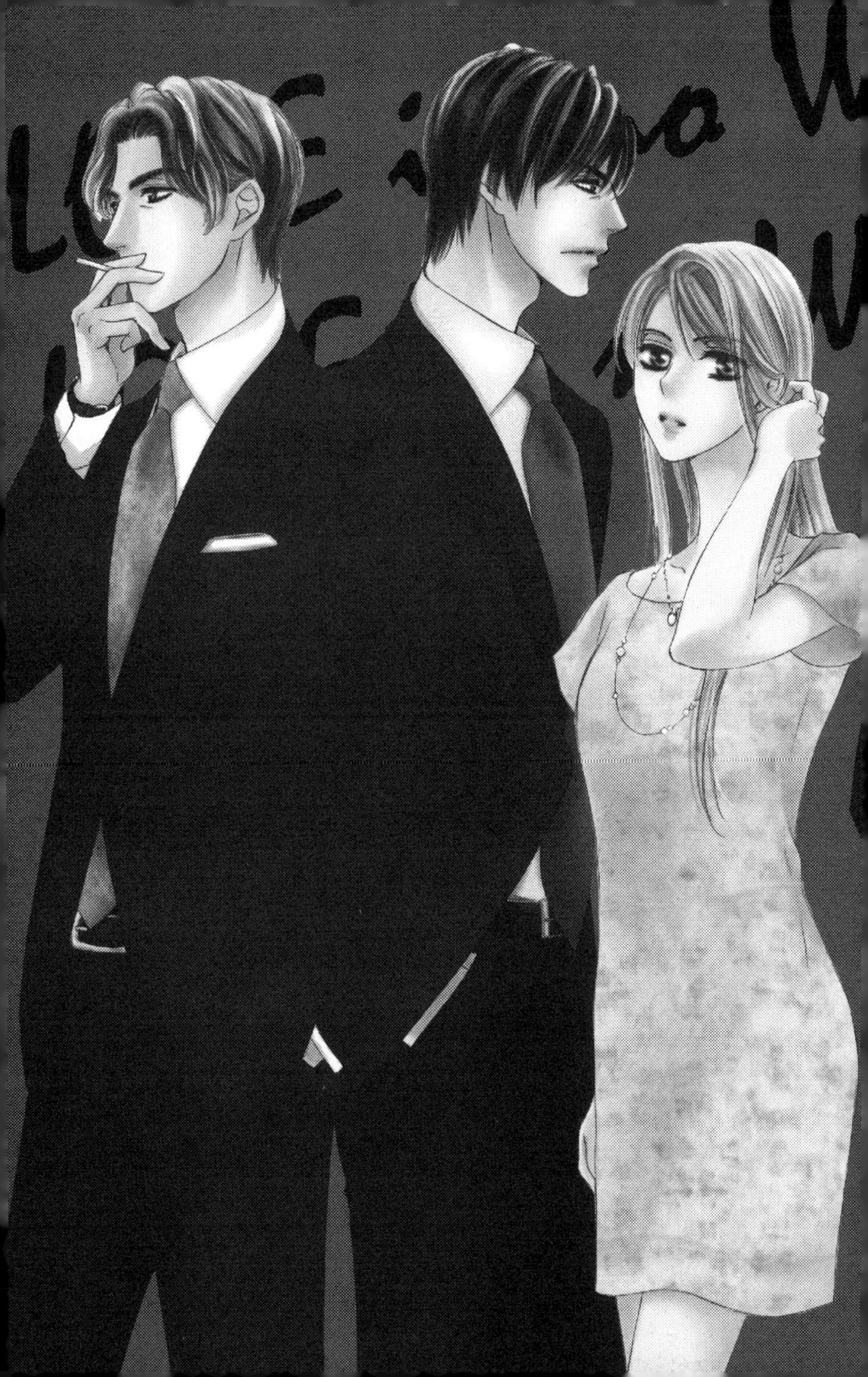

Everyone's
Getting
Married

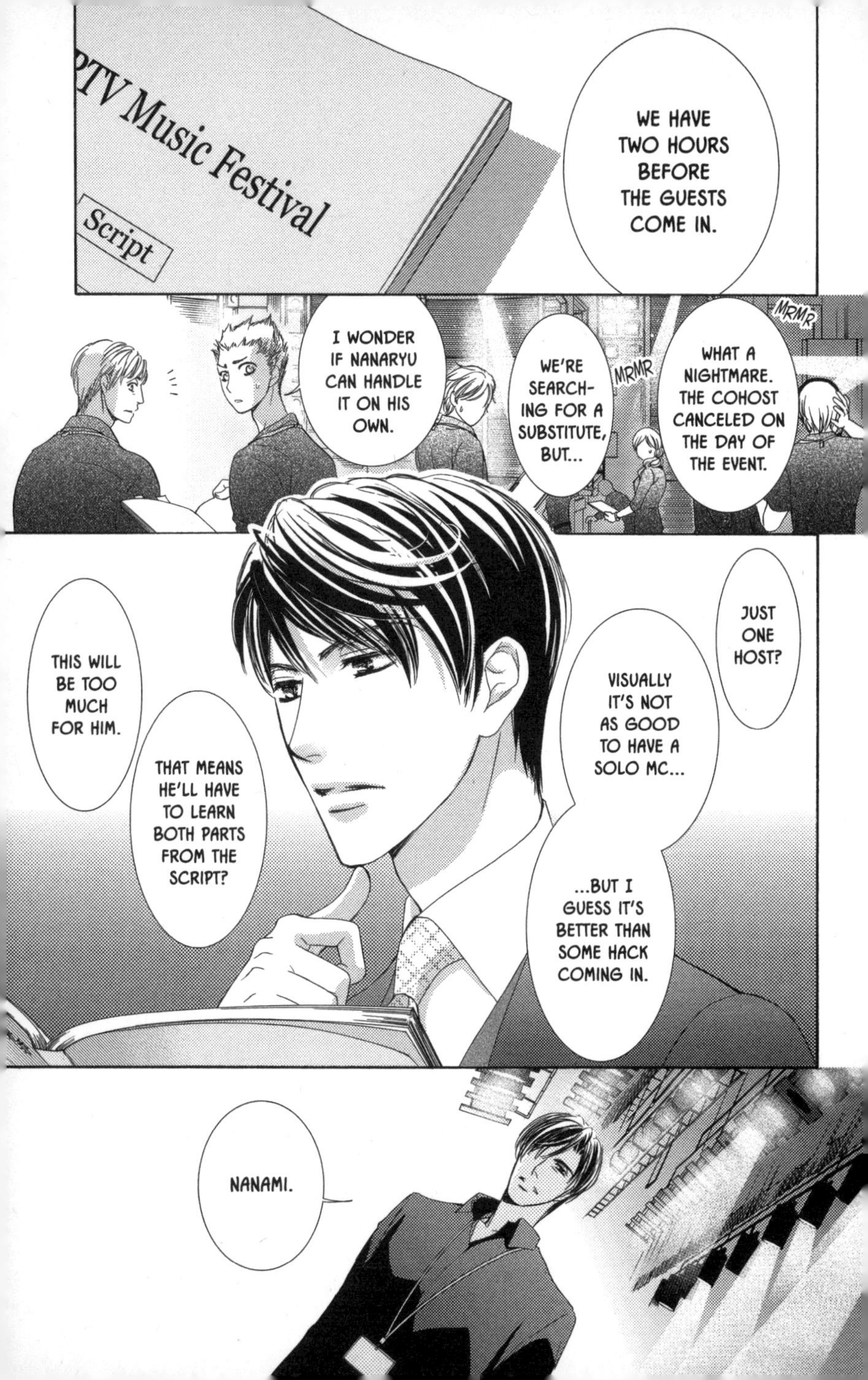
WE HAVE TWO HOURS BEFORE THE GUESTS COME IN.
RTV Music Festival
Script
MRMR
WHAT A NIGHTMARE. THE COHOST CANCELED ON THE DAY OF THE EVENT.
MRMR
WE'RE SEARCH-ING FOR A SUBSTITUTE, BUT...
I WONDER IF NANARYU CAN HANDLE IT ON HIS OWN.
JUST ONE HOST?
VISUALLY IT'S NOT AS GOOD TO HAVE A SOLO MC...
...BUT I GUESS IT'S BETTER THAN SOME HACK COMING IN.
THAT MEANS HE'LL HAVE TO LEARN BOTH PARTS FROM THE SCRIPT?
THIS WILL BE TOO MUCH FOR HIM.
NANAMI.

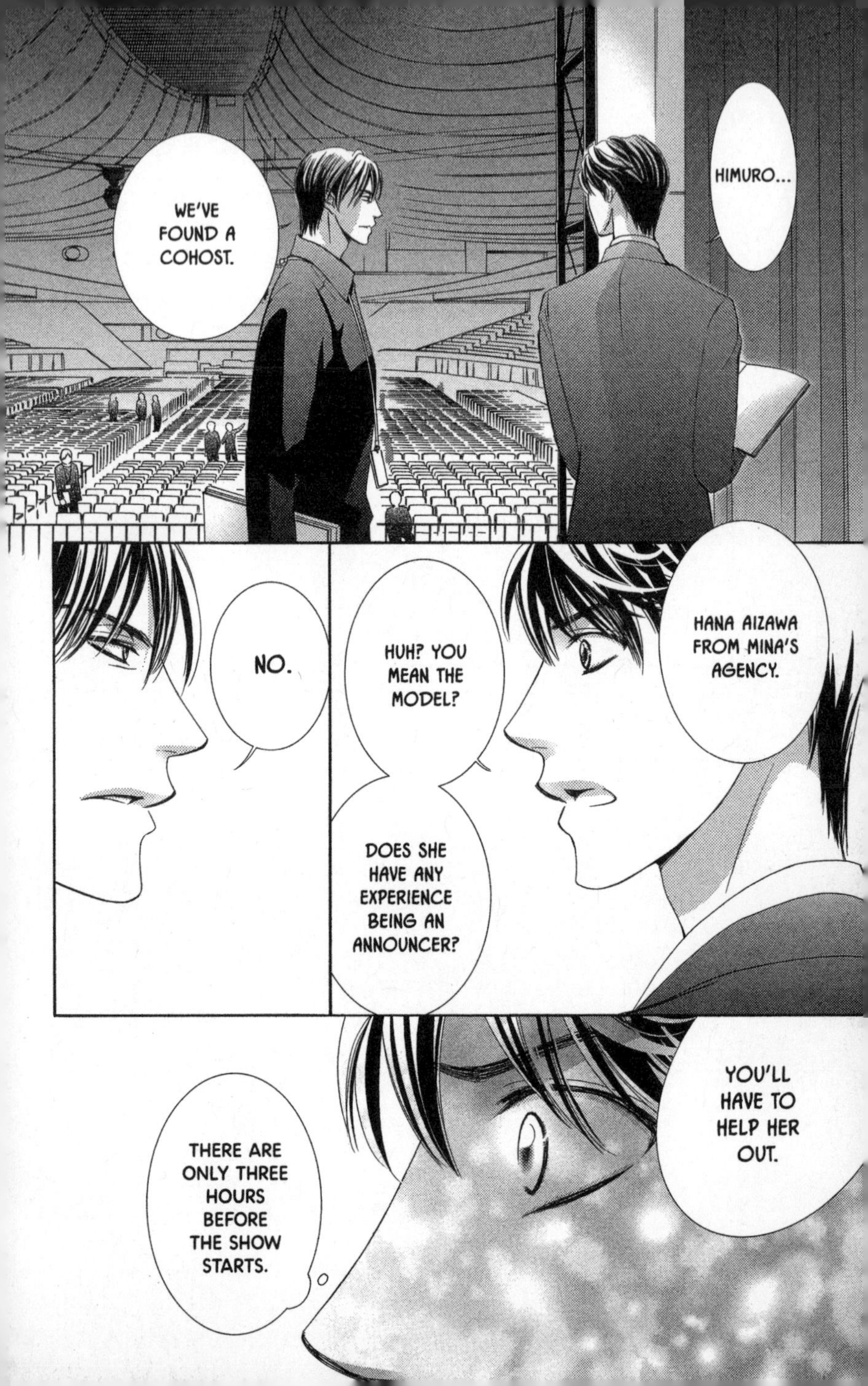
HIMURO...
WE'VE FOUND A COHOST.
HANA AIZAWA FROM MINA'S AGENCY.
HUH? YOU MEAN THE MODEL?
DOES SHE HAVE ANY EXPERIENCE BEING AN ANNOUNCER?
NO.
YOU'LL HAVE TO HELP HER OUT.
THERE ARE ONLY THREE HOURS BEFORE THE SHOW STARTS.

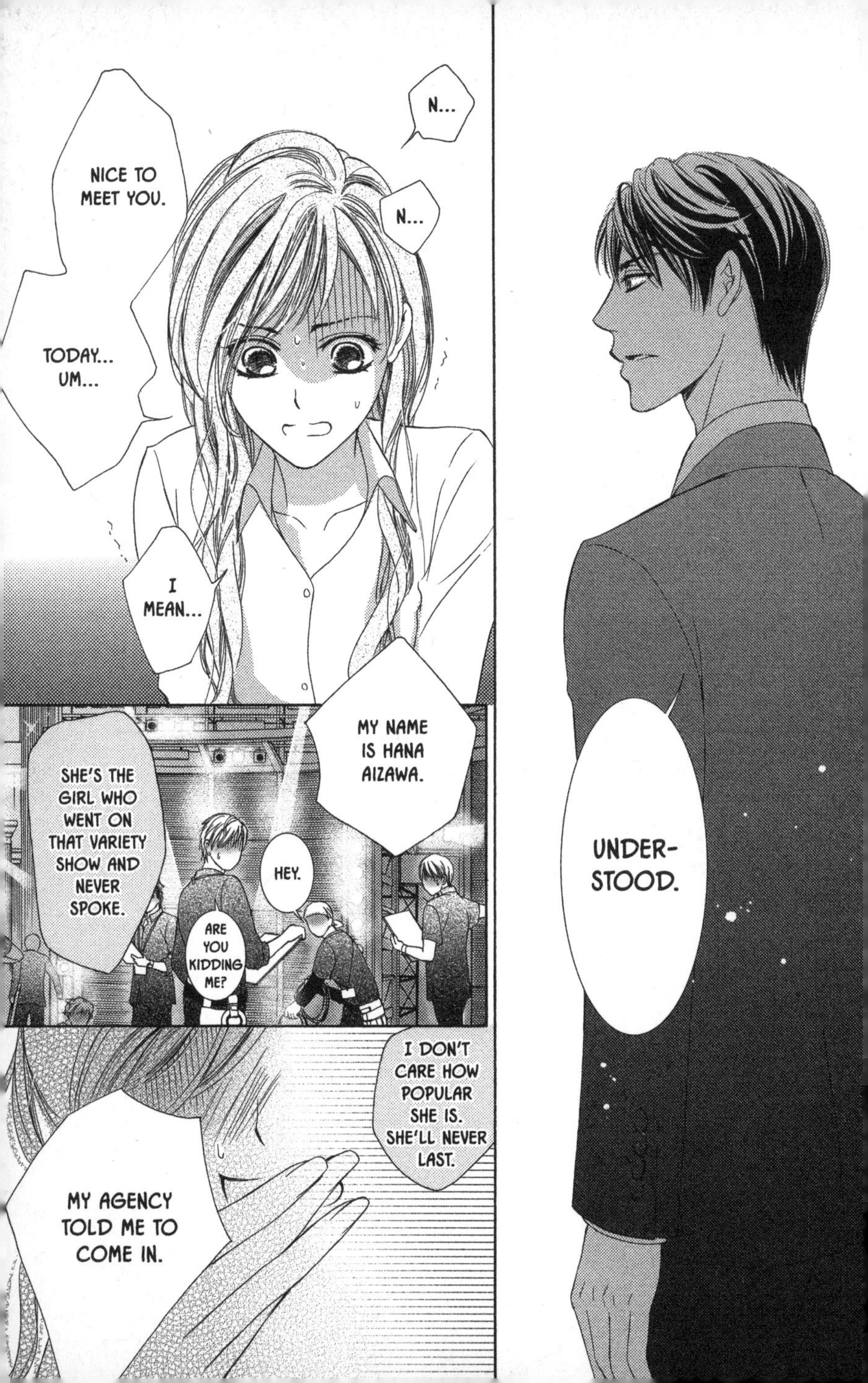
UNDER-STOOD.
N...
N...
NICE TO MEET YOU.
TODAY... UM...
I MEAN...
MY NAME IS HANA AIZAWA.
HEY.
ARE YOU KIDDING ME?
SHE'S THE GIRL WHO WENT ON THAT VARIETY SHOW AND NEVER SPOKE.
I DON'T CARE HOW POPULAR SHE IS. SHE'LL NEVER LAST.
MY AGENCY TOLD ME TO COME IN.

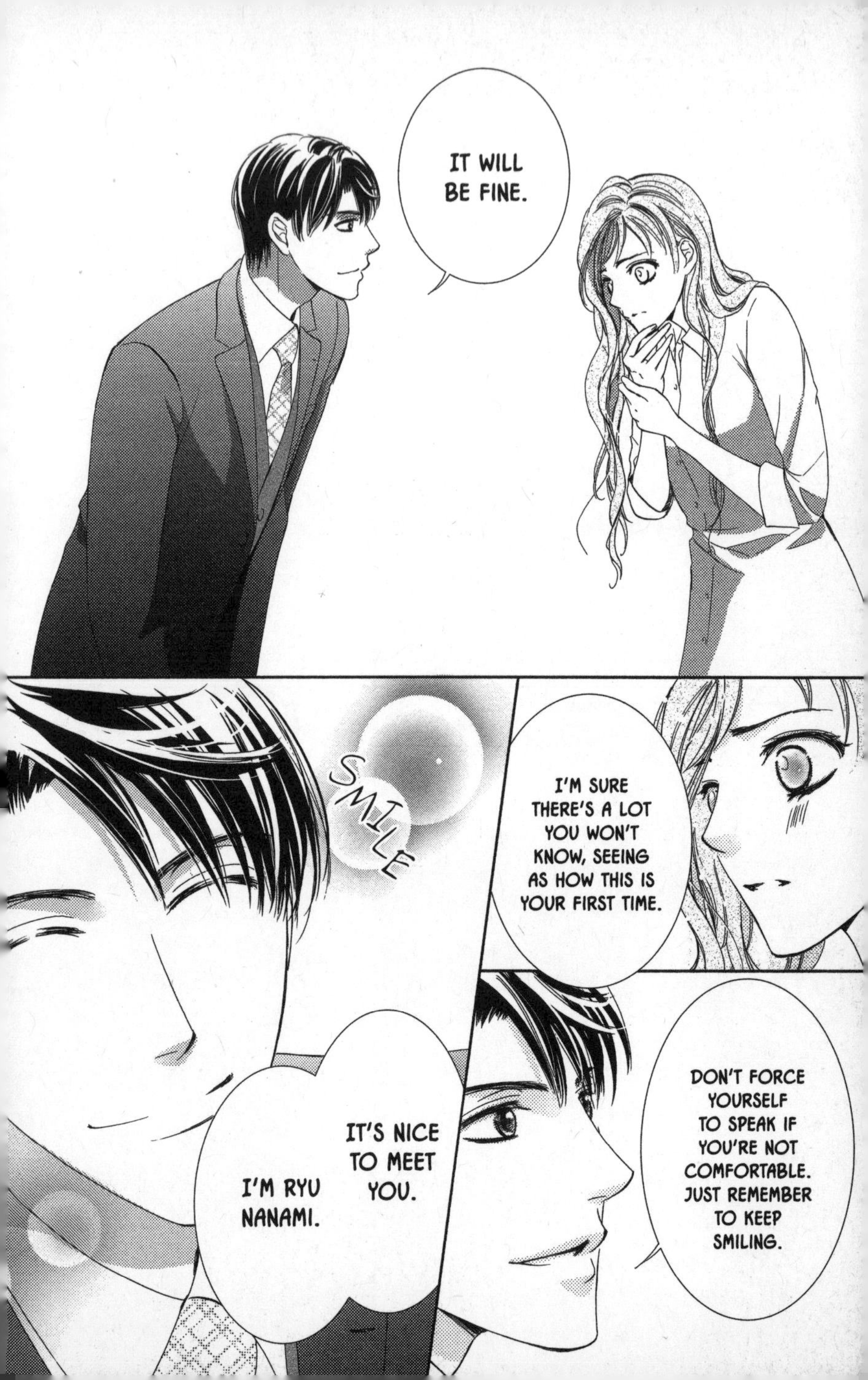
IT WILL BE FINE.
I'M SURE THERE'S A LOT YOU WON'T KNOW, SEEING AS HOW THIS IS YOUR FIRST TIME.
DON'T FORCE YOURSELF TO SPEAK IF YOU'RE NOT COMFORTABLE. JUST REMEMBER TO KEEP SMILING.
SMILE
IT'S NICE TO MEET YOU.
I'M RYU NANAMI.

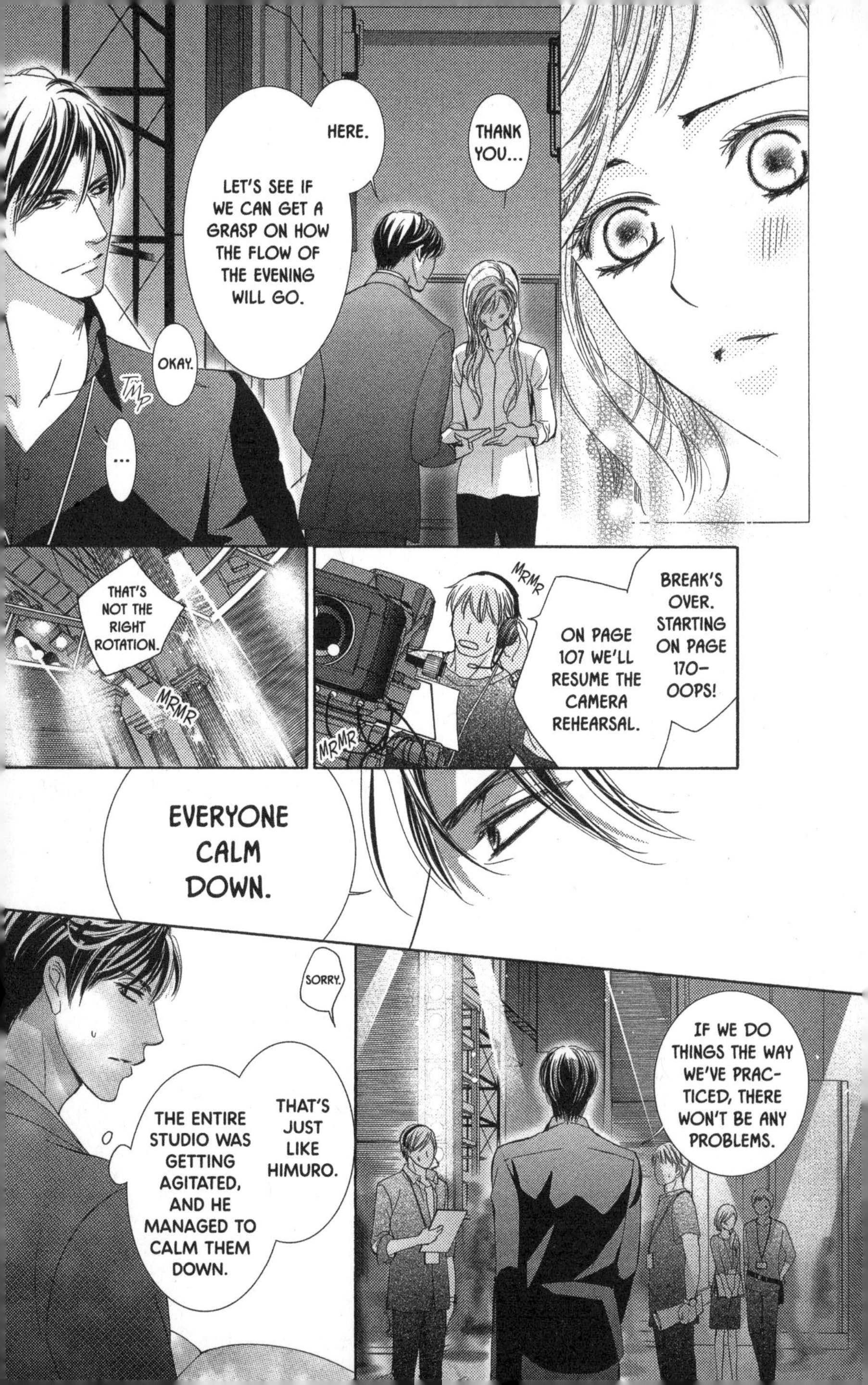
THANK YOU...
HERE.
LET'S SEE IF WE CAN GET A GRASP ON HOW THE FLOW OF THE EVENING WILL GO.
OKAY.
TMP
...
MRMR
BREAK'S OVER. STARTING ON PAGE 170— OOPS!
ON PAGE 107 WE'LL RESUME THE CAMERA REHEARSAL.
MRMR
THAT'S NOT THE RIGHT ROTATION.
MRMR
EVERYONE CALM DOWN.
IF WE DO THINGS THE WAY WE'VE PRAC-TICED, THERE WON'T BE ANY PROBLEMS.
SORRY.
THAT'S JUST LIKE HIMURO.
THE ENTIRE STUDIO WAS GETTING AGITATED, AND HE MANAGED TO CALM THEM DOWN.

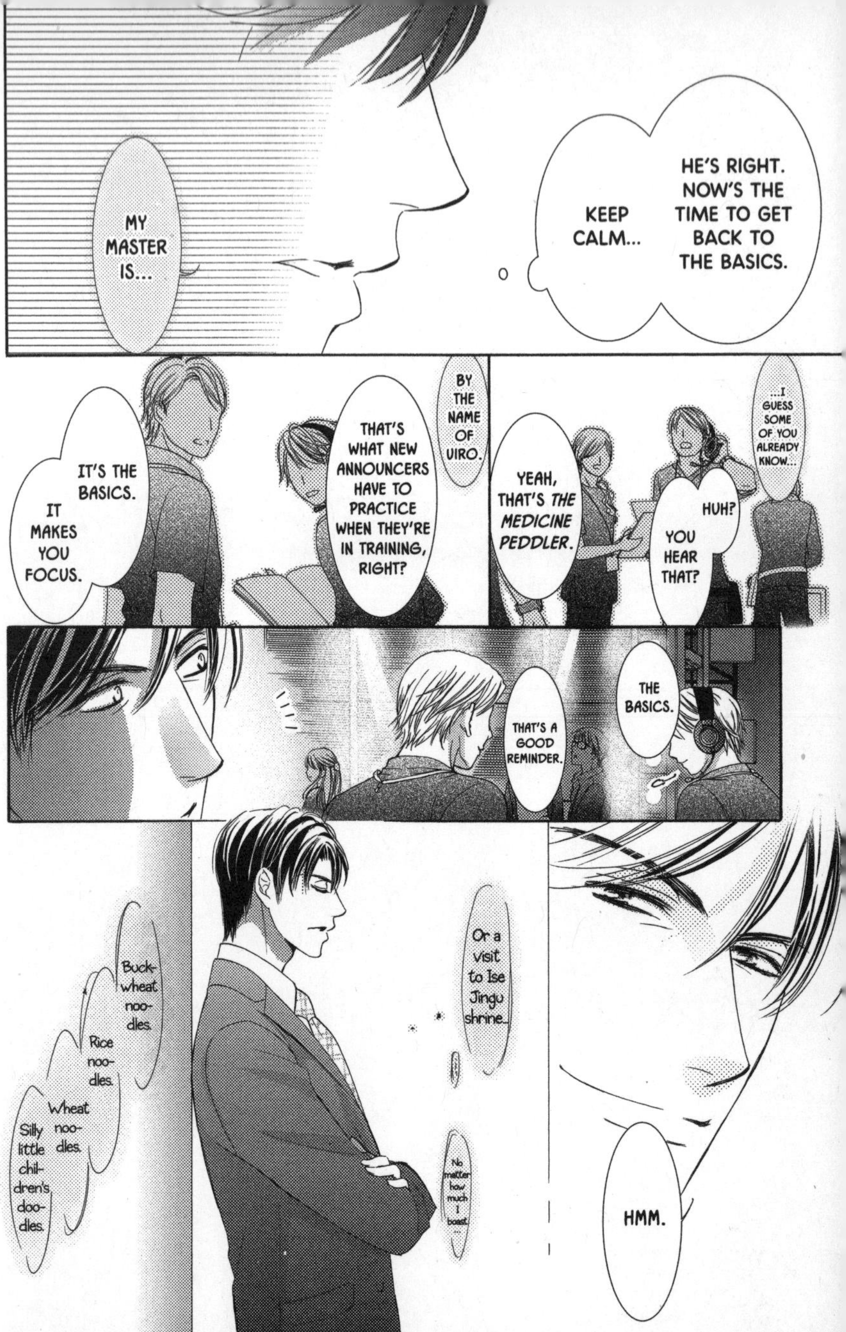
HE'S RIGHT. NOW'S THE TIME TO GET BACK TO THE BASICS.
KEEP CALM...
MY MASTER IS...
...I GUESS SOME OF YOU ALREADY KNOW...
HUH? YOU HEAR THAT?
YEAH, THAT'S *THE MEDICINE PEDDLER*.
BY THE NAME OF UIRO.
THAT'S WHAT NEW ANNOUNCERS HAVE TO PRACTICE WHEN THEY'RE IN TRAINING, RIGHT?
IT'S THE BASICS. IT MAKES YOU FOCUS.
THE BASICS.
THAT'S A GOOD REMINDER.
HMM.
Or a visit to Ise Jingu shrine...
No matter how much I boast...
Buck-wheat noo-dles.
Rice noo-dles.
Wheat noo-dles.
Silly little chil-dren's doo-dles.

**The Medicine Peddler* is a famous Kabuki play with a long and convoluted monologue. Sections from it are used as an oral test when recruiting newscasters and sports announcers.

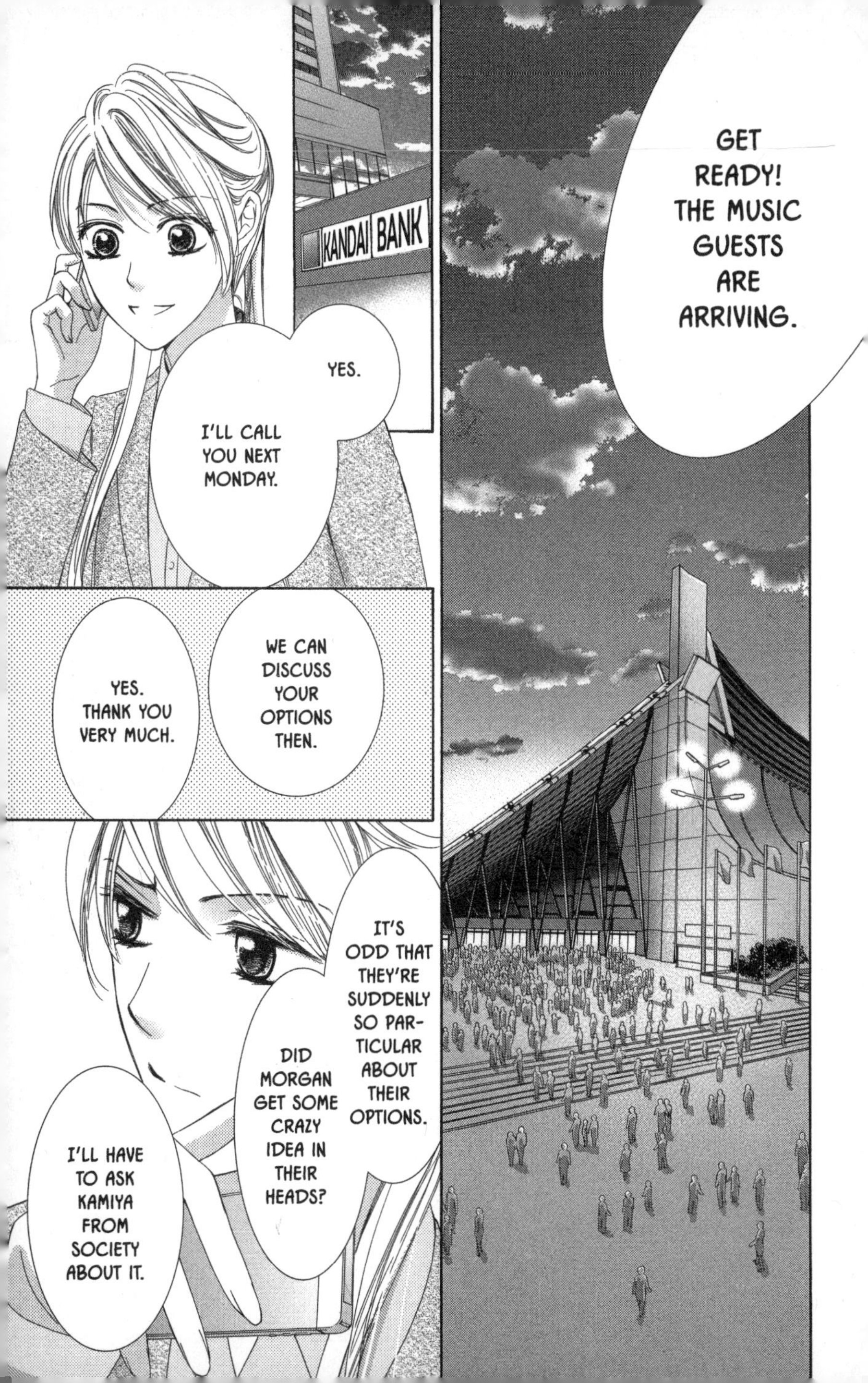
GET READY! THE MUSIC GUESTS ARE ARRIVING.
KANDAI BANK
YES.
I'LL CALL YOU NEXT MONDAY.
WE CAN DISCUSS YOUR OPTIONS THEN.
YES. THANK YOU VERY MUCH.
IT'S ODD THAT THEY'RE SUDDENLY SO PAR-TICULAR ABOUT THEIR OPTIONS.
DID MORGAN GET SOME CRAZY IDEA IN THEIR HEADS?
I'LL HAVE TO ASK KAMIYA FROM SOCIETY ABOUT IT.

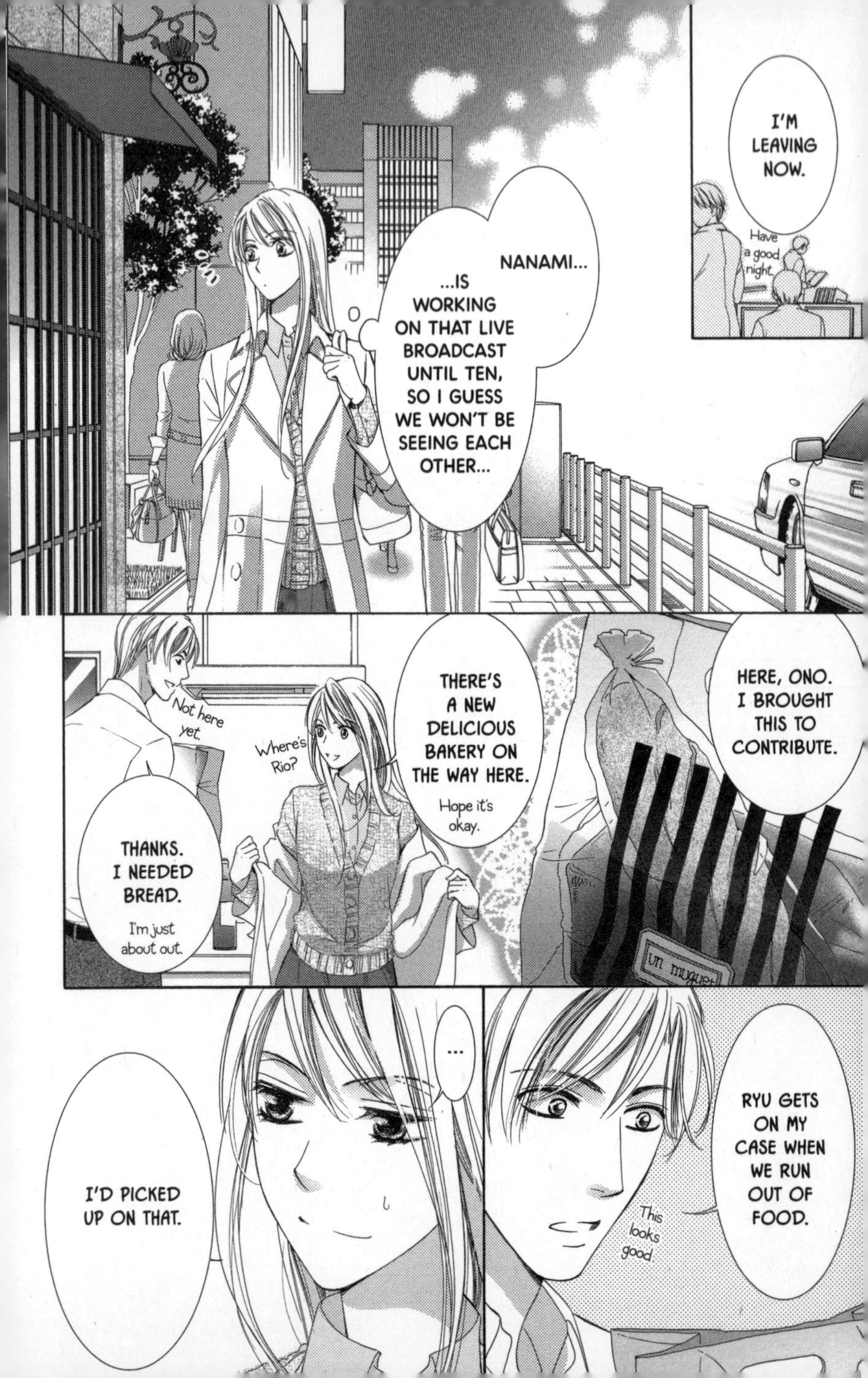
I'M LEAVING NOW.
Have a good night.
NANAMI...
...IS WORKING ON THAT LIVE BROADCAST UNTIL TEN, SO I GUESS WE WON'T BE SEEING EACH OTHER...
HERE, ONO. I BROUGHT THIS TO CONTRIBUTE.
THERE'S A NEW DELICIOUS BAKERY ON THE WAY HERE.
Hope it's okay.
Where's Rio?
Not here yet.
THANKS. I NEEDED BREAD.
I'm just about out.
RYU GETS ON MY CASE WHEN WE RUN OUT OF FOOD.
This looks good.
...
I'D PICKED UP ON THAT.

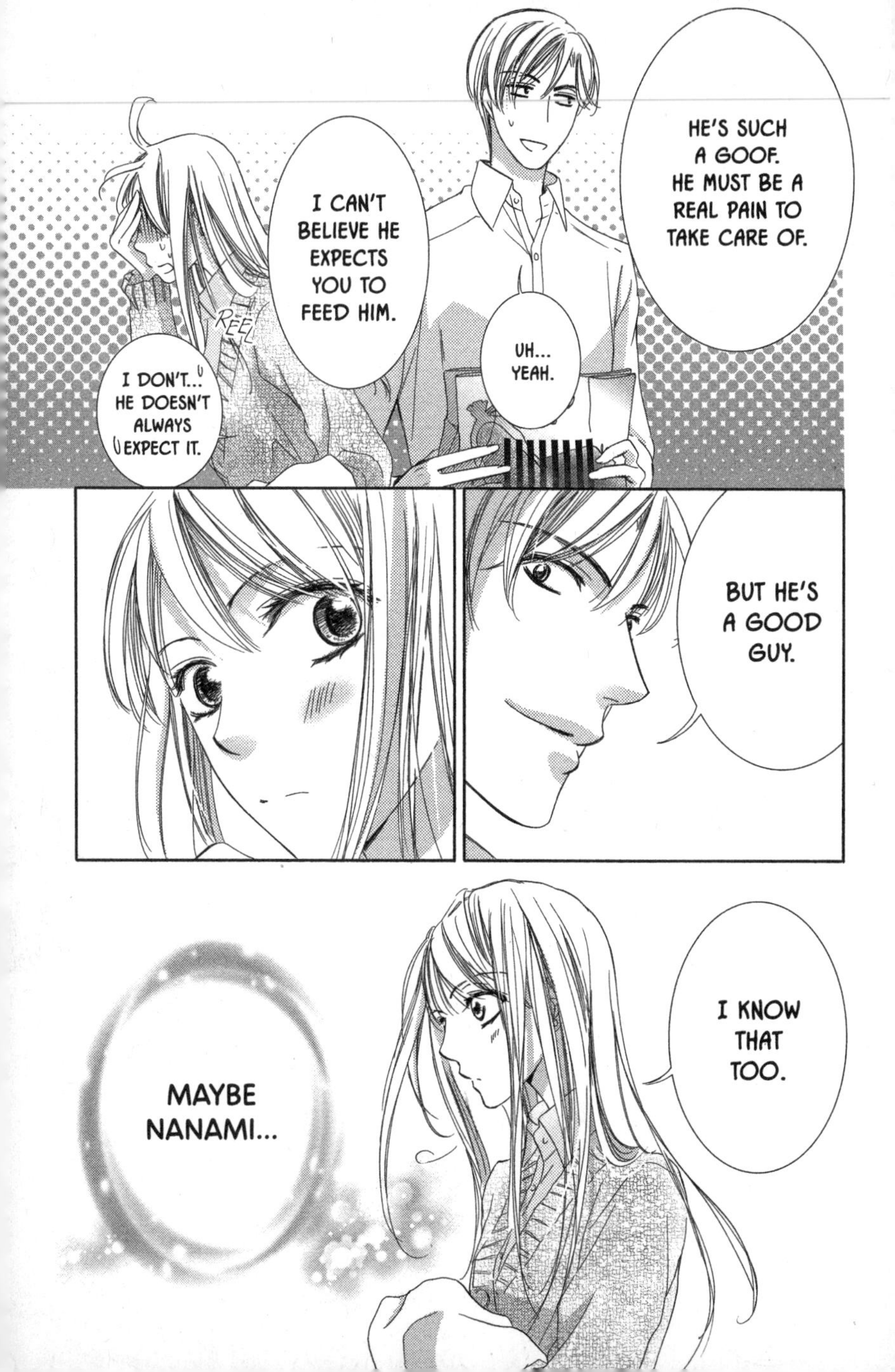
HE'S SUCH A GOOF. HE MUST BE A REAL PAIN TO TAKE CARE OF.
UH... YEAH.
I CAN'T BELIEVE HE EXPECTS YOU TO FEED HIM.
REEL
I DON'T... HE DOESN'T ALWAYS EXPECT IT.
BUT HE'S A GOOD GUY.
I KNOW THAT TOO.
MAYBE NANAMI...

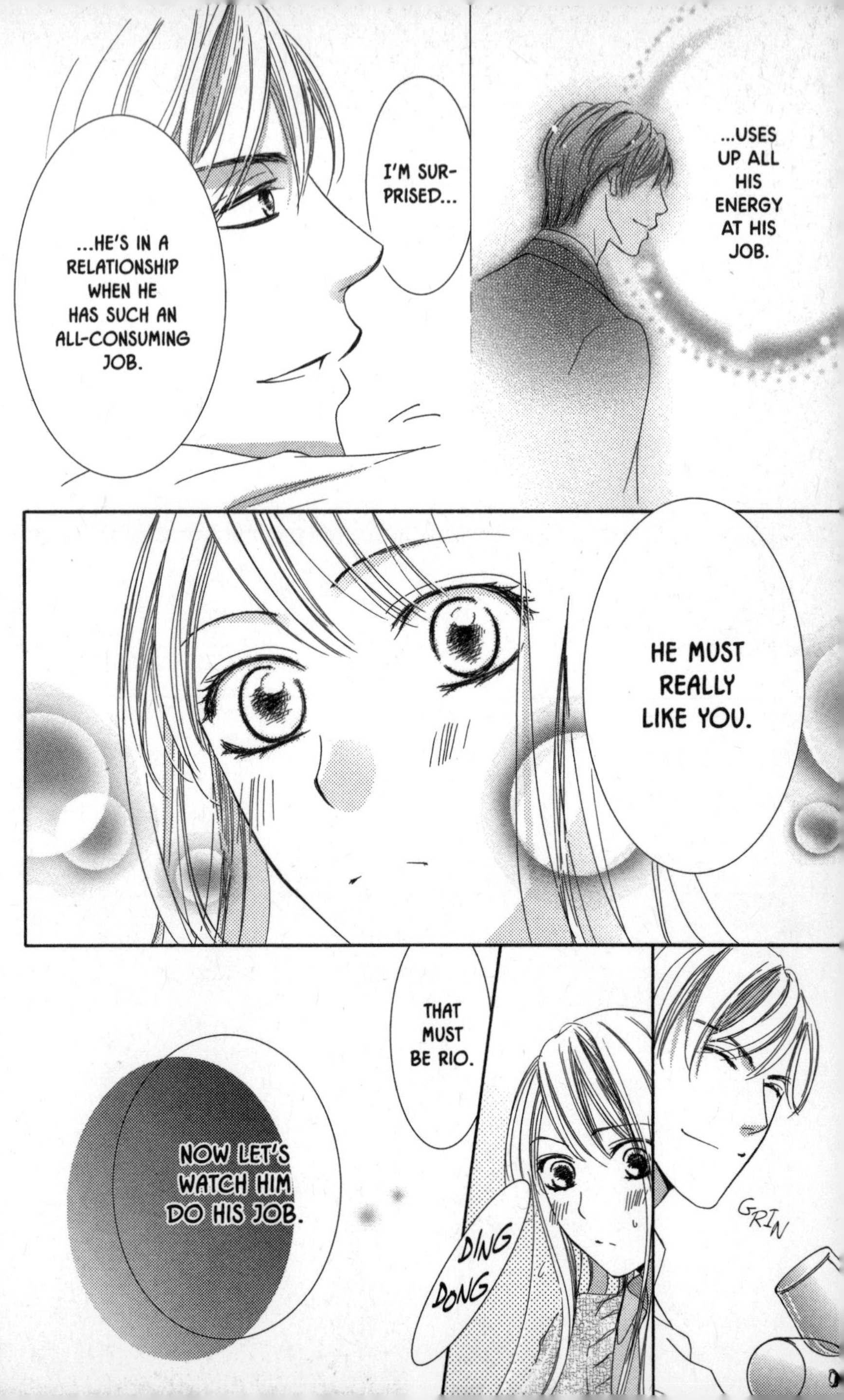
...USES UP ALL HIS ENERGY AT HIS JOB.
I'M SUR-PRISED...
...HE'S IN A RELATIONSHIP WHEN HE HAS SUCH AN ALL-CONSUMING JOB.
HE MUST REALLY LIKE YOU.
GRIN
THAT MUST BE RIO.
DING DONG
NOW LET'S WATCH HIM DO HIS JOB.

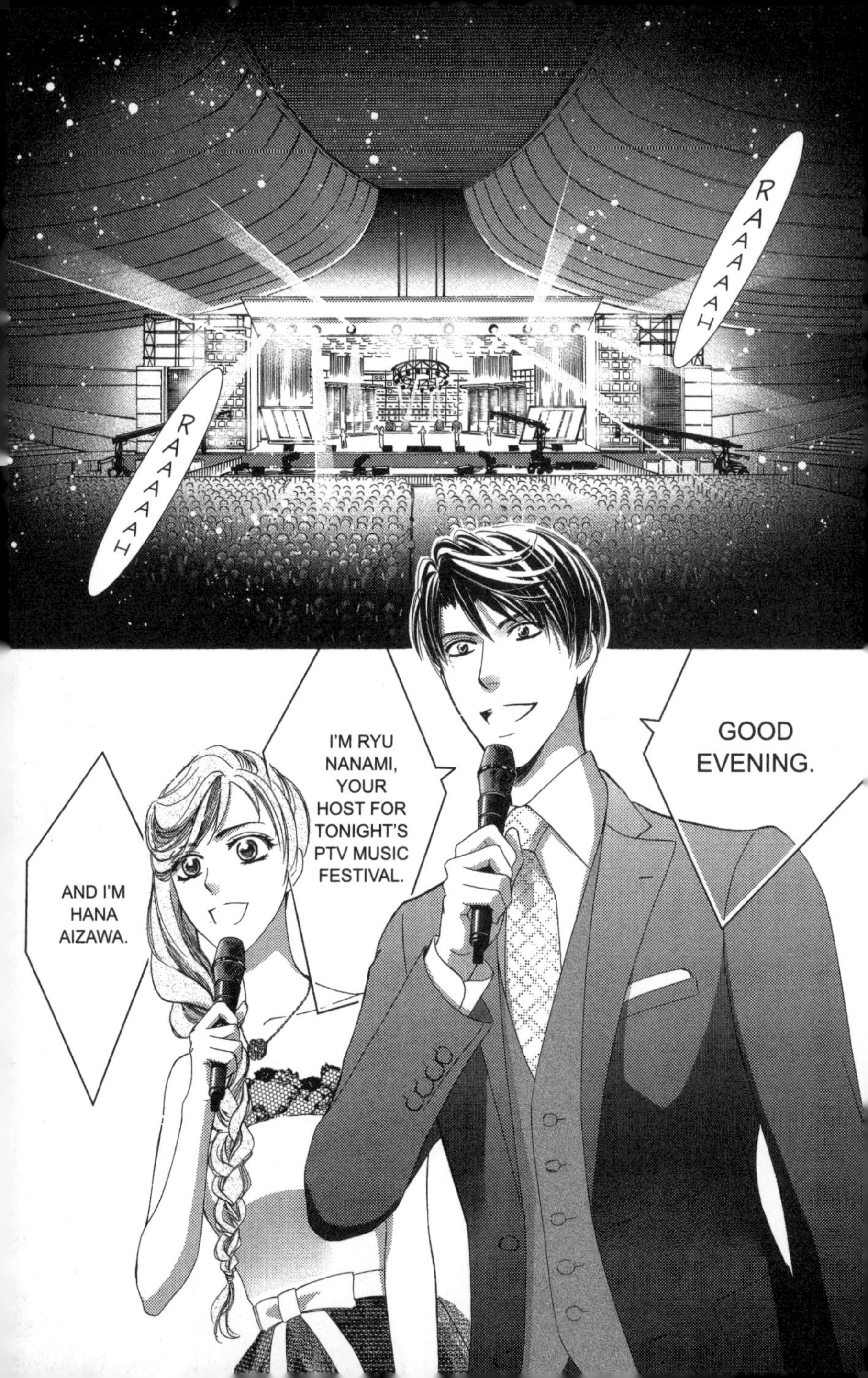
RAAAAAH
RAAAAAH
GOOD EVENING.
I'M RYU NANAMI, YOUR HOST FOR TONIGHT'S PTV MUSIC FESTIVAL.
AND I'M HANA AIZAWA.

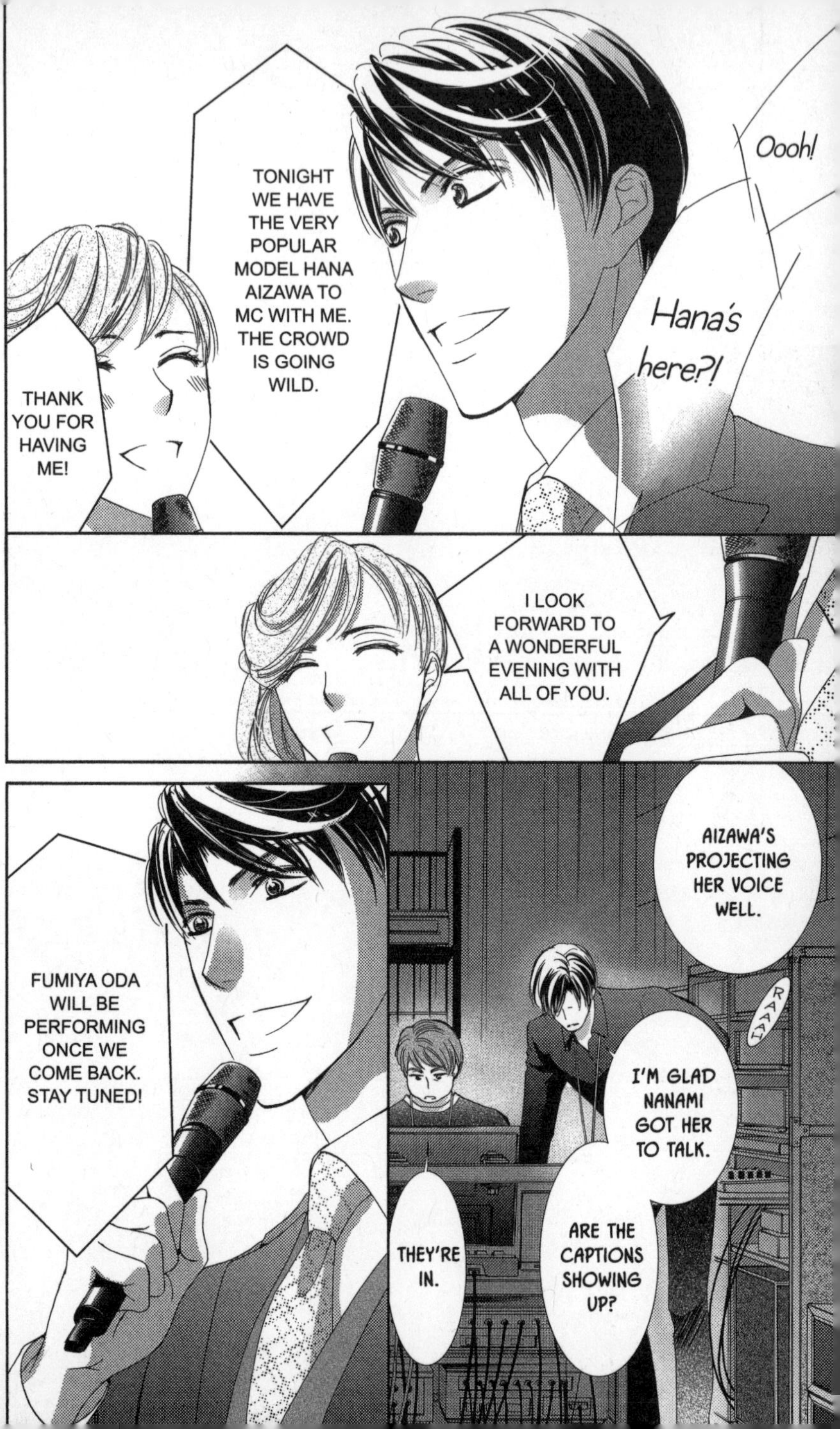
Oooh!
Hana's here?!
TONIGHT WE HAVE THE VERY POPULAR MODEL HANA AIZAWA TO MC WITH ME. THE CROWD IS GOING WILD.
THANK YOU FOR HAVING ME!
I LOOK FORWARD TO A WONDERFUL EVENING WITH ALL OF YOU.
AIZAWA'S PROJECTING HER VOICE WELL.
I'M GLAD NANAMI GOT HER TO TALK.
ARE THE CAPTIONS SHOWING UP?
THEY'RE IN.
FUMIYA ODA WILL BE PERFORMING ONCE WE COME BACK. STAY TUNED!

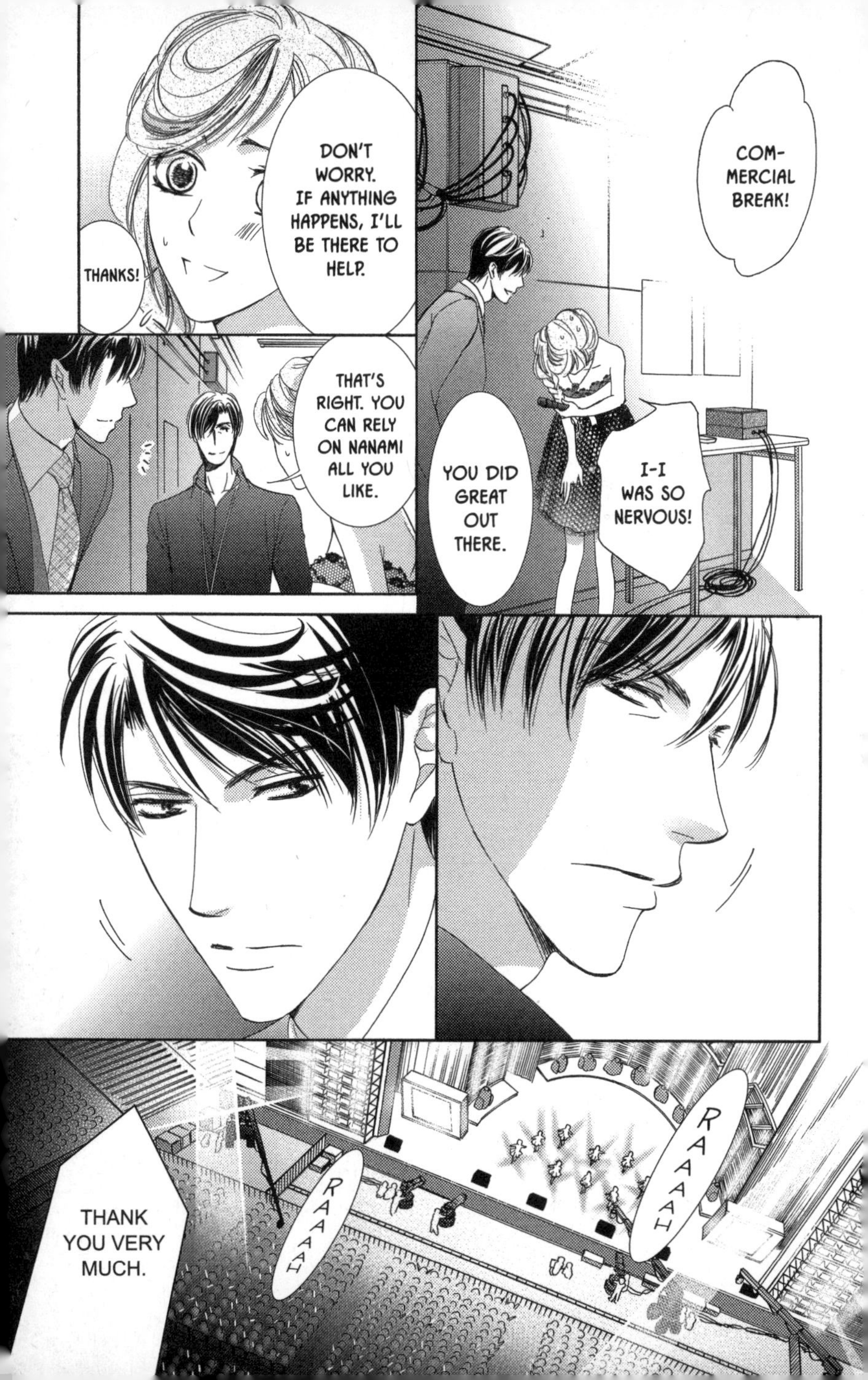
COM-MERCIAL BREAK!
I-I WAS SO NERVOUS!
YOU DID GREAT OUT THERE.
DON'T WORRY. IF ANYTHING HAPPENS, I'LL BE THERE TO HELP.
THANKS!
THAT'S RIGHT. YOU CAN RELY ON NANAMI ALL YOU LIKE.
RAAAAH
RAAAAH
THANK YOU VERY MUCH.

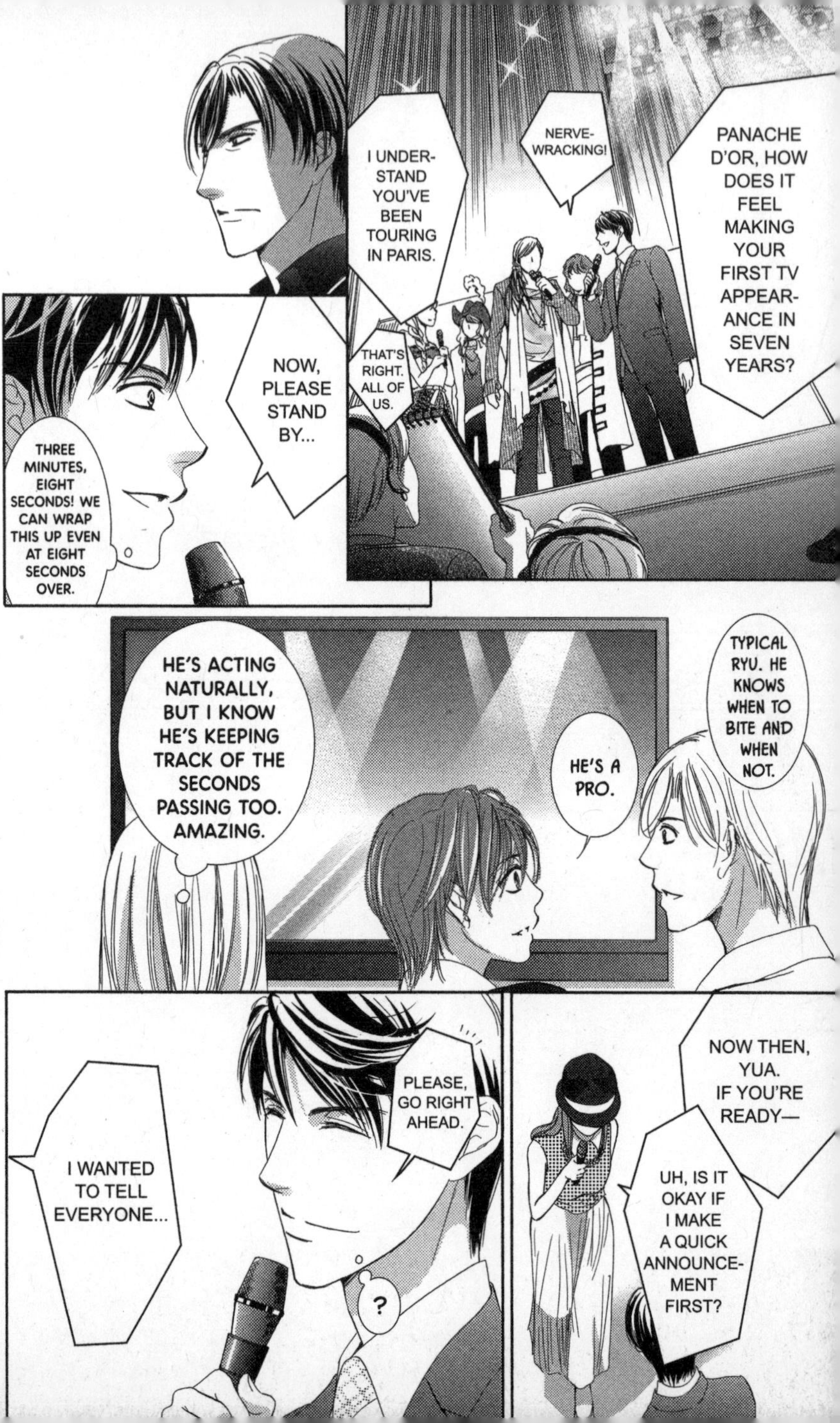
PANACHE D'OR, HOW DOES IT FEEL MAKING YOUR FIRST TV APPEARANCE IN SEVEN YEARS?
NERVE-WRACKING!
I UNDERSTAND YOU'VE BEEN TOURING IN PARIS.
THAT'S RIGHT. ALL OF US.
NOW, PLEASE STAND BY...
THREE MINUTES, EIGHT SECONDS! WE CAN WRAP THIS UP EVEN AT EIGHT SECONDS OVER.
TYPICAL RYU. HE KNOWS WHEN TO BITE AND WHEN NOT.
HE'S A PRO.
HE'S ACTING NATURALLY, BUT I KNOW HE'S KEEPING TRACK OF THE SECONDS PASSING TOO. AMAZING.
NOW THEN, YUA. IF YOU'RE READY—
UH, IS IT OKAY IF I MAKE A QUICK ANNOUNCEMENT FIRST?
PLEASE, GO RIGHT AHEAD.
?
I WANTED TO TELL EVERYONE...

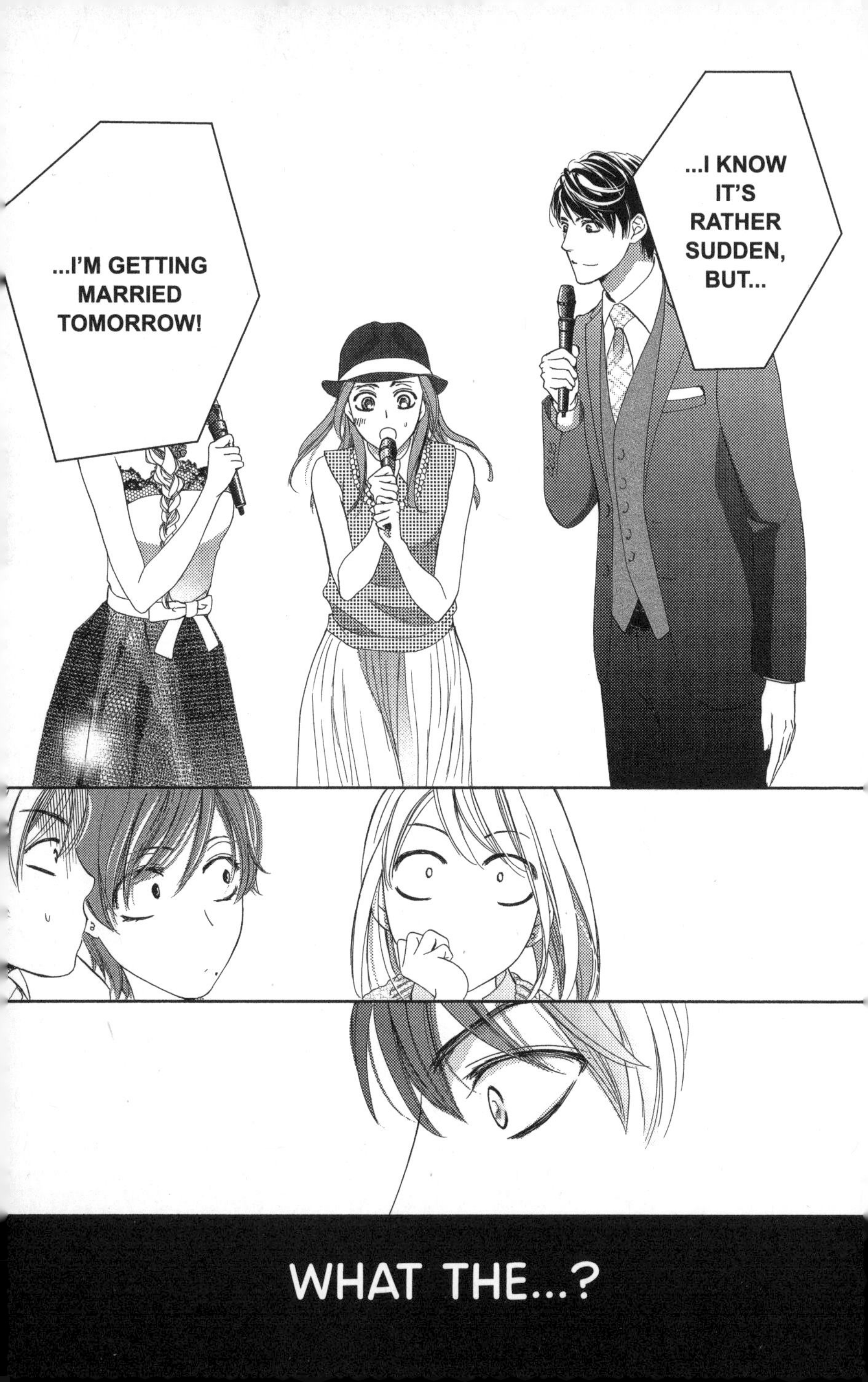
...I KNOW IT'S RATHER SUDDEN, BUT...
...I'M GETTING MARRIED TOMORROW!
WHAT THE...?

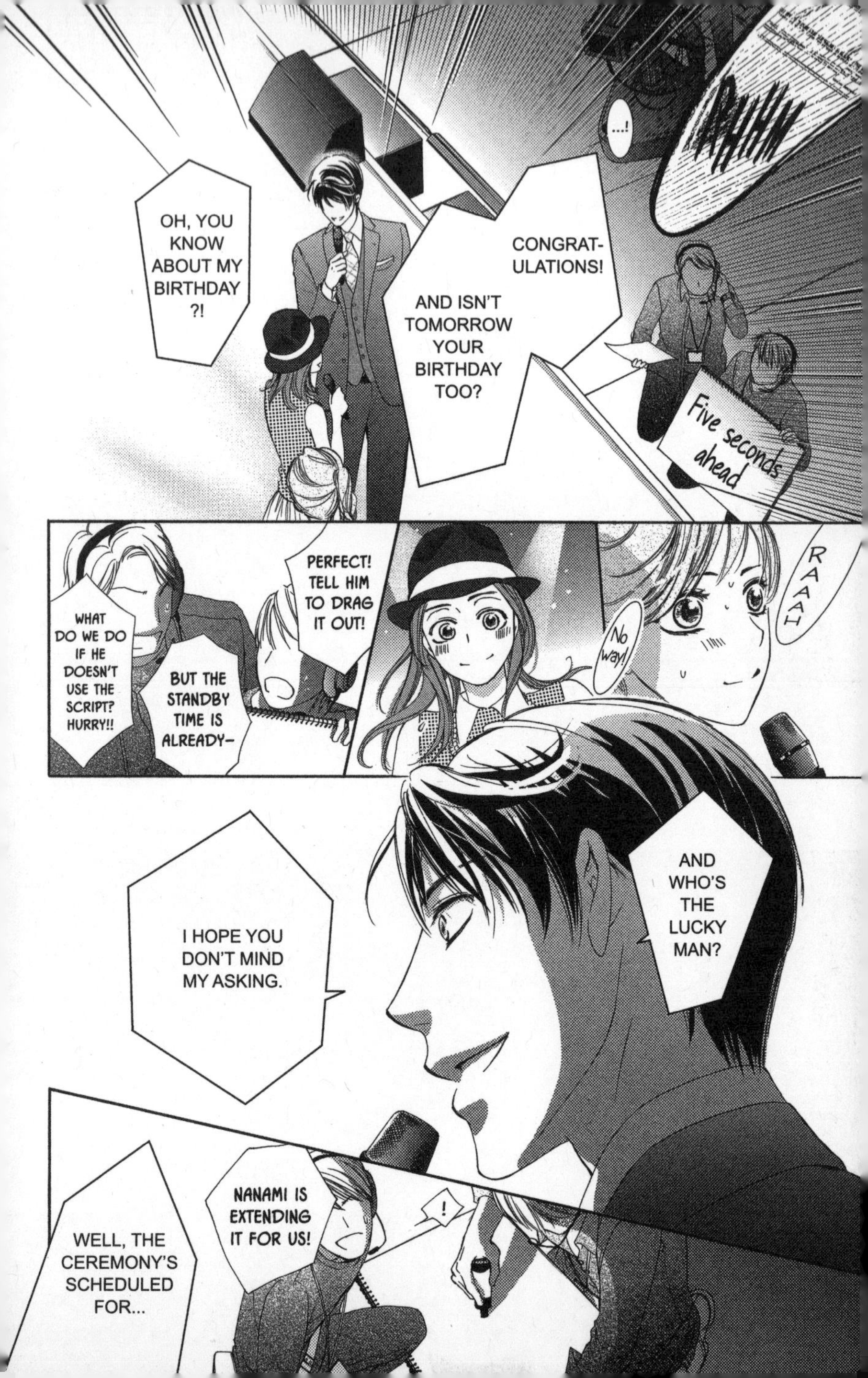
RAHH
...!
CONGRAT-ULATIONS!
Five seconds ahead
AND ISN'T TOMORROW YOUR BIRTHDAY TOO?
OH, YOU KNOW ABOUT MY BIRTHDAY?!
RAAAH
No way!
PERFECT! TELL HIM TO DRAG IT OUT!
WHAT DO WE DO IF HE DOESN'T USE THE SCRIPT? HURRY!!
BUT THE STANDBY TIME IS ALREADY–
AND WHO'S THE LUCKY MAN?
I HOPE YOU DON'T MIND MY ASKING.
!
NANAMI IS EXTENDING IT FOR US!
WELL, THE CEREMONY'S SCHEDULED FOR...

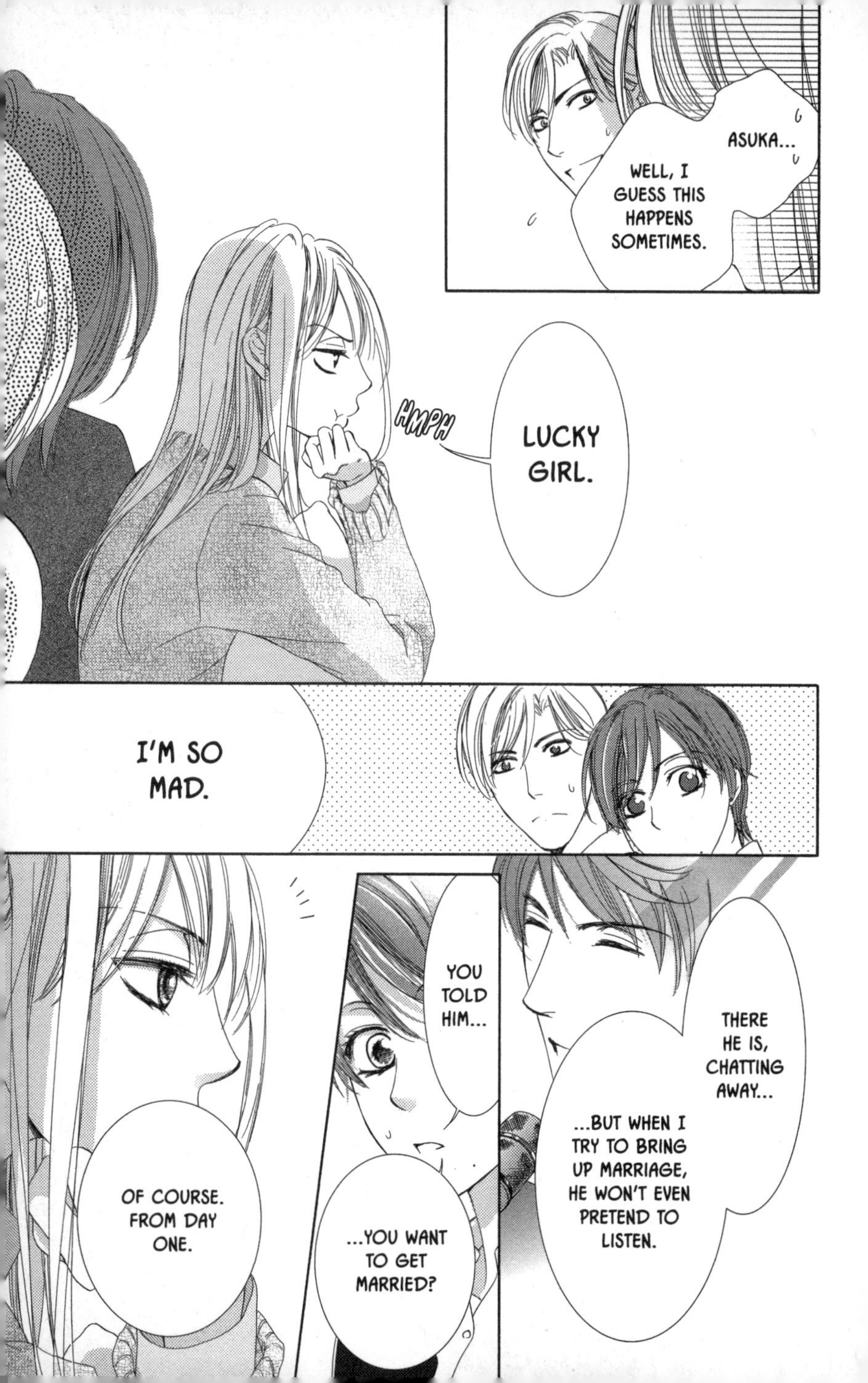
ASUKA...
WELL, I GUESS THIS HAPPENS SOMETIMES.
HMPH
LUCKY GIRL.
I'M SO MAD.
THERE HE IS, CHATTING AWAY...
...BUT WHEN I TRY TO BRING UP MARRIAGE, HE WON'T EVEN PRETEND TO LISTEN.
YOU TOLD HIM...
...YOU WANT TO GET MARRIED?
OF COURSE. FROM DAY ONE.

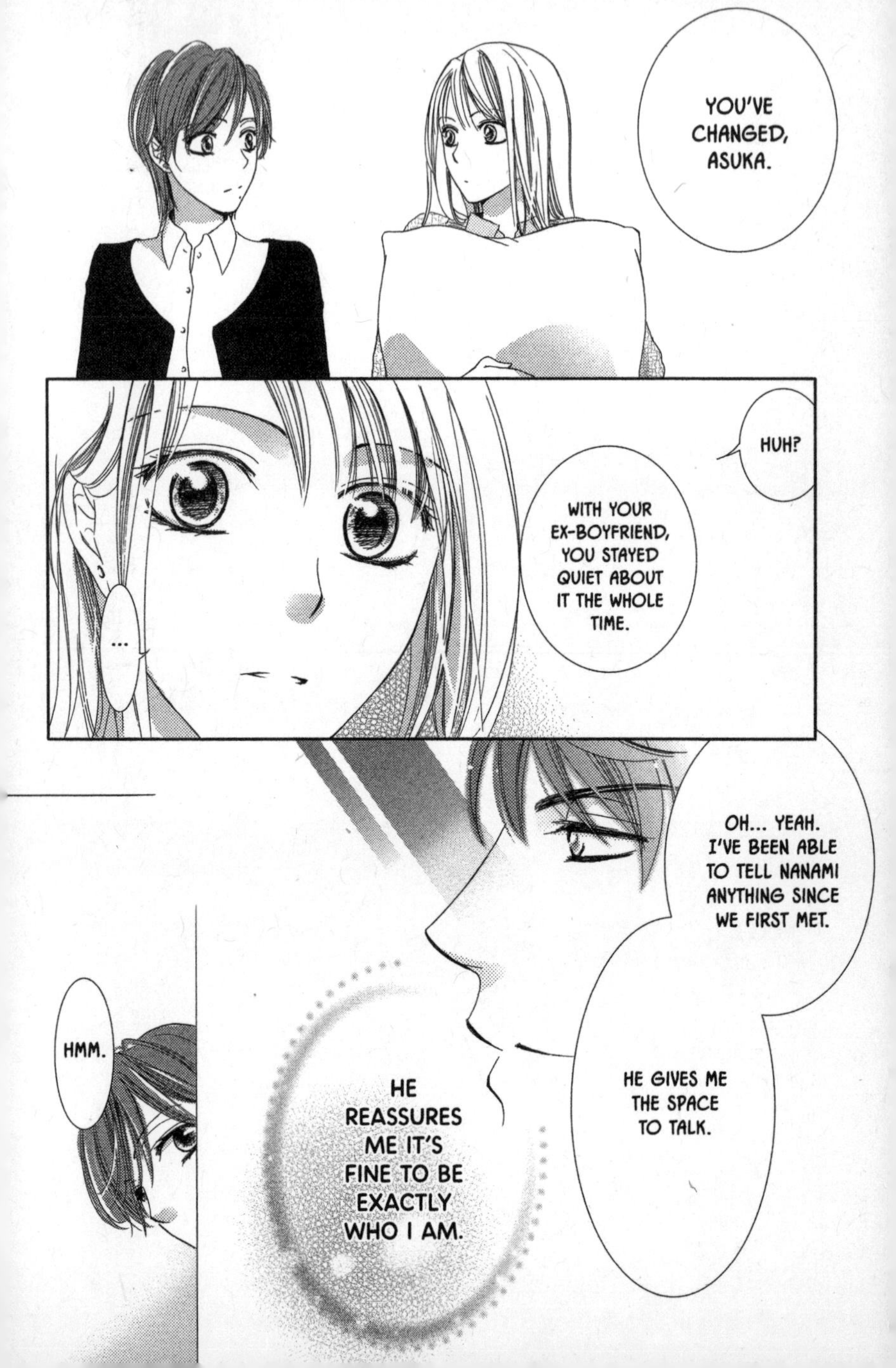
YOU'VE CHANGED, ASUKA.
HUH?
WITH YOUR EX-BOYFRIEND, YOU STAYED QUIET ABOUT IT THE WHOLE TIME.
...
OH... YEAH. I'VE BEEN ABLE TO TELL NANAMI ANYTHING SINCE WE FIRST MET.
HE GIVES ME THE SPACE TO TALK.
HE REASSURES ME IT'S FINE TO BE EXACTLY WHO I AM.
HMM.

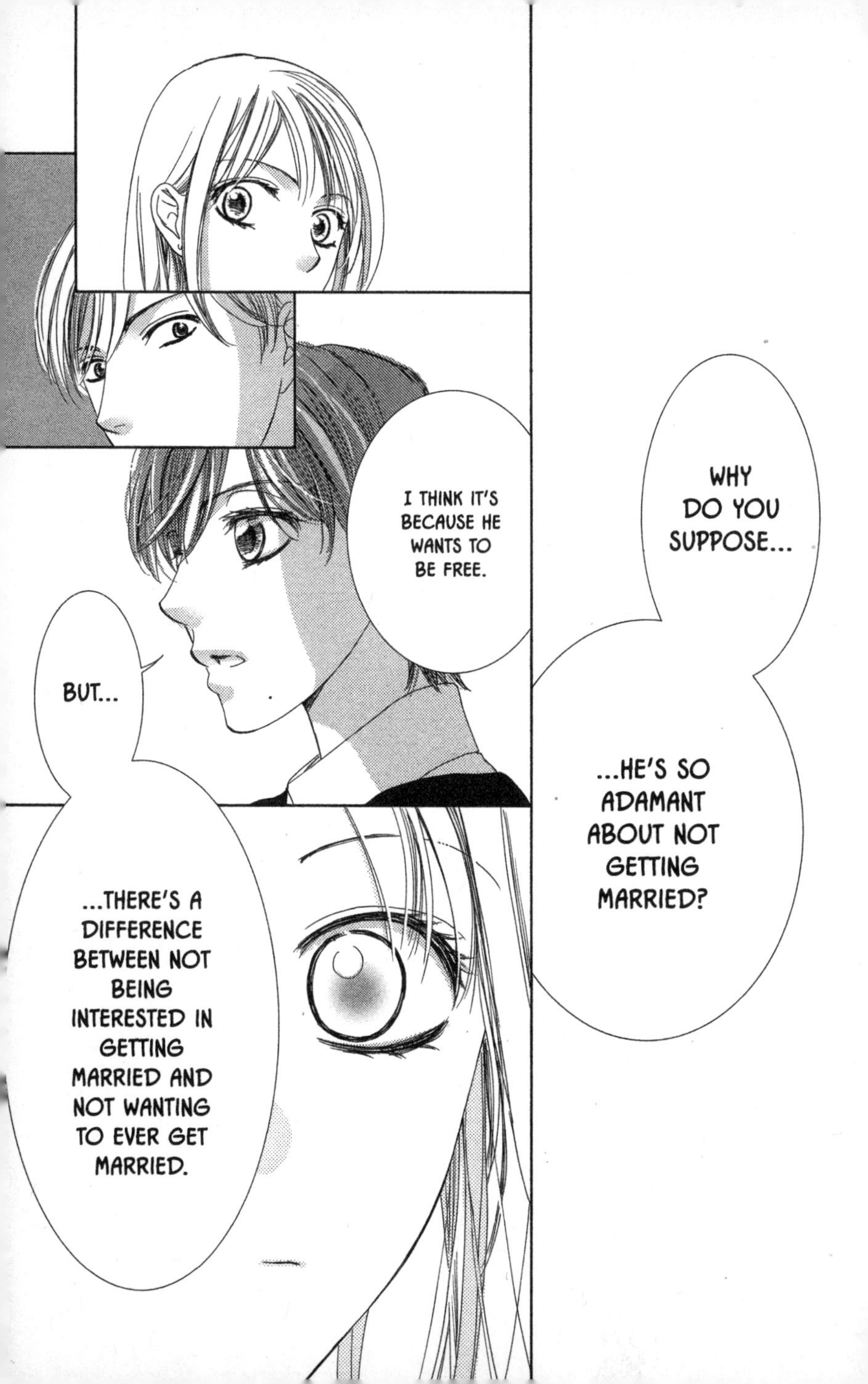
WHY DO YOU SUPPOSE...
...HE'S SO ADAMANT ABOUT NOT GETTING MARRIED?
I THINK IT'S BECAUSE HE WANTS TO BE FREE.
BUT...
...THERE'S A DIFFERENCE BETWEEN NOT BEING INTERESTED IN GETTING MARRIED AND NOT WANTING TO EVER GET MARRIED.

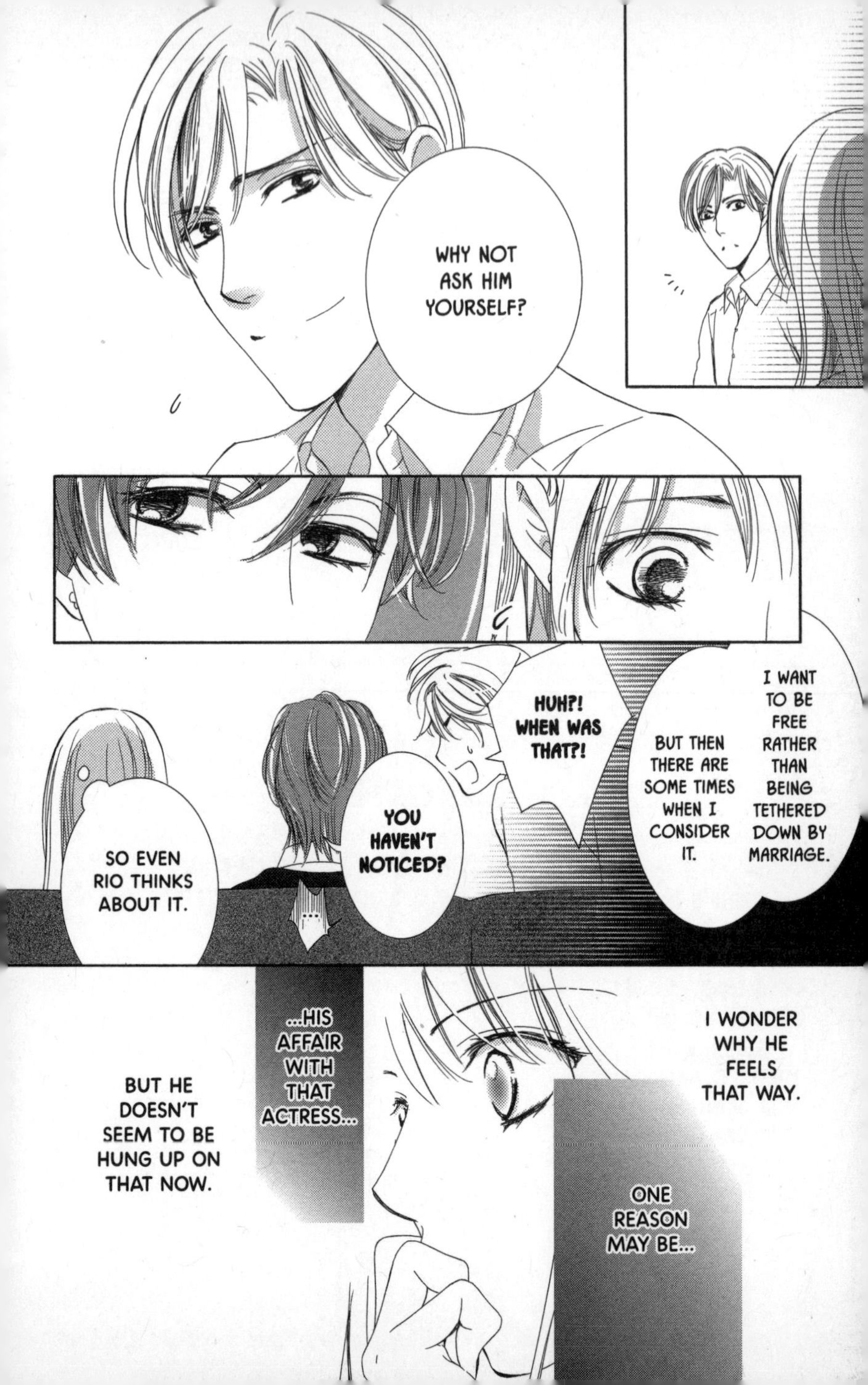
WHY NOT ASK HIM YOURSELF?
I WANT TO BE FREE RATHER THAN BEING TETHERED DOWN BY MARRIAGE.
BUT THEN THERE ARE SOME TIMES WHEN I CONSIDER IT.
HUH?! WHEN WAS THAT?!
YOU HAVEN'T NOTICED?
SO EVEN RIO THINKS ABOUT IT.
I WONDER WHY HE FEELS THAT WAY.
ONE REASON MAY BE...
...HIS AFFAIR WITH THAT ACTRESS...
BUT HE DOESN'T SEEM TO BE HUNG UP ON THAT NOW.

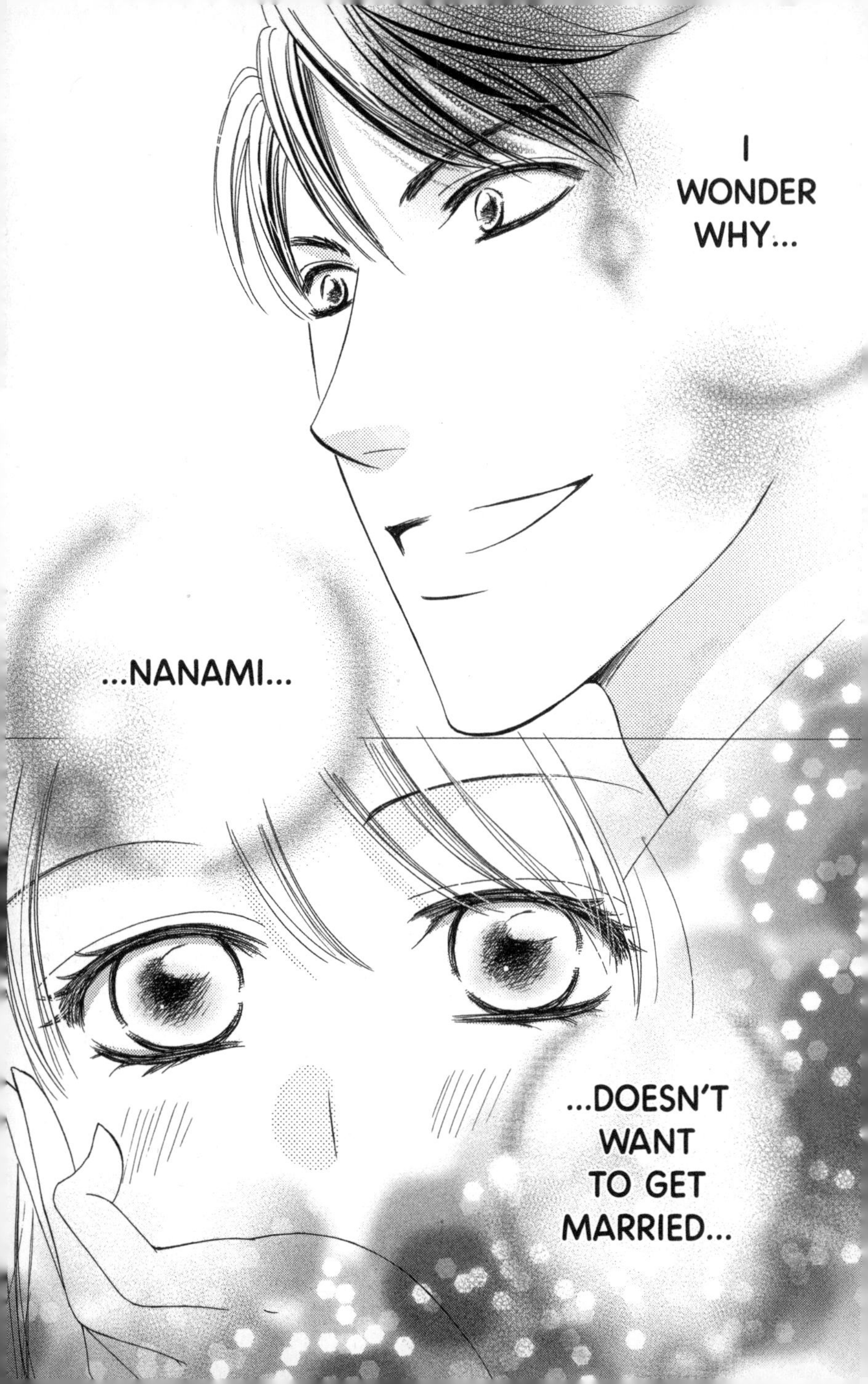
I WONDER WHY...
...NANAMI...
...DOESN'T WANT TO GET MARRIED...

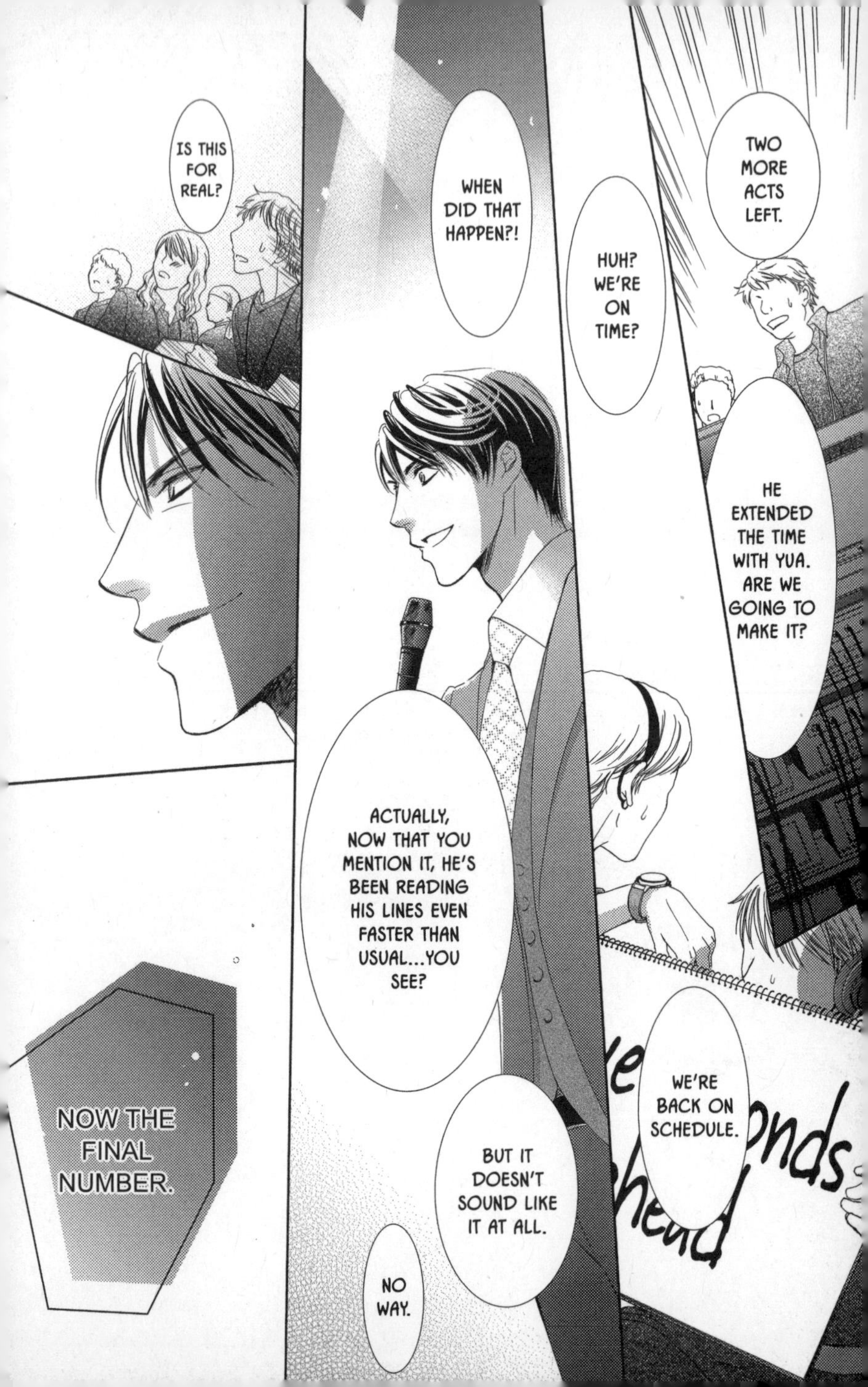
TWO MORE ACTS LEFT.
HE EXTENDED THE TIME WITH YUA. ARE WE GOING TO MAKE IT?
WE'RE BACK ON SCHEDULE.
HUH? WE'RE ON TIME?
WHEN DID THAT HAPPEN?!
ACTUALLY, NOW THAT YOU MENTION IT, HE'S BEEN READING HIS LINES EVEN FASTER THAN USUAL...YOU SEE?
BUT IT DOESN'T SOUND LIKE IT AT ALL.
NO WAY.
IS THIS FOR REAL?
NOW THE FINAL NUMBER.

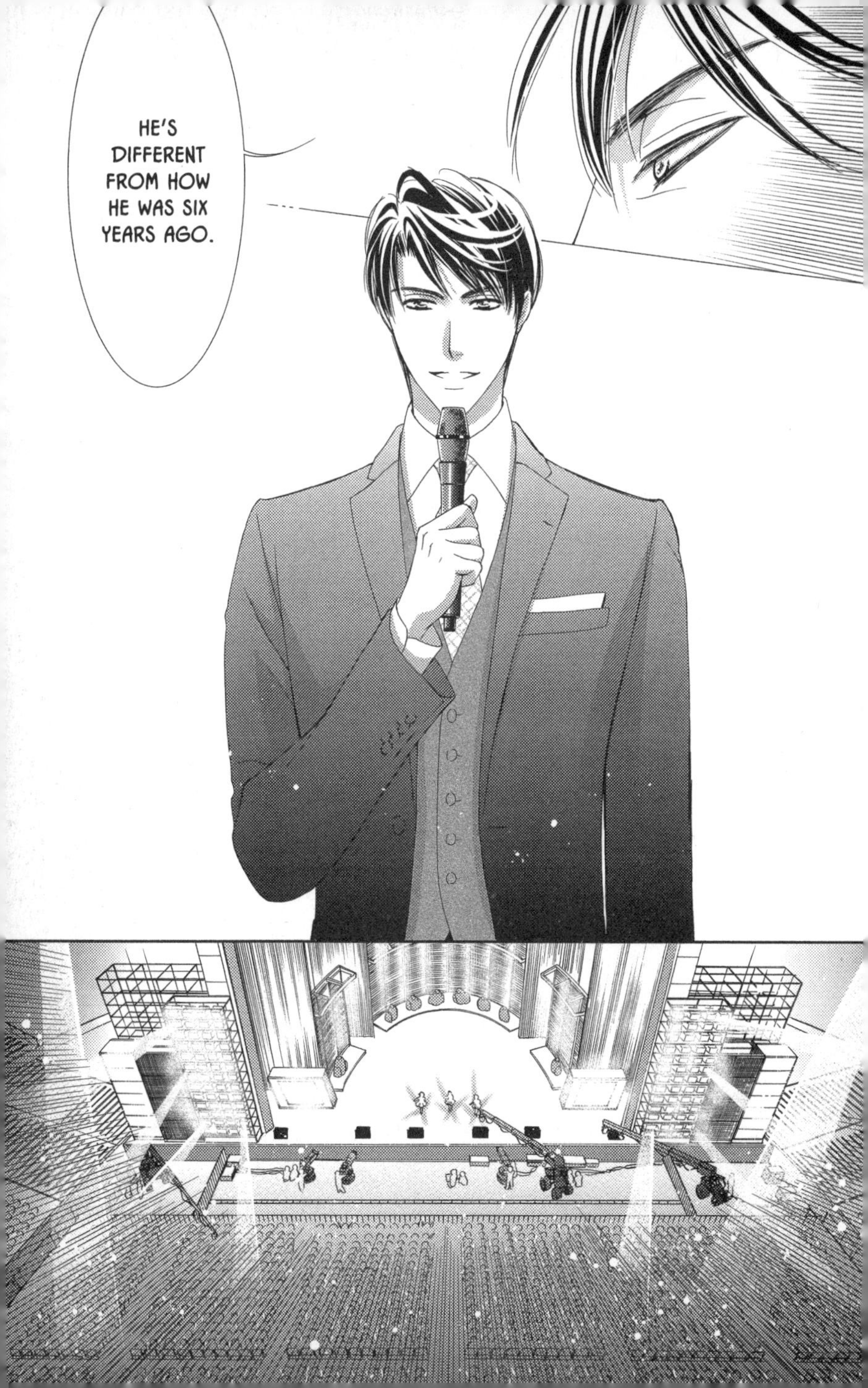
HE'S DIFFERENT FROM HOW HE WAS SIX YEARS AGO.

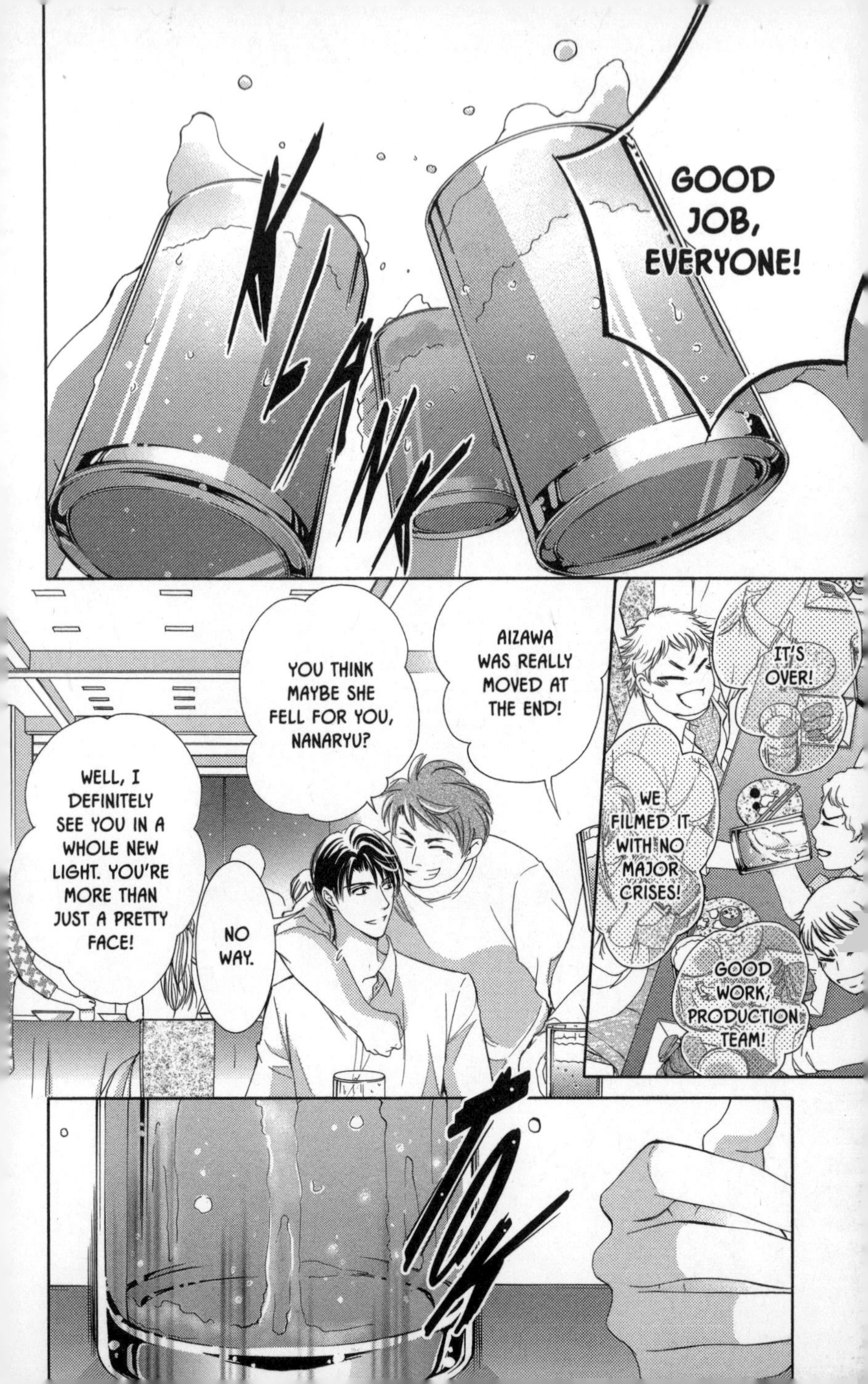
GOOD JOB, EVERYONE!
KLANK
IT'S OVER!
WE FILMED IT WITH NO MAJOR CRISES!
GOOD WORK, PRODUCTION TEAM!
AIZAWA WAS REALLY MOVED AT THE END!
YOU THINK MAYBE SHE FELL FOR YOU, NANARYU?
WELL, I DEFINITELY SEE YOU IN A WHOLE NEW LIGHT. YOU'RE MORE THAN JUST A PRETTY FACE!
NO WAY.
TOK

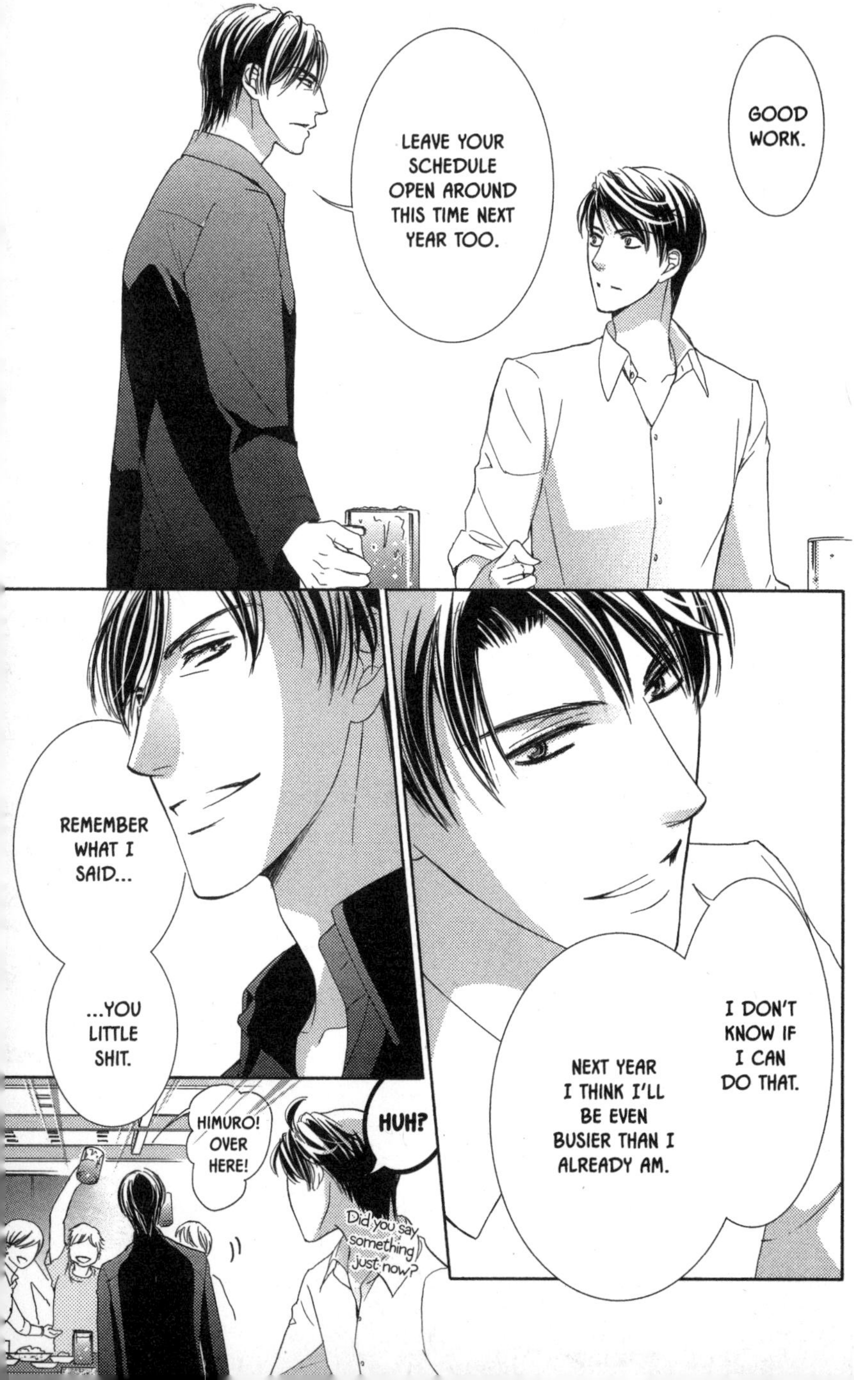
GOOD WORK.
LEAVE YOUR SCHEDULE OPEN AROUND THIS TIME NEXT YEAR TOO.
I DON'T KNOW IF I CAN DO THAT.
NEXT YEAR I THINK I'LL BE EVEN BUSIER THAN I ALREADY AM.
REMEMBER WHAT I SAID...
...YOU LITTLE SHIT.
HUH?
Did you say something just now?
HIMURO! OVER HERE!

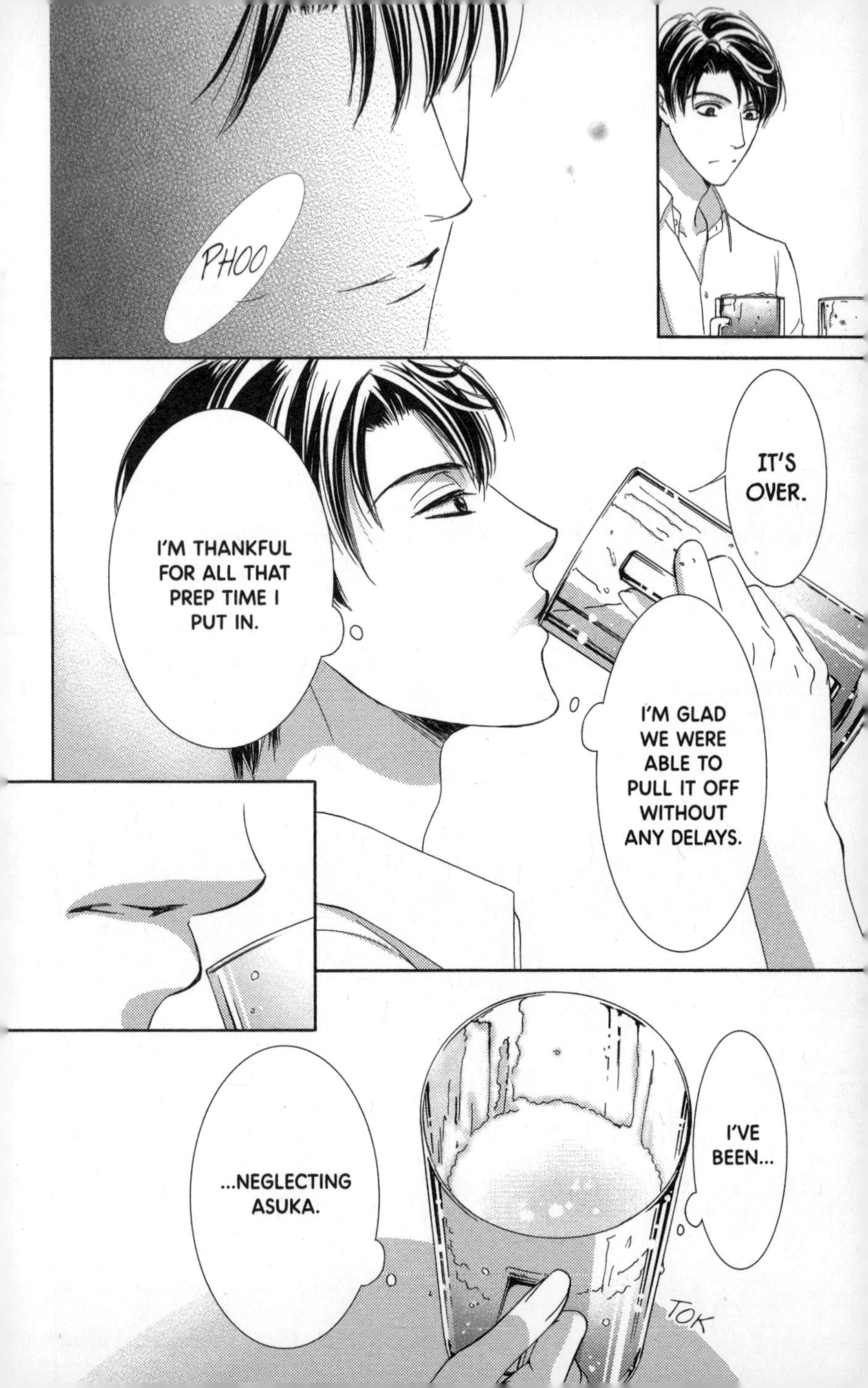
PHOO
IT'S OVER.
I'M GLAD WE WERE ABLE TO PULL IT OFF WITHOUT ANY DELAYS.
I'M THANKFUL FOR ALL THAT PREP TIME I PUT IN.
I'VE BEEN...
...NEGLECTING ASUKA.
TOK

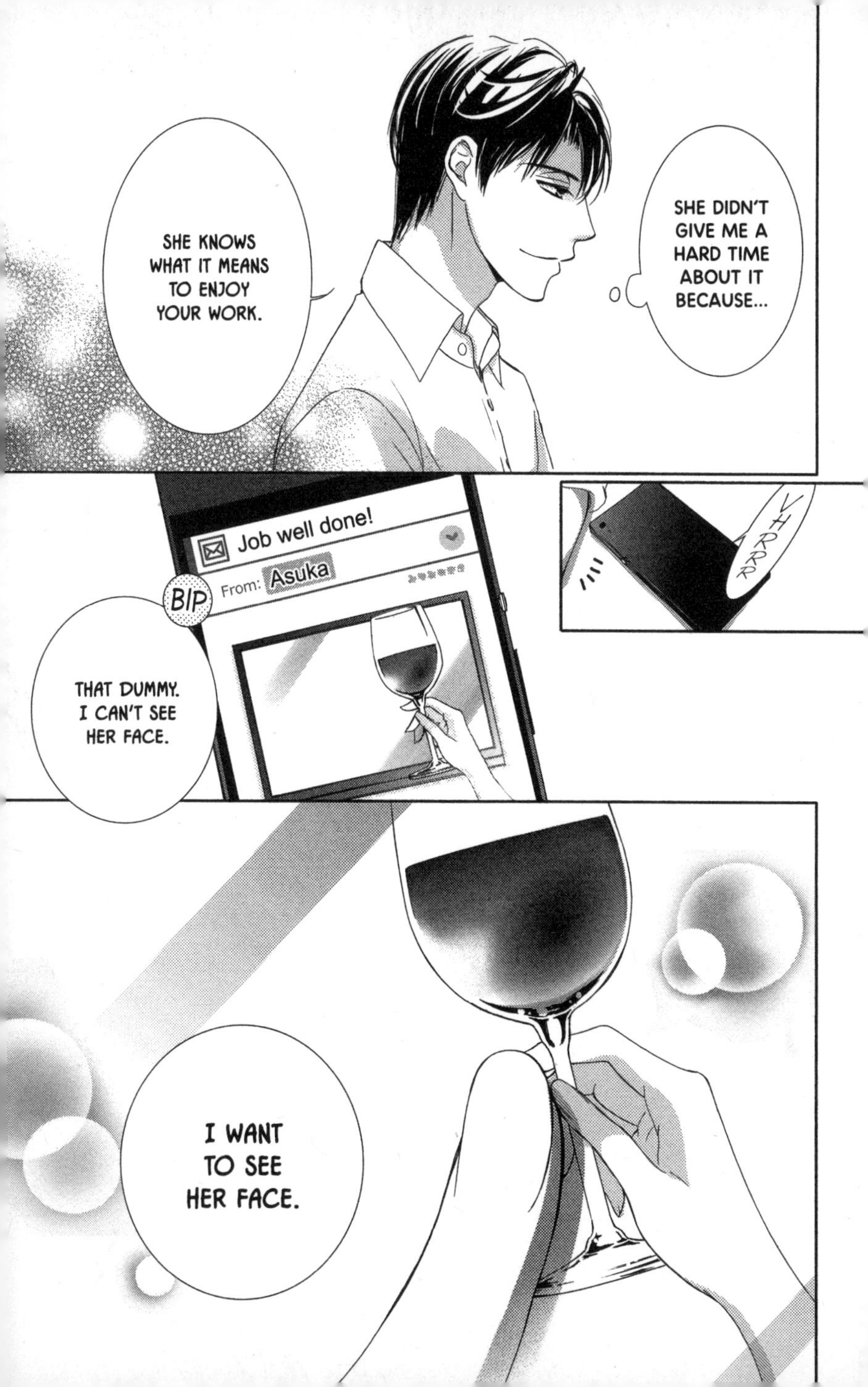
SHE DIDN'T GIVE ME A HARD TIME ABOUT IT BECAUSE...
SHE KNOWS WHAT IT MEANS TO ENJOY YOUR WORK.
VHRRR
Job well done!
From: Asuka
BIP
THAT DUMMY. I CAN'T SEE HER FACE.
I WANT TO SEE HER FACE.

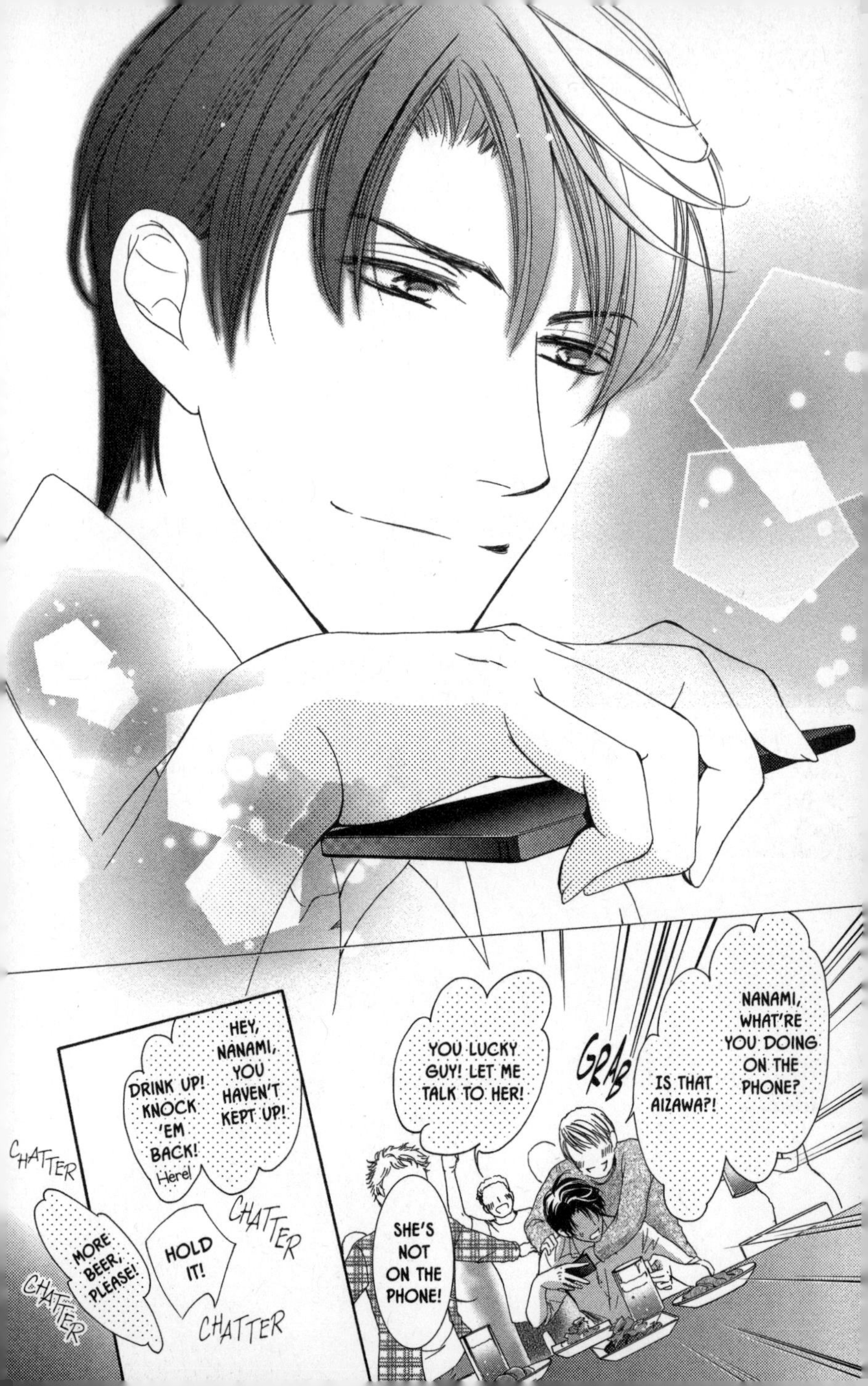
NANAMI, WHAT'RE YOU DOING ON THE PHONE?
IS THAT AIZAWA?!
GRAB
YOU LUCKY GUY! LET ME TALK TO HER!
SHE'S NOT ON THE PHONE!
HEY, NANAMI, YOU HAVEN'T KEPT UP!
DRINK UP! KNOCK 'EM BACK!
Here!
CHATTER
HOLD IT!
CHATTER
CHATTER
MORE BEER, PLEASE!
CHATTER

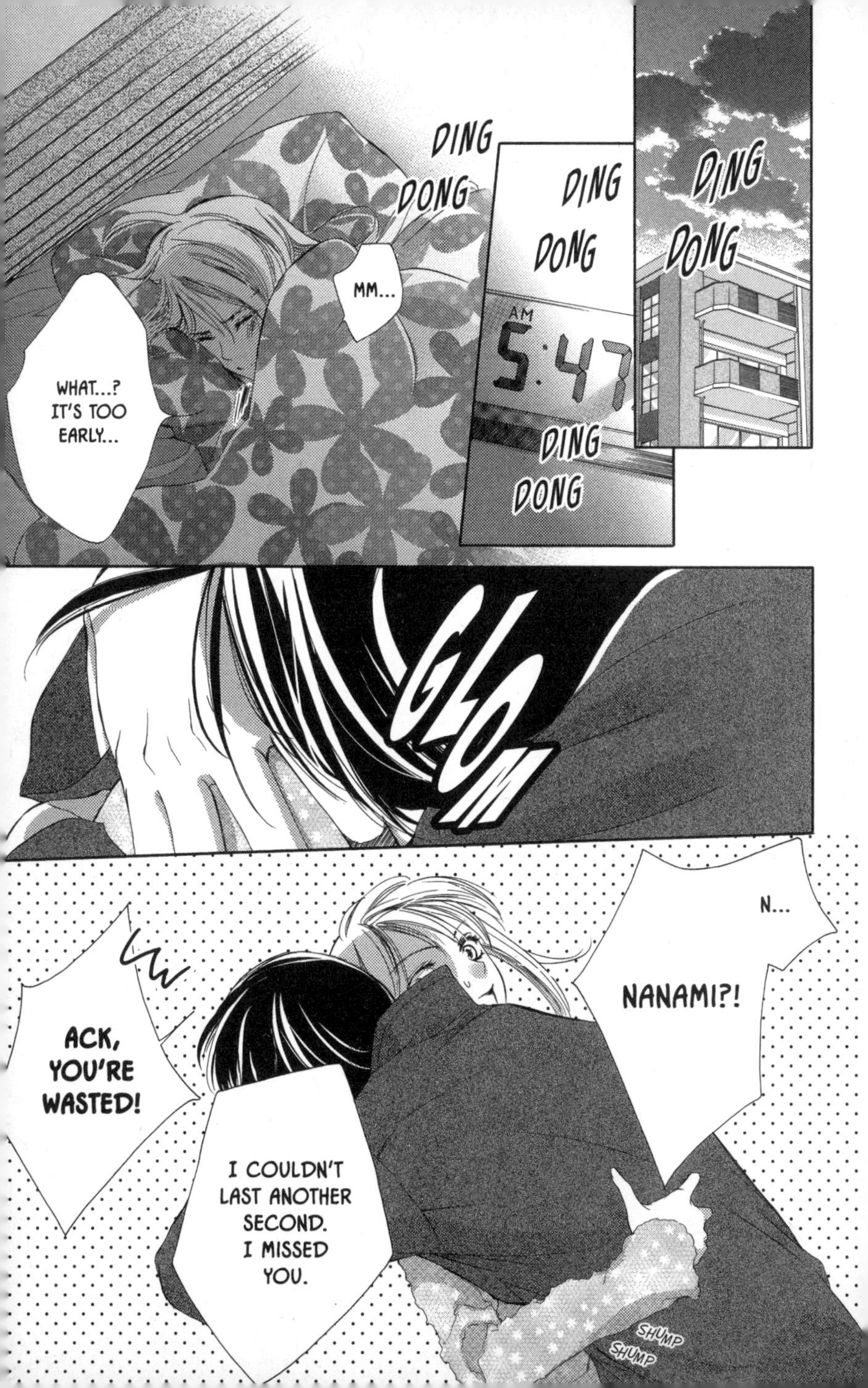
DING DONG
DING DONG
AM 5:47
DING DONG
DING DONG
MM...
WHAT...? IT'S TOO EARLY...
GLOM
N...
NANAMI?!
ACK, YOU'RE WASTED!
I COULDN'T LAST ANOTHER SECOND. I MISSED YOU.
SHUMP SHUMP

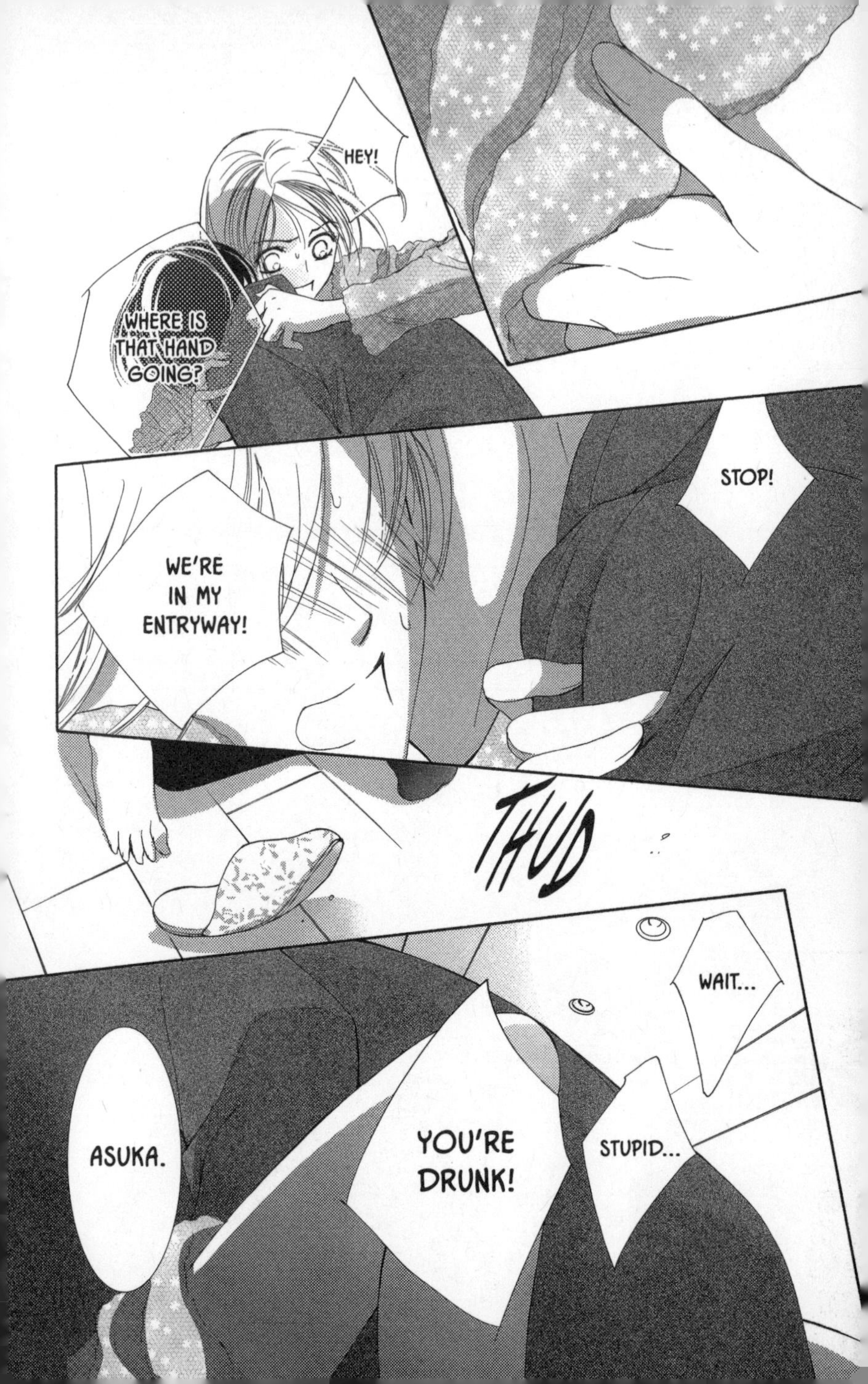
HEY!
WHERE IS THAT HAND GOING?
STOP!
WE'RE IN MY ENTRYWAY!
THUD
WAIT...
STUPID...
YOU'RE DRUNK!
ASUKA.

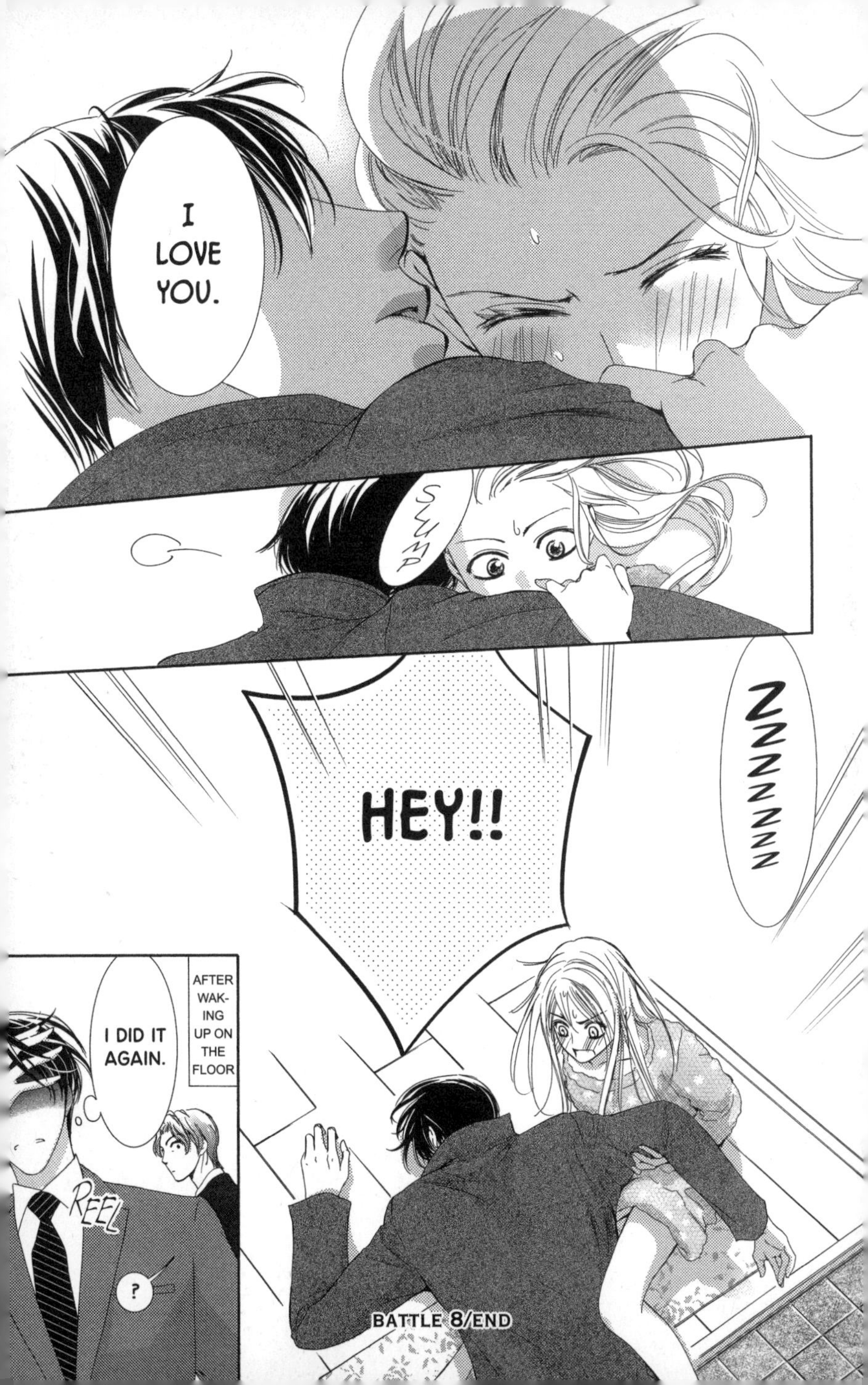
I LOVE YOU.
SLUMP
ZZZZZZZ
HEY!!
AFTER WAKING UP ON THE FLOOR
I DID IT AGAIN.
REEL
?
BATTLE 8/END

I love you,
but...

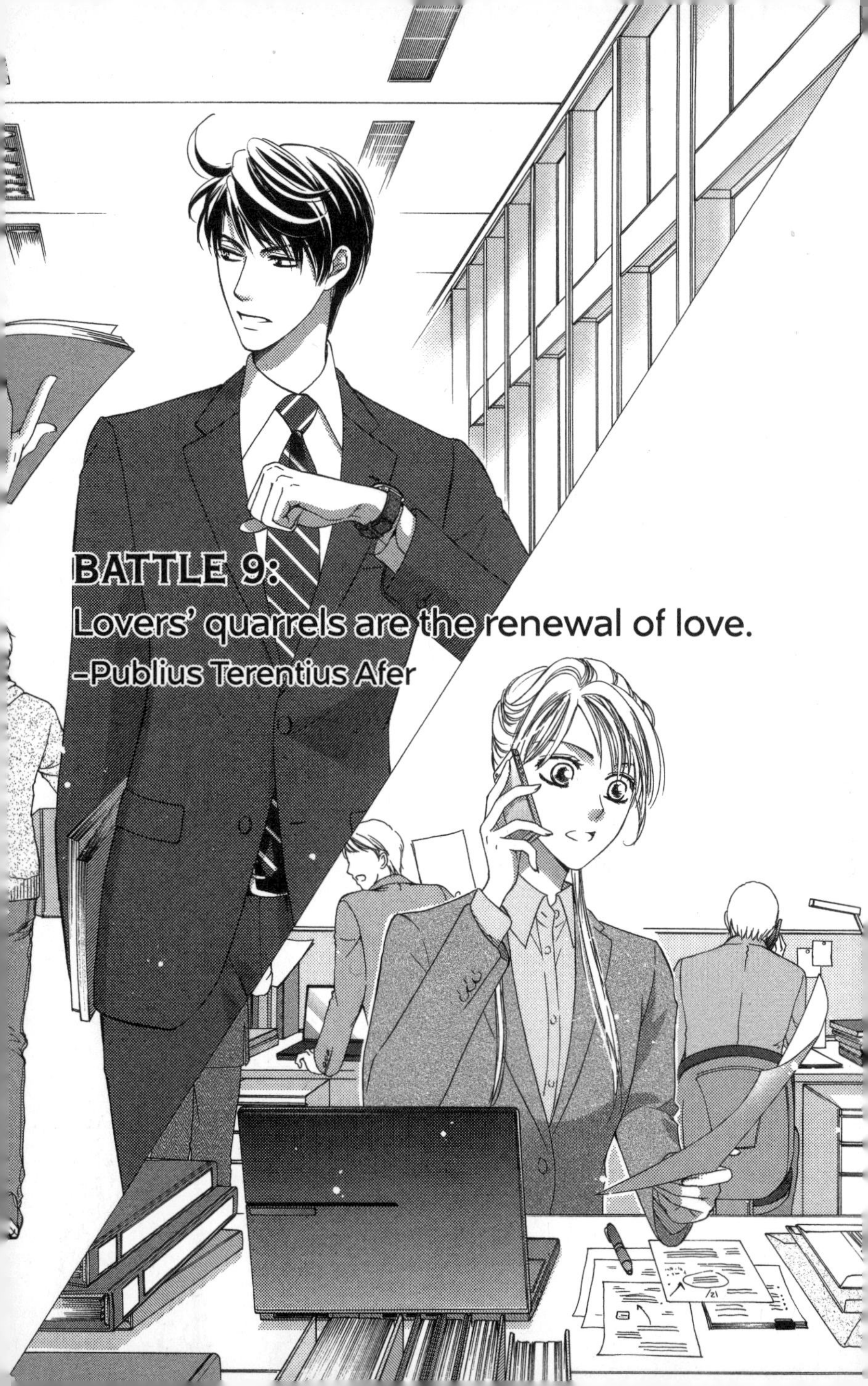

BATTLE 9:

Lovers' quarrels are the renewal of love.

–Publius Terentius Afer

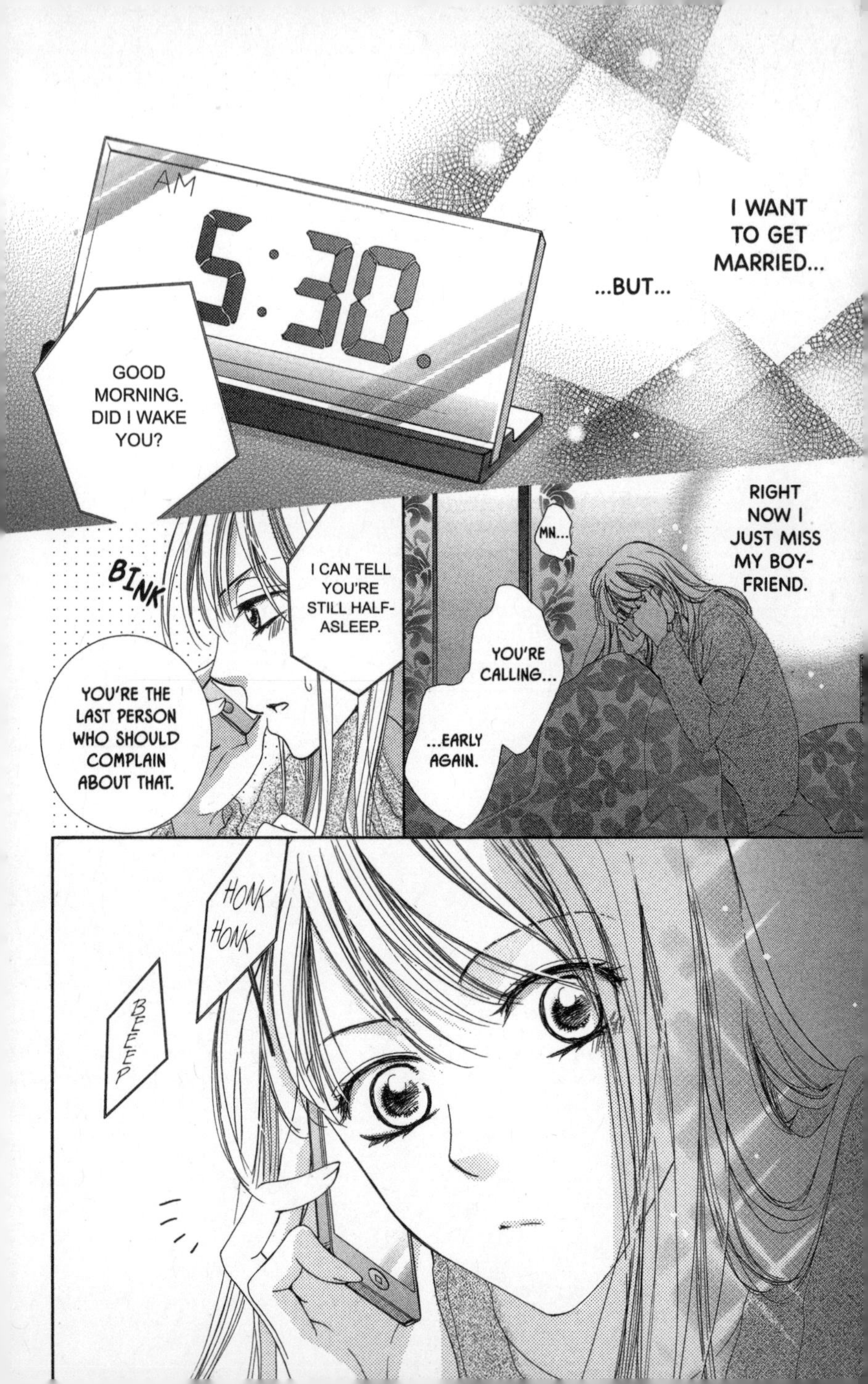
I WANT TO GET MARRIED...
...BUT...
AM
5:30
GOOD MORNING. DID I WAKE YOU?
RIGHT NOW I JUST MISS MY BOY-FRIEND.
MN...
YOU'RE CALLING...
...EARLY AGAIN.
I CAN TELL YOU'RE STILL HALF-ASLEEP.
BINK
YOU'RE THE LAST PERSON WHO SHOULD COMPLAIN ABOUT THAT.
HONK HONK
BEEEP

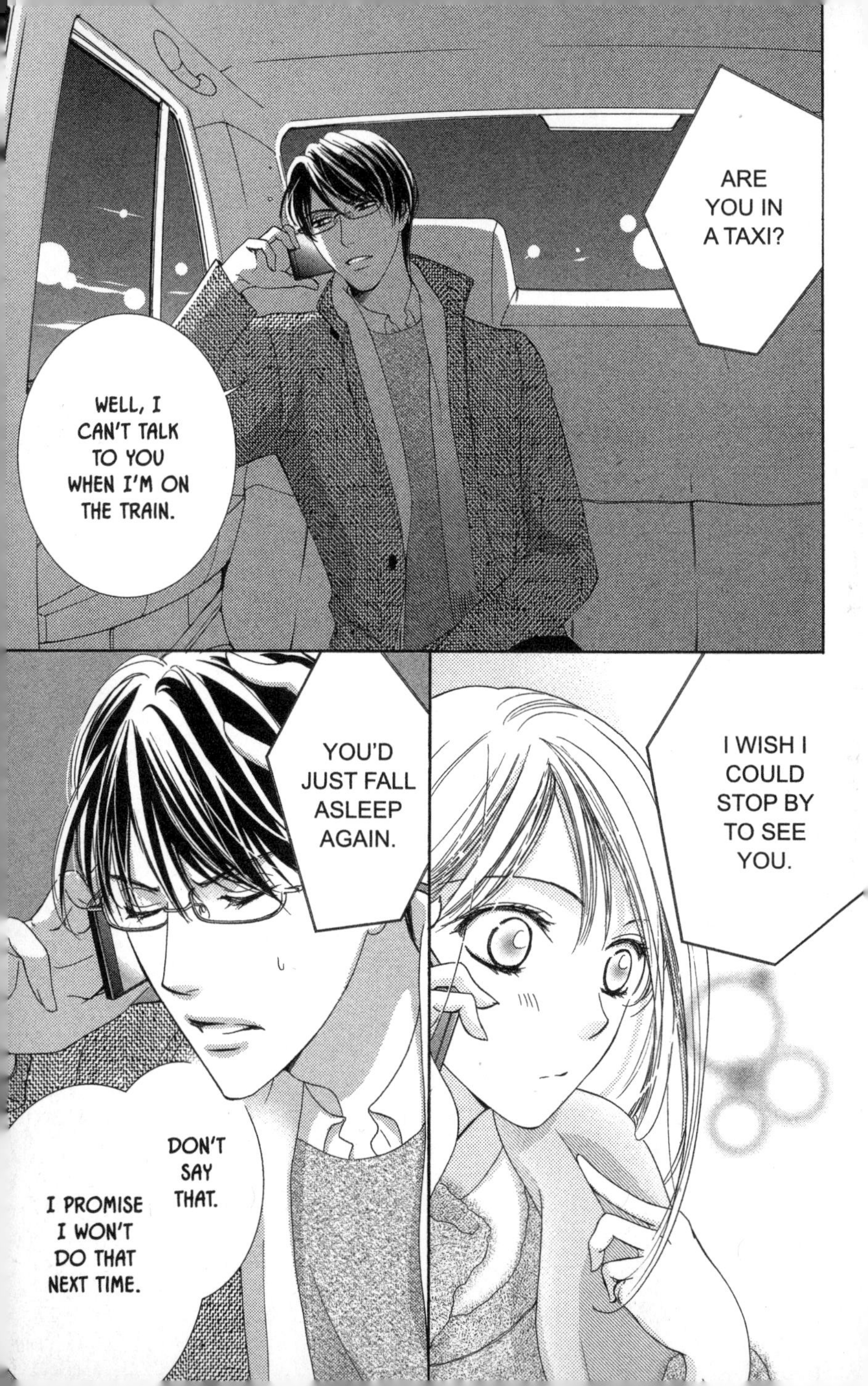
ARE YOU IN A TAXI?
WELL, I CAN'T TALK TO YOU WHEN I'M ON THE TRAIN.
I WISH I COULD STOP BY TO SEE YOU.
YOU'D JUST FALL ASLEEP AGAIN.
DON'T SAY THAT.
I PROMISE I WON'T DO THAT NEXT TIME.

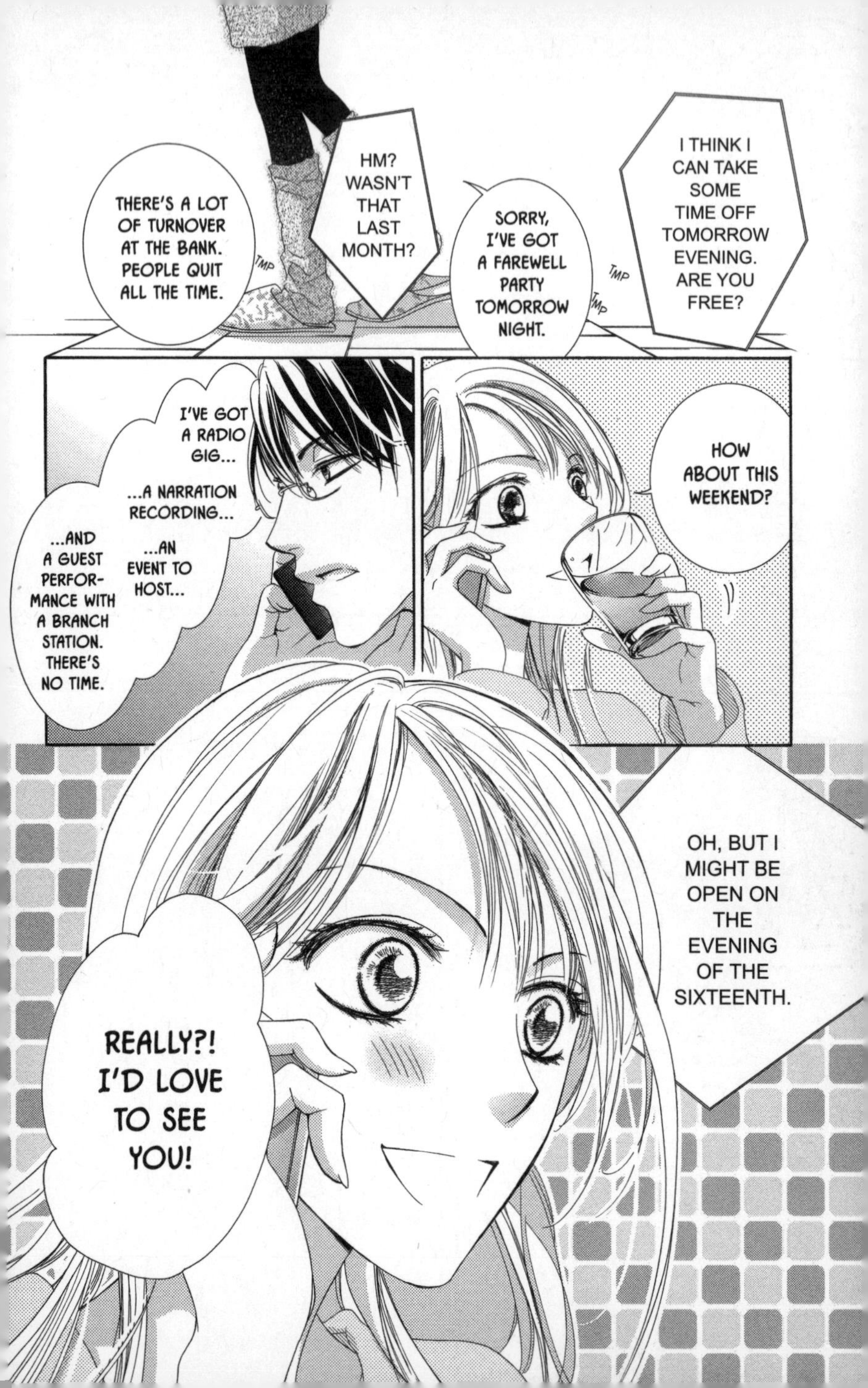

I THINK I CAN TAKE SOME TIME OFF TOMORROW EVENING. ARE YOU FREE?
TMP
TMP
SORRY, I'VE GOT A FAREWELL PARTY TOMORROW NIGHT.
HM? WASN'T THAT LAST MONTH?
TMP
THERE'S A LOT OF TURNOVER AT THE BANK. PEOPLE QUIT ALL THE TIME.
HOW ABOUT THIS WEEKEND?
I'VE GOT A RADIO GIG...
...A NARRATION RECORDING...
...AN EVENT TO HOST...
...AND A GUEST PERFORMANCE WITH A BRANCH STATION. THERE'S NO TIME.
OH, BUT I MIGHT BE OPEN ON THE EVENING OF THE SIXTEENTH.
REALLY?! I'D LOVE TO SEE YOU!

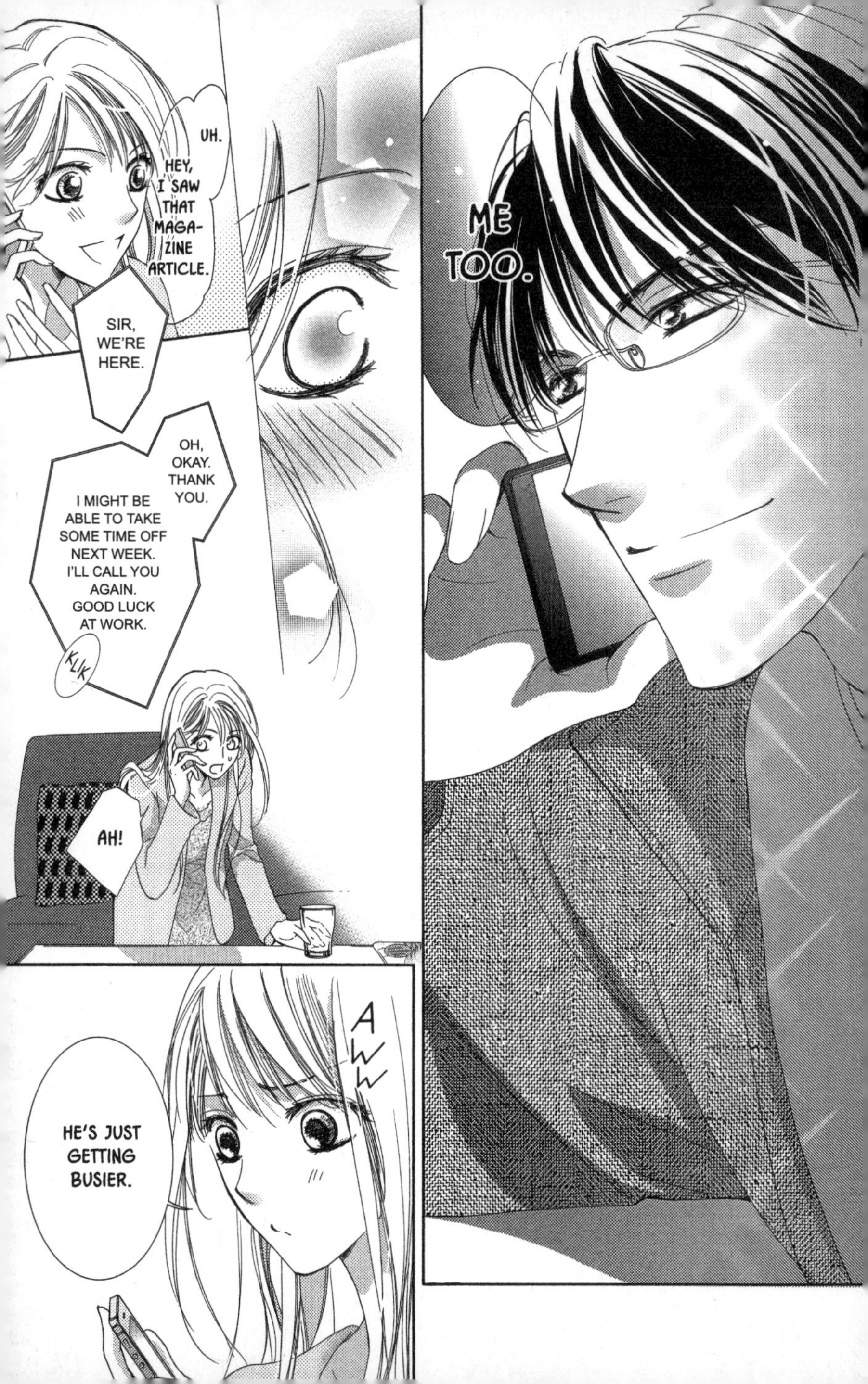
ME TOO.
UH.
HEY, I SAW THAT MAGAZINE ARTICLE.
SIR, WE'RE HERE.
OH, OKAY. THANK YOU.
I MIGHT BE ABLE TO TAKE SOME TIME OFF NEXT WEEK. I'LL CALL YOU AGAIN. GOOD LUCK AT WORK.
KLIK
AH!
AWW
HE'S JUST GETTING BUSIER.

1st	Ryu Nanami	PTV
2nd	Taiga Miyano	UNX

THIS IS PROBABLY PARTLY THE CAUSE.

FLIP

FLIP

Special Interview

PTV Newscaster

Ryu Nanami

...some, so how has it been readjusting?

...en six months home, you've returned it's good to be back.

...s a TV mate question: Are you seeing anyone right now? No, I'm only focusing on my work at the moment, so don't even have time to go out and meet girls. (laughs)

Any plans for marriage? None at the moment. I'm ...appy to be busy with work ...t now, I don't have time to ...er marriage.

...hat must ...espe-...for me

Year-End Newsca... Ranking First Place "Nanaryu"

Oh, hardly. My main inspiratio... have to be Mikami. I feel li... ropes. I'm always learn... job. I get butterflies... do a live broadc... veteran colle... All in all... day.

Any plans for marriage?

None at the moment. I'm happy to be busy with work right now. I don't have time to consider marriage.

HE IS REALLY BUSY, BUT...

...THAT SOUNDS LIKE A LAME EXCUSE TO ME.

NOT THAT HE WOULD CONFESS HOW HE FEELS ABOUT MARRIAGE IN AN INTERVIEW.

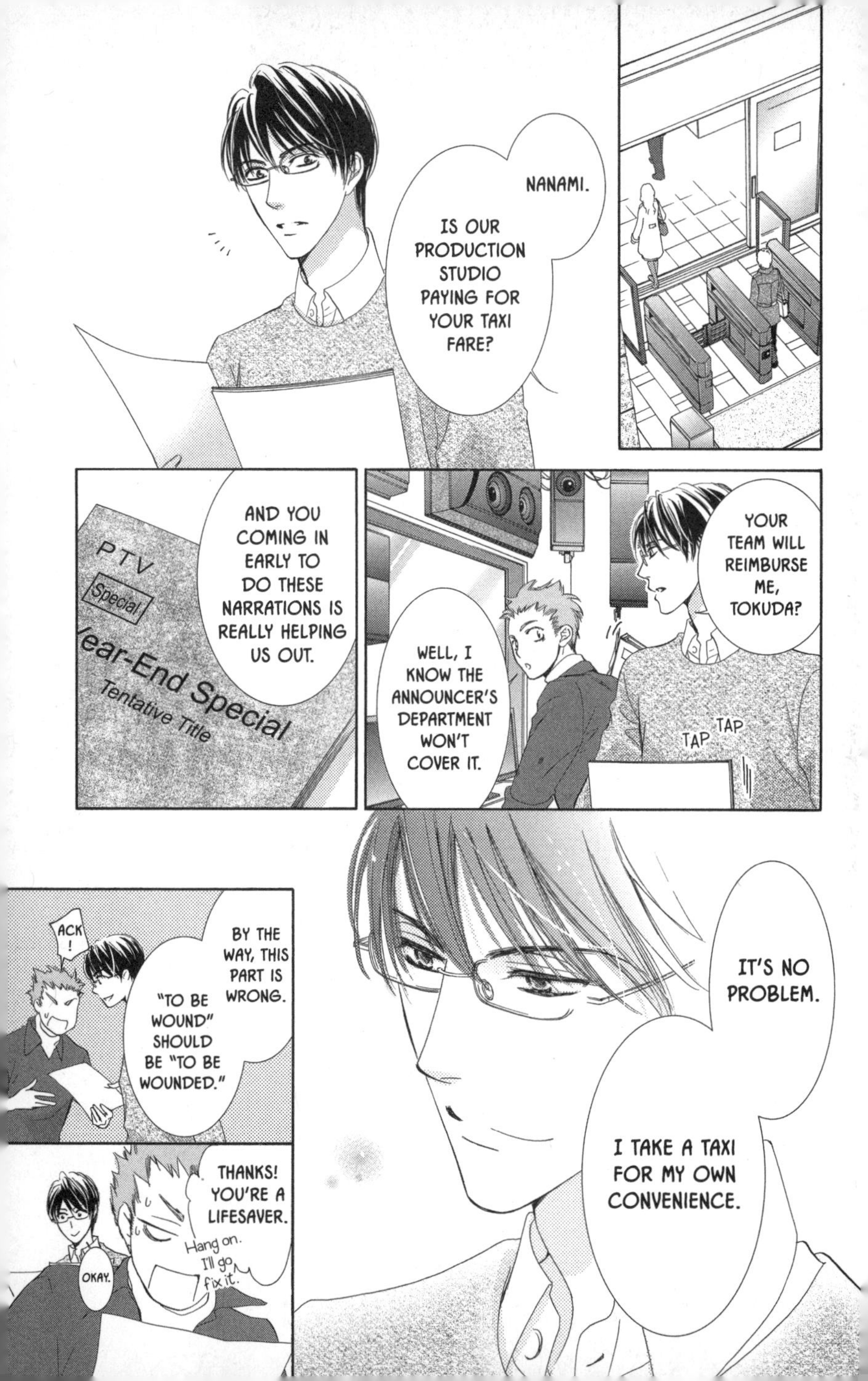
NANAMI.
IS OUR PRODUCTION STUDIO PAYING FOR YOUR TAXI FARE?
YOUR TEAM WILL REIMBURSE ME, TOKUDA?
WELL, I KNOW THE ANNOUNCER'S DEPARTMENT WON'T COVER IT.
TAP TAP
AND YOU COMING IN EARLY TO DO THESE NARRATIONS IS REALLY HELPING US OUT.
PTV
Special
Year-End Special
Tentative Title
IT'S NO PROBLEM.
I TAKE A TAXI FOR MY OWN CONVENIENCE.
BY THE WAY, THIS PART IS WRONG.
"TO BE WOUND" SHOULD BE "TO BE WOUNDED."
ACK!
THANKS! YOU'RE A LIFESAVER.
Hang on. I'll go fix it.
OKAY.

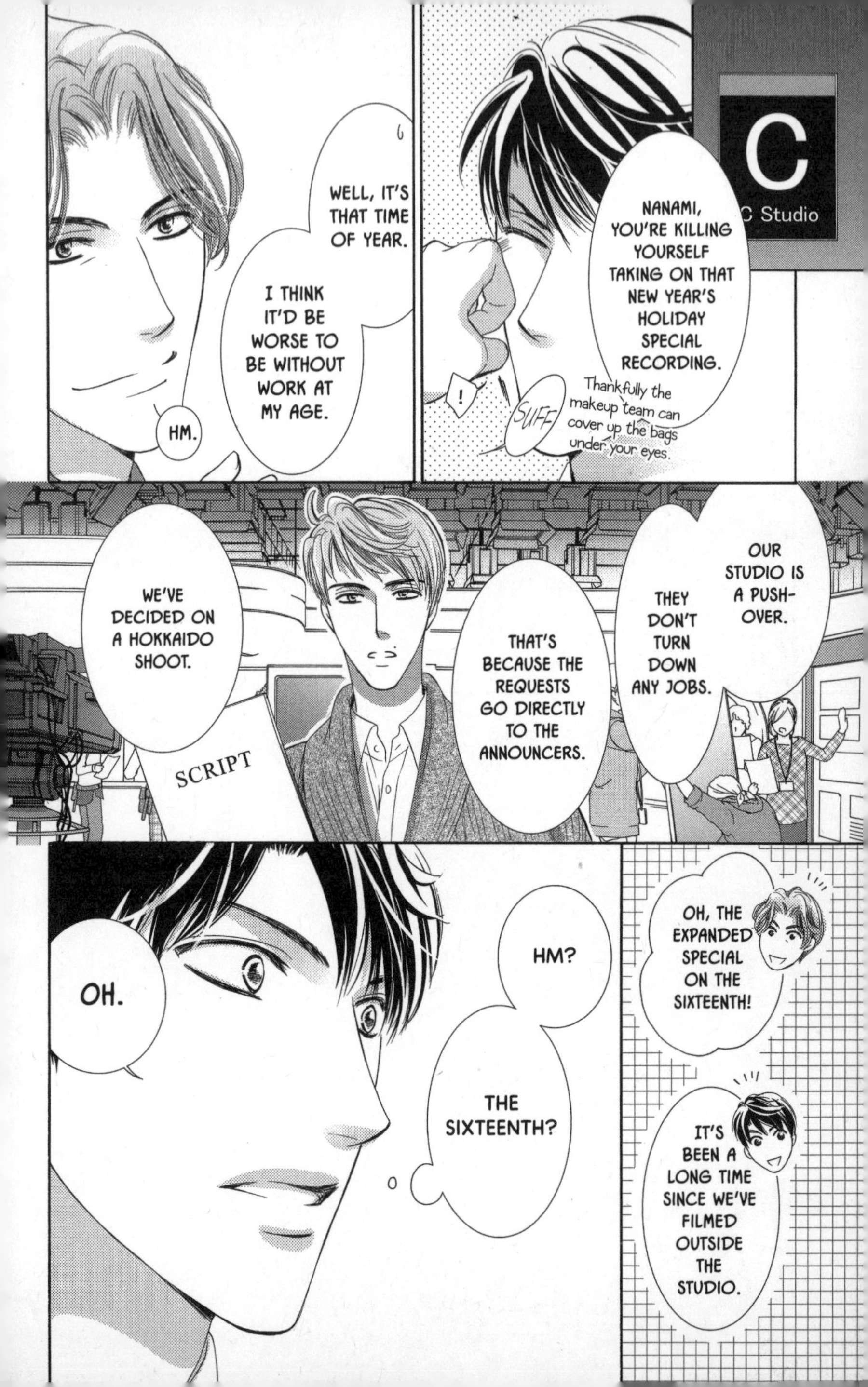
C
C Studio
NANAMI, YOU'RE KILLING YOURSELF TAKING ON THAT NEW YEAR'S HOLIDAY SPECIAL RECORDING.
Thankfully the makeup team can cover up the bags under your eyes.
SUFF
!
WELL, IT'S THAT TIME OF YEAR.
I THINK IT'D BE WORSE TO BE WITHOUT WORK AT MY AGE.
HM.
OUR STUDIO IS A PUSH-OVER.
THEY DON'T TURN DOWN ANY JOBS.
THAT'S BECAUSE THE REQUESTS GO DIRECTLY TO THE ANNOUNCERS.
WE'VE DECIDED ON A HOKKAIDO SHOOT.
SCRIPT
OH, THE EXPANDED SPECIAL ON THE SIXTEENTH!
IT'S BEEN A LONG TIME SINCE WE'VE FILMED OUTSIDE THE STUDIO.
HM?
THE SIXTEENTH?
OH.

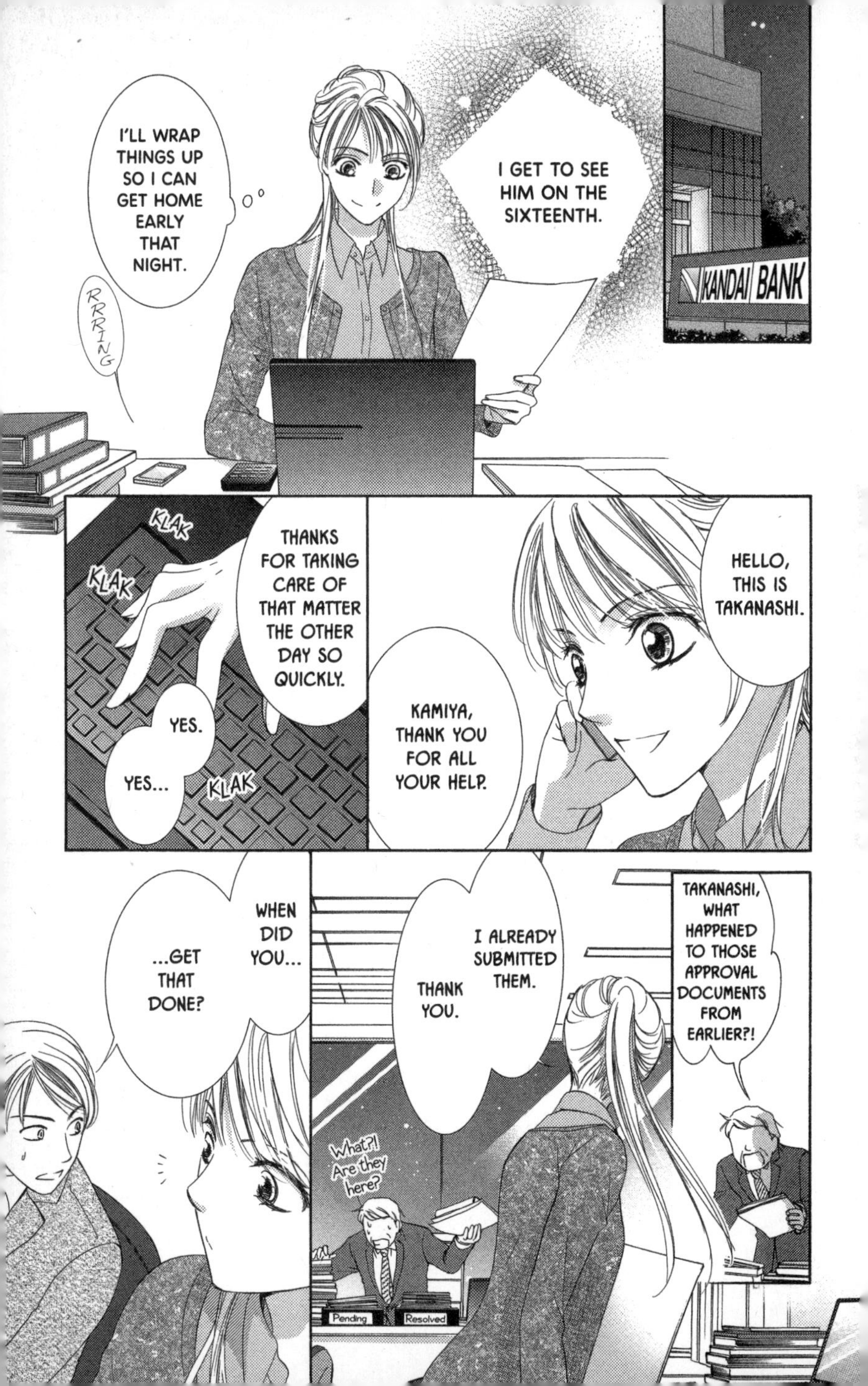
KANDAI BANK
I GET TO SEE HIM ON THE SIXTEENTH.
I'LL WRAP THINGS UP SO I CAN GET HOME EARLY THAT NIGHT.
RRRING
HELLO, THIS IS TAKANASHI.
KAMIYA, THANK YOU FOR ALL YOUR HELP.
THANKS FOR TAKING CARE OF THAT MATTER THE OTHER DAY SO QUICKLY.
KLAK
KLAK
YES.
YES...
KLAK
TAKANASHI, WHAT HAPPENED TO THOSE APPROVAL DOCUMENTS FROM EARLIER?!
I ALREADY SUBMITTED THEM.
THANK YOU.
What?! Are they here?
Pending
Resolved
WHEN DID YOU...
...GET THAT DONE?

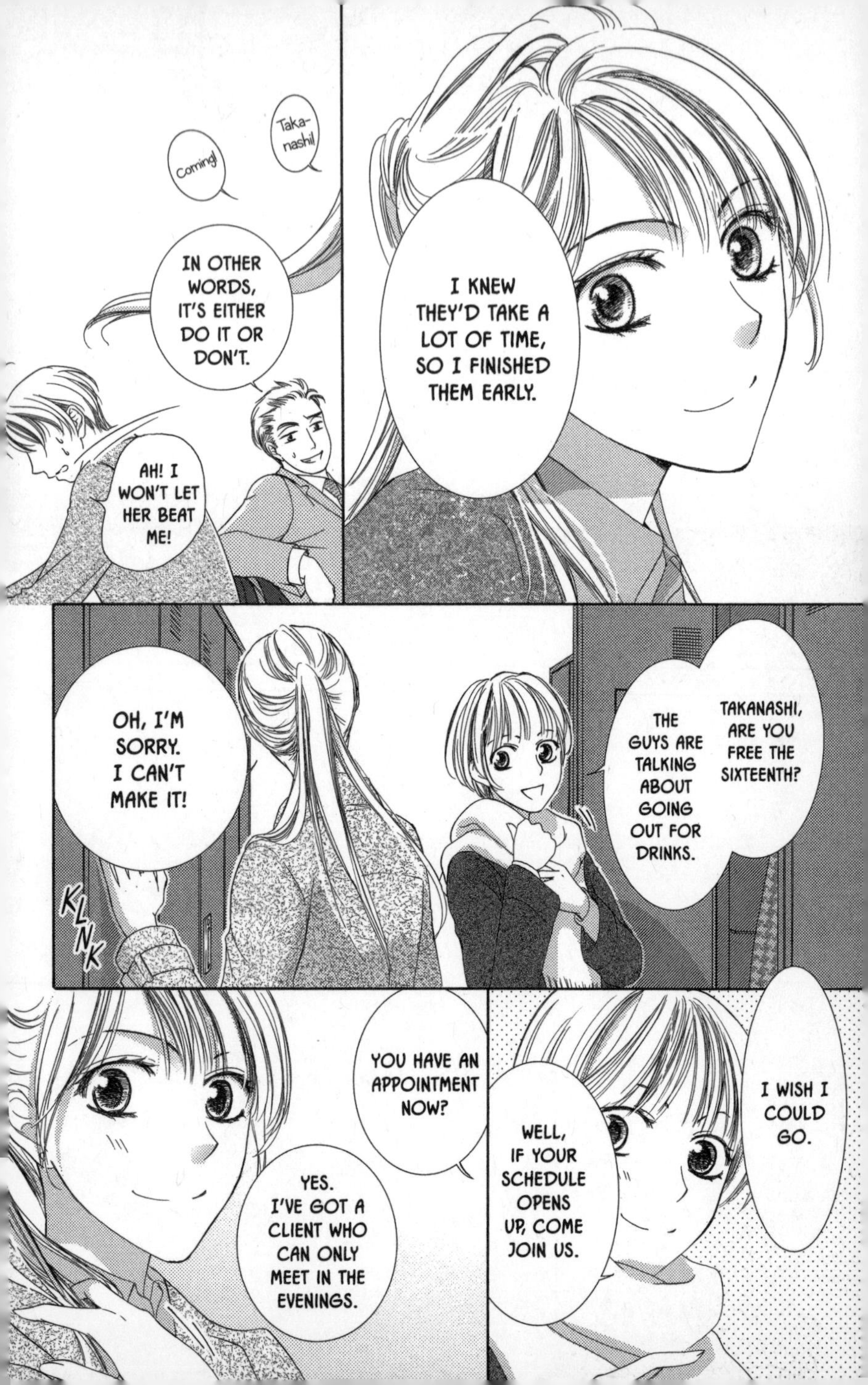
I KNEW THEY'D TAKE A LOT OF TIME, SO I FINISHED THEM EARLY.
Taka-nashi!
Coming!
IN OTHER WORDS, IT'S EITHER DO IT OR DON'T.
AH! I WON'T LET HER BEAT ME!
TAKANASHI, ARE YOU FREE THE SIXTEENTH?
THE GUYS ARE TALKING ABOUT GOING OUT FOR DRINKS.
OH, I'M SORRY. I CAN'T MAKE IT!
KLNK
I WISH I COULD GO.
WELL, IF YOUR SCHEDULE OPENS UP, COME JOIN US.
YOU HAVE AN APPOINTMENT NOW?
YES. I'VE GOT A CLIENT WHO CAN ONLY MEET IN THE EVENINGS.

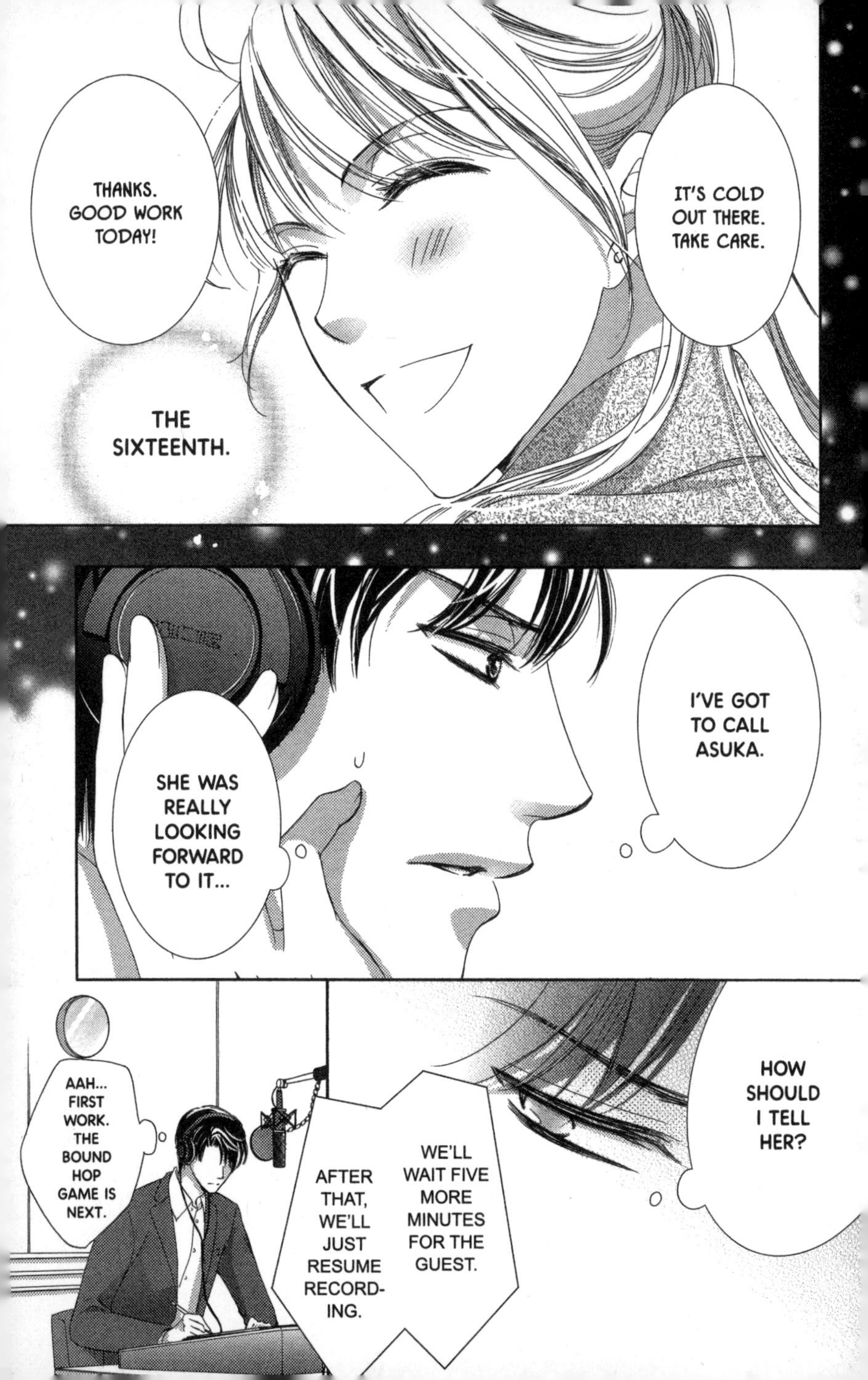
IT'S COLD OUT THERE. TAKE CARE.
THANKS. GOOD WORK TODAY!
THE SIXTEENTH.
I'VE GOT TO CALL ASUKA.
SHE WAS REALLY LOOKING FORWARD TO IT...
HOW SHOULD I TELL HER?
WE'LL WAIT FIVE MORE MINUTES FOR THE GUEST.
AFTER THAT, WE'LL JUST RESUME RECORD-ING.
AAH... FIRST WORK. THE BOUND HOP GAME IS NEXT.

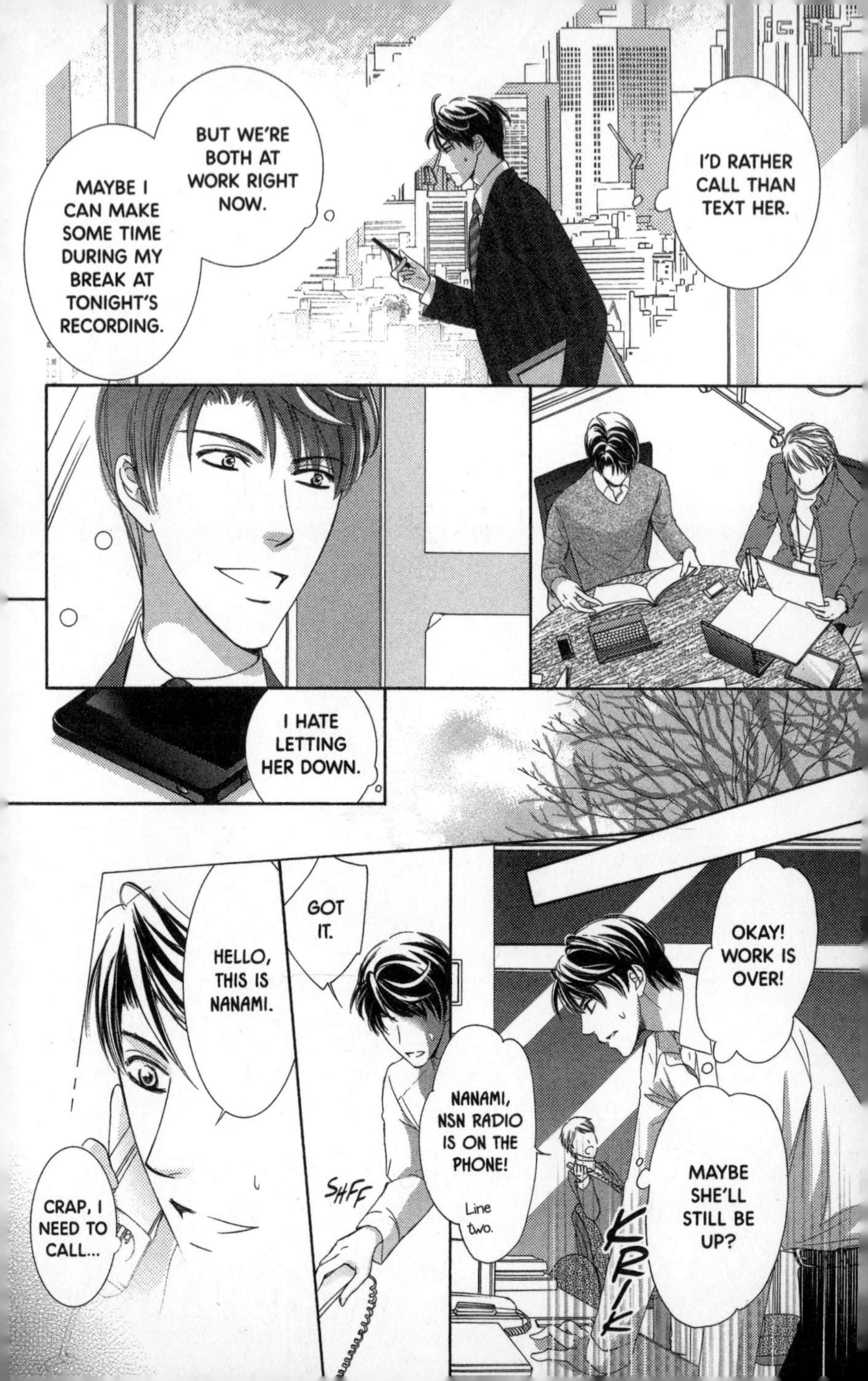
I'D RATHER CALL THAN TEXT HER.
BUT WE'RE BOTH AT WORK RIGHT NOW.
MAYBE I CAN MAKE SOME TIME DURING MY BREAK AT TONIGHT'S RECORDING.
I HATE LETTING HER DOWN.
OKAY! WORK IS OVER!
MAYBE SHE'LL STILL BE UP?
KRIK
NANAMI, NSN RADIO IS ON THE PHONE!
Line two.
GOT IT.
SHFF
HELLO, THIS IS NANAMI.
CRAP, I NEED TO CALL...

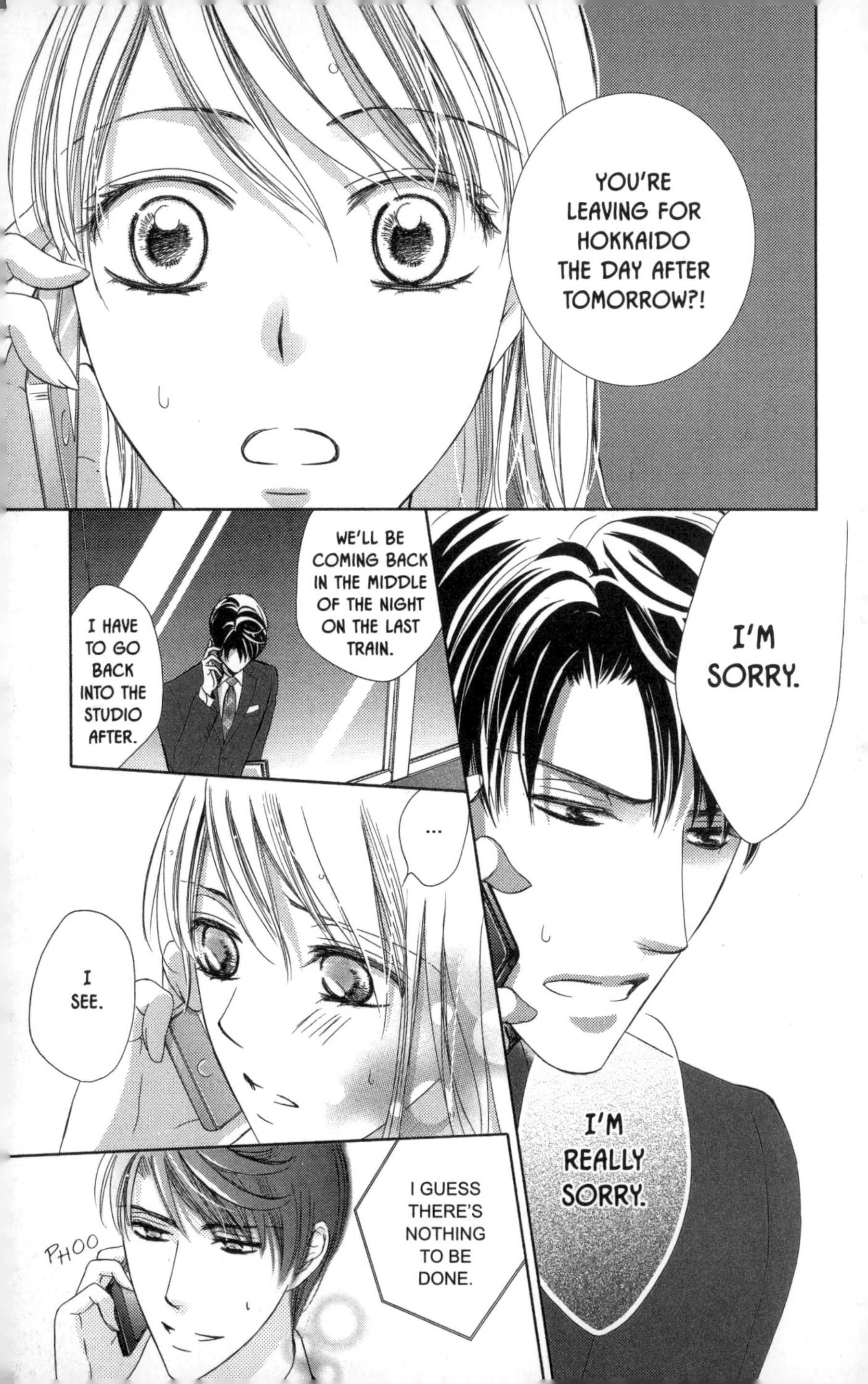
YOU'RE LEAVING FOR HOKKAIDO THE DAY AFTER TOMORROW?!
I'M SORRY.
I'M REALLY SORRY.
WE'LL BE COMING BACK IN THE MIDDLE OF THE NIGHT ON THE LAST TRAIN.
I HAVE TO GO BACK INTO THE STUDIO AFTER.
...
I SEE.
I GUESS THERE'S NOTHING TO BE DONE.
PHOO

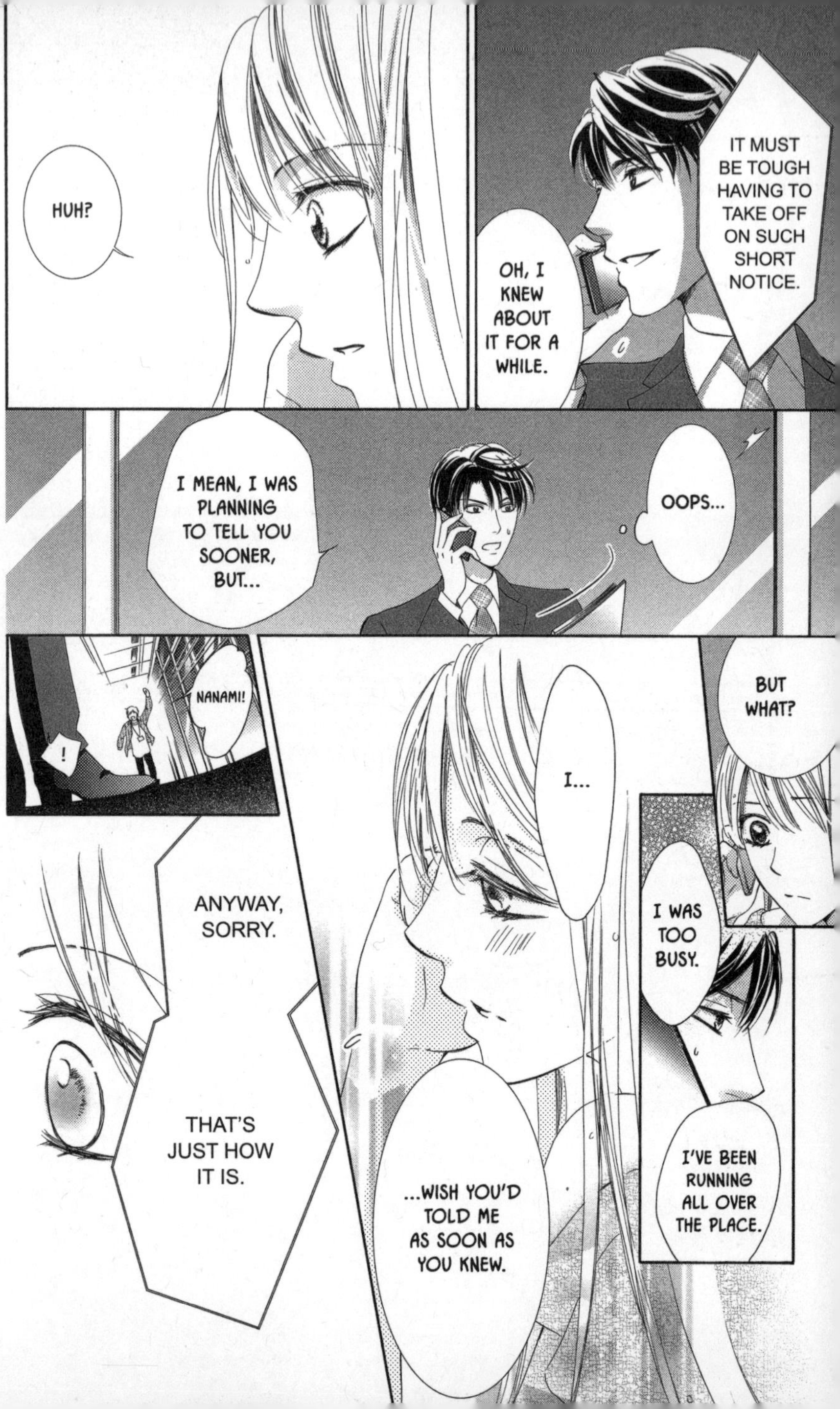
IT MUST BE TOUGH HAVING TO TAKE OFF ON SUCH SHORT NOTICE.
OH, I KNEW ABOUT IT FOR A WHILE.
HUH?
OOPS...
I MEAN, I WAS PLANNING TO TELL YOU SOONER, BUT...
BUT WHAT?
I WAS TOO BUSY.
I'VE BEEN RUNNING ALL OVER THE PLACE.
I...
...WISH YOU'D TOLD ME AS SOON AS YOU KNEW.
NANAMI!
!
ANYWAY, SORRY.
THAT'S JUST HOW IT IS.

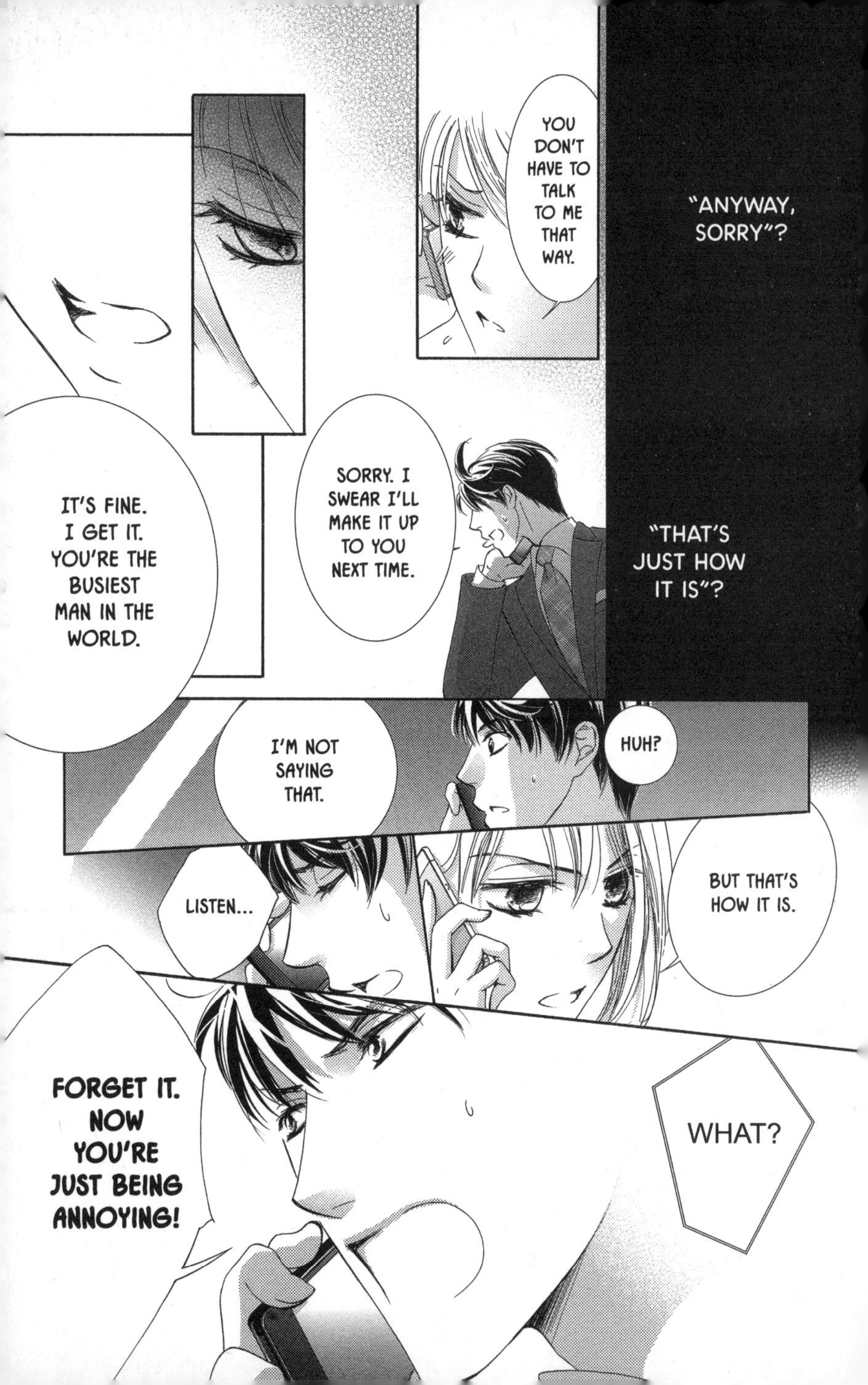
"ANYWAY, SORRY"?
"THAT'S JUST HOW IT IS"?
YOU DON'T HAVE TO TALK TO ME THAT WAY.
SORRY. I SWEAR I'LL MAKE IT UP TO YOU NEXT TIME.
IT'S FINE. I GET IT. YOU'RE THE BUSIEST MAN IN THE WORLD.
HUH?
I'M NOT SAYING THAT.
BUT THAT'S HOW IT IS.
LISTEN...
WHAT?
FORGET IT. NOW YOU'RE JUST BEING ANNOYING!

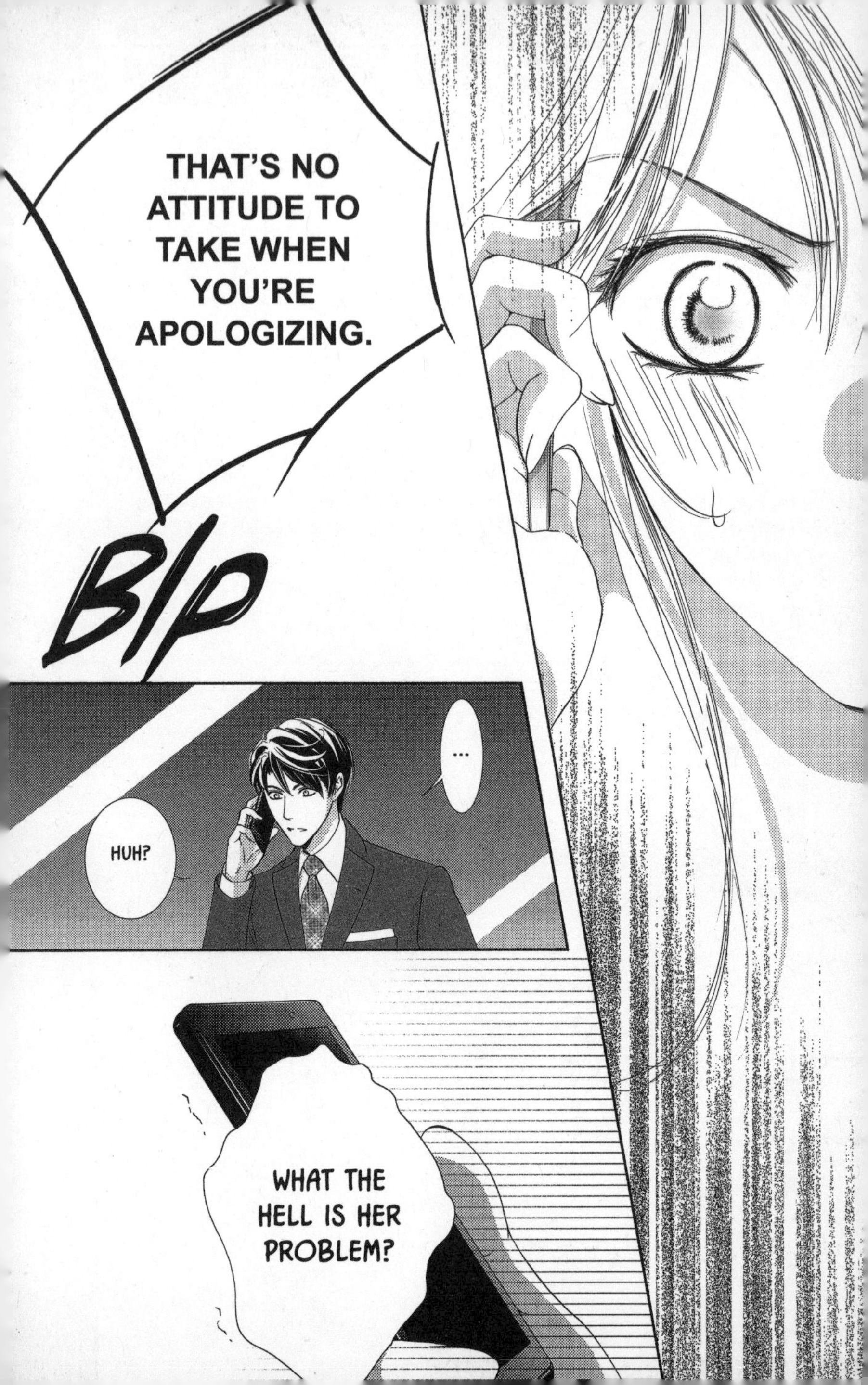
THAT'S NO ATTITUDE TO TAKE WHEN YOU'RE APOLOGIZING.
BIP
...
HUH?
WHAT THE HELL IS HER PROBLEM?

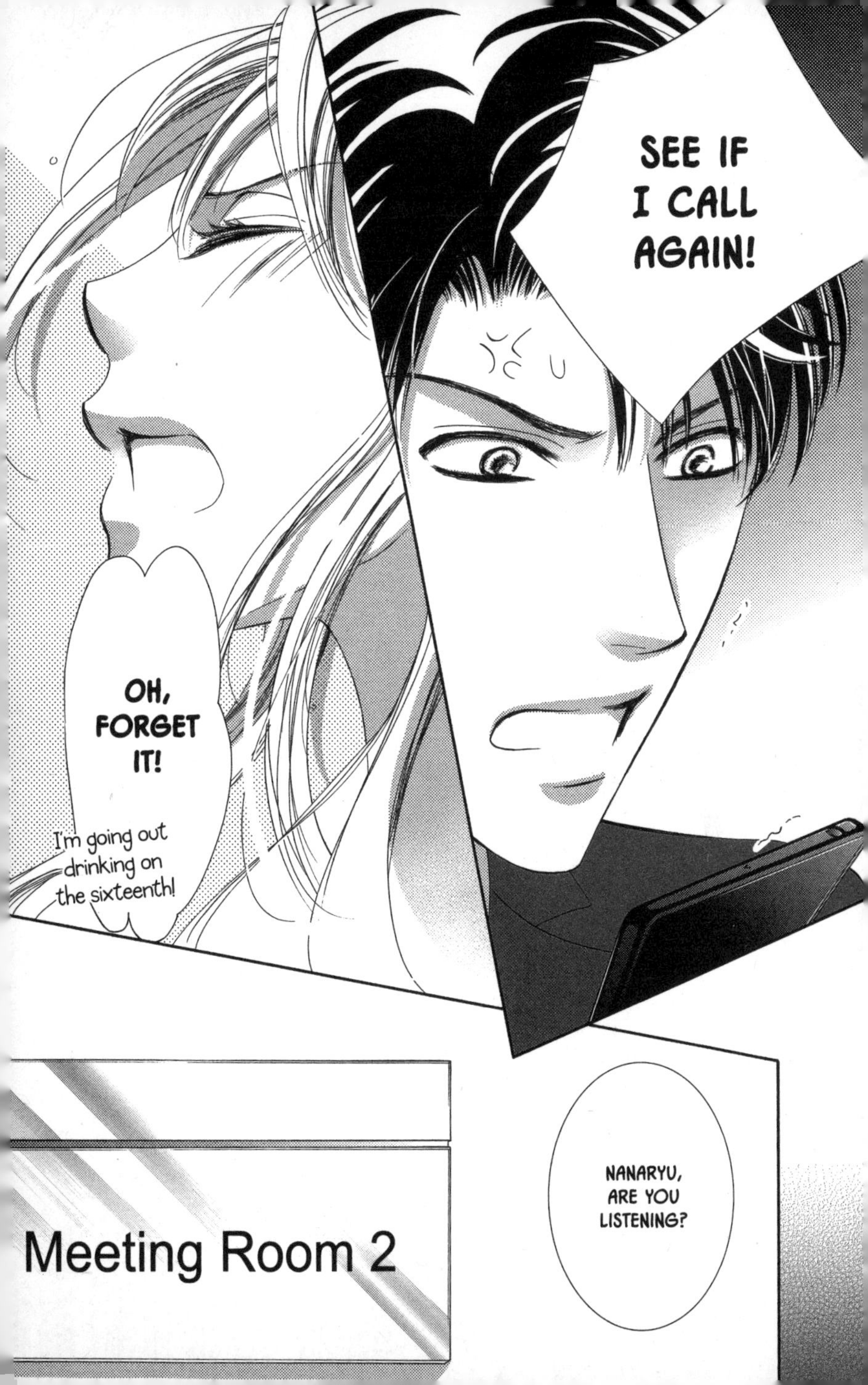
SEE IF I CALL AGAIN!
OH, FORGET IT!
I'm going out drinking on the sixteenth!
NANARYU, ARE YOU LISTENING?
Meeting Room 2

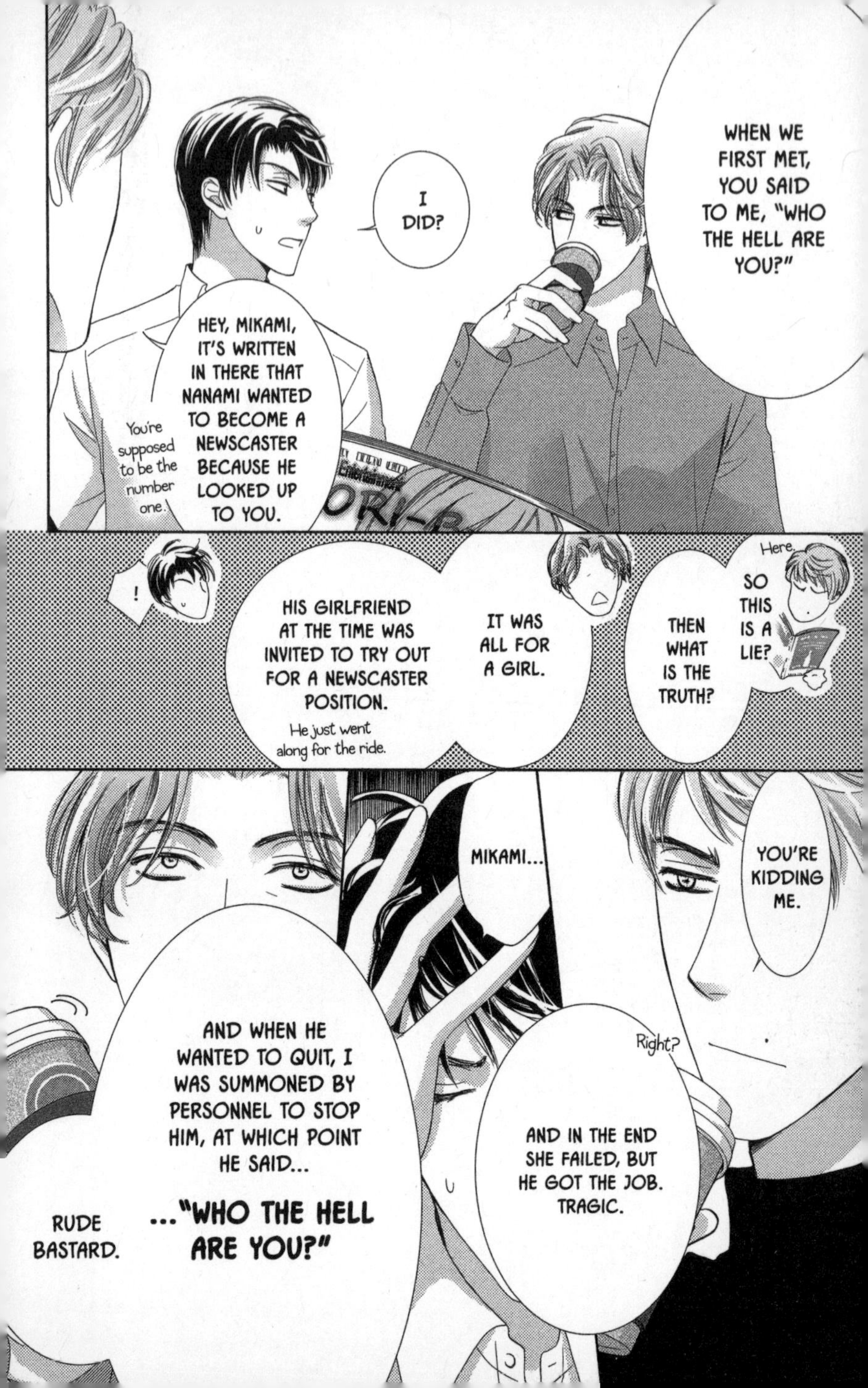
WHEN WE FIRST MET, YOU SAID TO ME, "WHO THE HELL ARE YOU?"
I DID?
HEY, MIKAMI, IT'S WRITTEN IN THERE THAT NANAMI WANTED TO BECOME A NEWSCASTER BECAUSE HE LOOKED UP TO YOU.
You're supposed to be the number one.
Here.
SO THIS IS A LIE?
THEN WHAT IS THE TRUTH?
IT WAS ALL FOR A GIRL.
HIS GIRLFRIEND AT THE TIME WAS INVITED TO TRY OUT FOR A NEWSCASTER POSITION.
He just went along for the ride.
!
YOU'RE KIDDING ME.
MIKAMI...
Right?
AND IN THE END SHE FAILED, BUT HE GOT THE JOB. TRAGIC.
AND WHEN HE WANTED TO QUIT, I WAS SUMMONED BY PERSONNEL TO STOP HIM, AT WHICH POINT HE SAID...
..."WHO THE HELL ARE YOU?"
RUDE BASTARD.

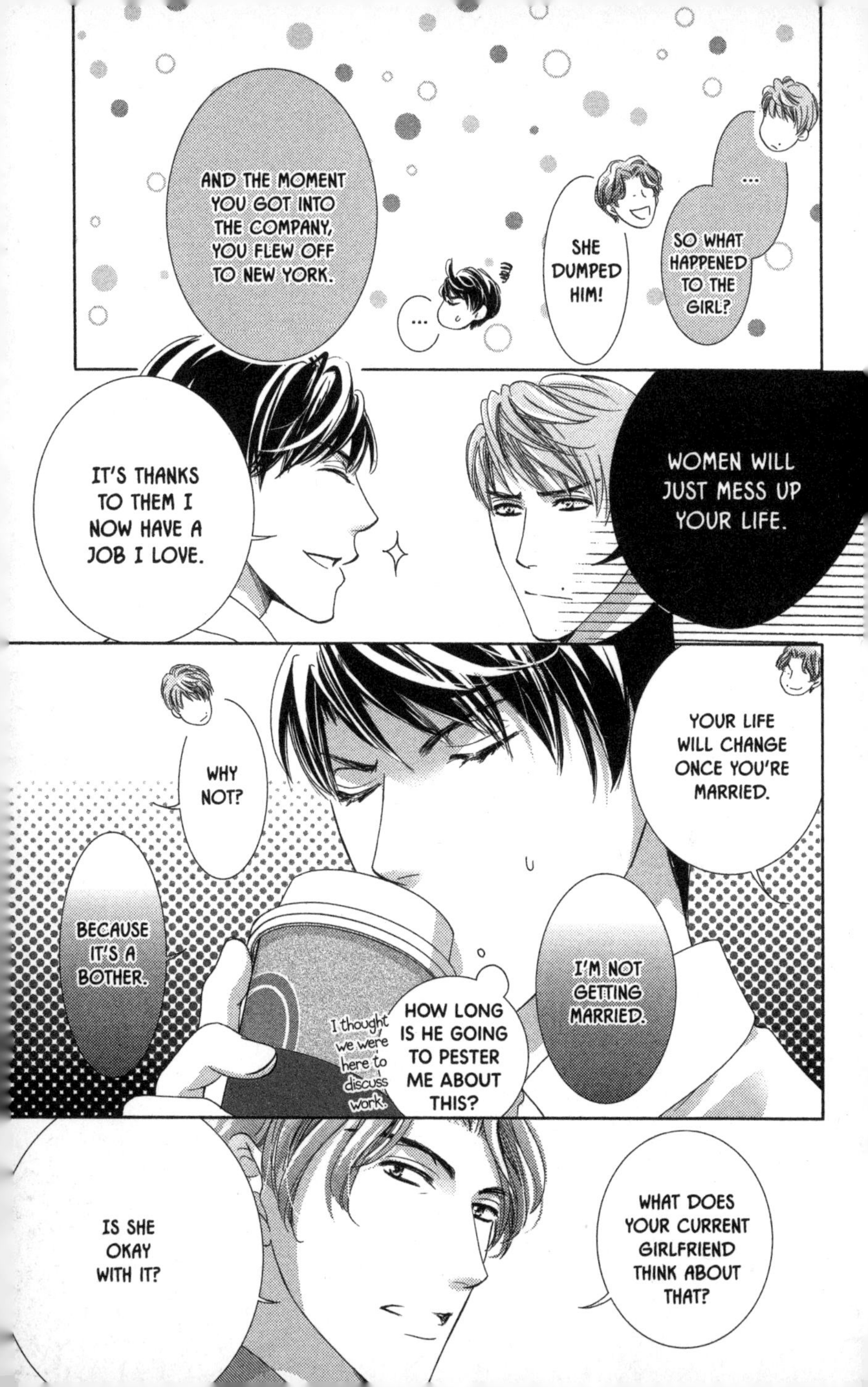
AND THE MOMENT YOU GOT INTO THE COMPANY, YOU FLEW OFF TO NEW YORK.
...
SO WHAT HAPPENED TO THE GIRL?
SHE DUMPED HIM!
...
WOMEN WILL JUST MESS UP YOUR LIFE.
IT'S THANKS TO THEM I NOW HAVE A JOB I LOVE.
YOUR LIFE WILL CHANGE ONCE YOU'RE MARRIED.
I'M NOT GETTING MARRIED.
WHY NOT?
BECAUSE IT'S A BOTHER.
HOW LONG IS HE GOING TO PESTER ME ABOUT THIS?
I thought we were here to discuss work.
WHAT DOES YOUR CURRENT GIRLFRIEND THINK ABOUT THAT?
IS SHE OKAY WITH IT?

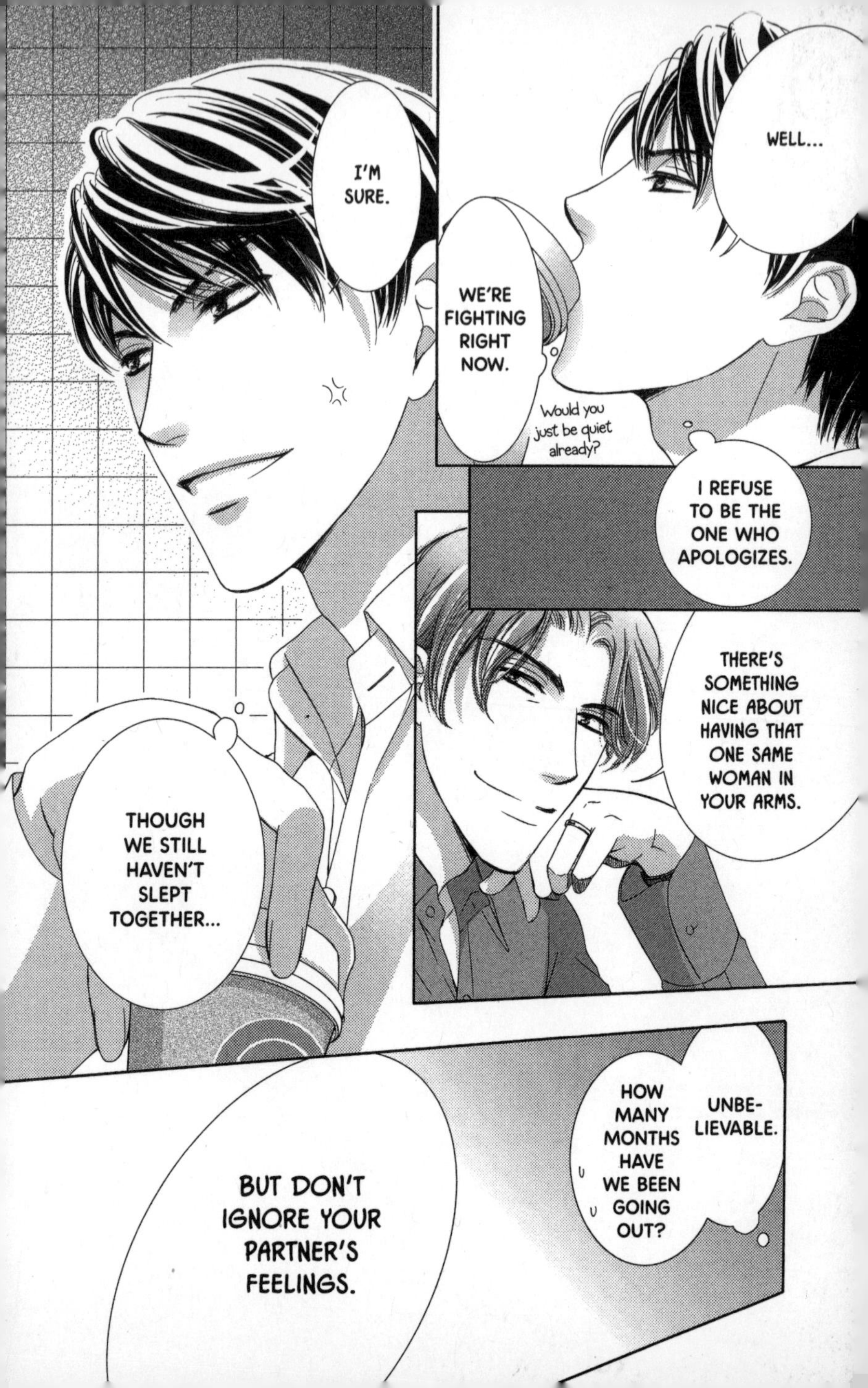
WELL...
WE'RE FIGHTING RIGHT NOW.
Would you just be quiet already?
I REFUSE TO BE THE ONE WHO APOLOGIZES.
THERE'S SOMETHING NICE ABOUT HAVING THAT ONE SAME WOMAN IN YOUR ARMS.
I'M SURE.
THOUGH WE STILL HAVEN'T SLEPT TOGETHER...
UNBE-LIEVABLE.
HOW MANY MONTHS HAVE WE BEEN GOING OUT?
BUT DON'T IGNORE YOUR PARTNER'S FEELINGS.

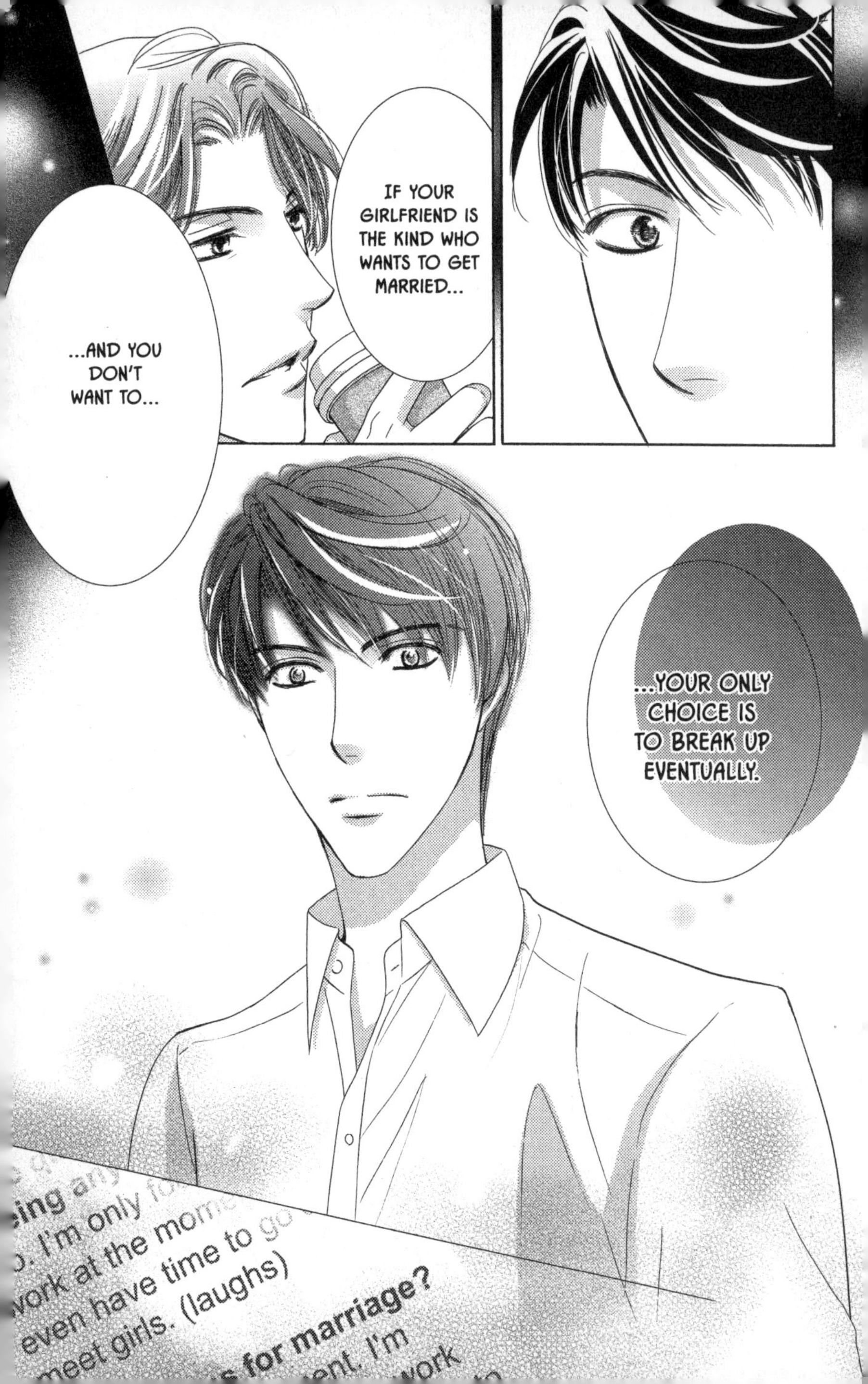
IF YOUR GIRLFRIEND IS THE KIND WHO WANTS TO GET MARRIED...
...AND YOU DON'T WANT TO...
...YOUR ONLY CHOICE IS TO BREAK UP EVENTUALLY.
even have time to
meet girls. (laughs)
for marriage?

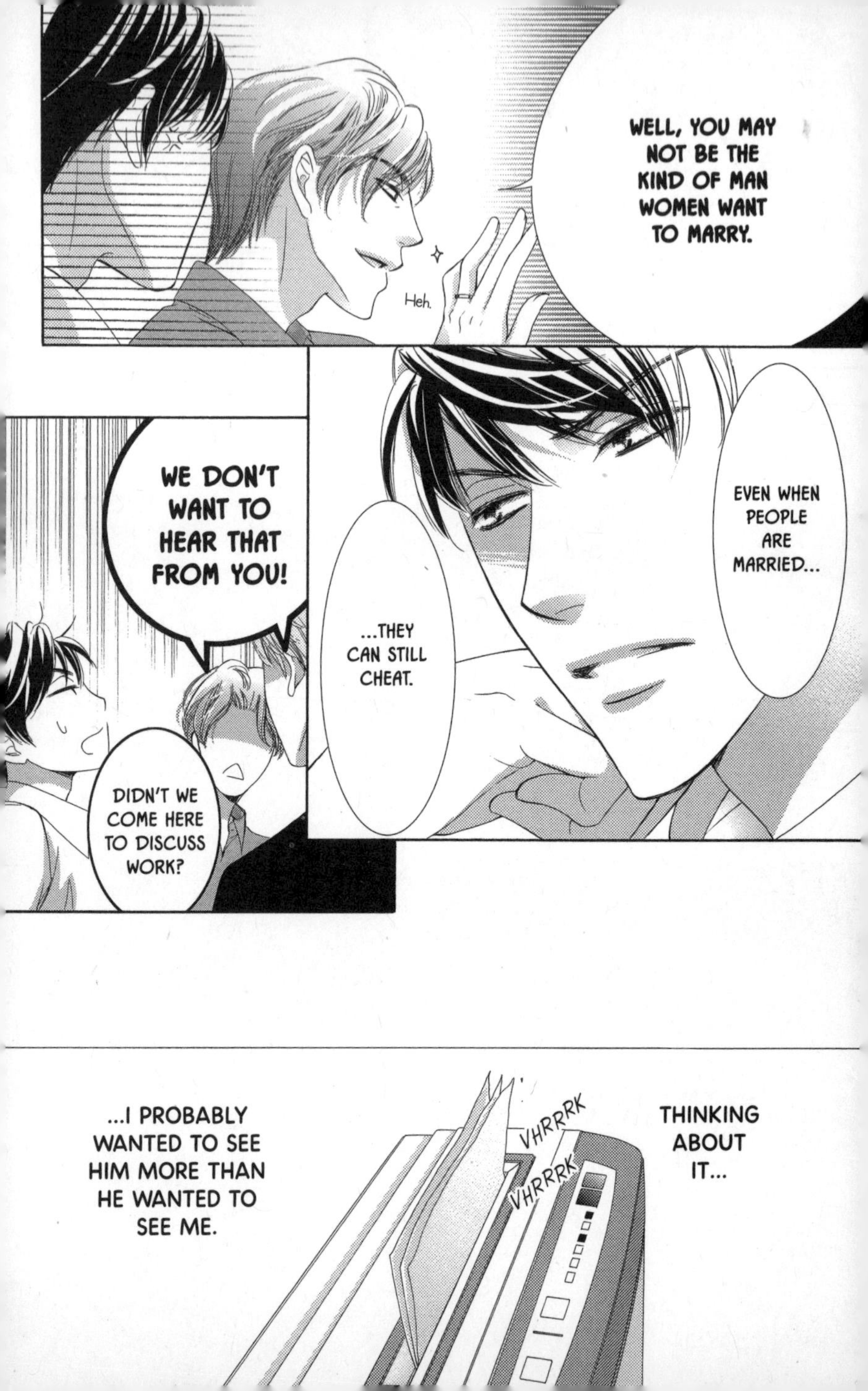
WELL, YOU MAY NOT BE THE KIND OF MAN WOMEN WANT TO MARRY.
Heh.
EVEN WHEN PEOPLE ARE MARRIED...
...THEY CAN STILL CHEAT.
WE DON'T WANT TO HEAR THAT FROM YOU!
DIDN'T WE COME HERE TO DISCUSS WORK?
THINKING ABOUT IT...
VHRRRK
VHRRRK
...I PROBABLY WANTED TO SEE HIM MORE THAN HE WANTED TO SEE ME.

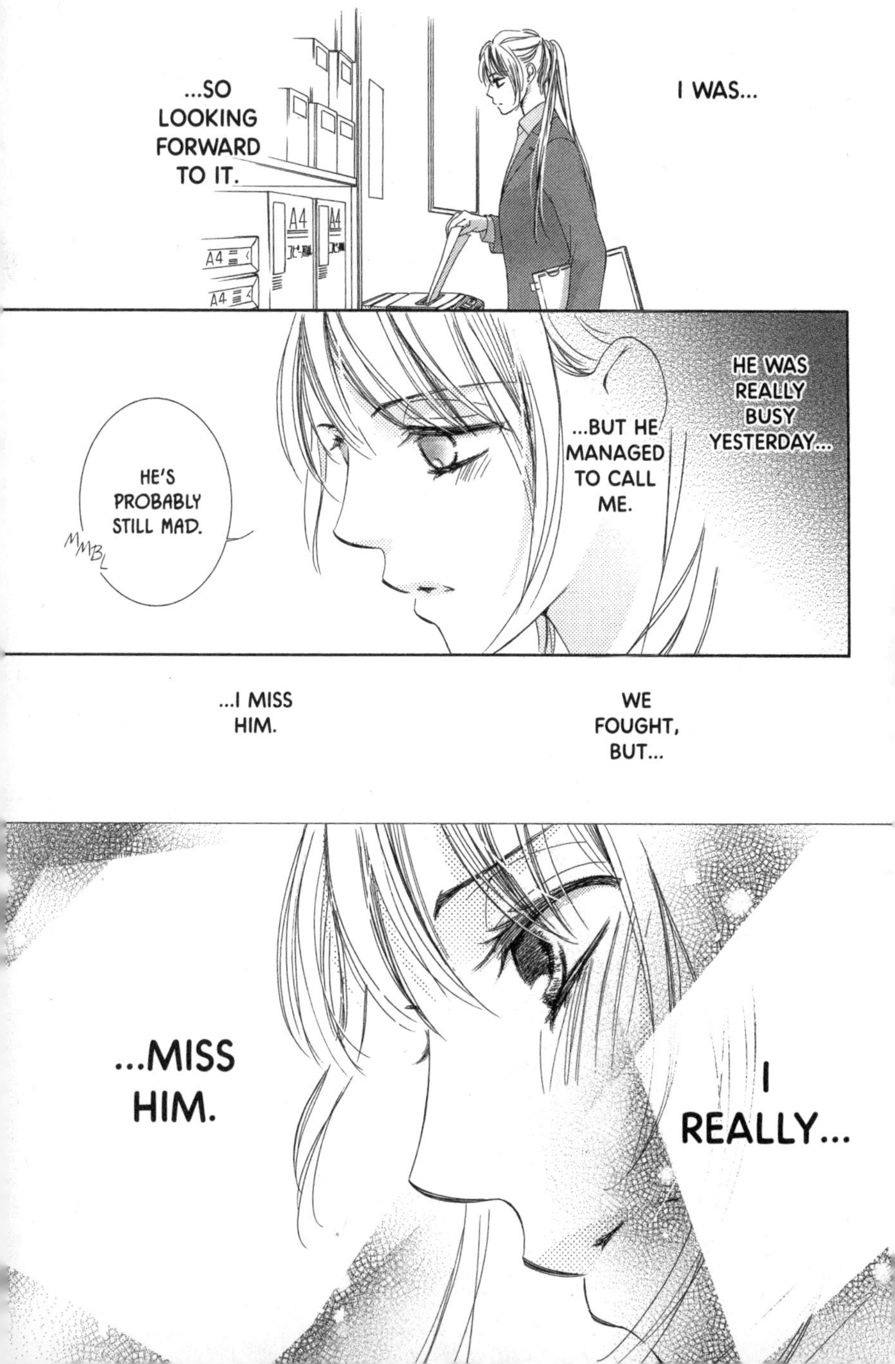
I WAS...
...SO LOOKING FORWARD TO IT.
HE WAS REALLY BUSY YESTERDAY...
...BUT HE MANAGED TO CALL ME.
HE'S PROBABLY STILL MAD.
MMBL
WE FOUGHT, BUT...
...I MISS HIM.
I REALLY...
...MISS HIM.

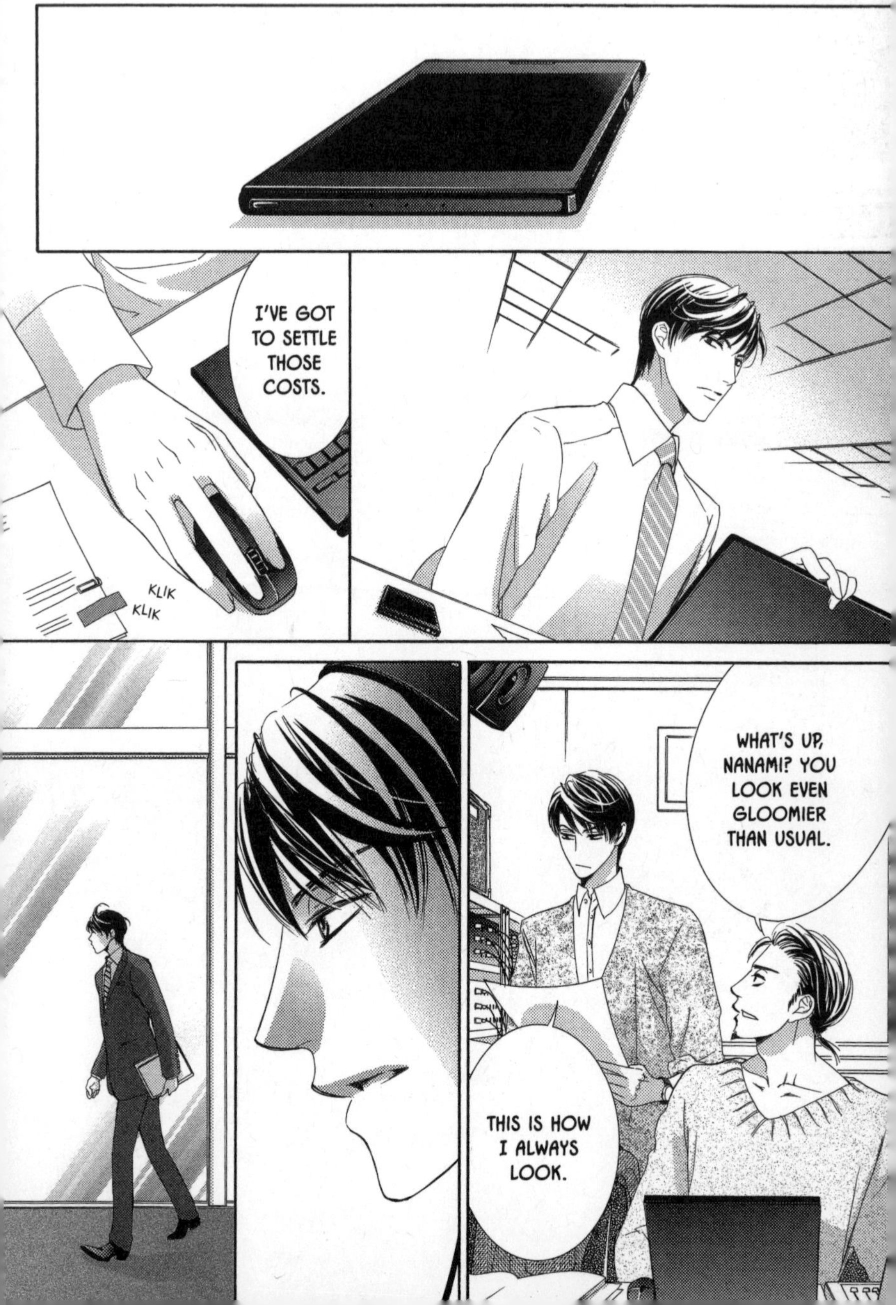
I'VE GOT TO SETTLE THOSE COSTS.
KLIK KLIK
WHAT'S UP, NANAMI? YOU LOOK EVEN GLOOMIER THAN USUAL.
THIS IS HOW I ALWAYS LOOK.

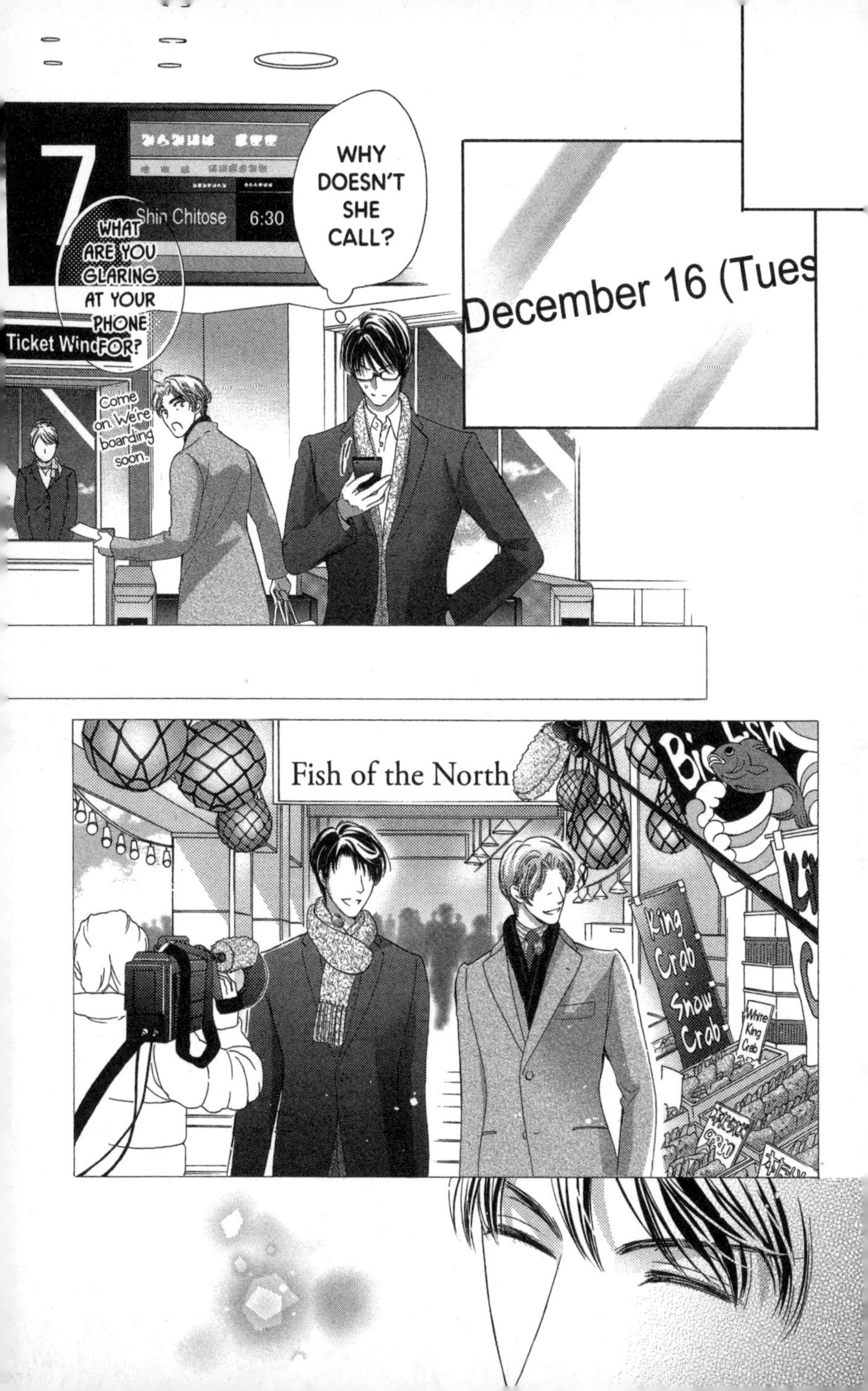
December 16 (Tues
WHY DOESN'T SHE CALL?
7
Shin Chitose 6:30
WHAT ARE YOU GLARING AT YOUR PHONE FOR?
Ticket Wind
Come on. We're boarding soon.
Fish of the North
King Crab
Snow Crab
White King Crab

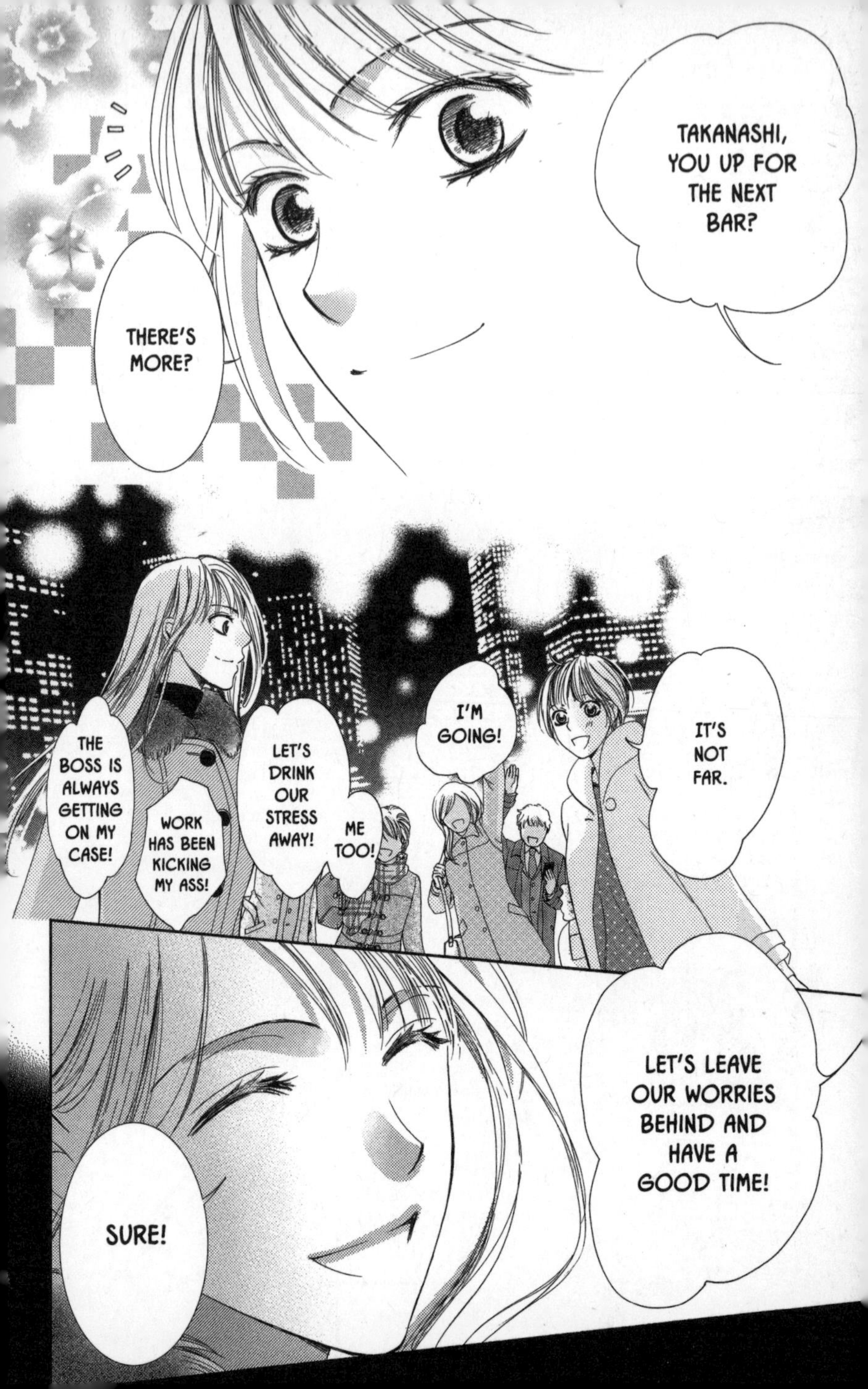
TAKANASHI, YOU UP FOR THE NEXT BAR?
THERE'S MORE?
IT'S NOT FAR.
I'M GOING!
ME TOO!
LET'S DRINK OUR STRESS AWAY!
WORK HAS BEEN KICKING MY ASS!
THE BOSS IS ALWAYS GETTING ON MY CASE!
LET'S LEAVE OUR WORRIES BEHIND AND HAVE A GOOD TIME!
SURE!

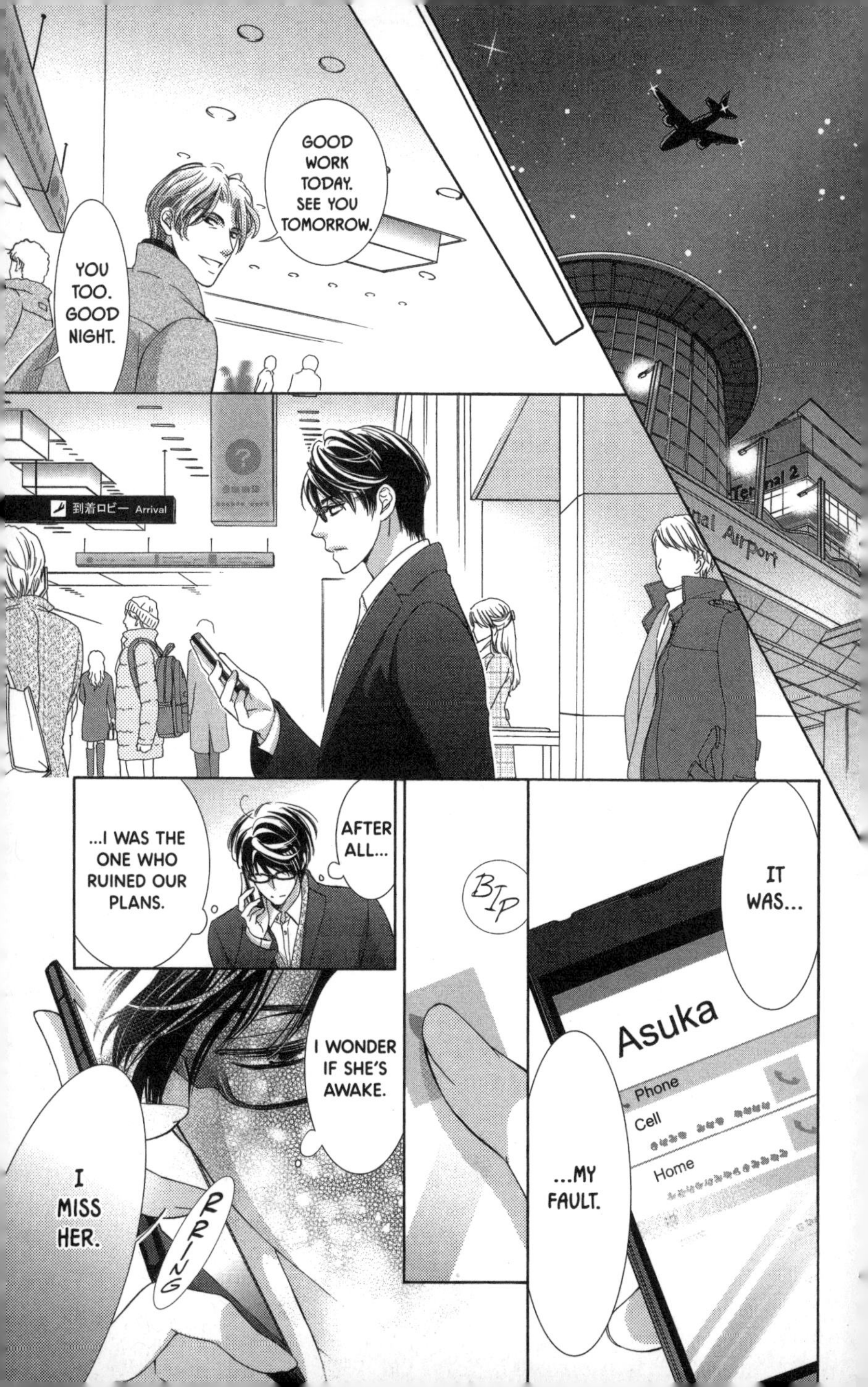
GOOD WORK TODAY. SEE YOU TOMORROW.
YOU TOO. GOOD NIGHT.
到着ロビー Arrival
IT WAS...
...MY FAULT.
Asuka
Phone
Cell
Home
BIP
AFTER ALL...
...I WAS THE ONE WHO RUINED OUR PLANS.
I WONDER IF SHE'S AWAKE.
I MISS HER.
RRING

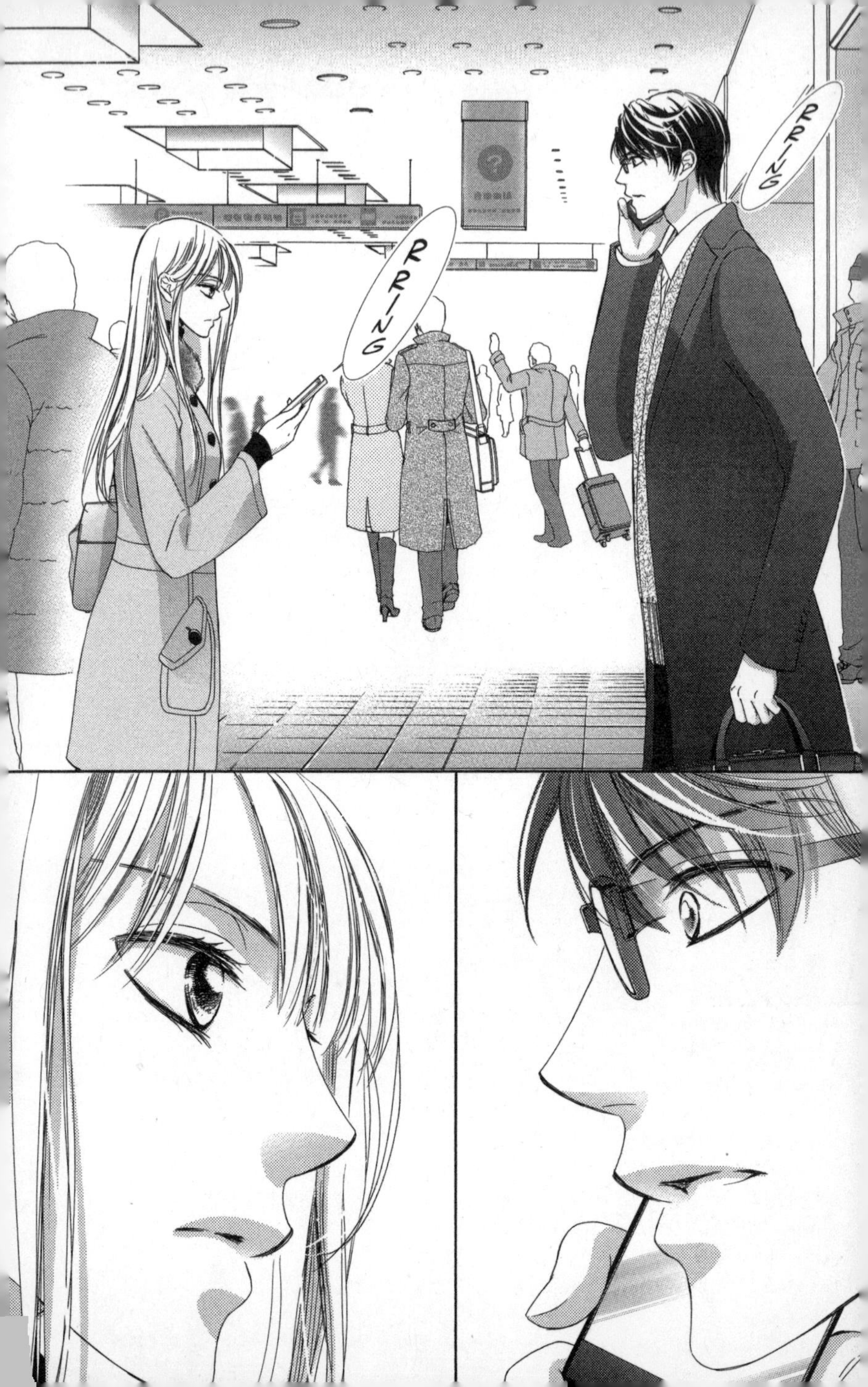
RRING
RRING

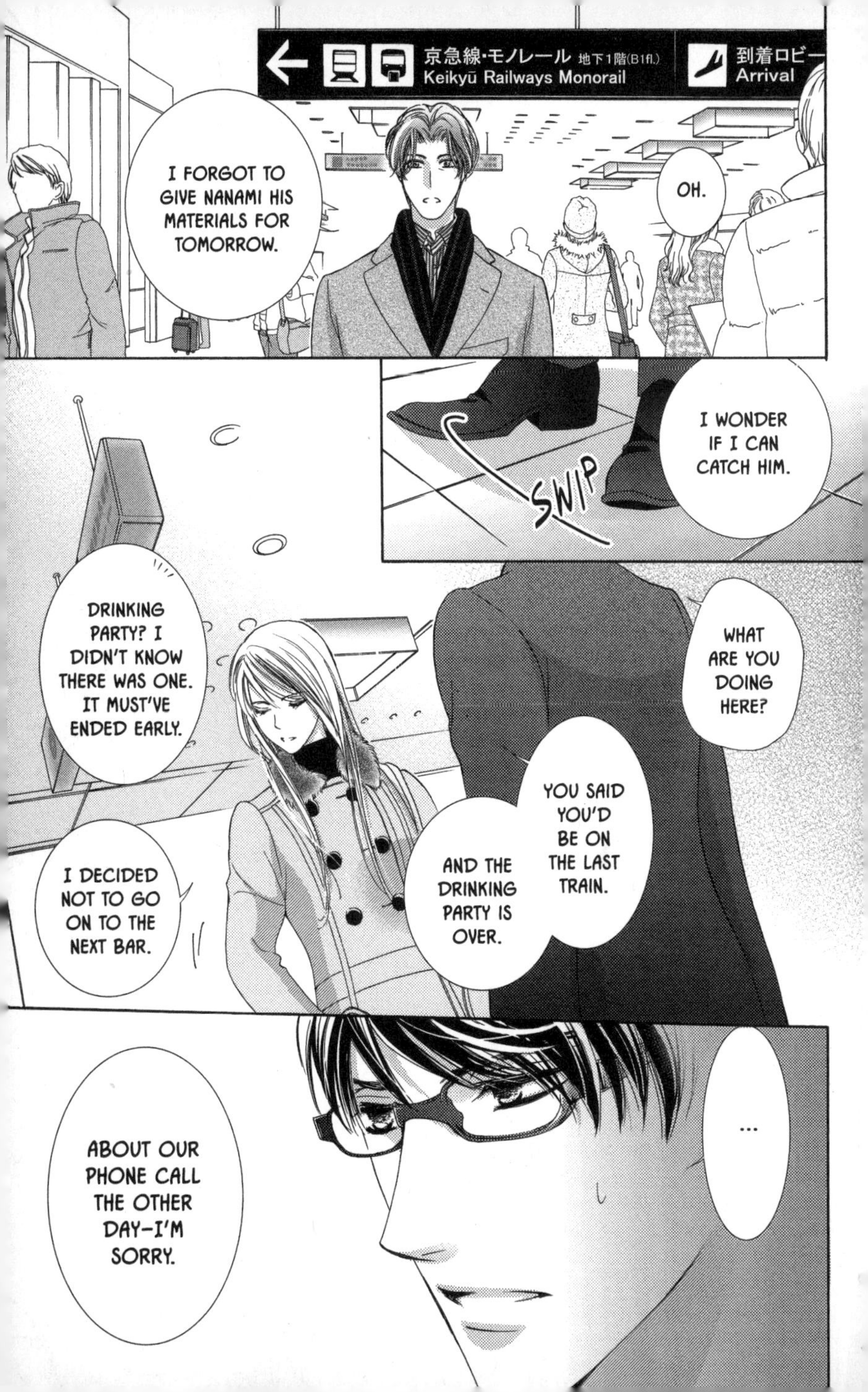

到着ロビー
Arrival
京急線・モノレール 地下1階(B1fl.)
Keikyū Railways Monorail
OH.
I FORGOT TO GIVE NANAMI HIS MATERIALS FOR TOMORROW.
I WONDER IF I CAN CATCH HIM.
SWIP
WHAT ARE YOU DOING HERE?
YOU SAID YOU'D BE ON THE LAST TRAIN.
AND THE DRINKING PARTY IS OVER.
DRINKING PARTY? I DIDN'T KNOW THERE WAS ONE. IT MUST'VE ENDED EARLY.
I DECIDED NOT TO GO ON TO THE NEXT BAR.
...
ABOUT OUR PHONE CALL THE OTHER DAY—I'M SORRY.

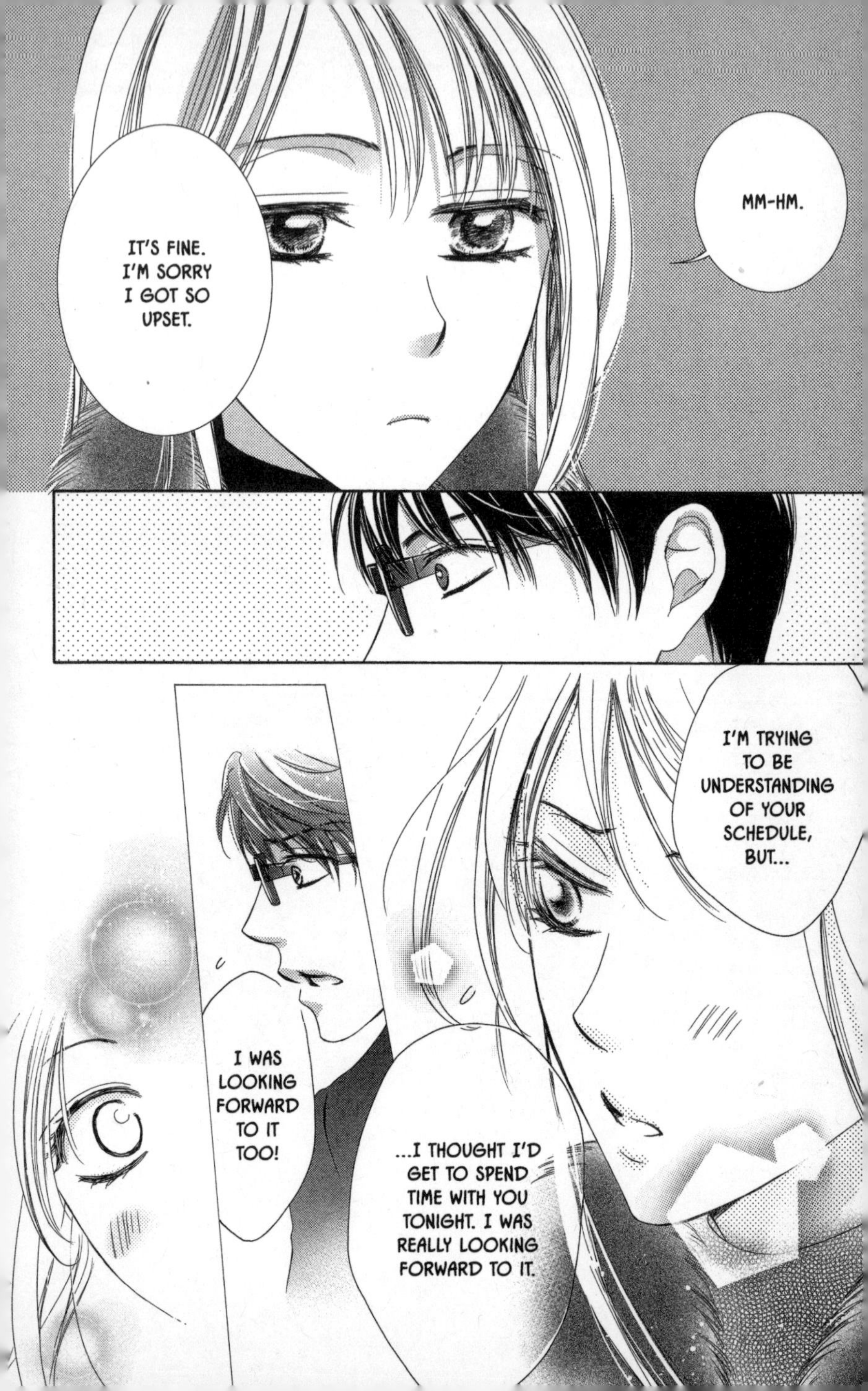
MM-HM.
IT'S FINE. I'M SORRY I GOT SO UPSET.
I'M TRYING TO BE UNDERSTANDING OF YOUR SCHEDULE, BUT...
...I THOUGHT I'D GET TO SPEND TIME WITH YOU TONIGHT. I WAS REALLY LOOKING FORWARD TO IT.
I WAS LOOKING FORWARD TO IT TOO!

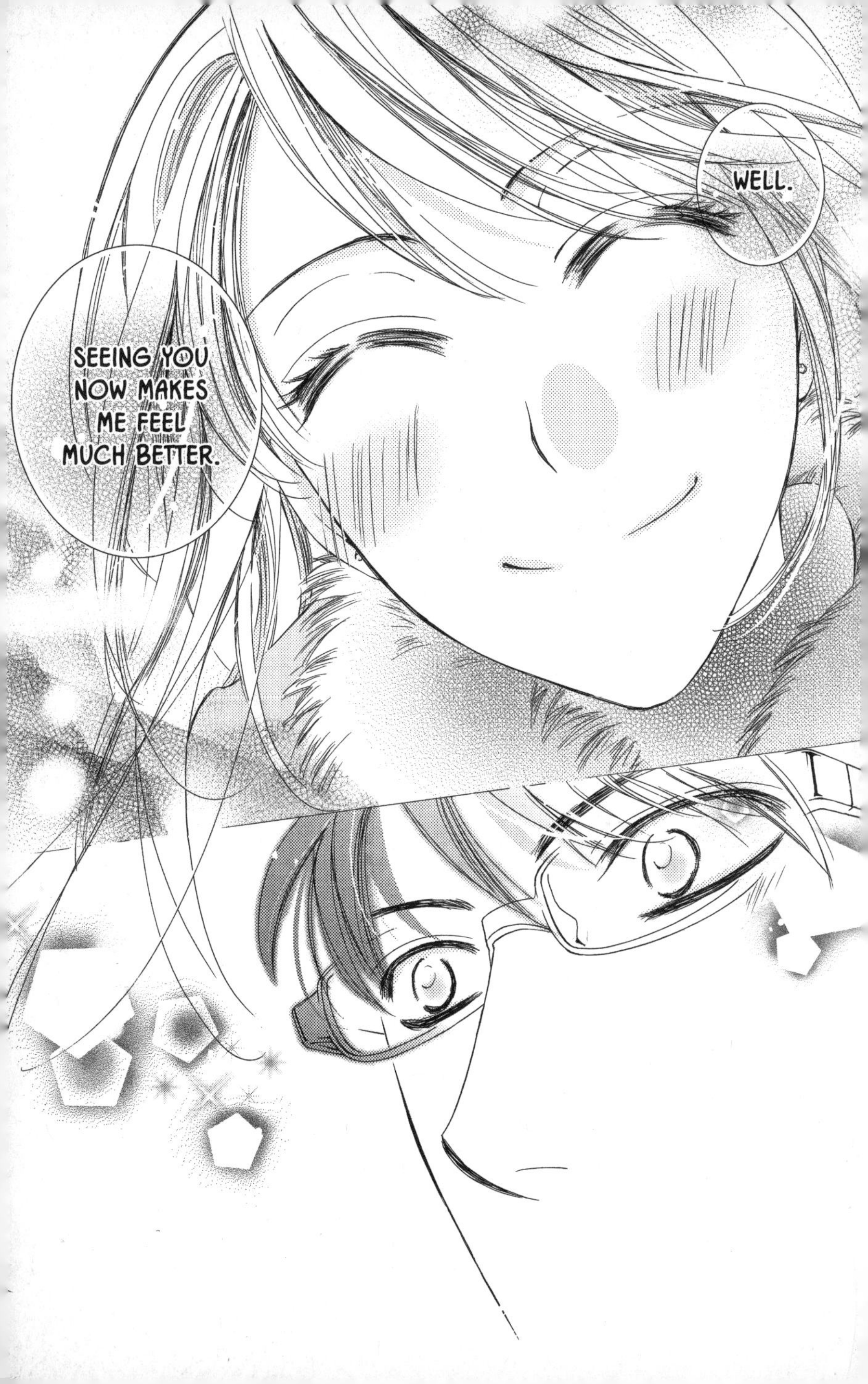
WELL.
SEEING YOU NOW MAKES ME FEEL MUCH BETTER.

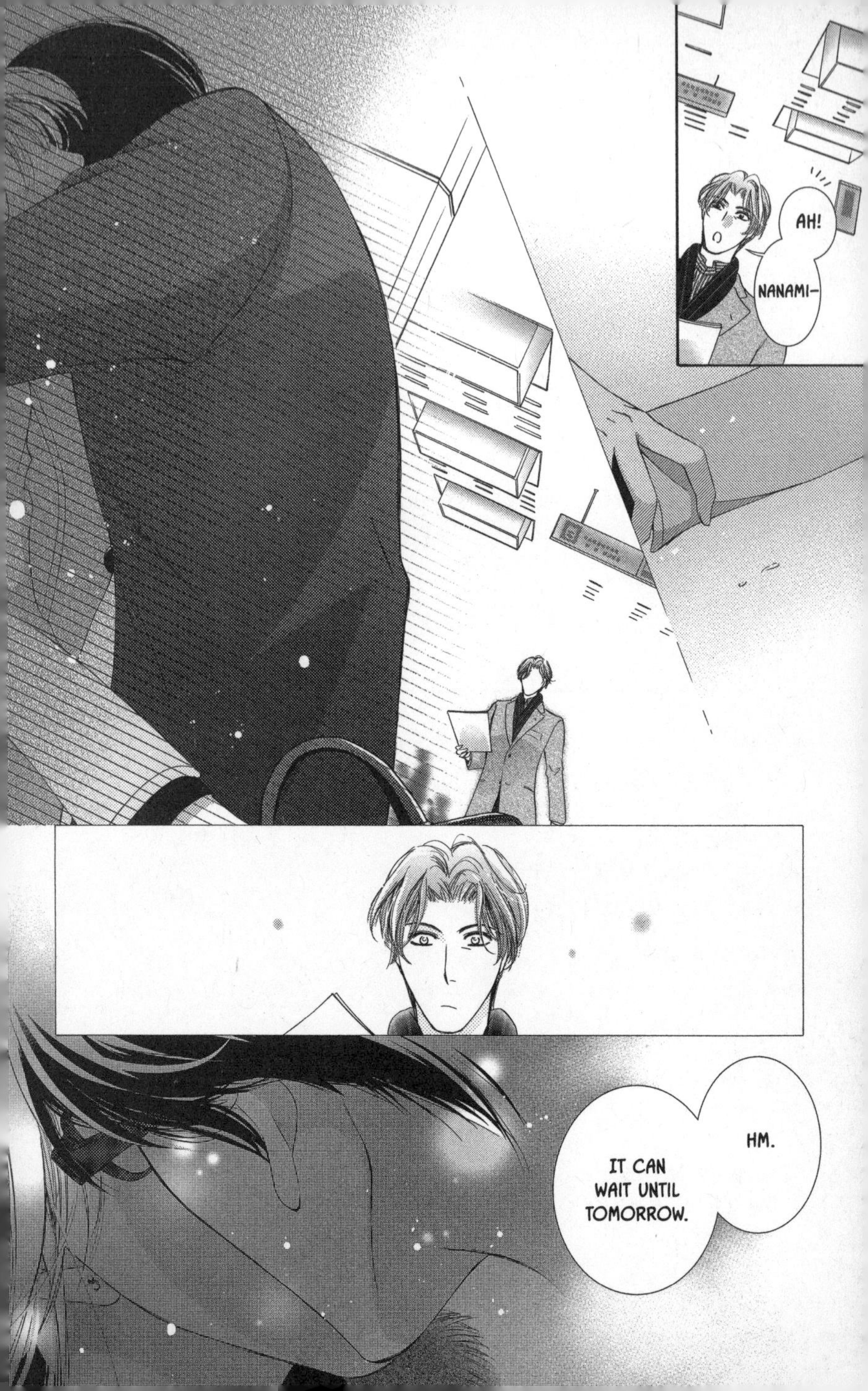
AH!
NANAMI—
HM.
IT CAN WAIT UNTIL TOMORROW.

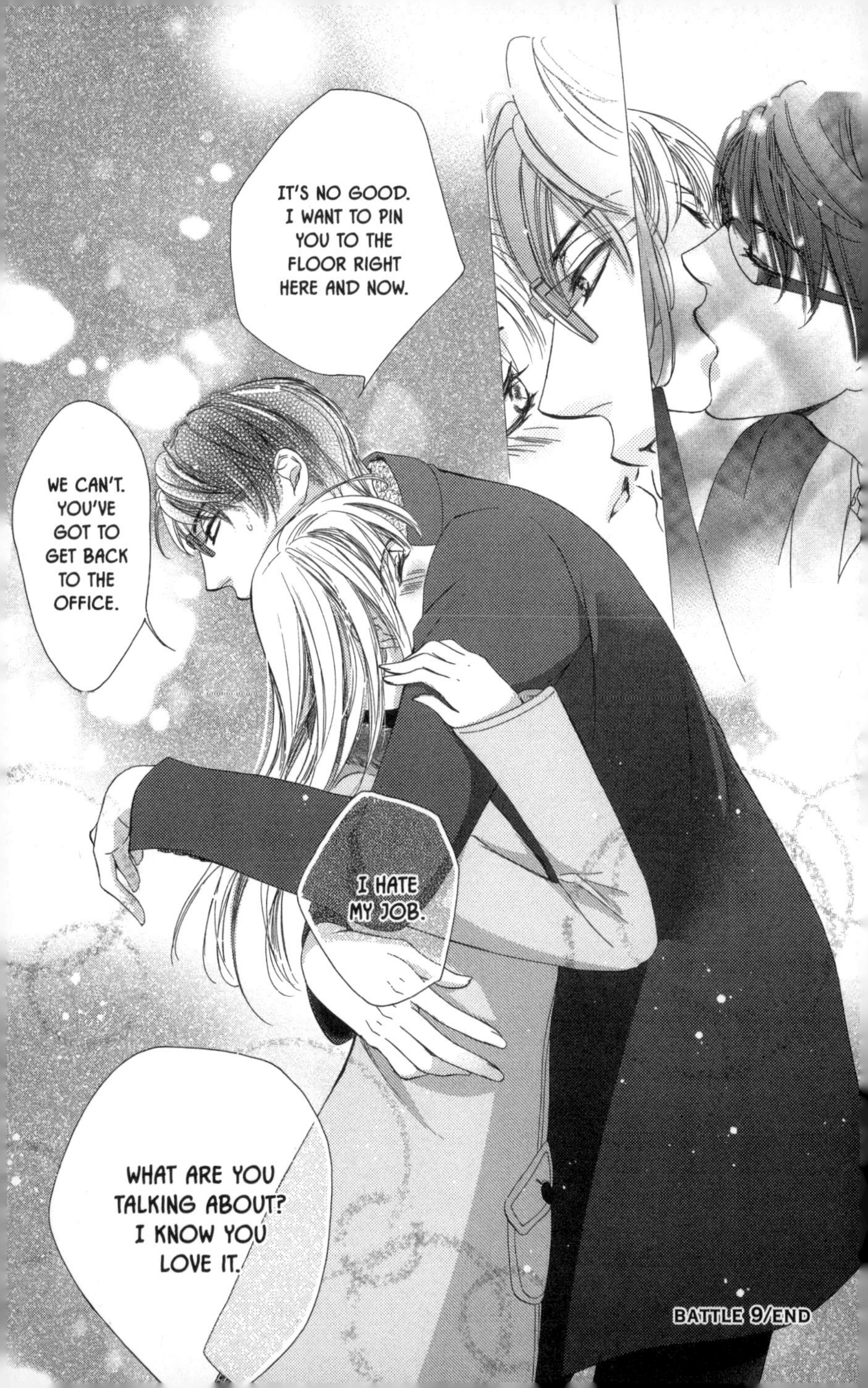
IT'S NO GOOD. I WANT TO PIN YOU TO THE FLOOR RIGHT HERE AND NOW.
WE CAN'T. YOU'VE GOT TO GET BACK TO THE OFFICE.
I HATE MY JOB.
WHAT ARE YOU TALKING ABOUT? I KNOW YOU LOVE IT.
BATTLE 9/END

Now
there is love...

BATTLE 10:

Romance calls for the faraway love of the troubadours; marriage for love of one's neighbor.

–Denis de Rougemont

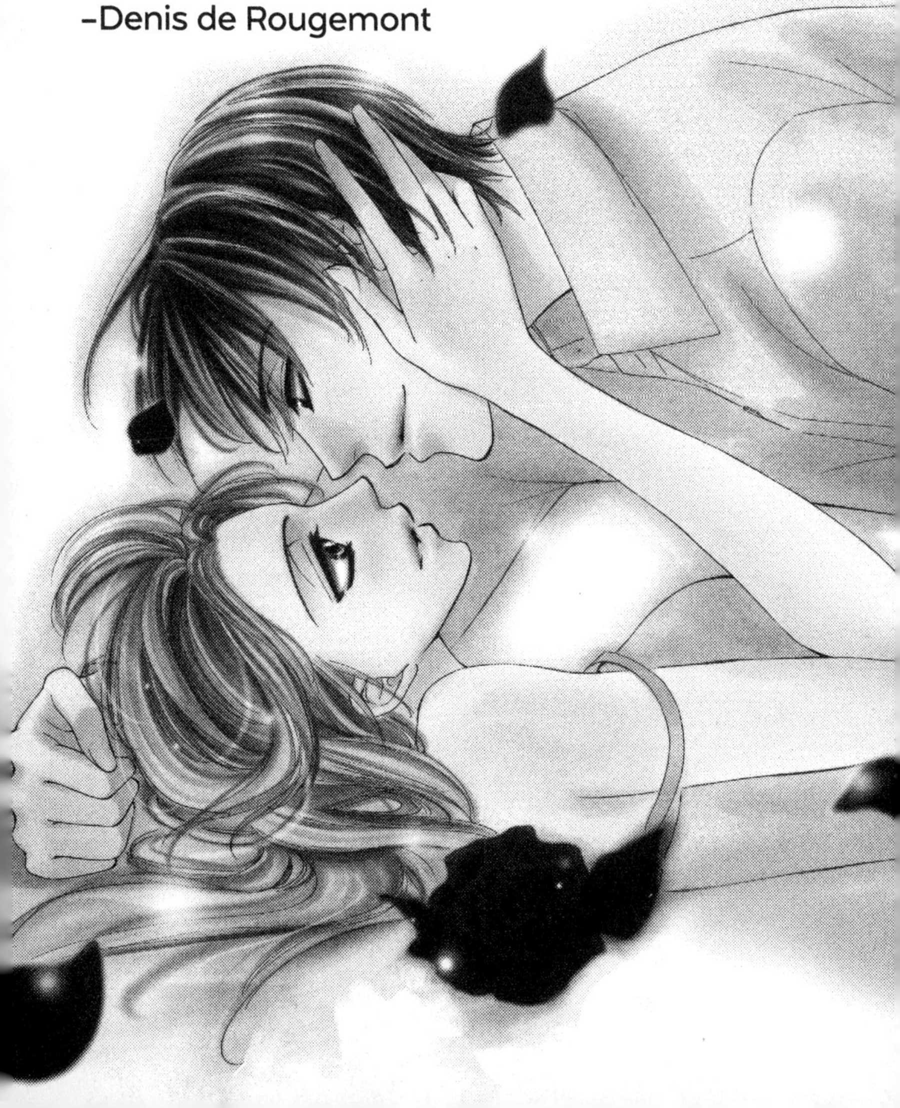

Everyone's
Getting
Married

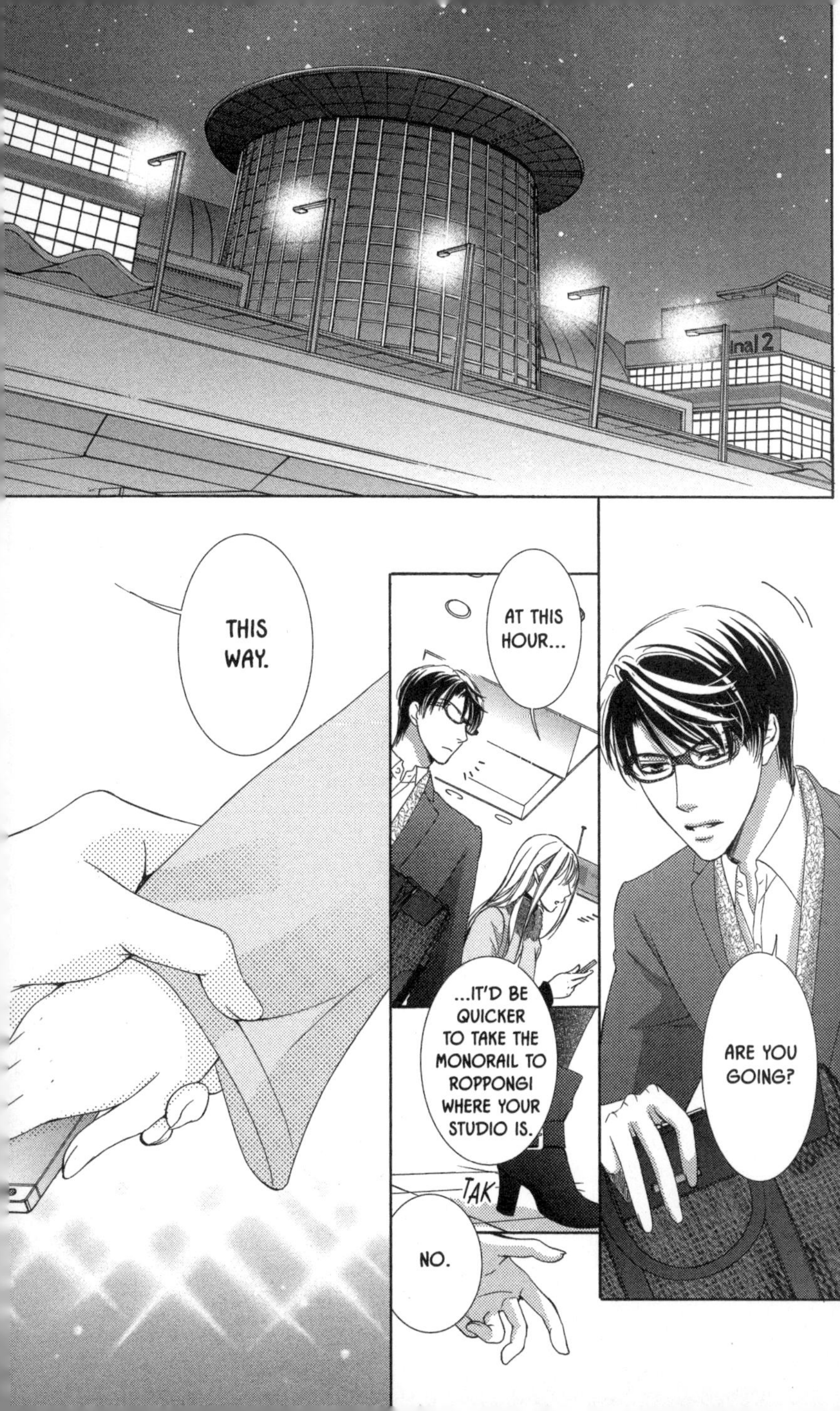
inal 2
ARE YOU GOING?
AT THIS HOUR...
...IT'D BE QUICKER TO TAKE THE MONORAIL TO ROPPONGI WHERE YOUR STUDIO IS.
TAK
NO.
THIS WAY.

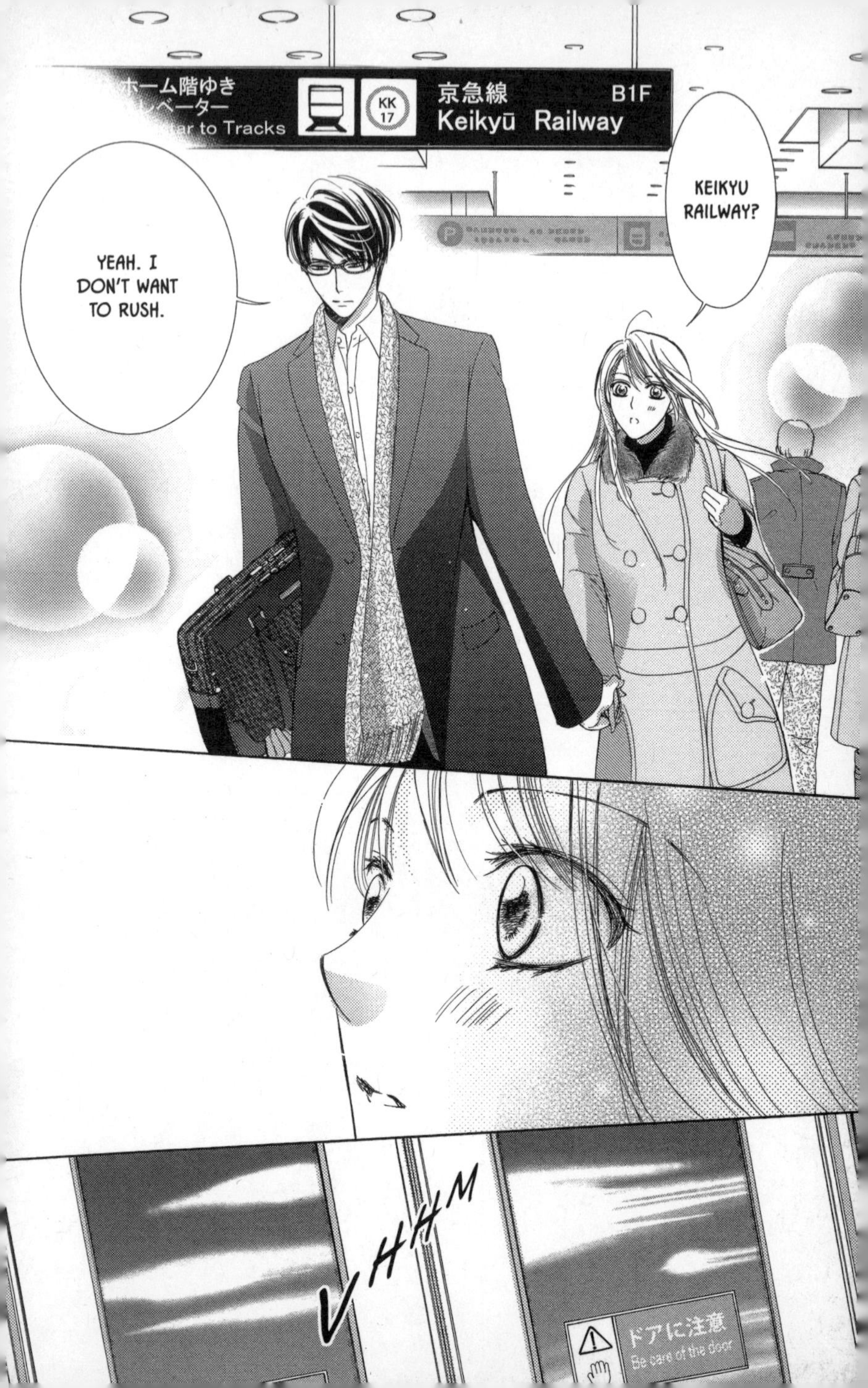
ホーム階ゆき
京急線 B1F
KK 17
Keikyū Railway
KEIKYU RAILWAY?
YEAH. I DON'T WANT TO RUSH.
VHHM
ドアに注意
Be care of the door

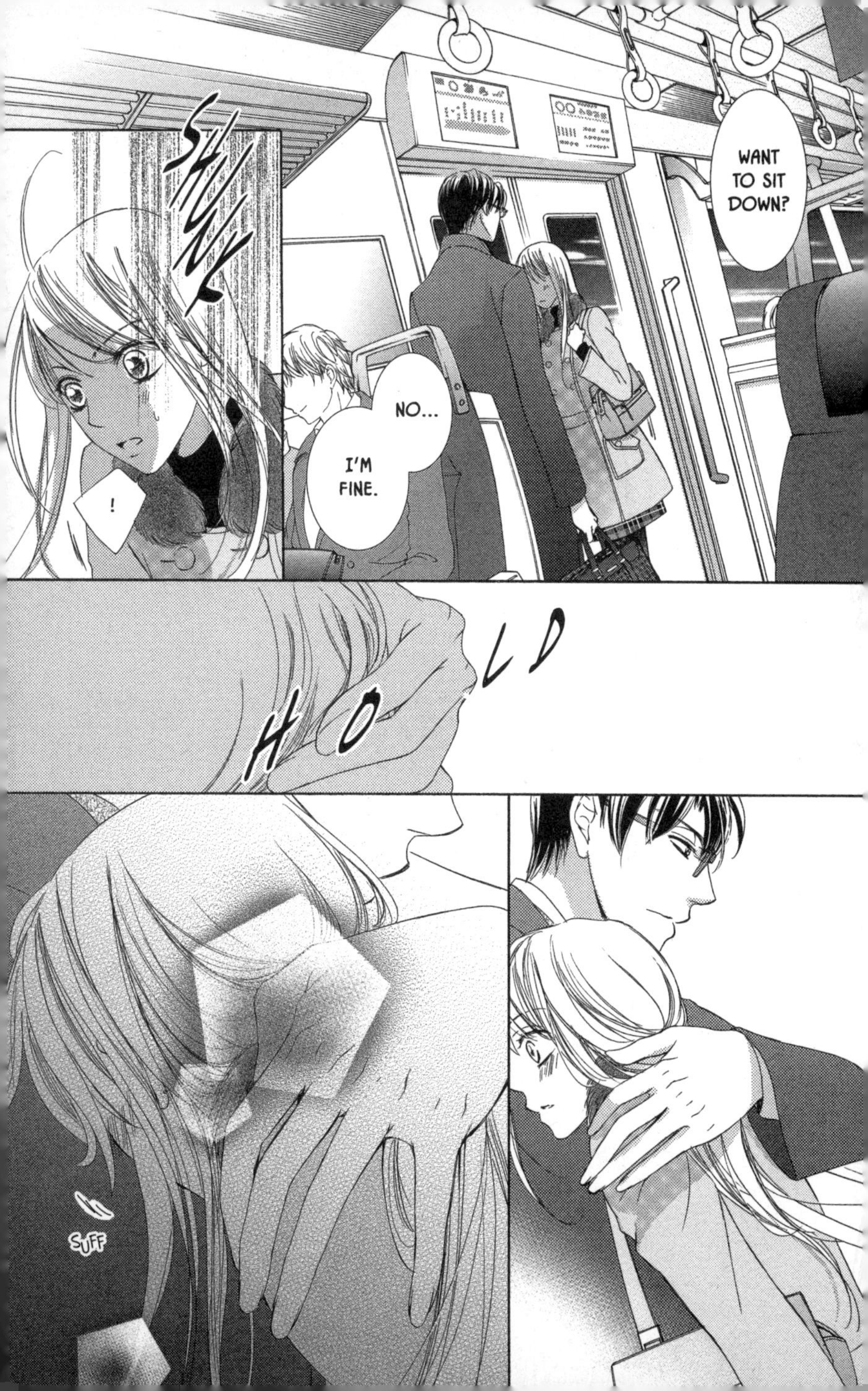
WANT TO SIT DOWN?
NO...
I'M FINE.
SHUNK
!
HOLD
SUFF

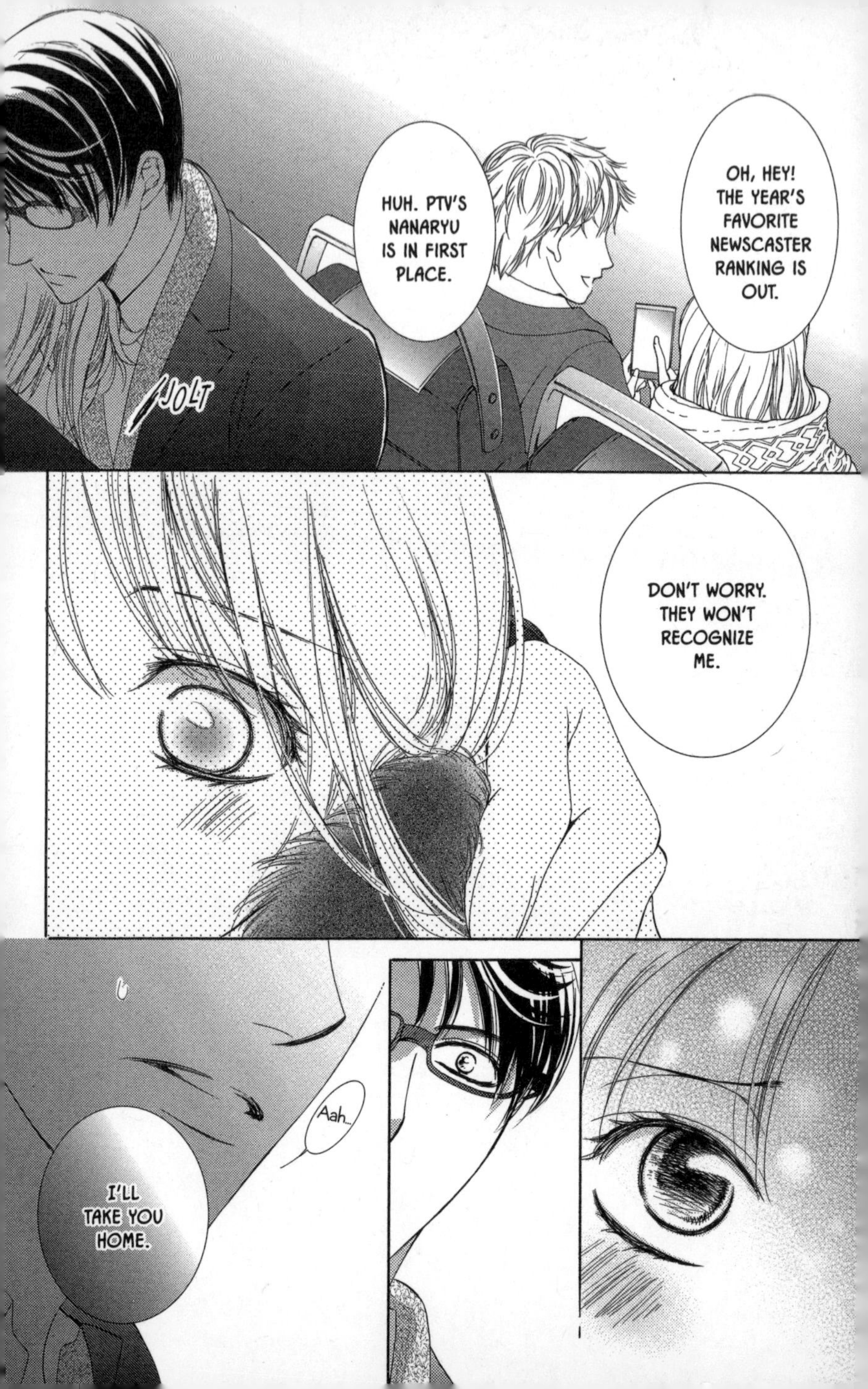
OH, HEY! THE YEAR'S FAVORITE NEWSCASTER RANKING IS OUT.
HUH. PTV'S NANARYU IS IN FIRST PLACE.
JOLT
DON'T WORRY. THEY WON'T RECOGNIZE ME.
Aah...
I'LL TAKE YOU HOME.

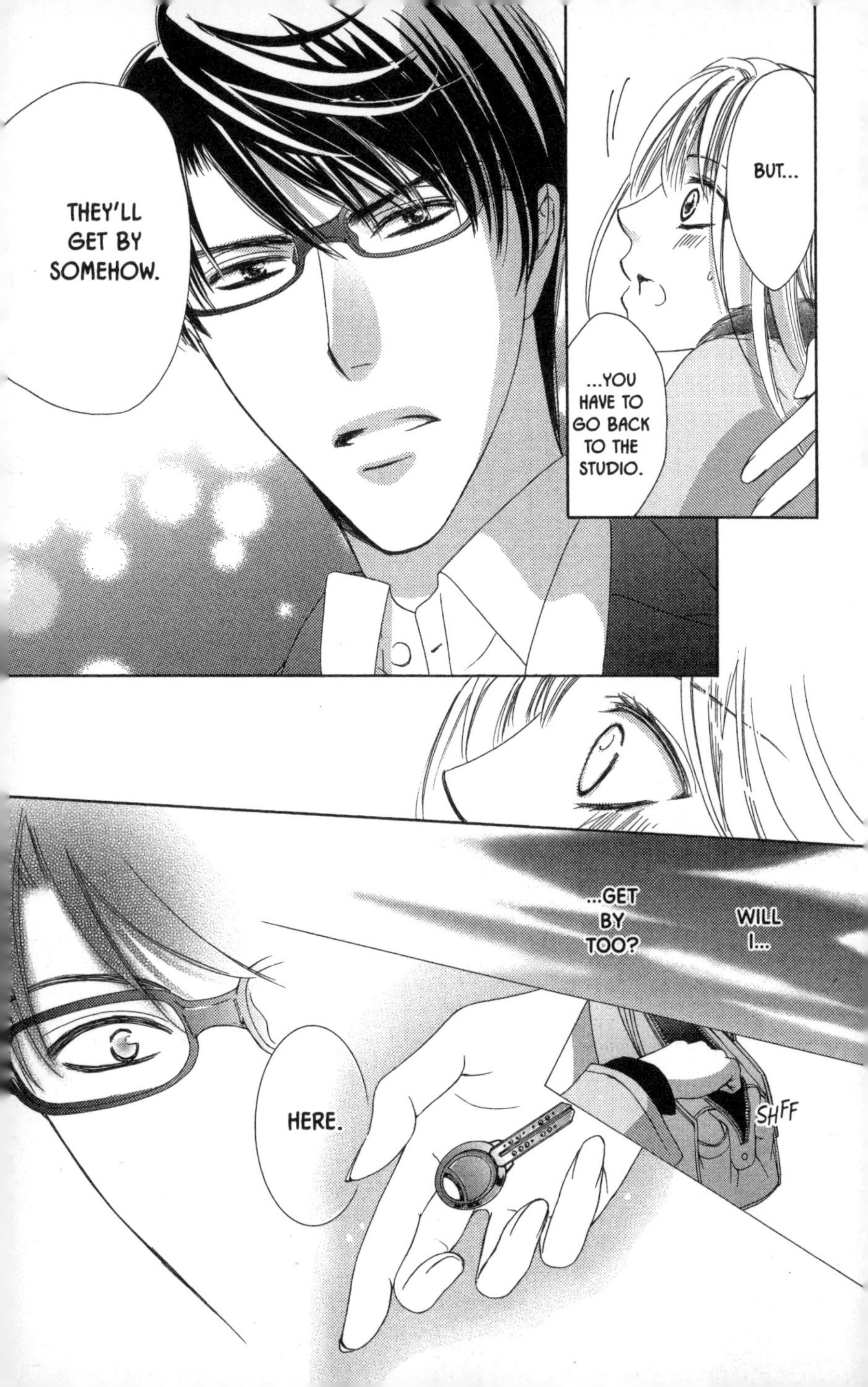
BUT...
...YOU HAVE TO GO BACK TO THE STUDIO.
THEY'LL GET BY SOMEHOW.
WILL I...
...GET BY TOO?
SHFF
HERE.

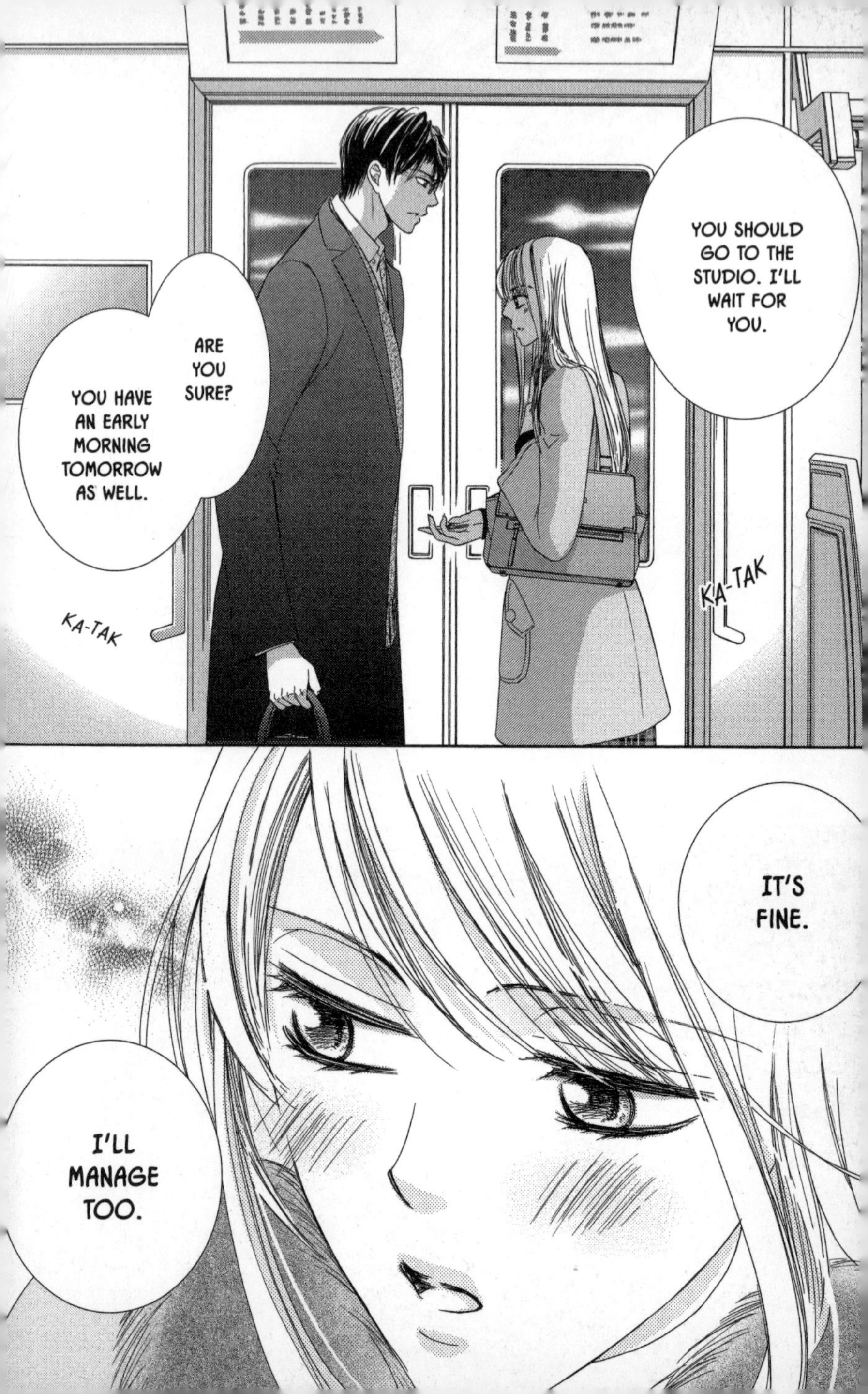
YOU SHOULD GO TO THE STUDIO. I'LL WAIT FOR YOU.
ARE YOU SURE?
YOU HAVE AN EARLY MORNING TOMORROW AS WELL.
KA-TAK
KA-TAK
IT'S FINE.
I'LL MANAGE TOO.

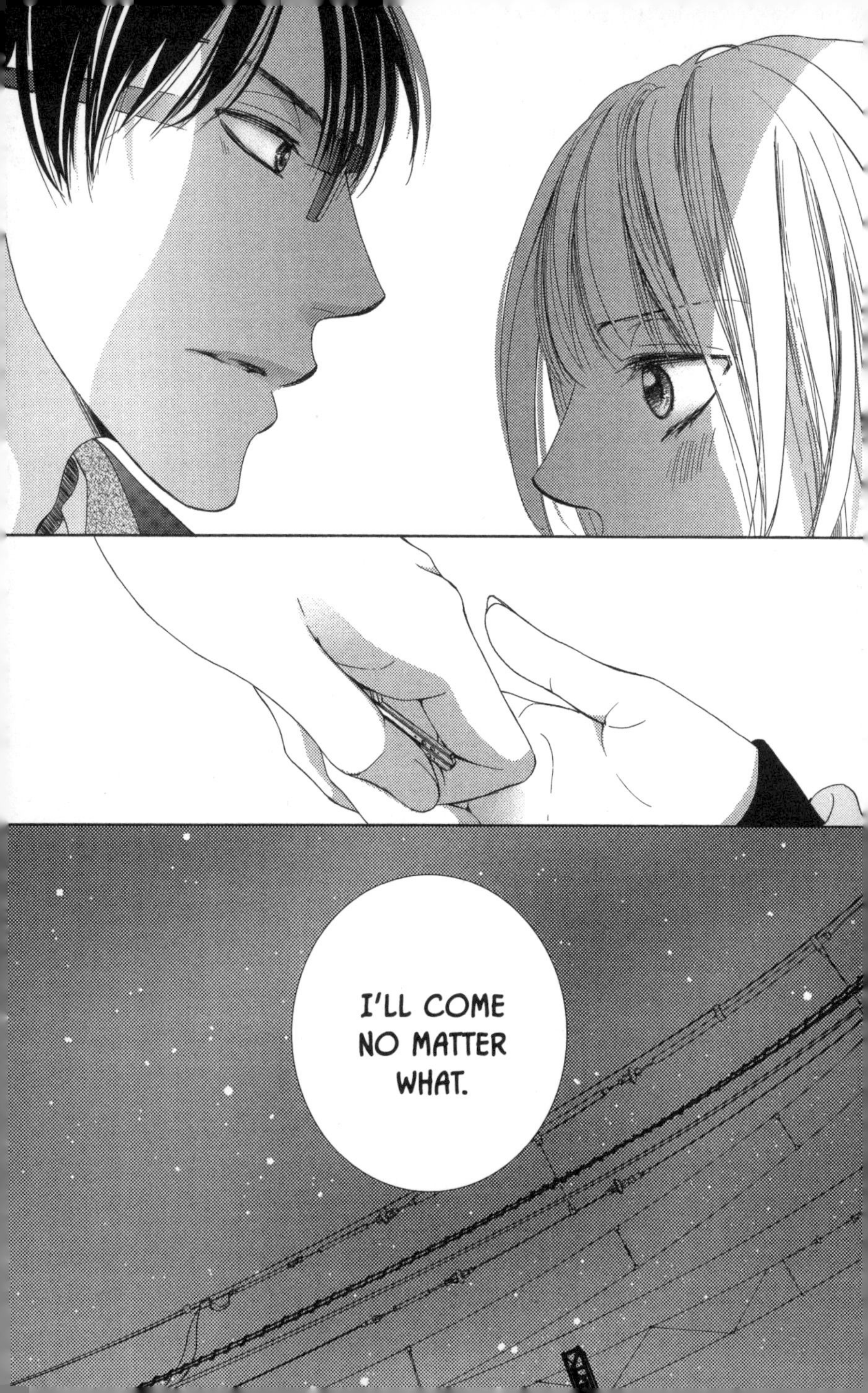
I'LL COME NO MATTER WHAT.

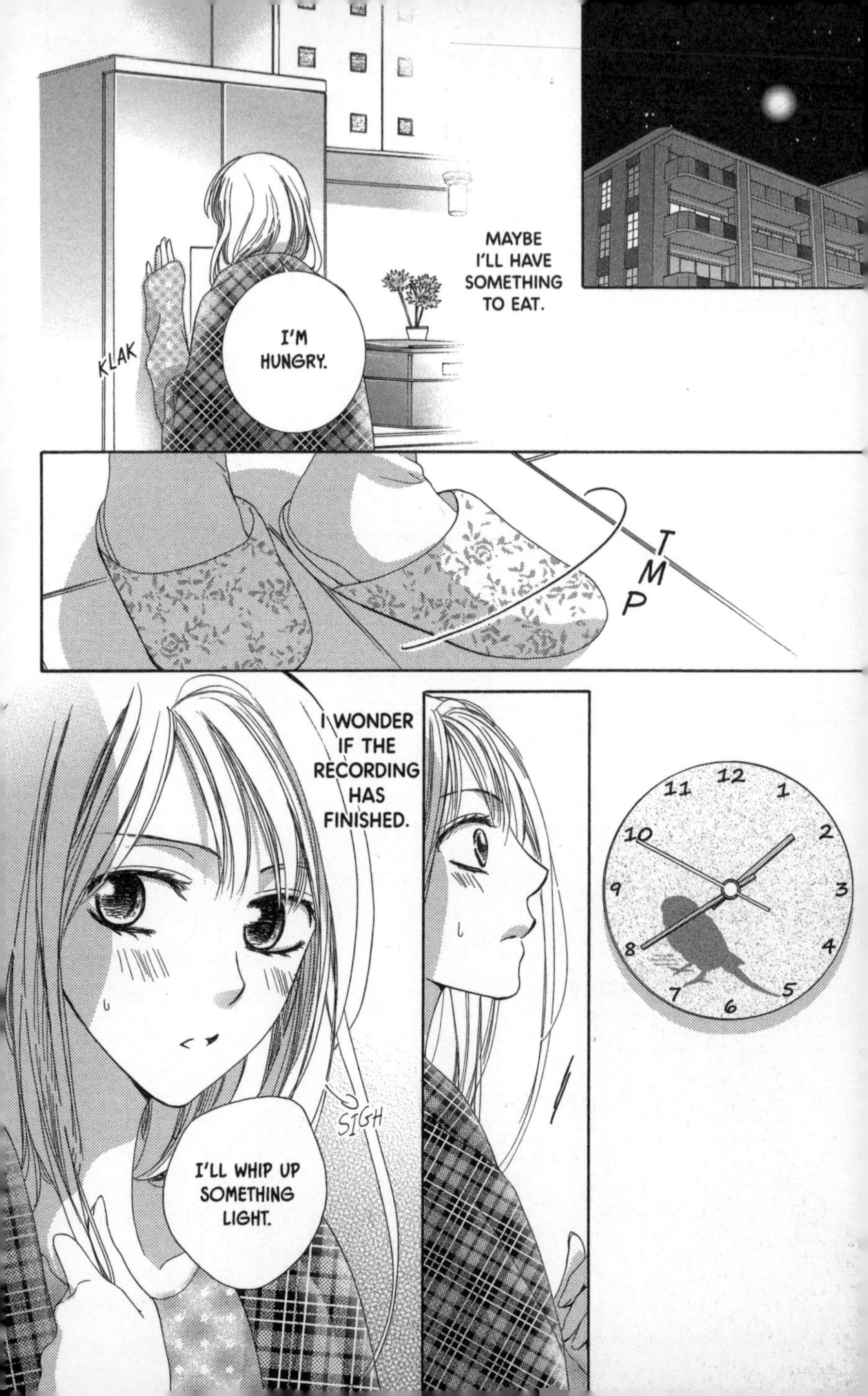
MAYBE I'LL HAVE SOMETHING TO EAT.
I'M HUNGRY.
KLAK
TMP
I WONDER IF THE RECORDING HAS FINISHED.
SIGH
I'LL WHIP UP SOMETHING LIGHT.

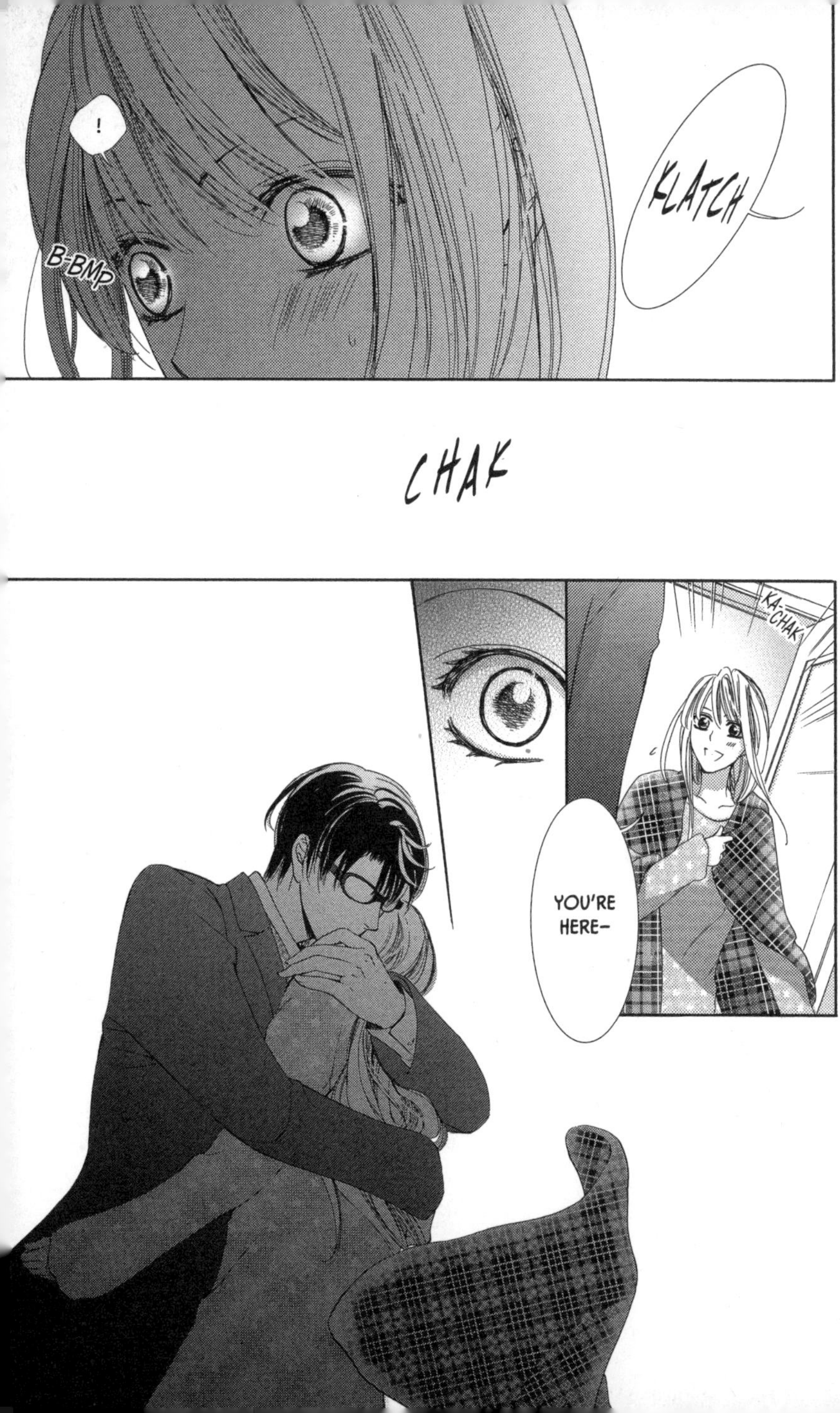
KLATCH
!
B-BMP
CHAK
KA-CHAK
YOU'RE HERE-

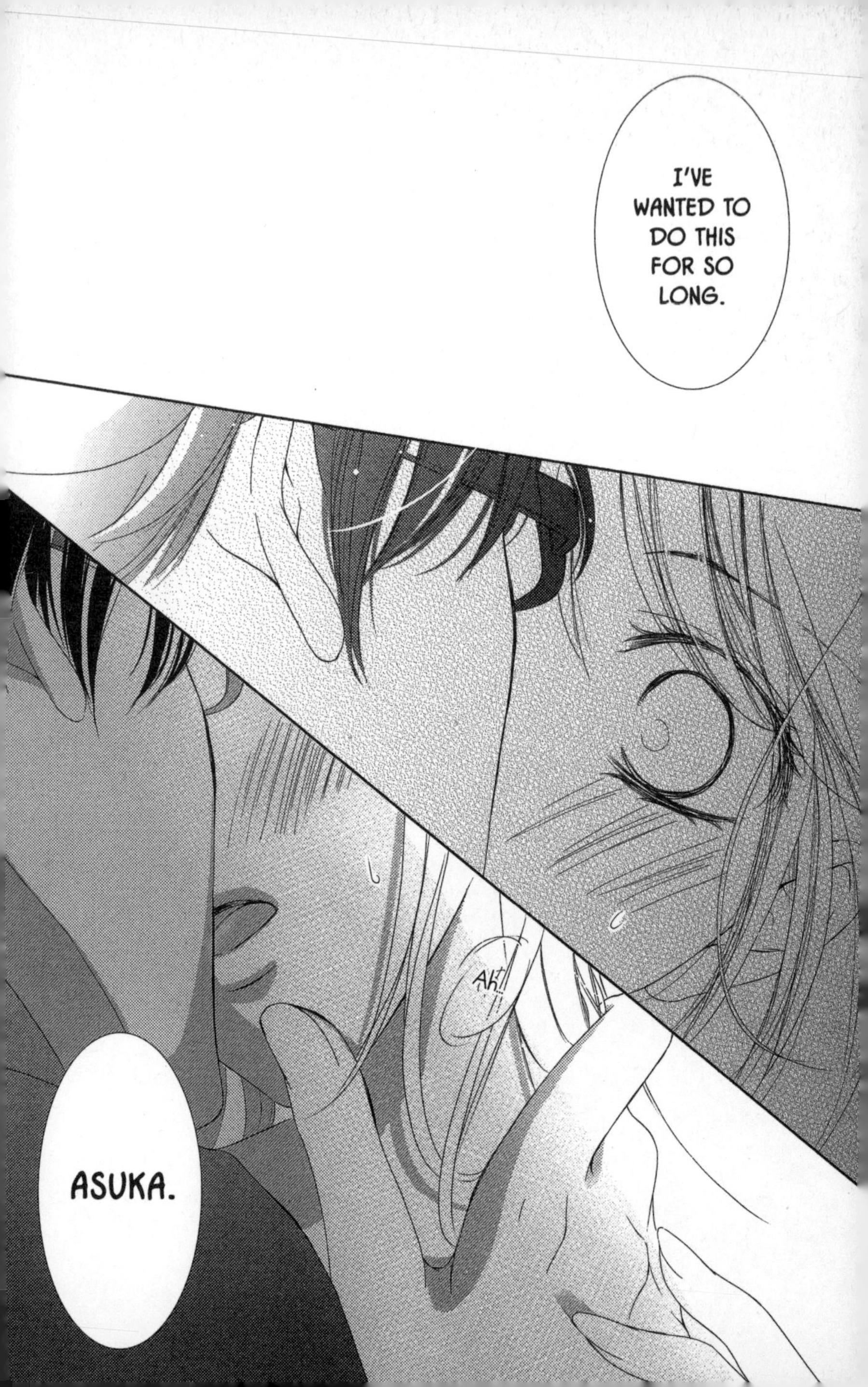
I'VE WANTED TO DO THIS FOR SO LONG.
Ah...
ASUKA.

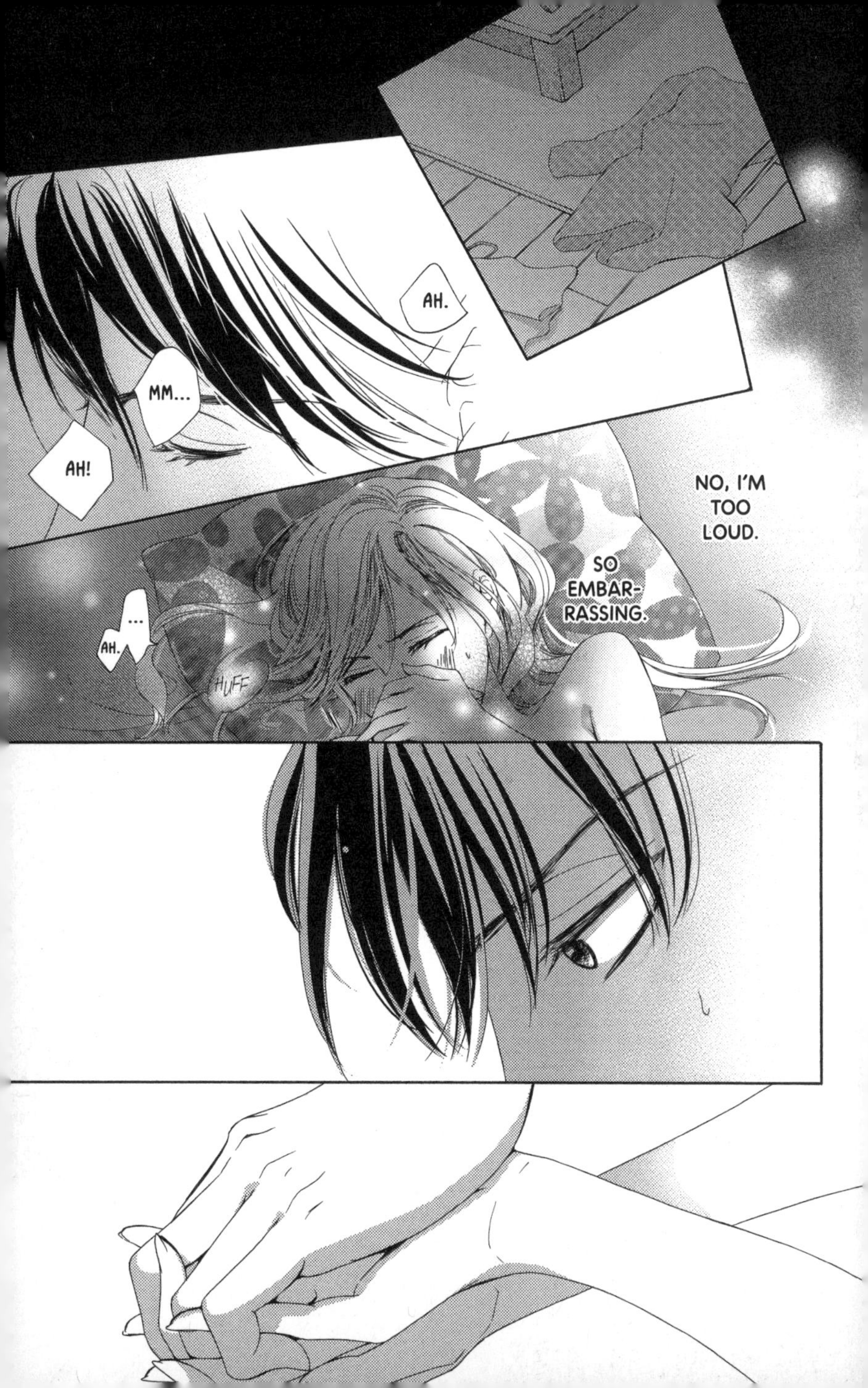
AH.
MM...
AH!
NO, I'M TOO LOUD.
SO EMBAR-RASSING.
...
AH.
HUFF

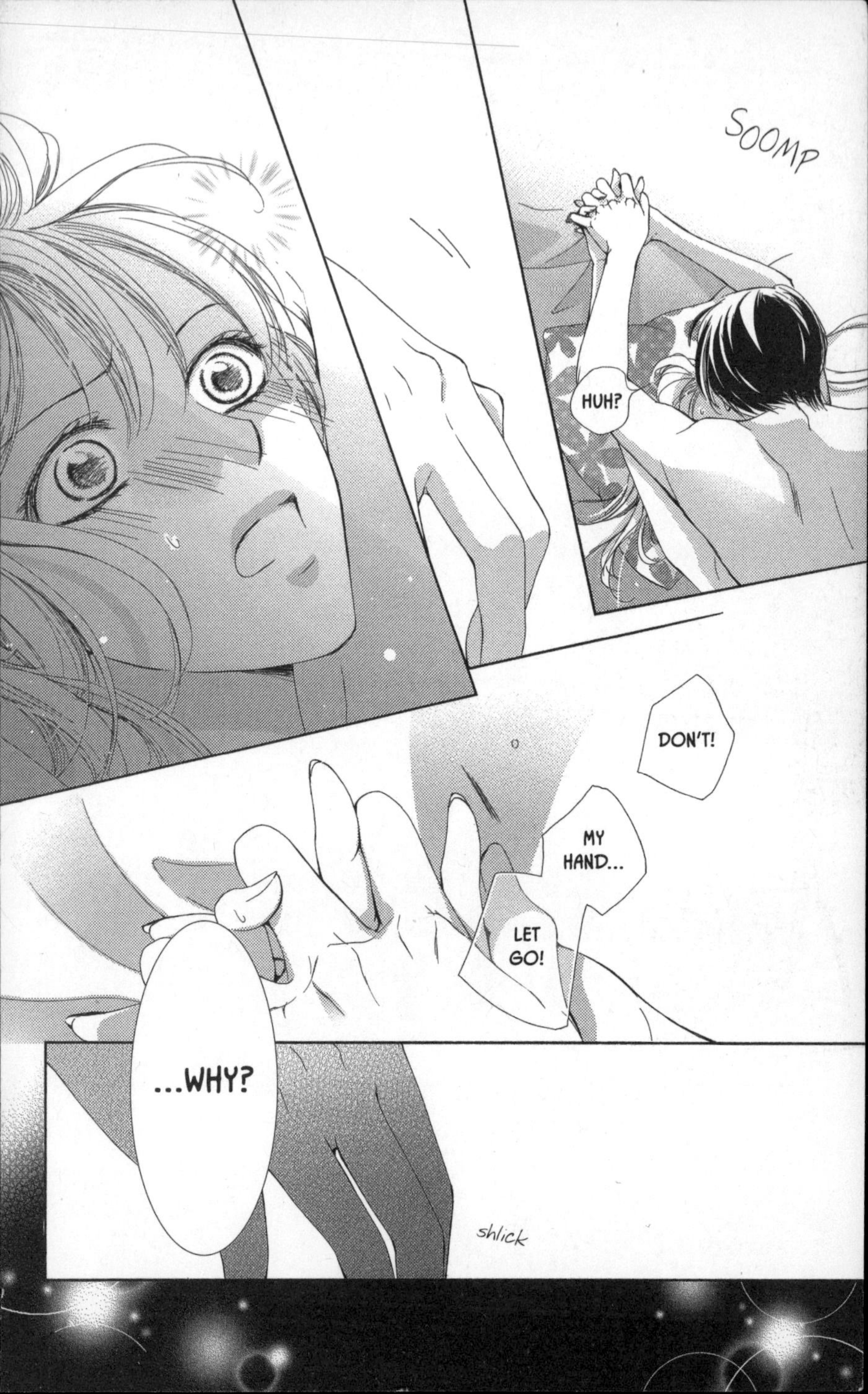
SOOMP
HUH?
DON'T!
MY HAND...
LET GO!
...WHY?
shlick

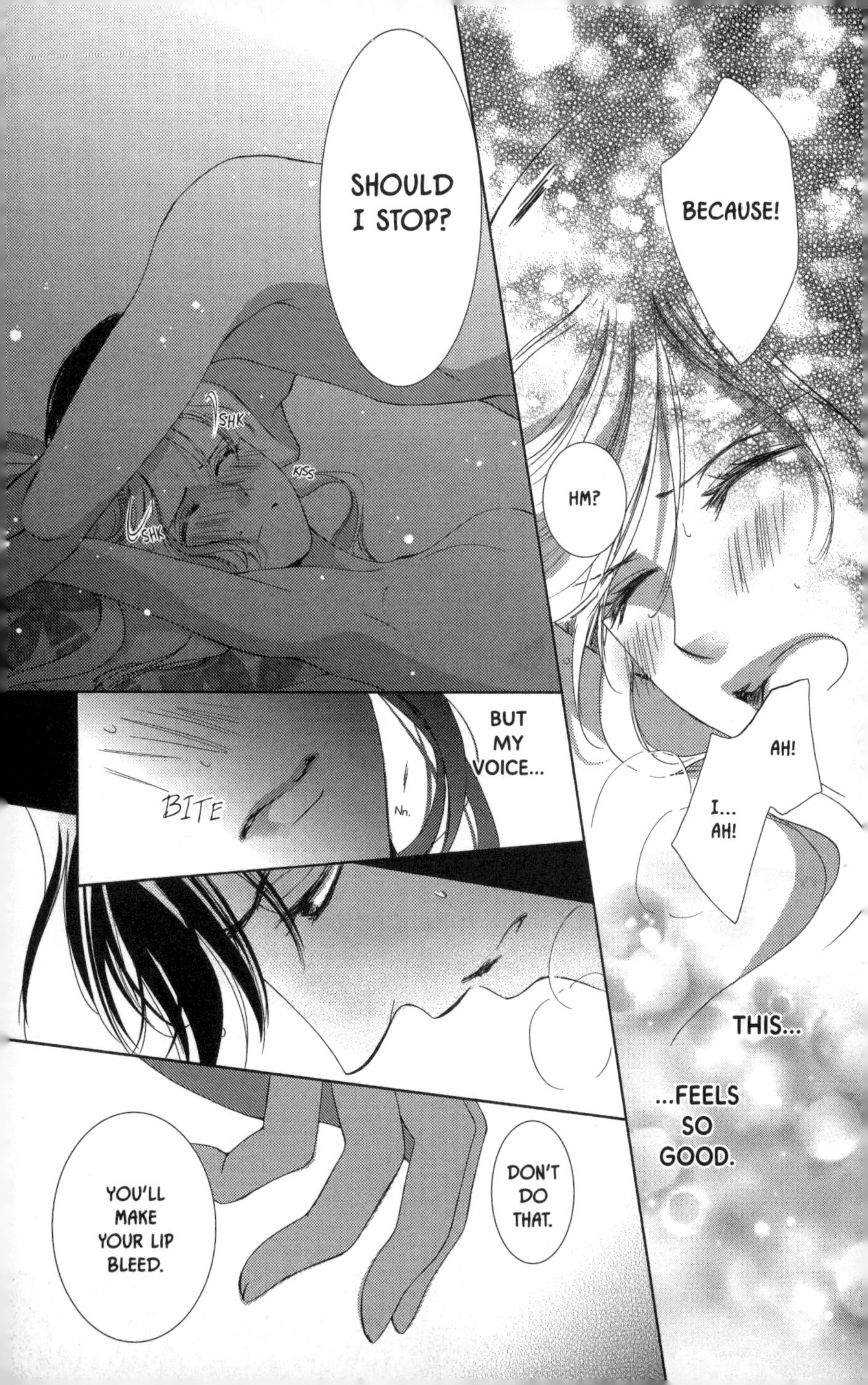
BECAUSE!
HM?
AH!
I... AH!
THIS...
...FEELS SO GOOD.
SHOULD I STOP?
SHK
KISS
SHK
BUT MY VOICE...
BITE
Nn.
DON'T DO THAT.
YOU'LL MAKE YOUR LIP BLEED.

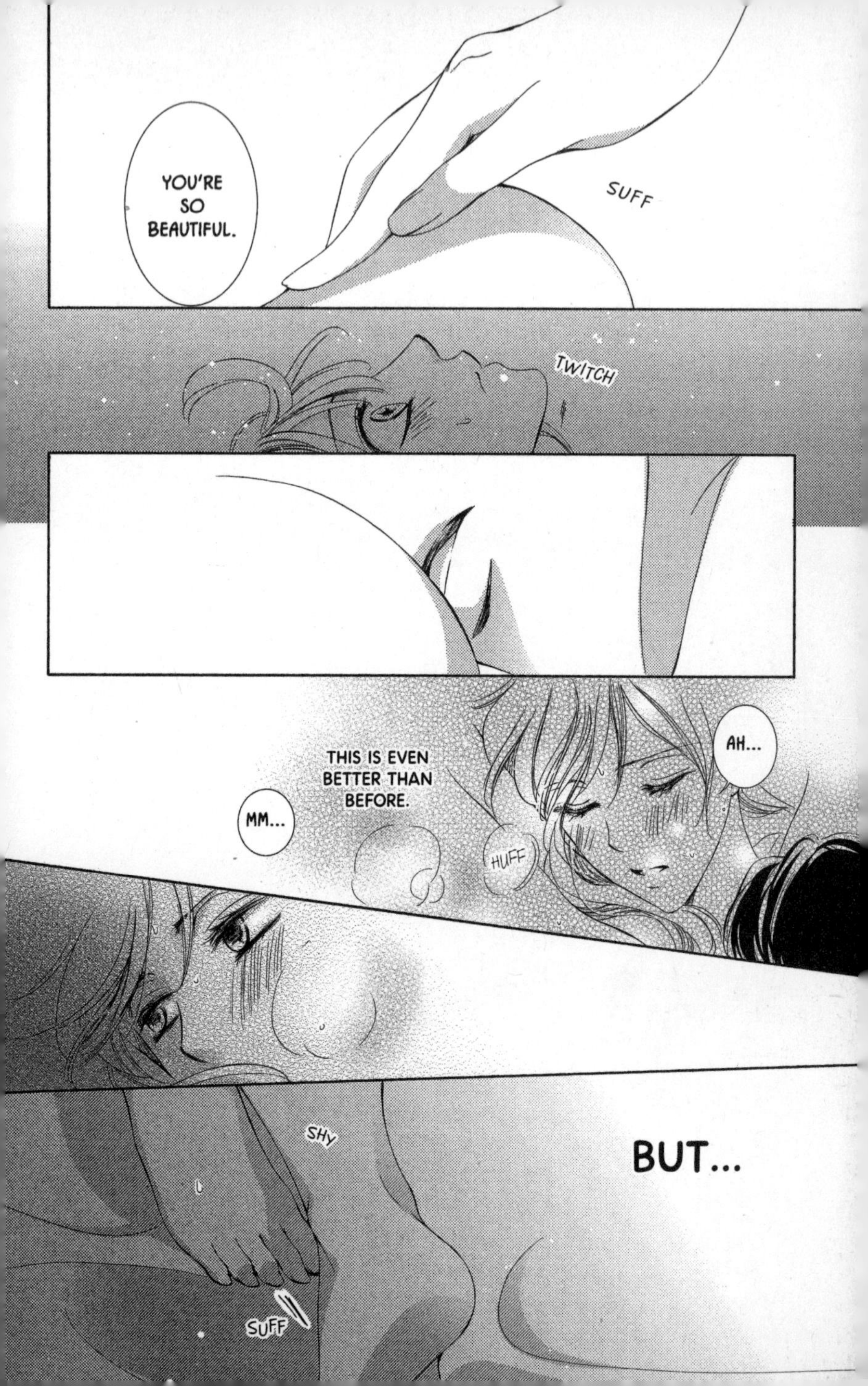
SUFF
YOU'RE SO BEAUTIFUL.
TWITCH
AH...
HUFF
THIS IS EVEN BETTER THAN BEFORE.
MM...
BUT...
SHY
SUFF

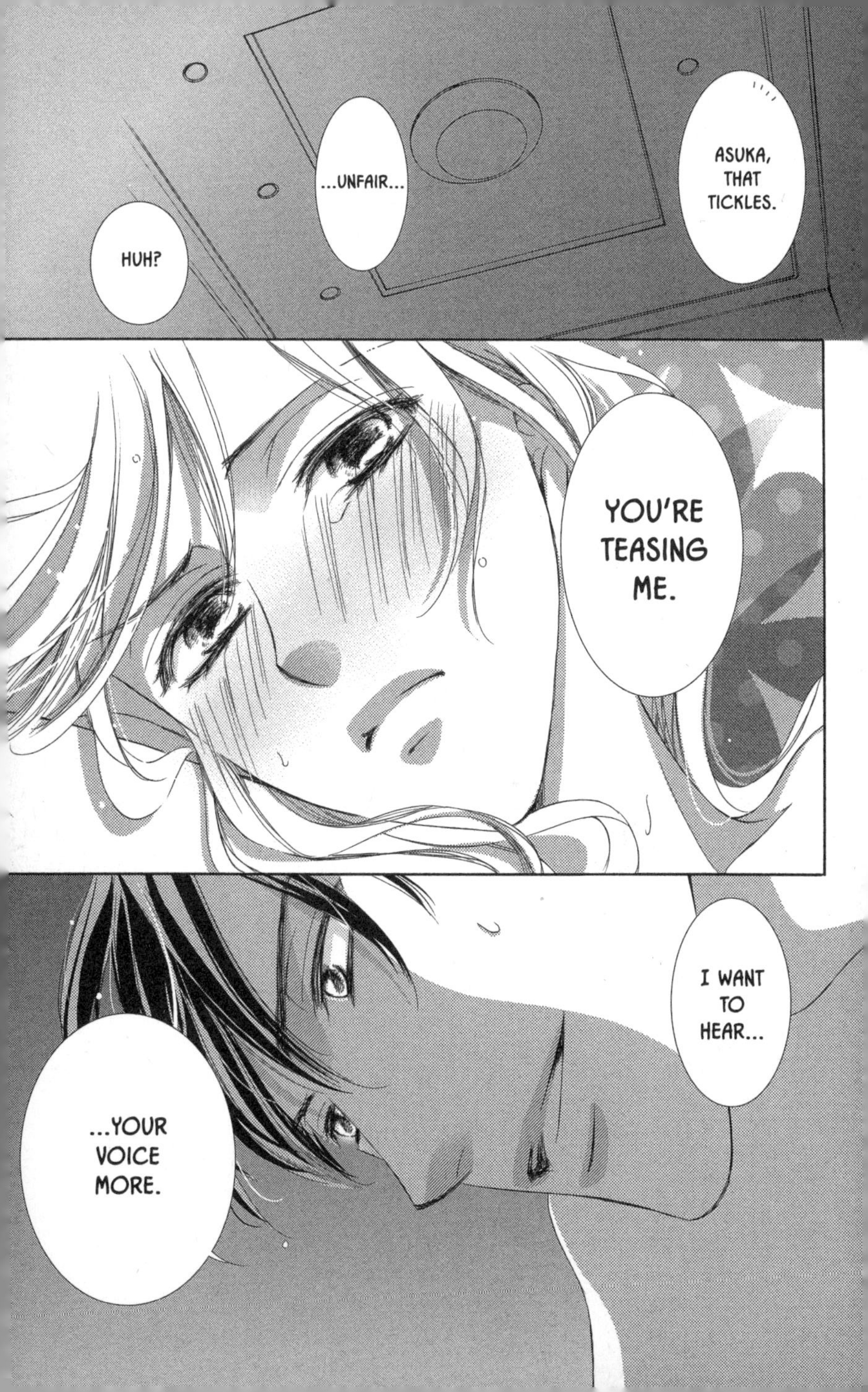
ASUKA, THAT TICKLES.
...UNFAIR...
HUH?
YOU'RE TEASING ME.
I WANT TO HEAR...
...YOUR VOICE MORE.

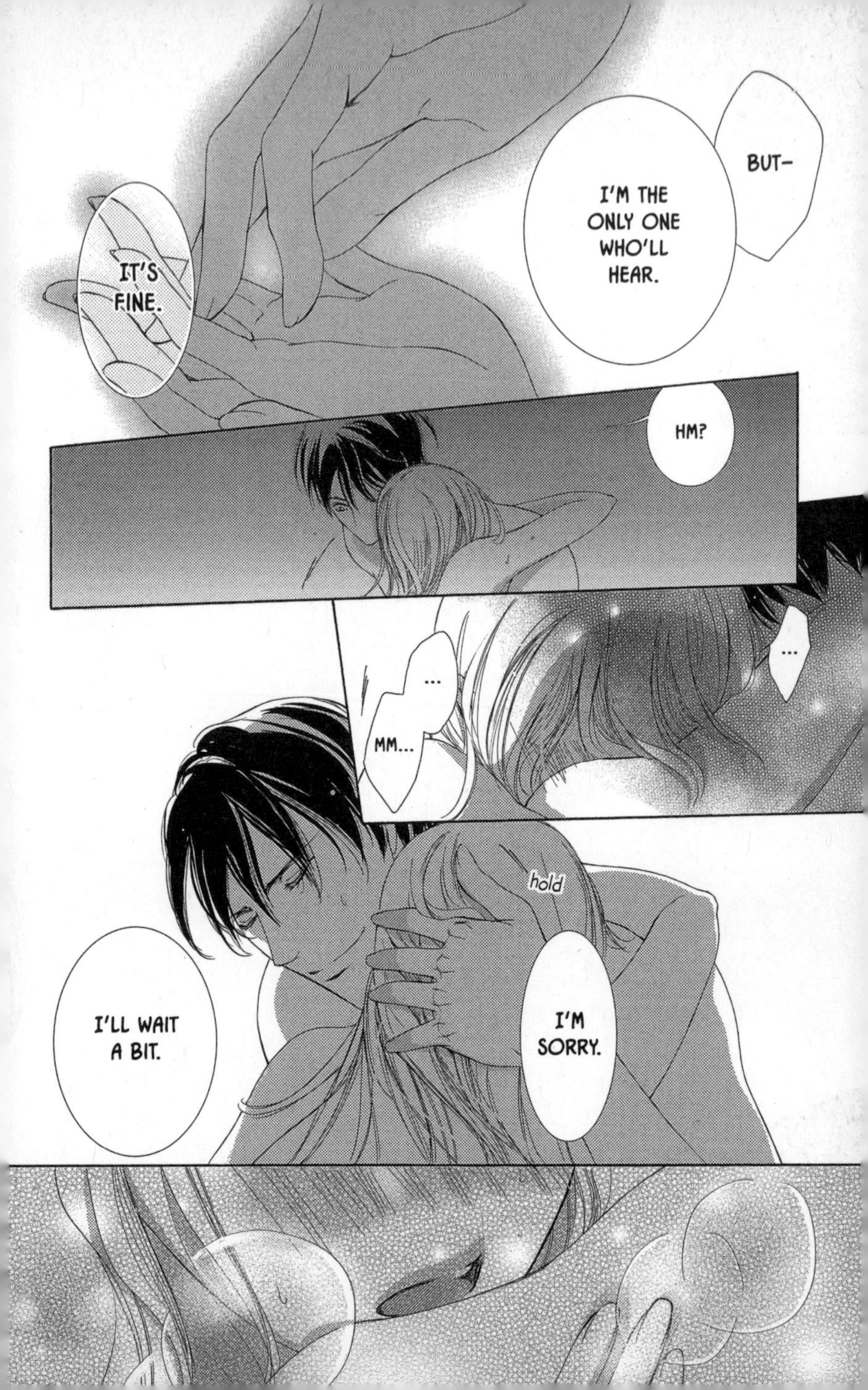
BUT–
I'M THE ONLY ONE WHO'LL HEAR.
IT'S FINE.
HM?
...
...
MM...
hold
I'M SORRY.
I'LL WAIT A BIT.

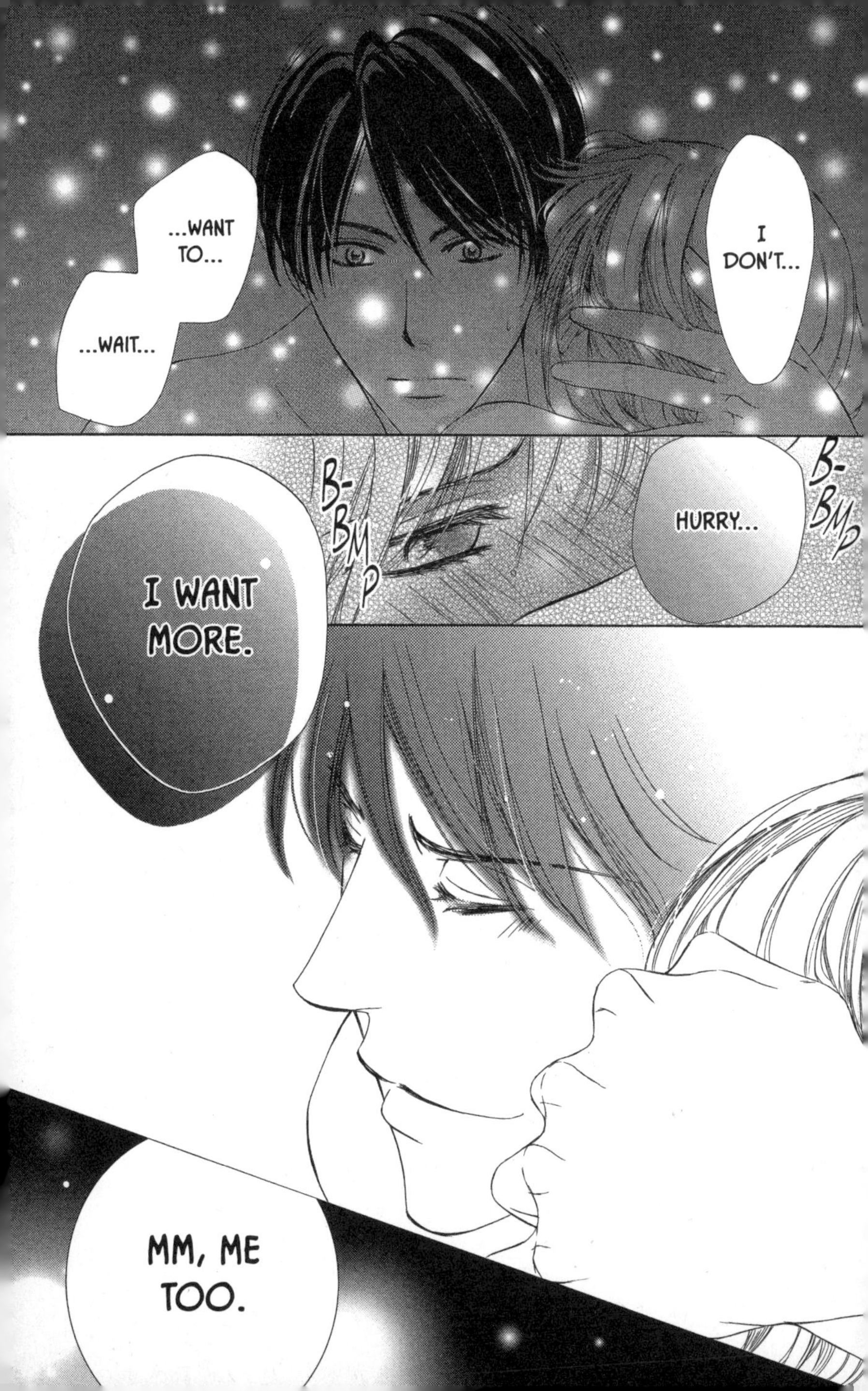
I DON'T...
...WANT TO...
...WAIT...
B-BMP
HURRY...
B-BMP
I WANT MORE.
MM, ME TOO.

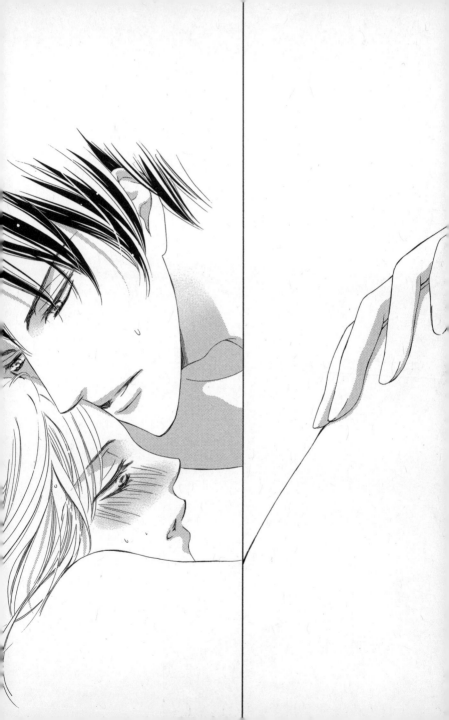

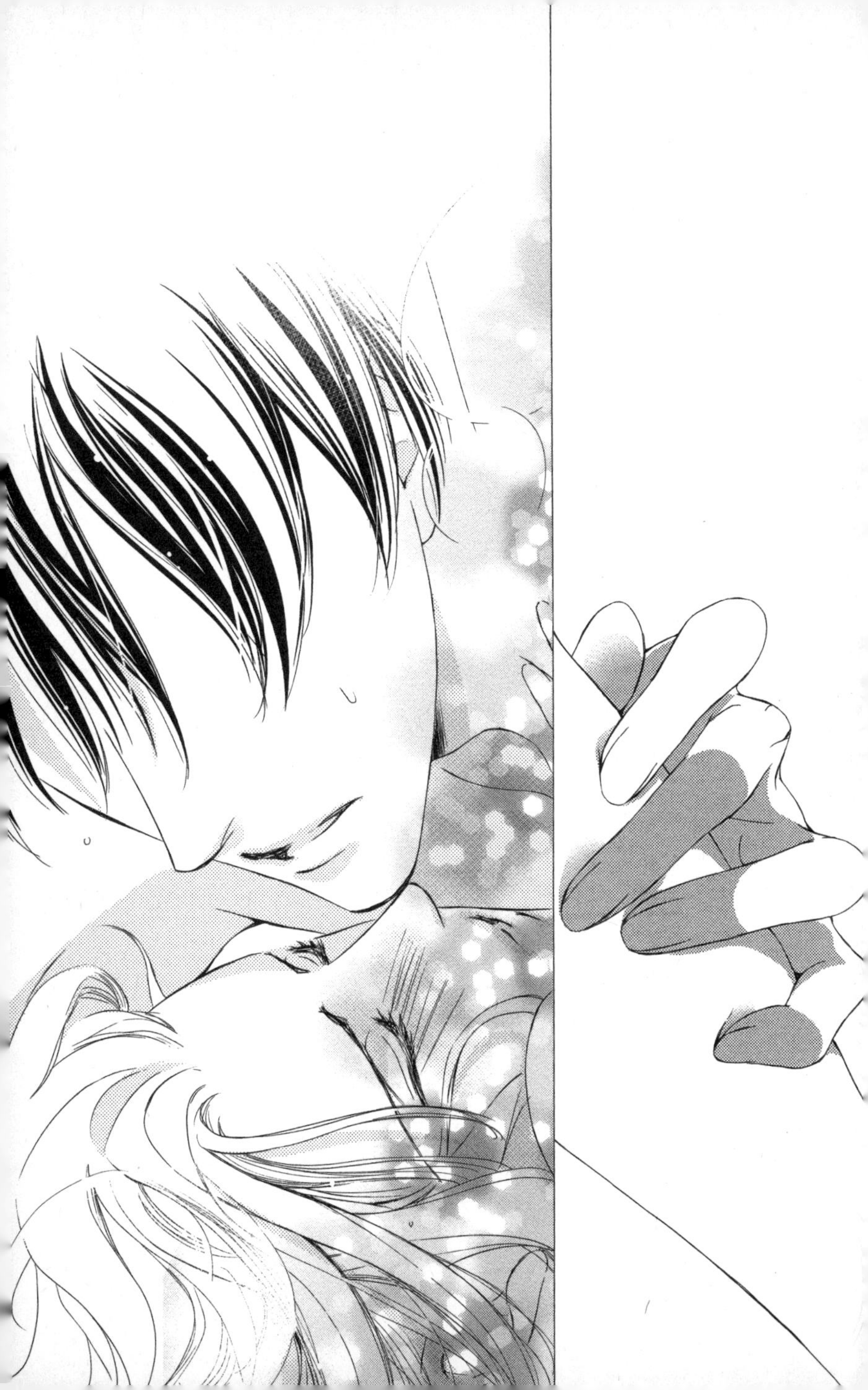

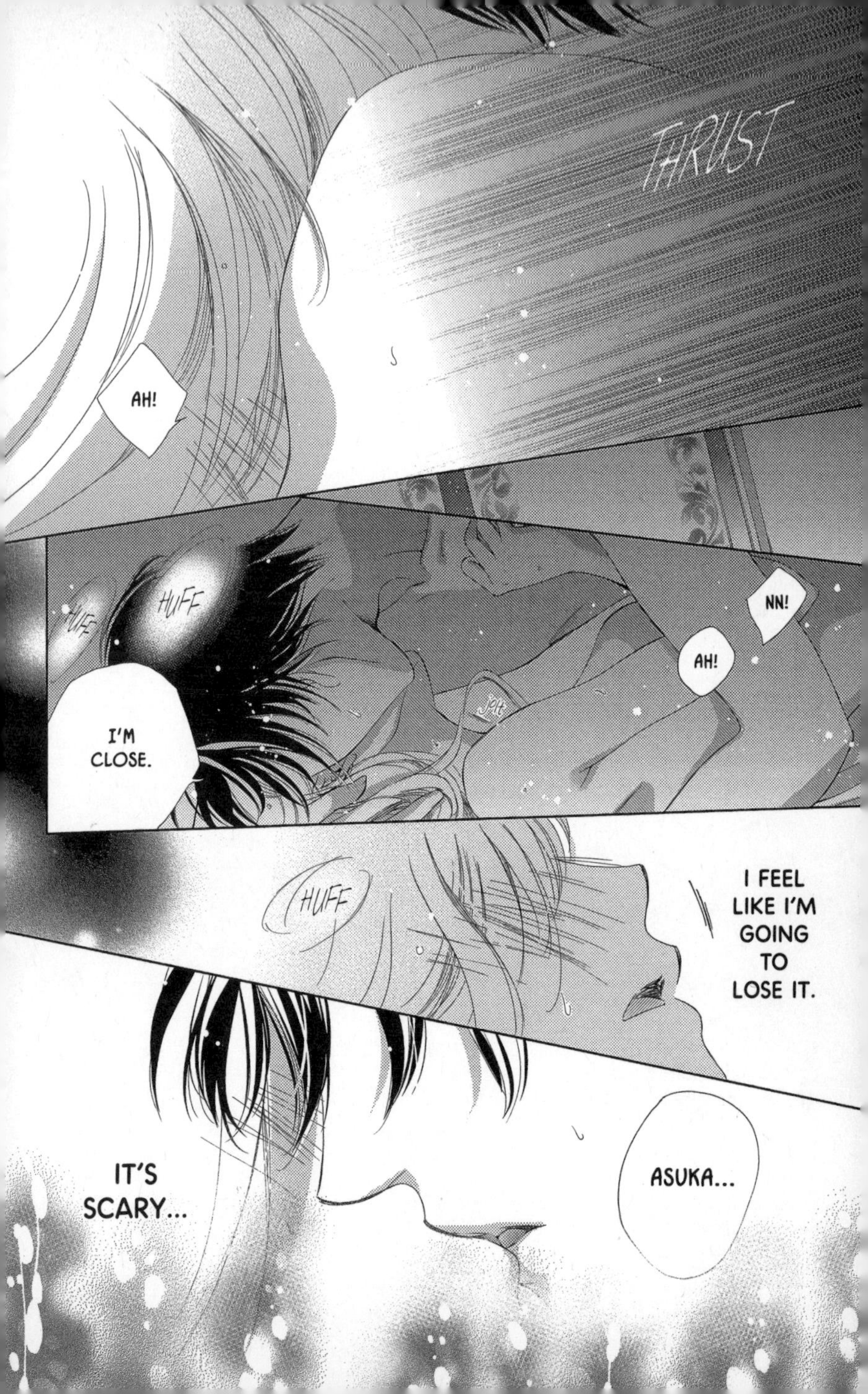
THRUST
AH!
NN!
AH!
jolt
HUFF
HUFF
I'M CLOSE.
I FEEL LIKE I'M GOING TO LOSE IT.
HUFF
ASUKA...
IT'S SCARY...

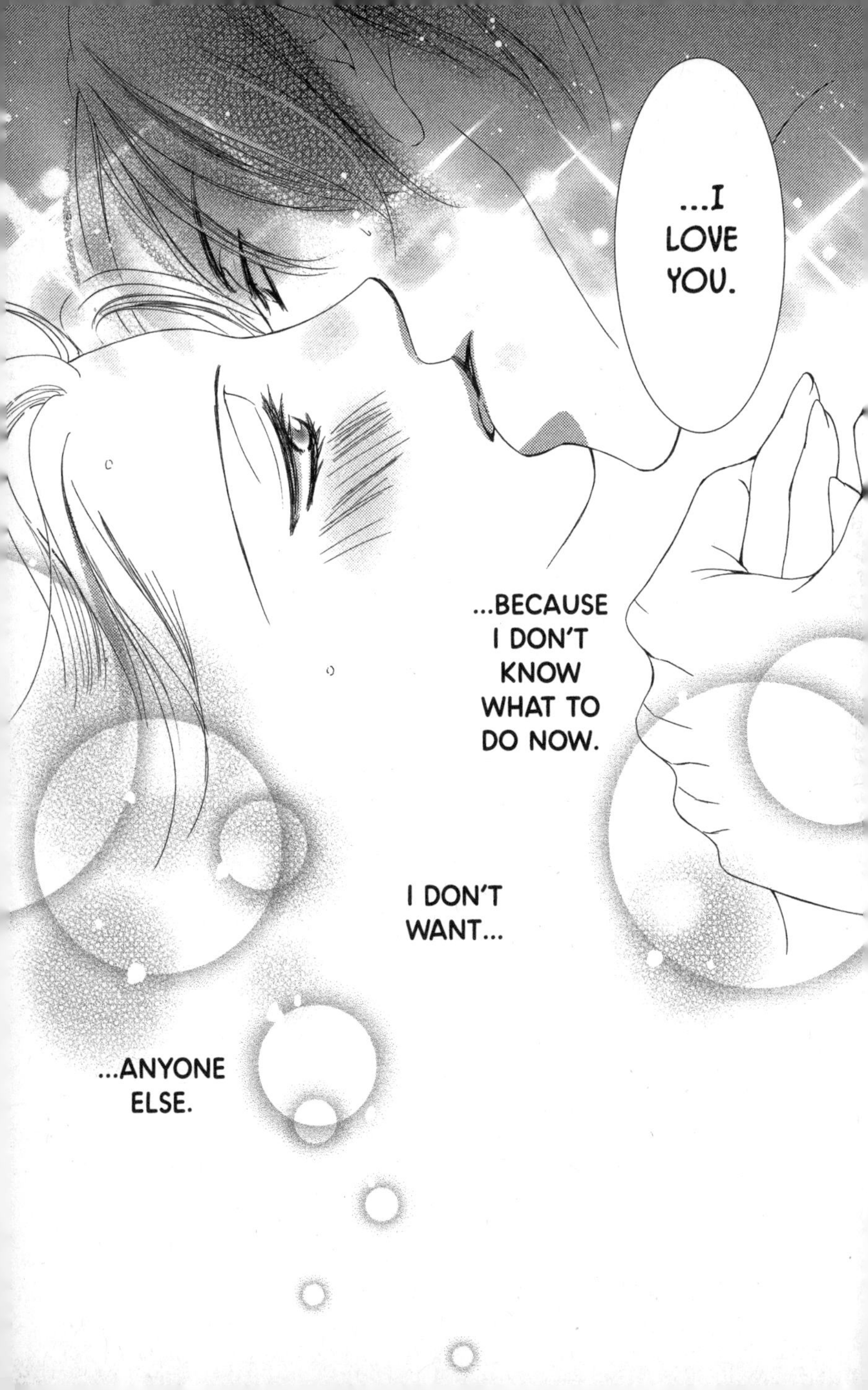
...I LOVE YOU.
...BECAUSE I DON'T KNOW WHAT TO DO NOW.
I DON'T WANT...
...ANYONE ELSE.

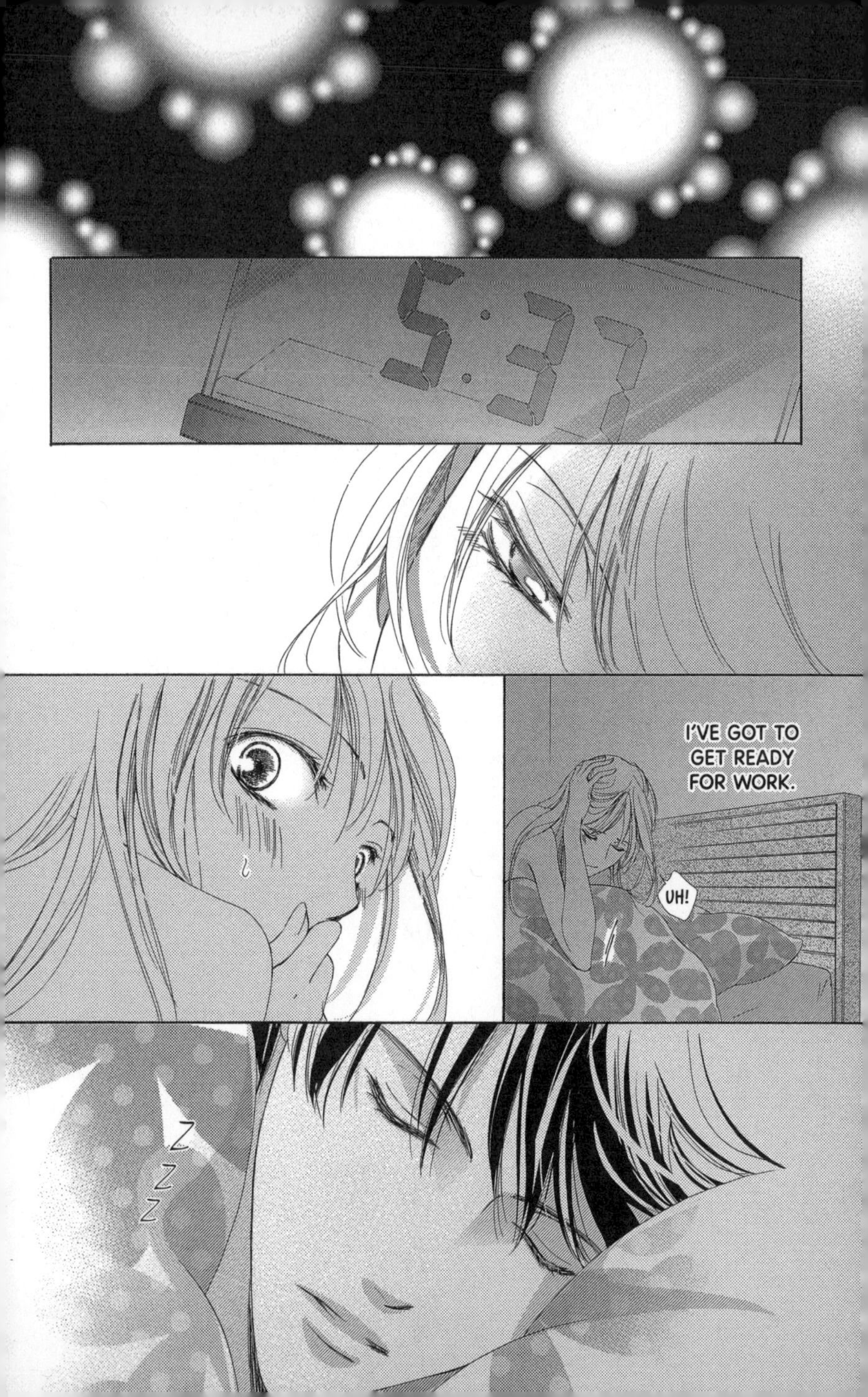
5:37
I'VE GOT TO GET READY FOR WORK.
UH!
Z
Z
Z

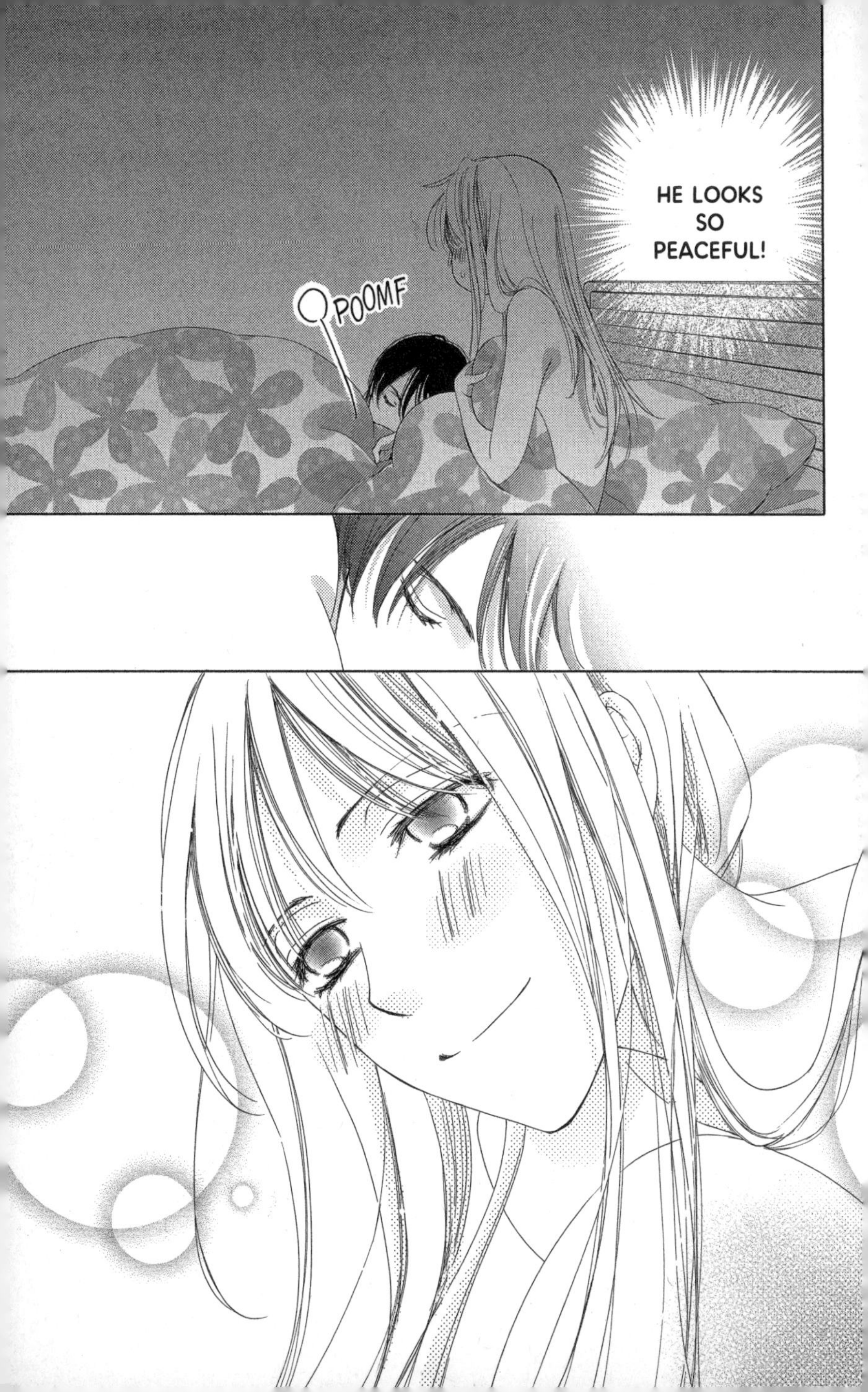
HE LOOKS SO PEACEFUL!
POOMF

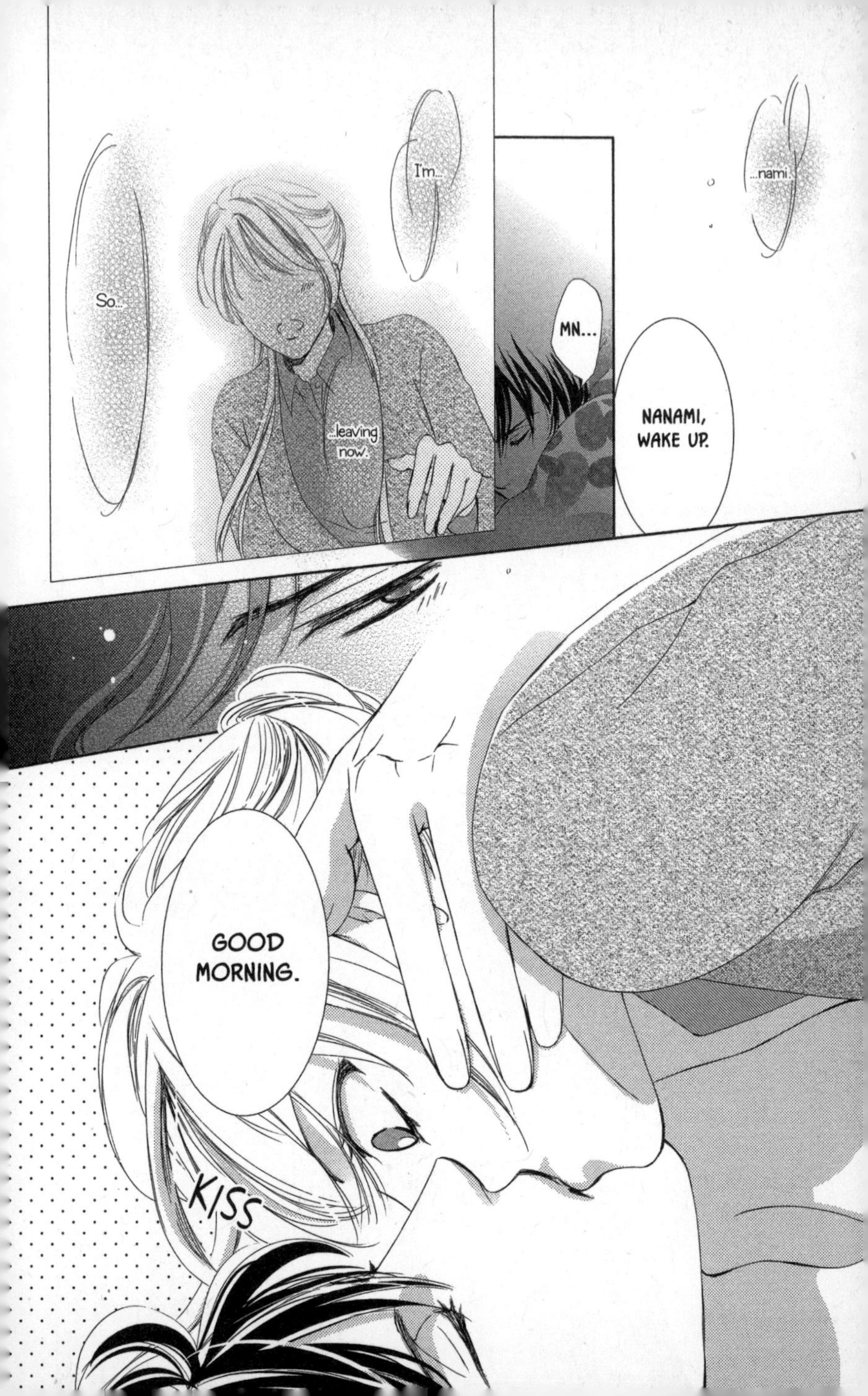

...nami.
NANAMI, WAKE UP.
MN...
I'm...
...leaving now.
So...
GOOD MORNING.
KISS

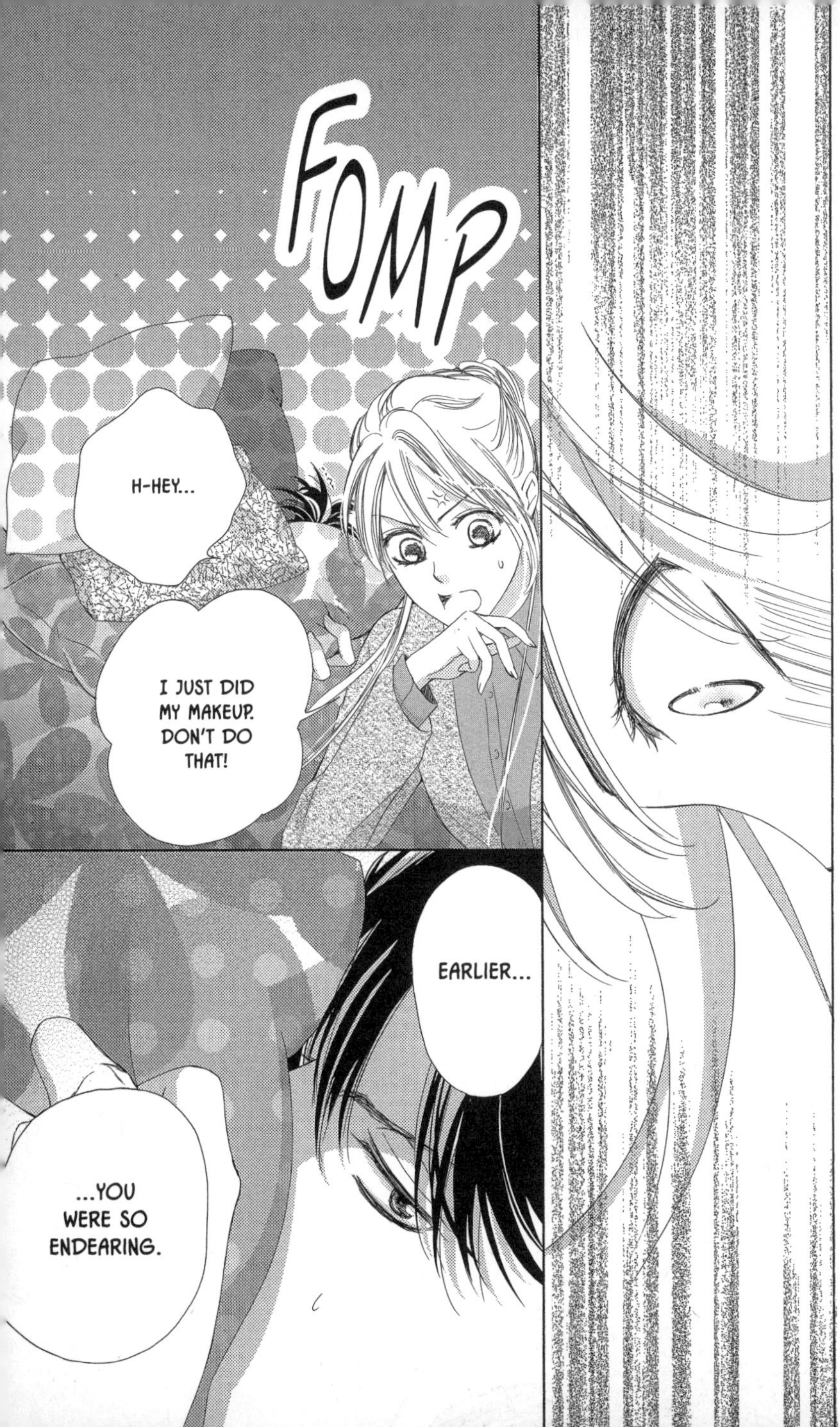
FOMP
H-HEY...
I JUST DID MY MAKEUP. DON'T DO THAT!
EARLIER...
...YOU WERE SO ENDEARING.

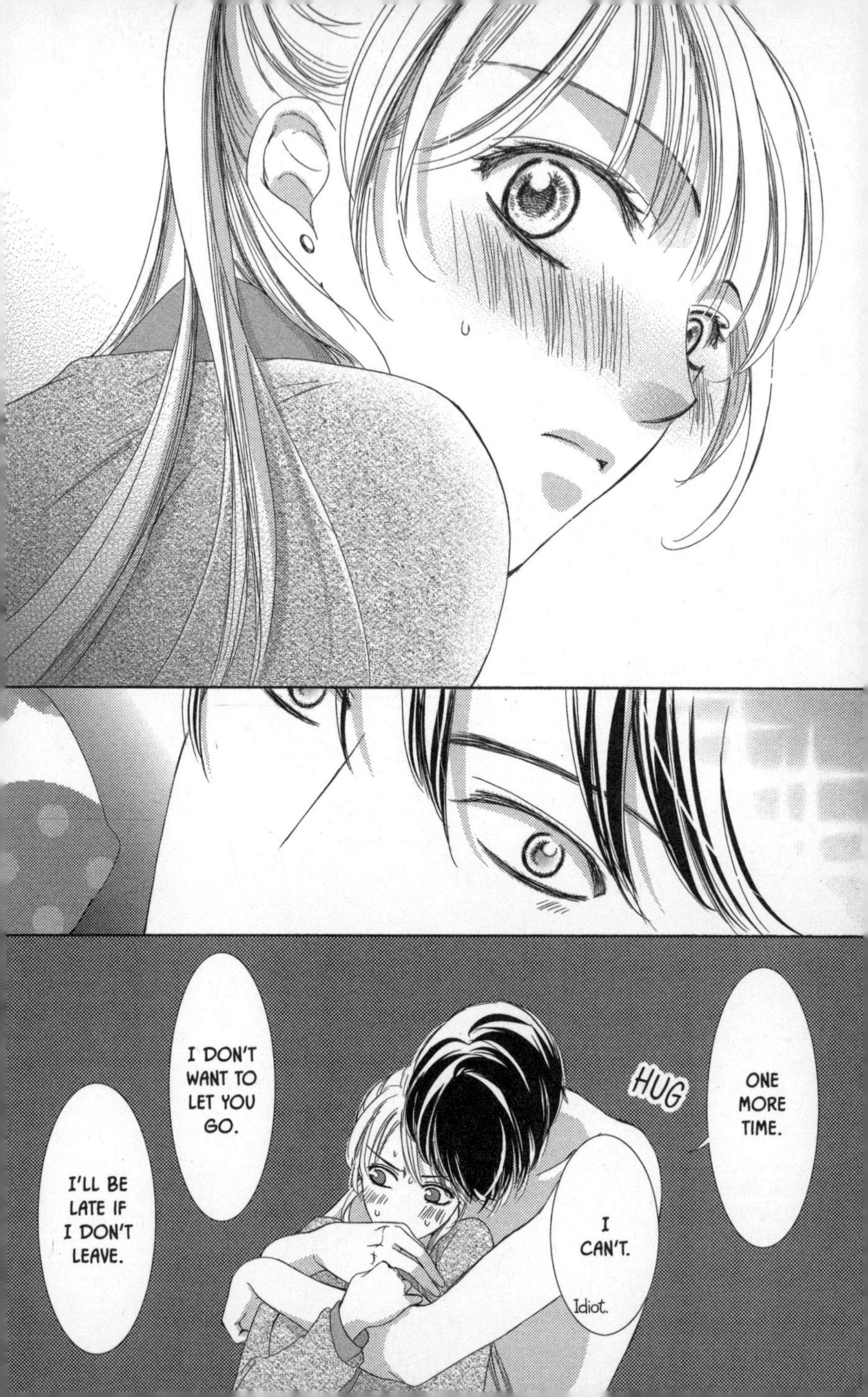
ONE MORE TIME.
HUG
I CAN'T.
Idiot.
I DON'T WANT TO LET YOU GO.
I'LL BE LATE IF I DON'T LEAVE.

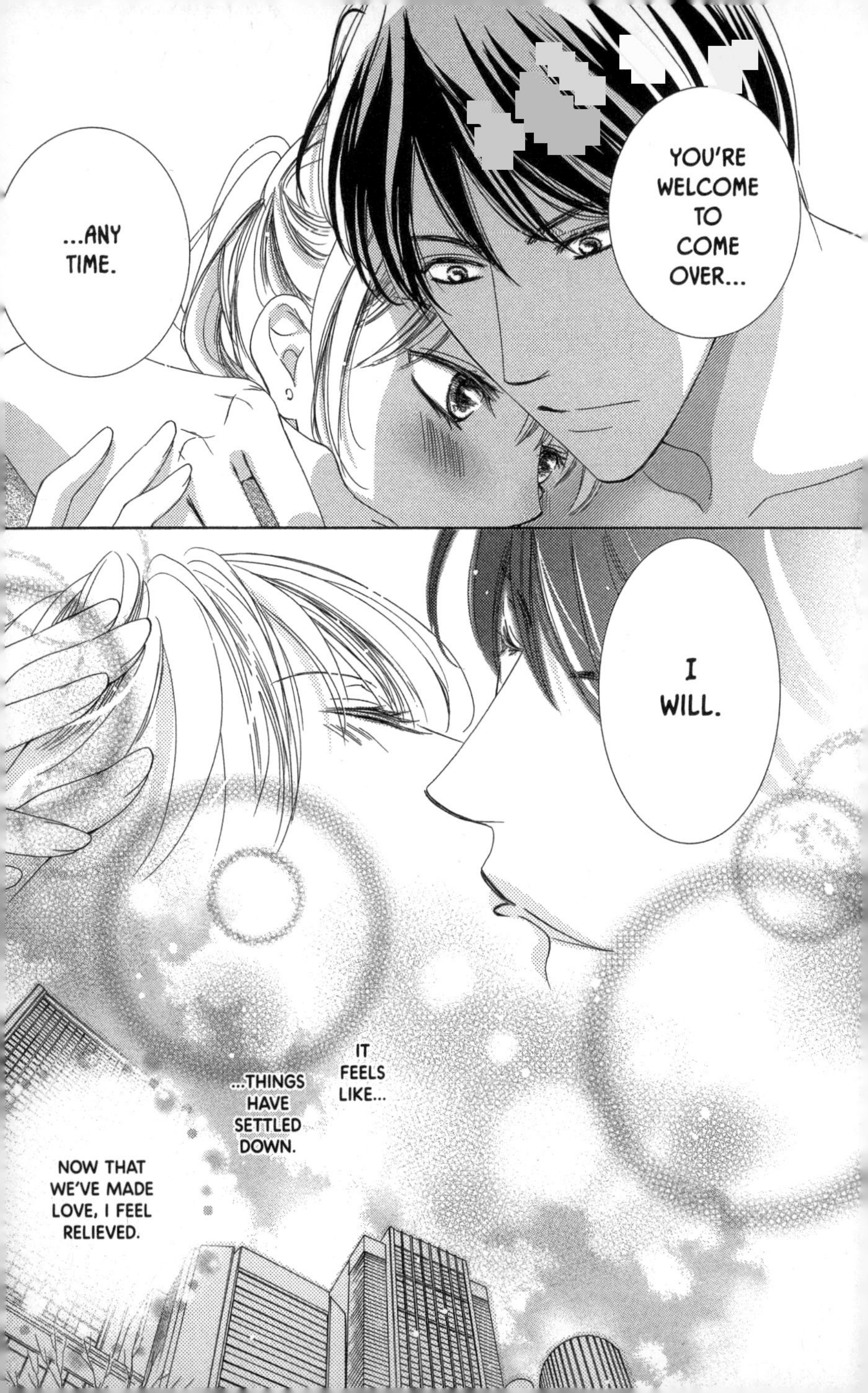
YOU'RE WELCOME TO COME OVER...
...ANY TIME.
I WILL.
IT FEELS LIKE...
...THINGS HAVE SETTLED DOWN.
NOW THAT WE'VE MADE LOVE, I FEEL RELIEVED.

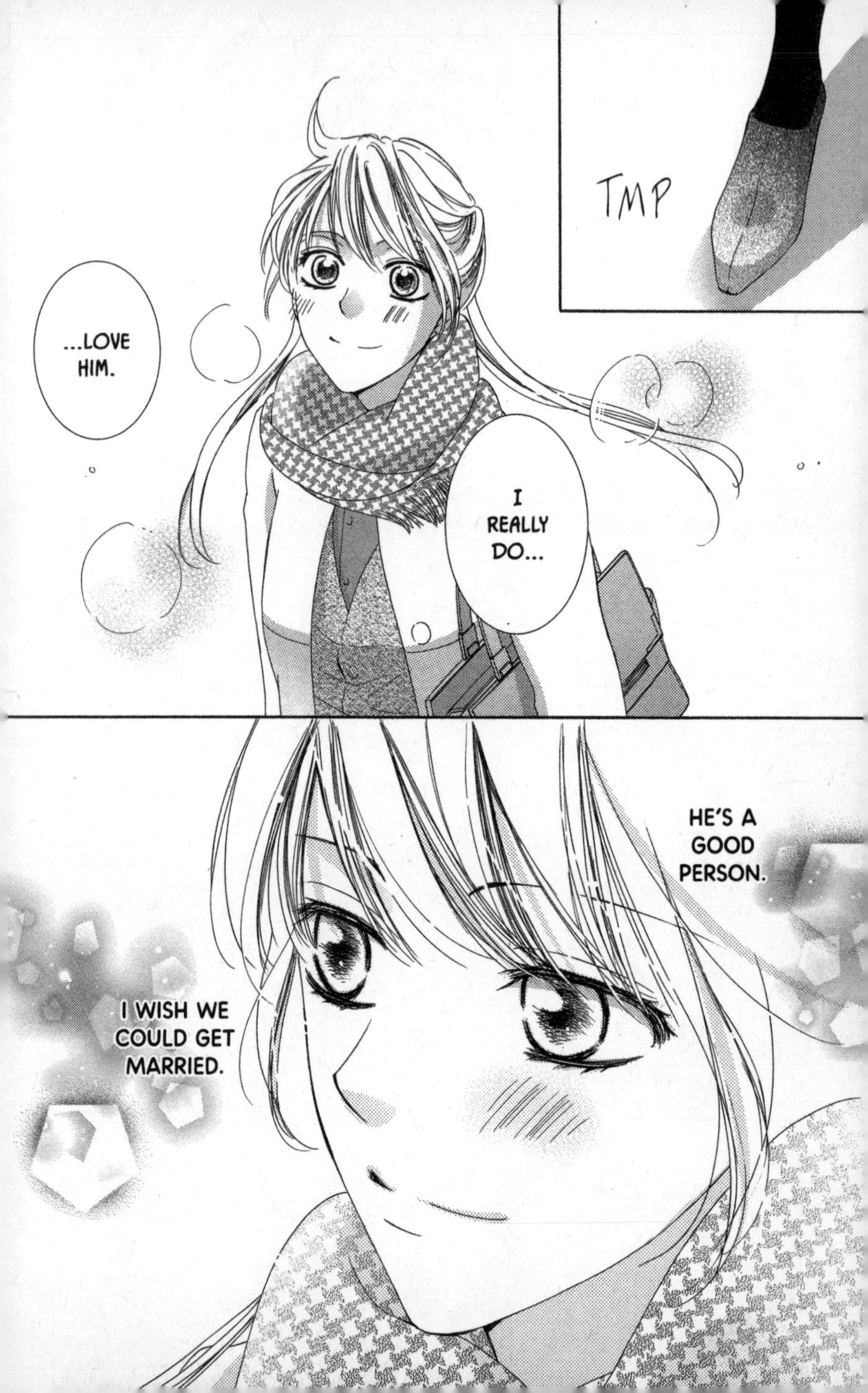
TMP
...LOVE HIM.
I REALLY DO...
HE'S A GOOD PERSON.
I WISH WE COULD GET MARRIED.

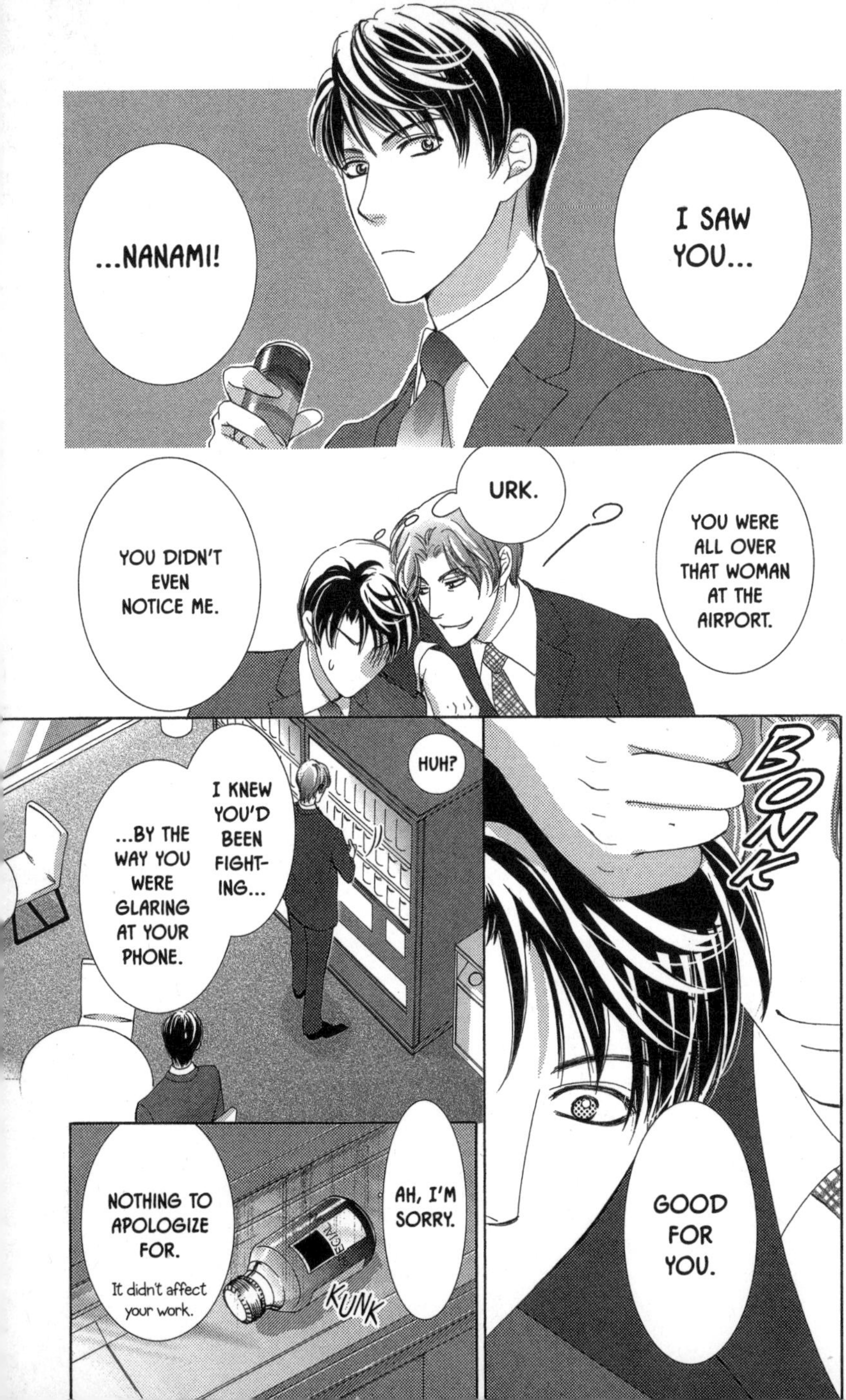
I SAW YOU...
...NANAMI!
YOU WERE ALL OVER THAT WOMAN AT THE AIRPORT.
URK.
YOU DIDN'T EVEN NOTICE ME.
BONK
GOOD FOR YOU.
HUH?
I KNEW YOU'D BEEN FIGHT-ING...
...BY THE WAY YOU WERE GLARING AT YOUR PHONE.
AH, I'M SORRY.
KUNK
NOTHING TO APOLOGIZE FOR.
It didn't affect your work.

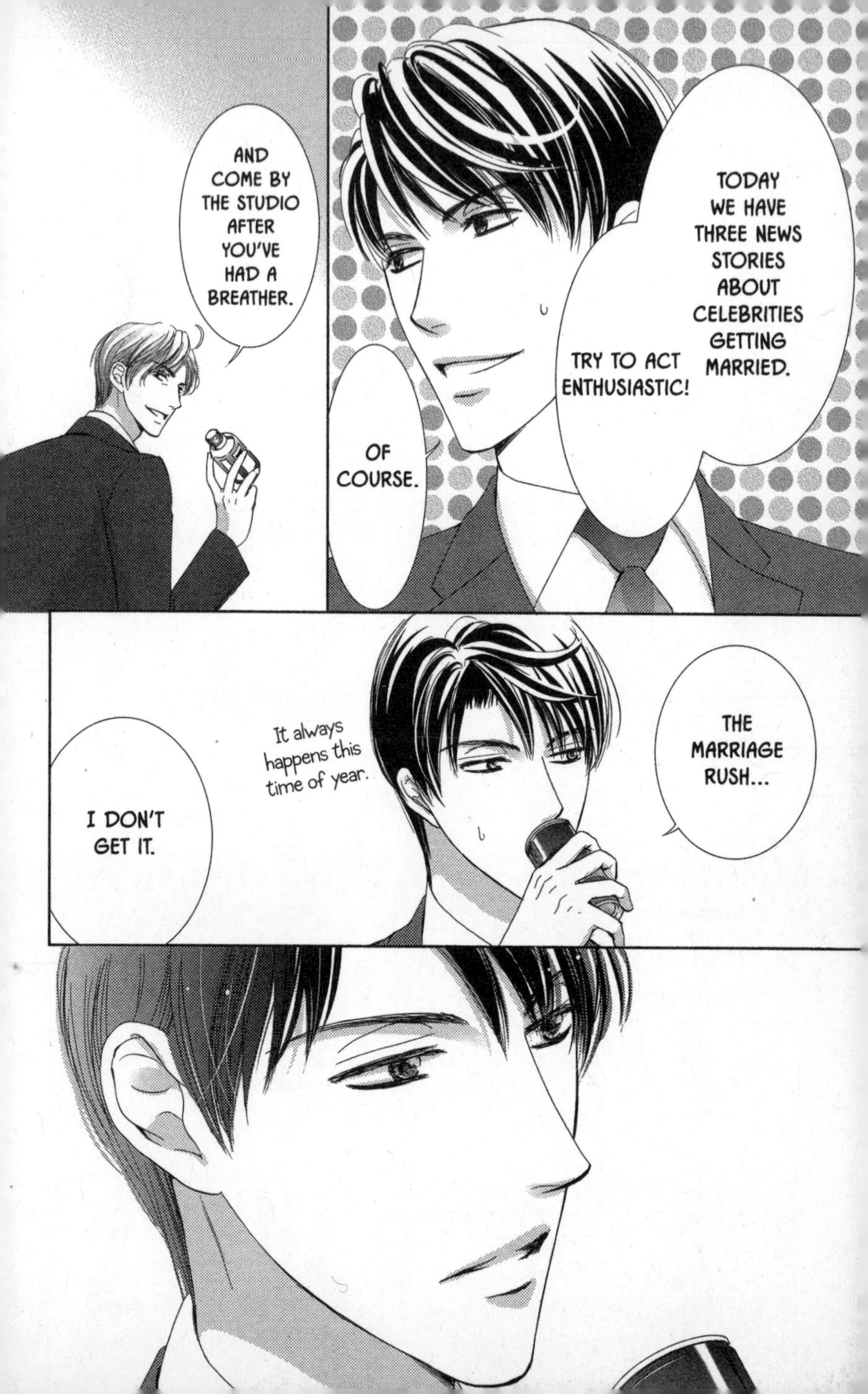
TODAY WE HAVE THREE NEWS STORIES ABOUT CELEBRITIES GETTING MARRIED.
TRY TO ACT ENTHUSIASTIC!
OF COURSE.
AND COME BY THE STUDIO AFTER YOU'VE HAD A BREATHER.
THE MARRIAGE RUSH...
It always happens this time of year.
I DON'T GET IT.

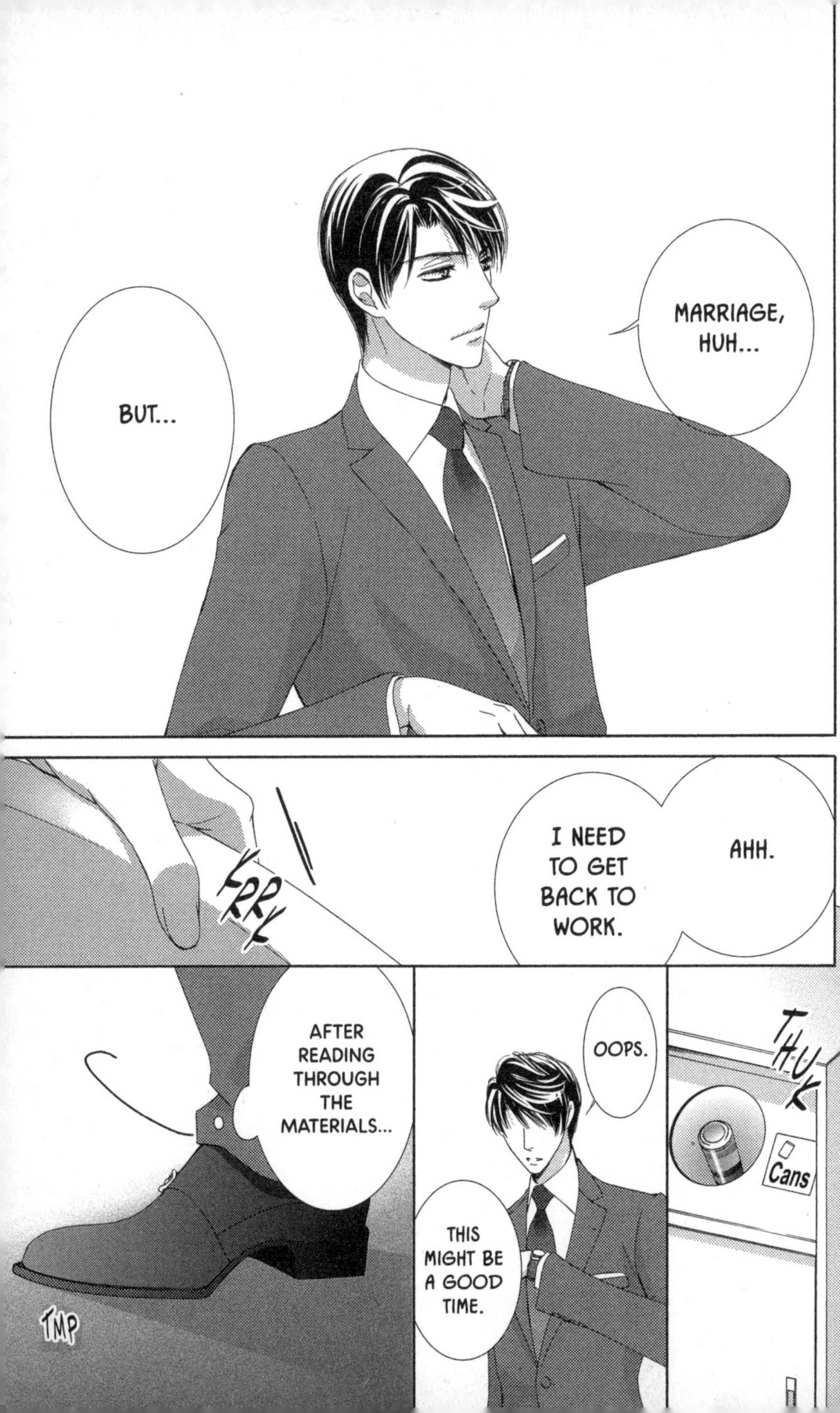
MARRIAGE, HUH...
BUT...
AHH.
I NEED TO GET BACK TO WORK.
KRRK
THUK
Cans
OOPS.
THIS MIGHT BE A GOOD TIME.
AFTER READING THROUGH THE MATERIALS...
TMP

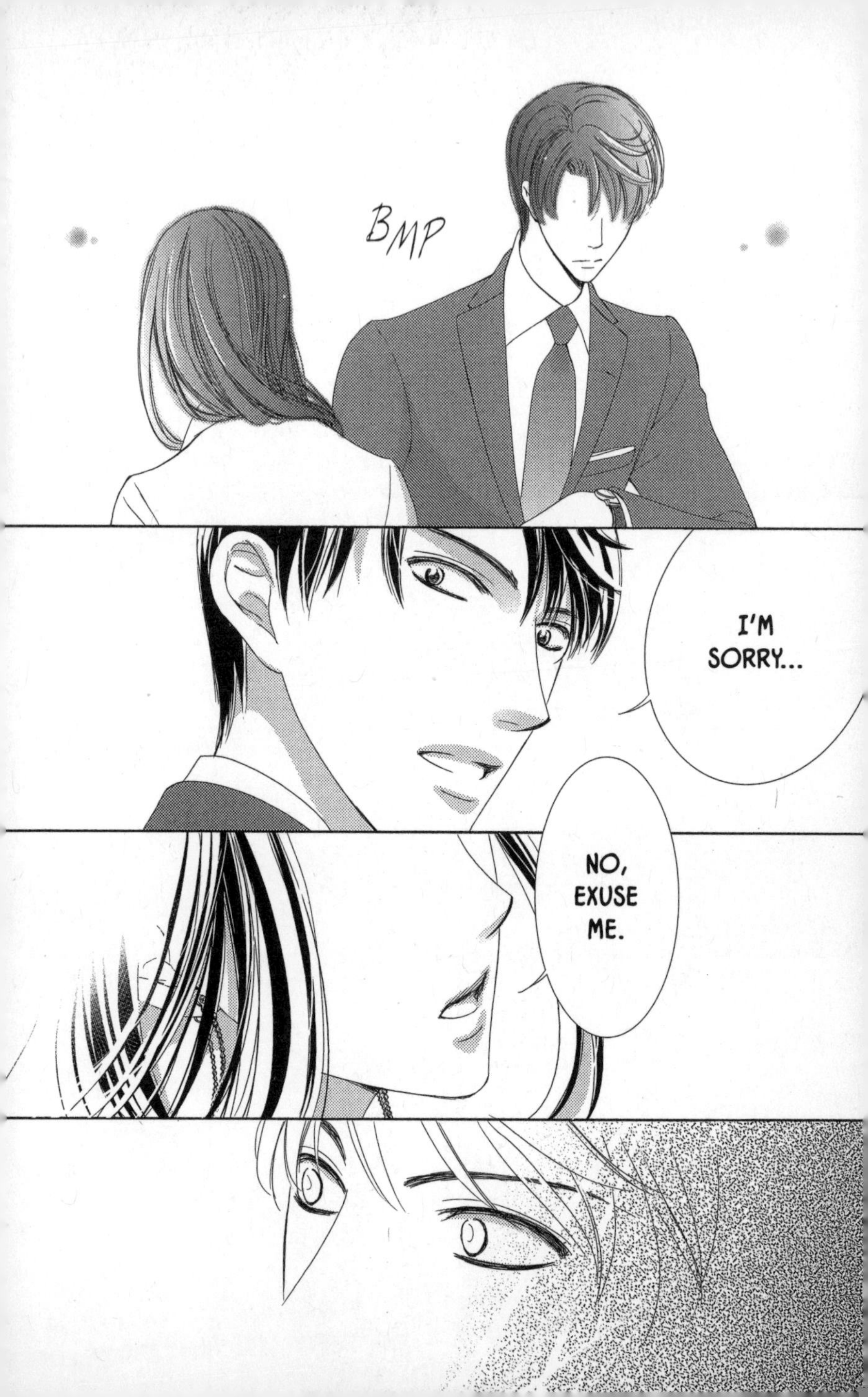
BMP
I'M SORRY...
NO, EXUSE ME.

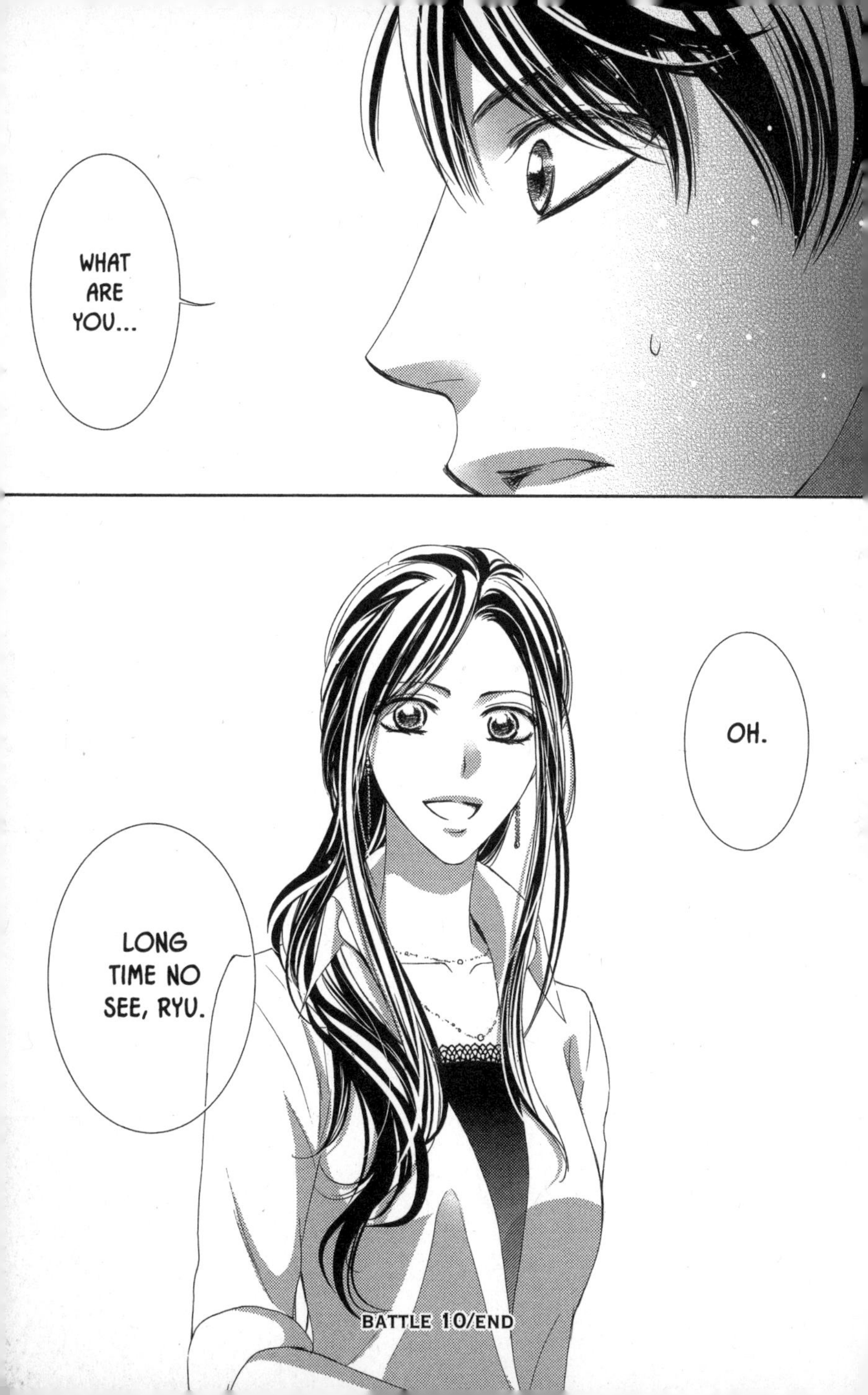
WHAT ARE YOU...
OH.
LONG TIME NO SEE, RYU.
BATTLE 10/END

GREETINGS

Hello, this is Izumi Miyazono. Thank you very much for picking up volume 2 of *Everyone's Getting Married*. Asuka and Ryu's love battle has a long way to go. On to volume 3!

I received a lot of reference material this time around.

NHK's Hirotake Kai-san
NHK's Gen Hamura-san

Thank you so much for all your help despite your busy schedules!

I wrote a bonus story for the end of this volume. It seems that the "Nanaryu" stories are becoming something of a series. I wonder what situation I'll draw him in next... Heh heh heh! (*smile*) I've never done bonus stories like this before, so it's an exciting new feeling.

I hope everyone enjoys these side stories about Nanaryu.♥

I hope we get to see each other again in volume 3.

Thank you very much!

Special thanks ♥: Keiko S., Megumi M., Emi Y., my family, my editor and everyone else involved.

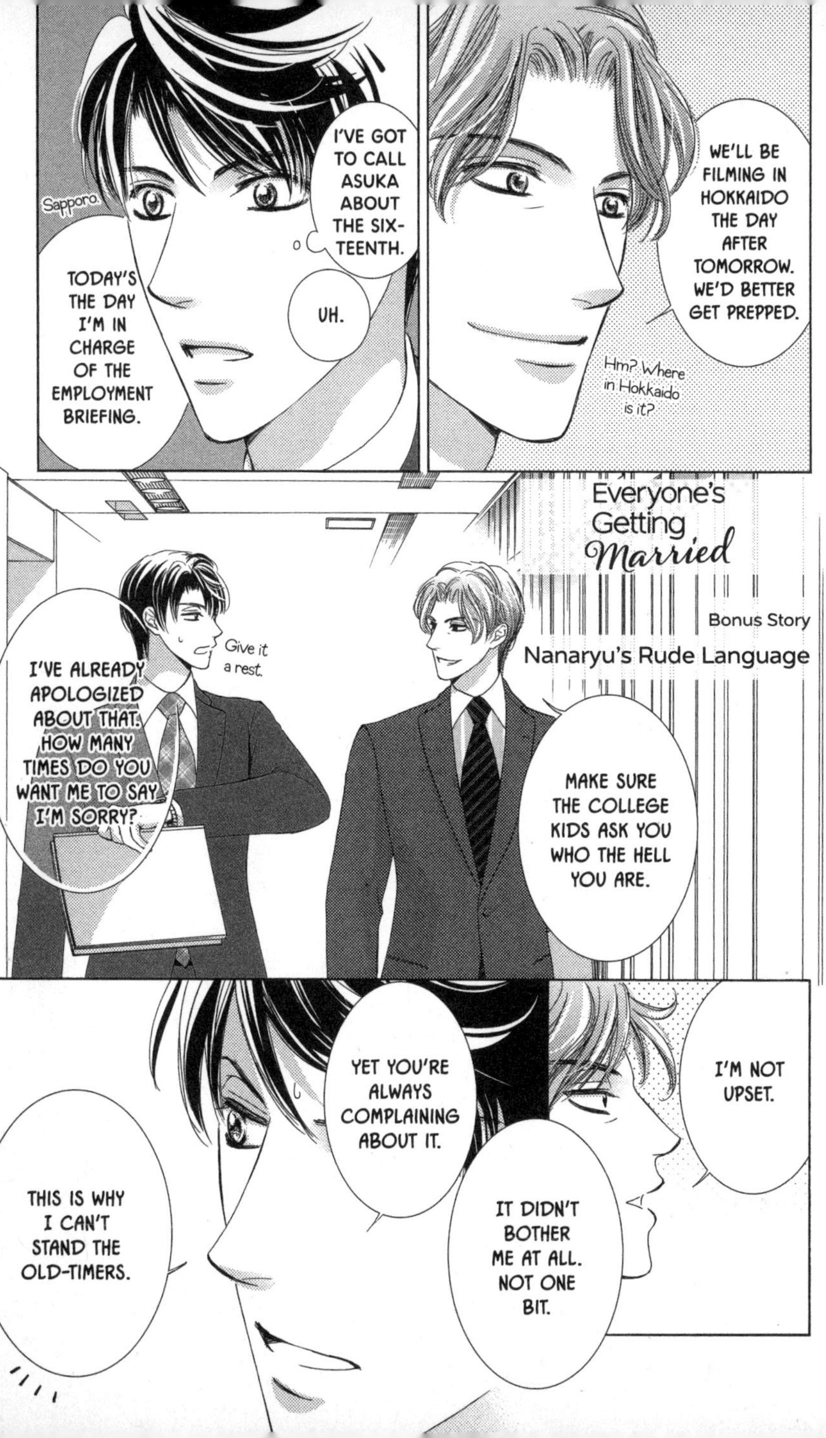
WE'LL BE FILMING IN HOKKAIDO THE DAY AFTER TOMORROW. WE'D BETTER GET PREPPED.
Hm? Where in Hokkaido is it?
I'VE GOT TO CALL ASUKA ABOUT THE SIXTEENTH.
UH.
Sapporo.
TODAY'S THE DAY I'M IN CHARGE OF THE EMPLOYMENT BRIEFING.
Everyone's Getting Married
Bonus Story
Nanaryu's Rude Language
MAKE SURE THE COLLEGE KIDS ASK YOU WHO THE HELL YOU ARE.
Give it a rest.
I'VE ALREADY APOLOGIZED ABOUT THAT. HOW MANY TIMES DO YOU WANT ME TO SAY I'M SORRY?
I'M NOT UPSET.
IT DIDN'T BOTHER ME AT ALL. NOT ONE BIT.
YET YOU'RE ALWAYS COMPLAINING ABOUT IT.
THIS IS WHY I CAN'T STAND THE OLD-TIMERS.

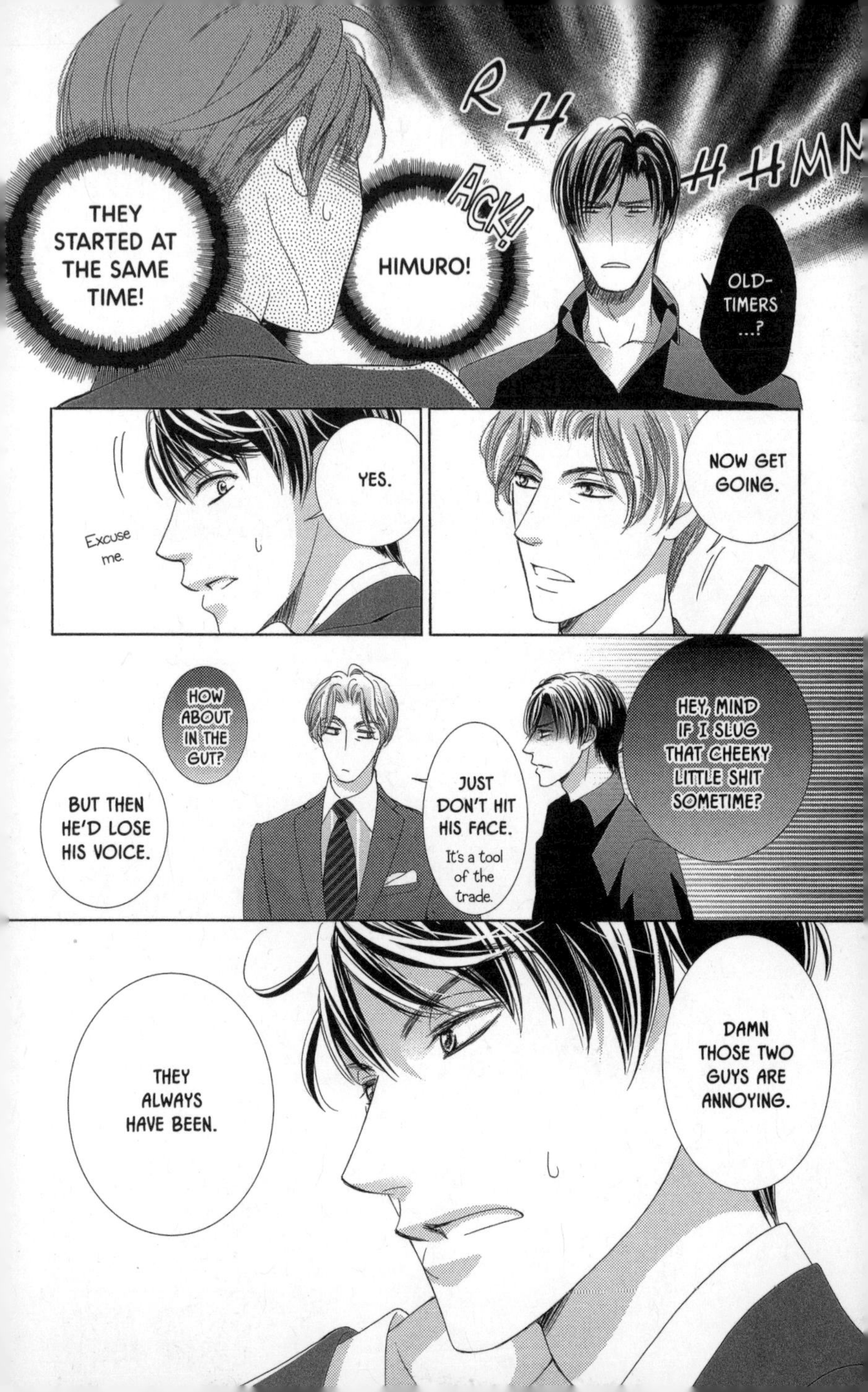
R H H HMN
OLD-TIMERS ...?
ACK!
HIMURO!
THEY STARTED AT THE SAME TIME!
NOW GET GOING.
YES.
Excuse me.
HEY, MIND IF I SLUG THAT CHEEKY LITTLE SHIT SOMETIME?
JUST DON'T HIT HIS FACE.
It's a tool of the trade.
HOW ABOUT IN THE GUT?
BUT THEN HE'D LOSE HIS VOICE.
DAMN THOSE TWO GUYS ARE ANNOYING.
THEY ALWAYS HAVE BEEN.

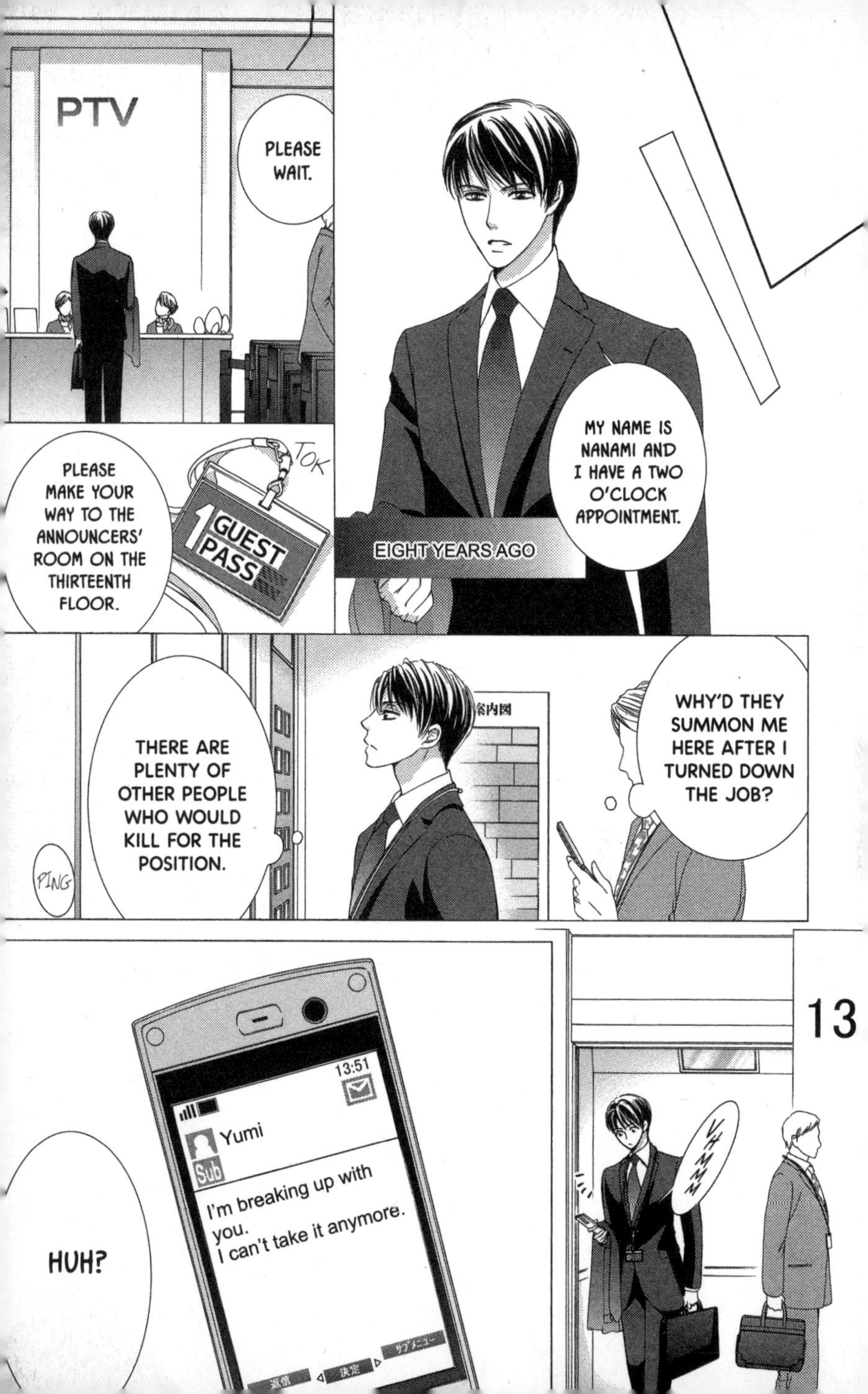
MY NAME IS NANAMI AND I HAVE A TWO O'CLOCK APPOINTMENT.
EIGHT YEARS AGO
PTV
PLEASE WAIT.
TOK
1 GUEST PASS
PLEASE MAKE YOUR WAY TO THE ANNOUNCERS' ROOM ON THE THIRTEENTH FLOOR.
WHY'D THEY SUMMON ME HERE AFTER I TURNED DOWN THE JOB?
案内図
THERE ARE PLENTY OF OTHER PEOPLE WHO WOULD KILL FOR THE POSITION.
PING
13
VHMMM
13:51
Yumi
Sub
I'm breaking up with you.
I can't take it anymore.
HUH?

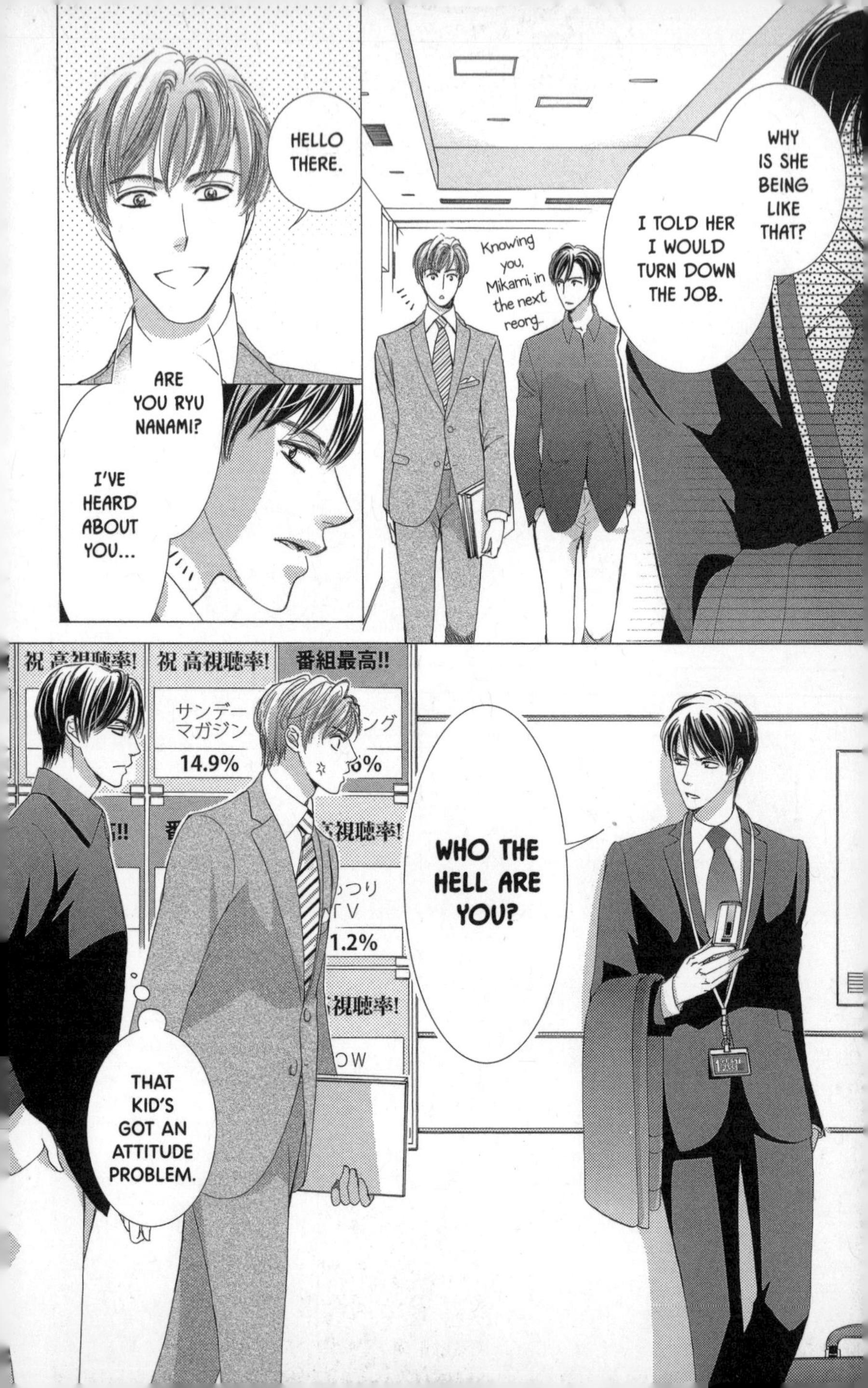
WHY IS SHE BEING LIKE THAT?
I TOLD HER I WOULD TURN DOWN THE JOB.
Knowing you, Mikami, in the next reorg...
HELLO THERE.
ARE YOU RYU NANAMI?
I'VE HEARD ABOUT YOU...
番組最高!!
祝 高視聴率!
祝 高視聴率!
サンデー マガジン
14.9%
WHO THE HELL ARE YOU?
THAT KID'S GOT AN ATTITUDE PROBLEM.

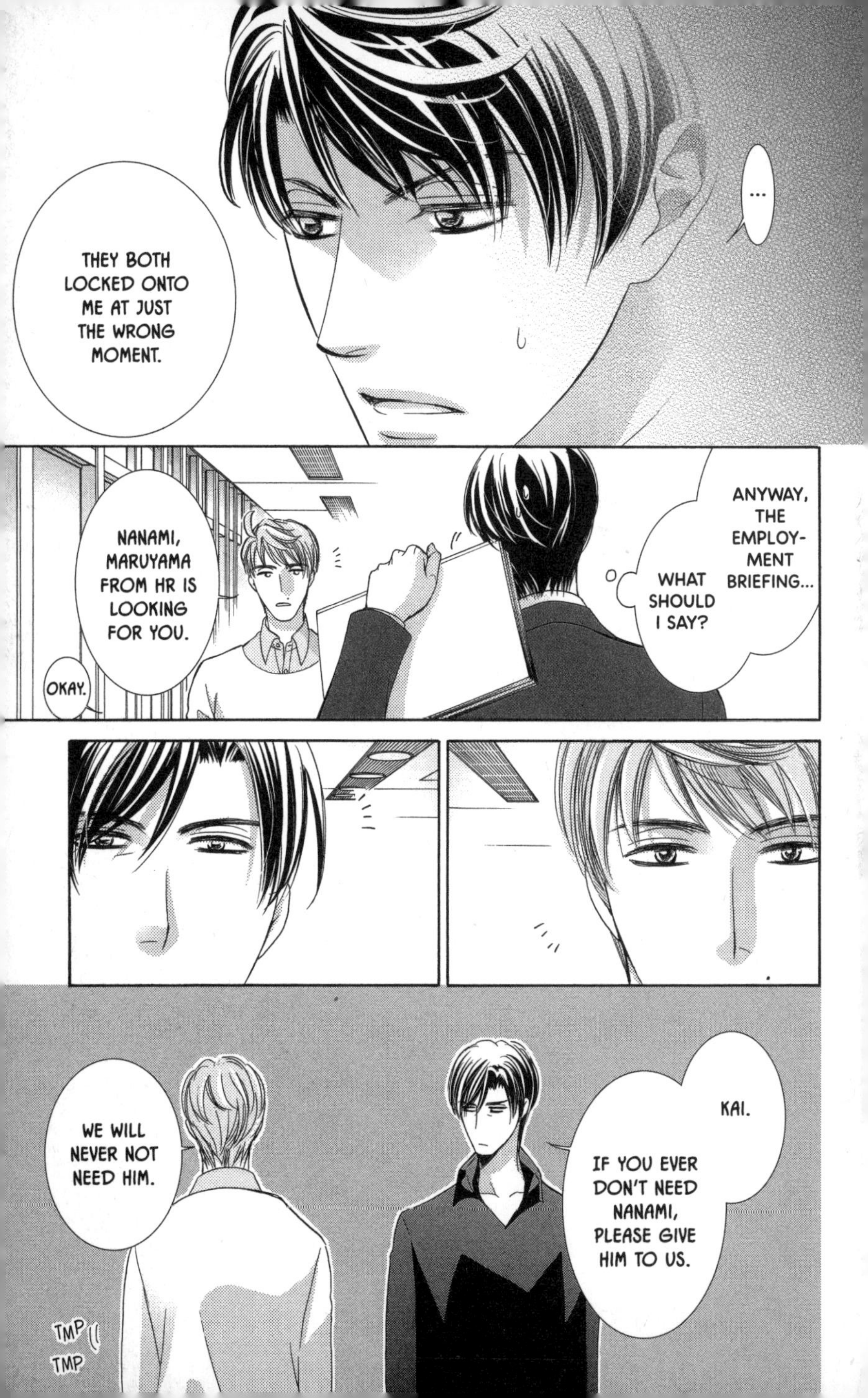
...
THEY BOTH LOCKED ONTO ME AT JUST THE WRONG MOMENT.
ANYWAY, THE EMPLOY-MENT BRIEFING...
WHAT SHOULD I SAY?
NANAMI, MARUYAMA FROM HR IS LOOKING FOR YOU.
OKAY.
KAI.
IF YOU EVER DON'T NEED NANAMI, PLEASE GIVE HIM TO US.
WE WILL NEVER NOT NEED HIM.
TMP TMP

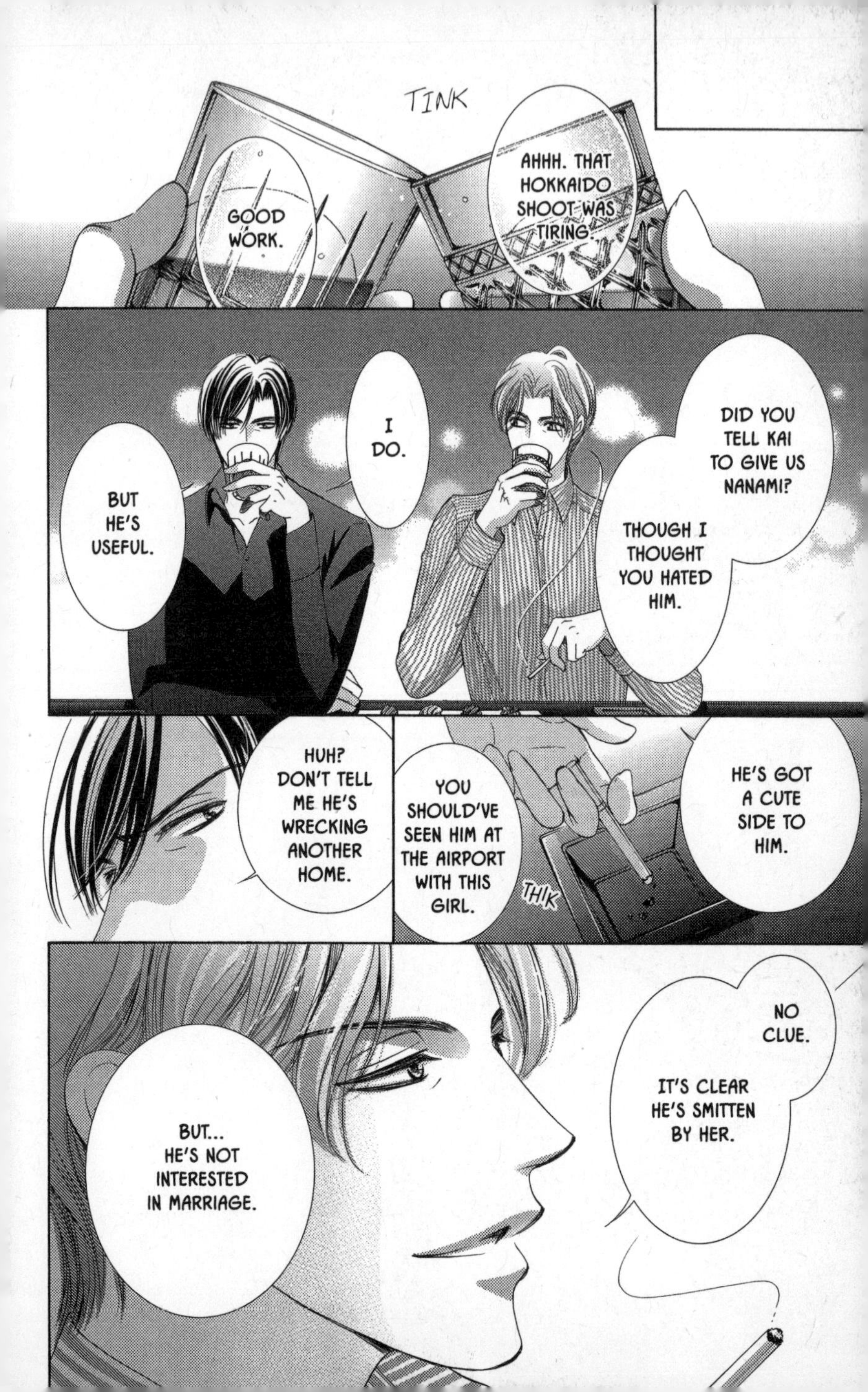
TINK
AHHH. THAT HOKKAIDO SHOOT WAS TIRING.
GOOD WORK.
DID YOU TELL KAI TO GIVE US NANAMI?
THOUGH I THOUGHT YOU HATED HIM.
I DO.
BUT HE'S USEFUL.
HE'S GOT A CUTE SIDE TO HIM.
THIK
YOU SHOULD'VE SEEN HIM AT THE AIRPORT WITH THIS GIRL.
HUH? DON'T TELL ME HE'S WRECKING ANOTHER HOME.
NO CLUE.
IT'S CLEAR HE'S SMITTEN BY HER.
BUT... HE'S NOT INTERESTED IN MARRIAGE.

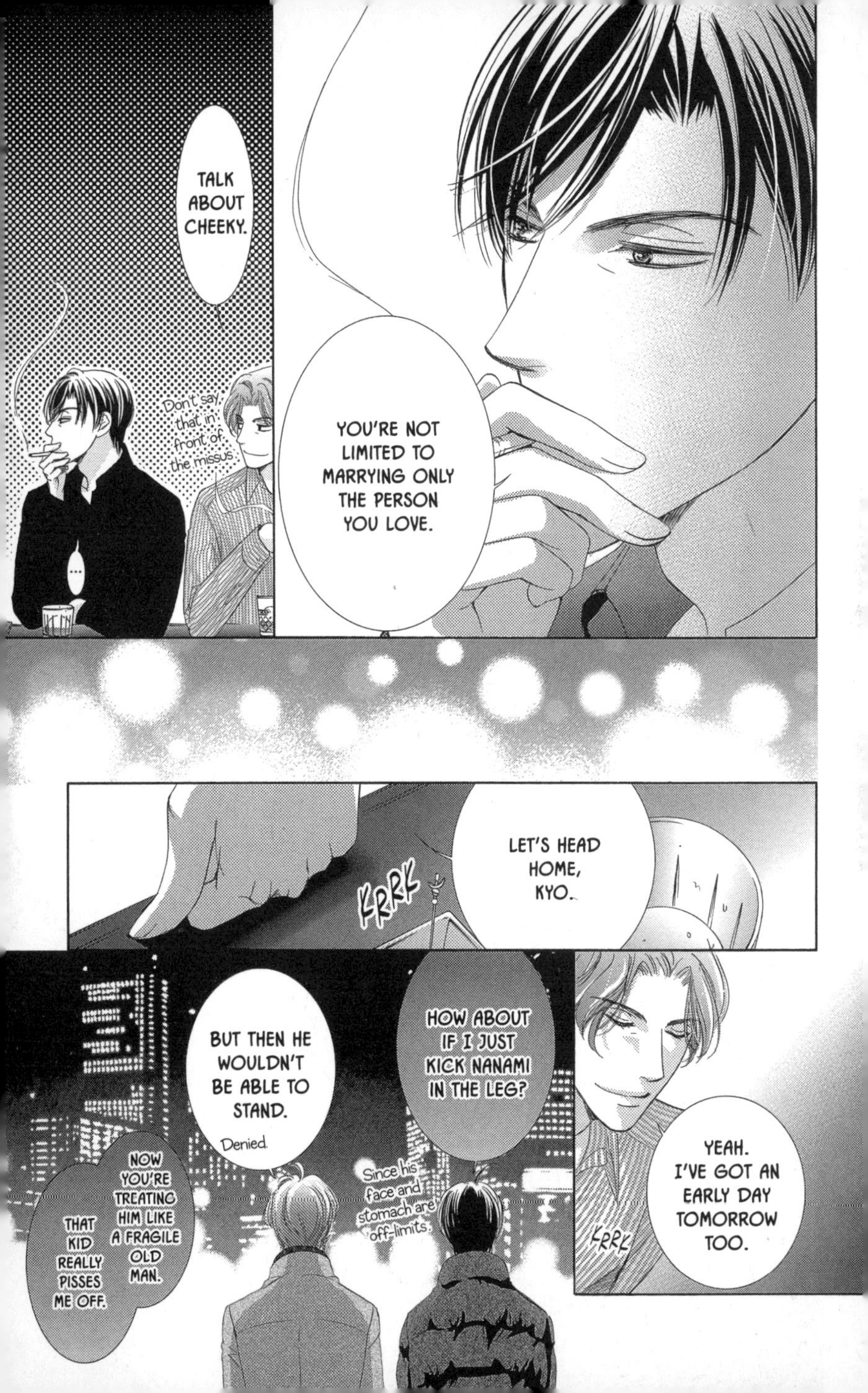
YOU'RE NOT LIMITED TO MARRYING ONLY THE PERSON YOU LOVE.
TALK ABOUT CHEEKY.
Don't say that in front of the missus.
...
LET'S HEAD HOME, KYO.
KRRK
KRRK
YEAH. I'VE GOT AN EARLY DAY TOMORROW TOO.
HOW ABOUT IF I JUST KICK NANAMI IN THE LEG?
Since his face and stomach are off-limits.
BUT THEN HE WOULDN'T BE ABLE TO STAND.
Denied.
NOW YOU'RE TREATING HIM LIKE A FRAGILE OLD MAN.
THAT KID REALLY PISSES ME OFF.

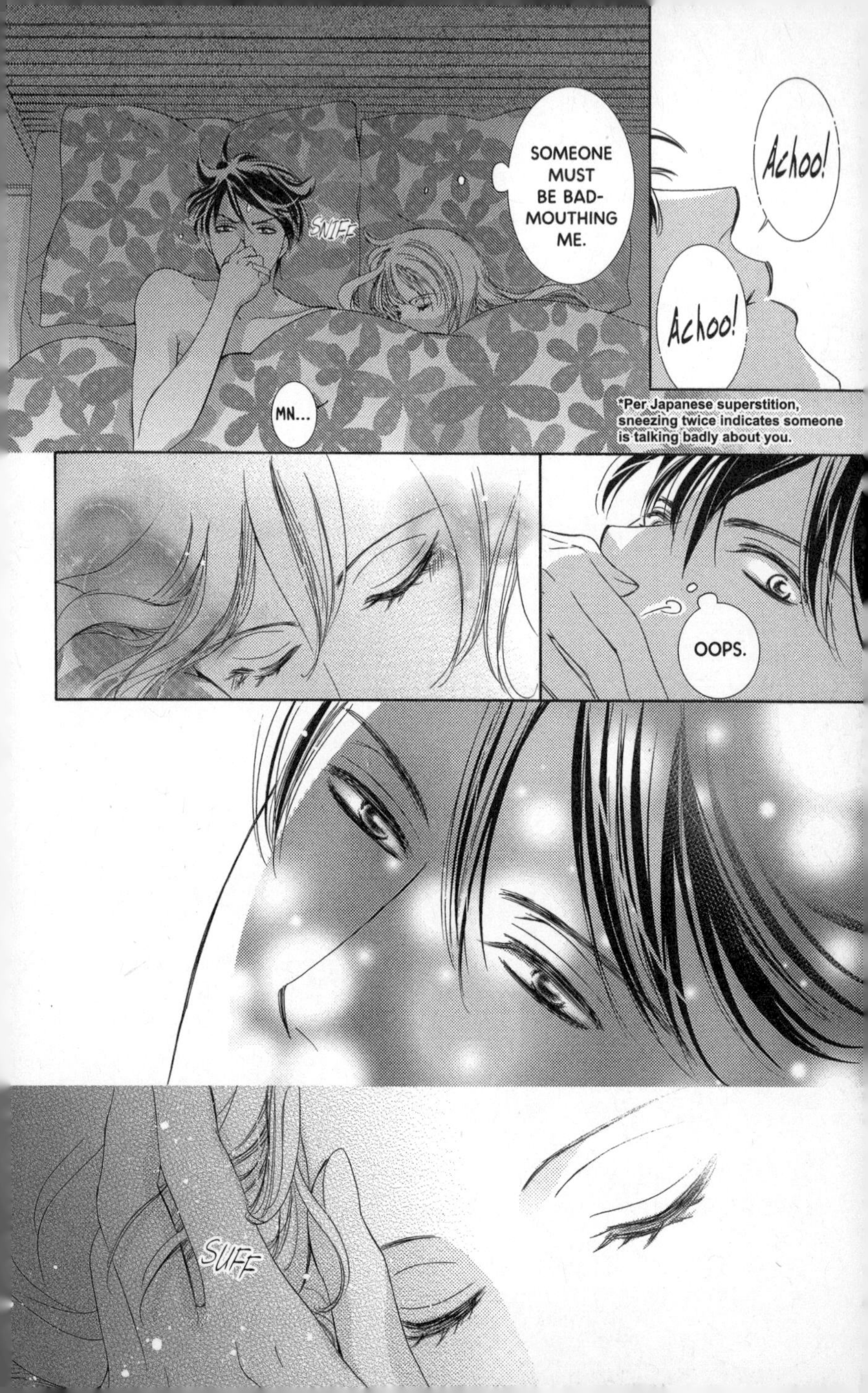
Achoo!
Achoo!
SOMEONE MUST BE BAD-MOUTHING ME.
SNIFF
MN...
*Per Japanese superstition, sneezing twice indicates someone is talking badly about you.
OOPS.
SUFF

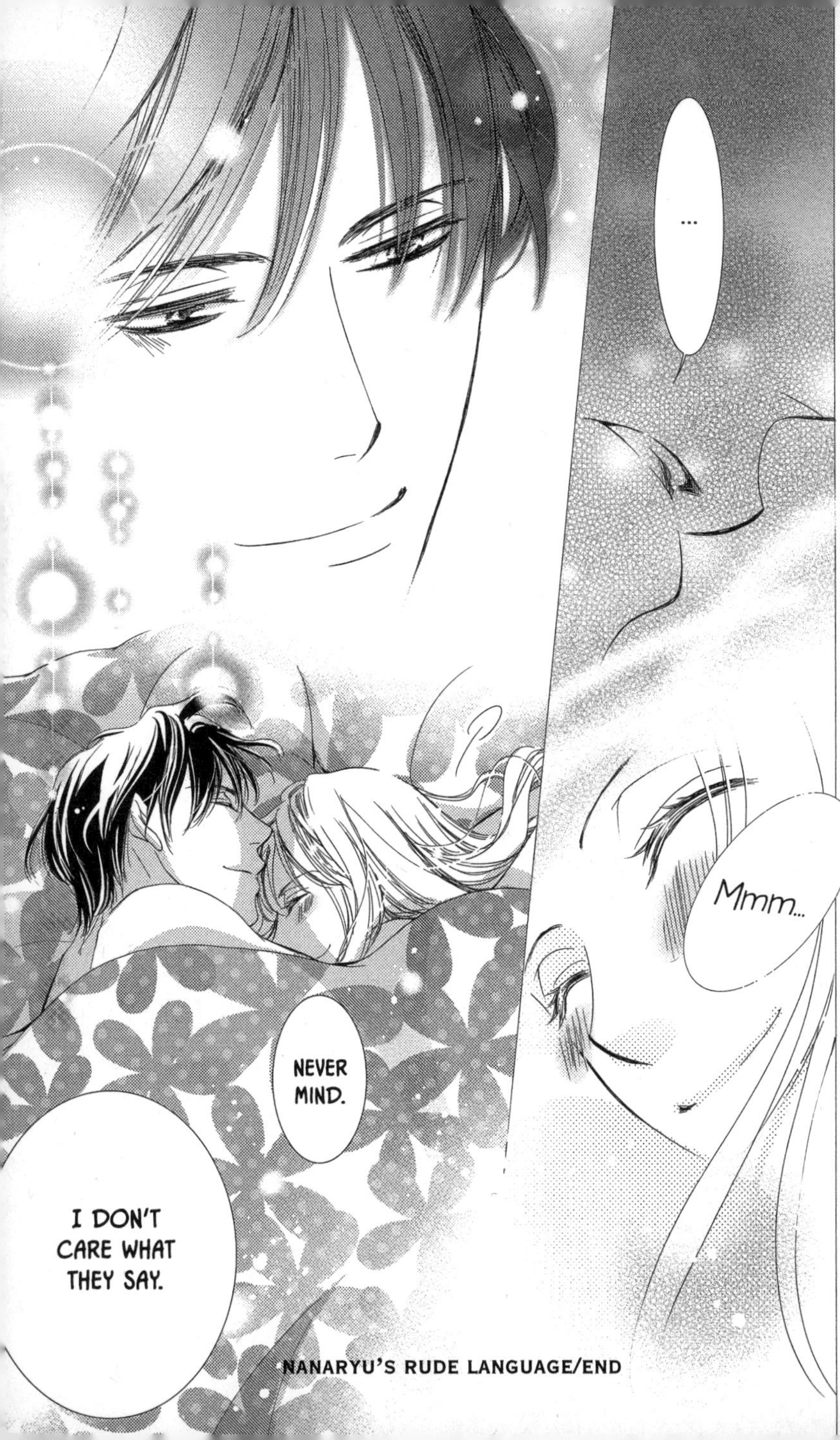
...
Mmm...
NEVER MIND.
I DON'T CARE WHAT THEY SAY.

NANARYU'S RUDE LANGUAGE/END

Announcer Mikami

I'm married.

It's volume 2. I think Asuka and Ryu are very similar and yet different at the same time. I personally like Mikami best and look forward to the scenes in which he makes an appearance. (*laugh*)

IZUMI MIYAZONO

IZUMI MIYAZONO is from Niigata Prefecture in Japan. She debuted in 2005 with *Shunmin Shohousen* (A Prescription for Sleep). In 2014 she began serializing *Everyone's Getting Married* in *Petit Comic*.

Everyone's Getting Married ②

SHOJO BEAT EDITION

STORY AND ART BY IZUMI MIYAZONO

TOTSUZEN DESUGA, ASHITA KEKKON SHIMASU Vol. 2
by Izumi MIYAZONO
© 2014 Izumi MIYAZONO
All rights reserved.
Original Japanese edition published by SHOGAKUKAN.
English translation rights in the United States of America, Canada,
the United Kingdom and Ireland arranged with SHOGAKUKAN.

ORIGINAL COVER DESIGN Kaoru KUROKI + Bay Bridge Studio

TRANSLATION Katherine Schilling
TOUCH-UP ART & LETTERING Inori Fukuda Trant
DESIGN Shawn Carrico
EDITOR Nancy Thistlethwaite

Printed in the U.S.A.

Published by VIZ Media, LLC
P.O. Box 77010
San Francisco, CA 94107

10 9 8 7 6 5 4 3 2 1
First printing, September 2016

www.viz.com

www.shojobeat.com

STOP!

YOU MAY BE READING THE WRONG WAY!

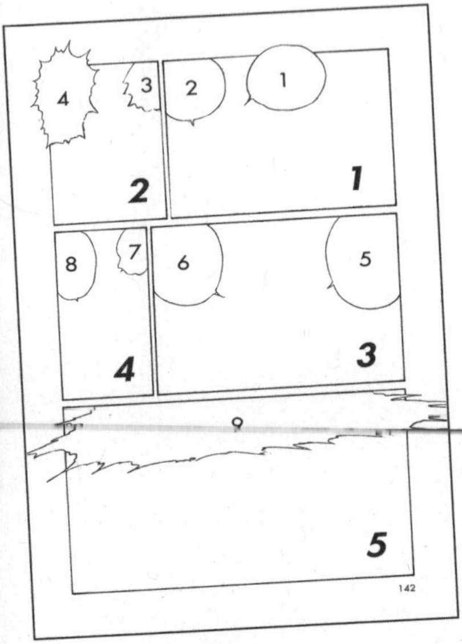
1
2
3
4
1
2
5
6
7
8
3
4
9
5
142

In keeping with the original Japanese comic format, this book reads from right to left—so action, sound effects and word balloons are completely reversed to preserve the orientation of the original artwork.

Check out the diagram shown here to get the hang of things, and then turn to the other side of the book to get started!

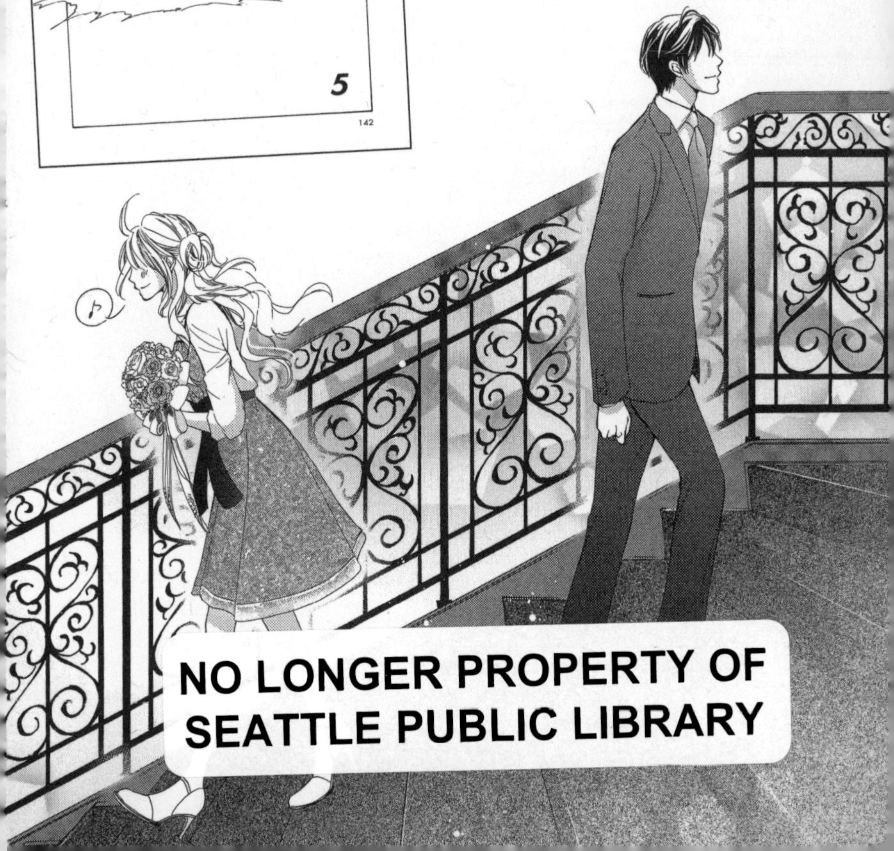